DRUNK STONED BRILLIANT DEAD
THE WRITERS AND ARTISTS
WHO MADE THE NATIONAL LAMPOON
INSANELY GREAT

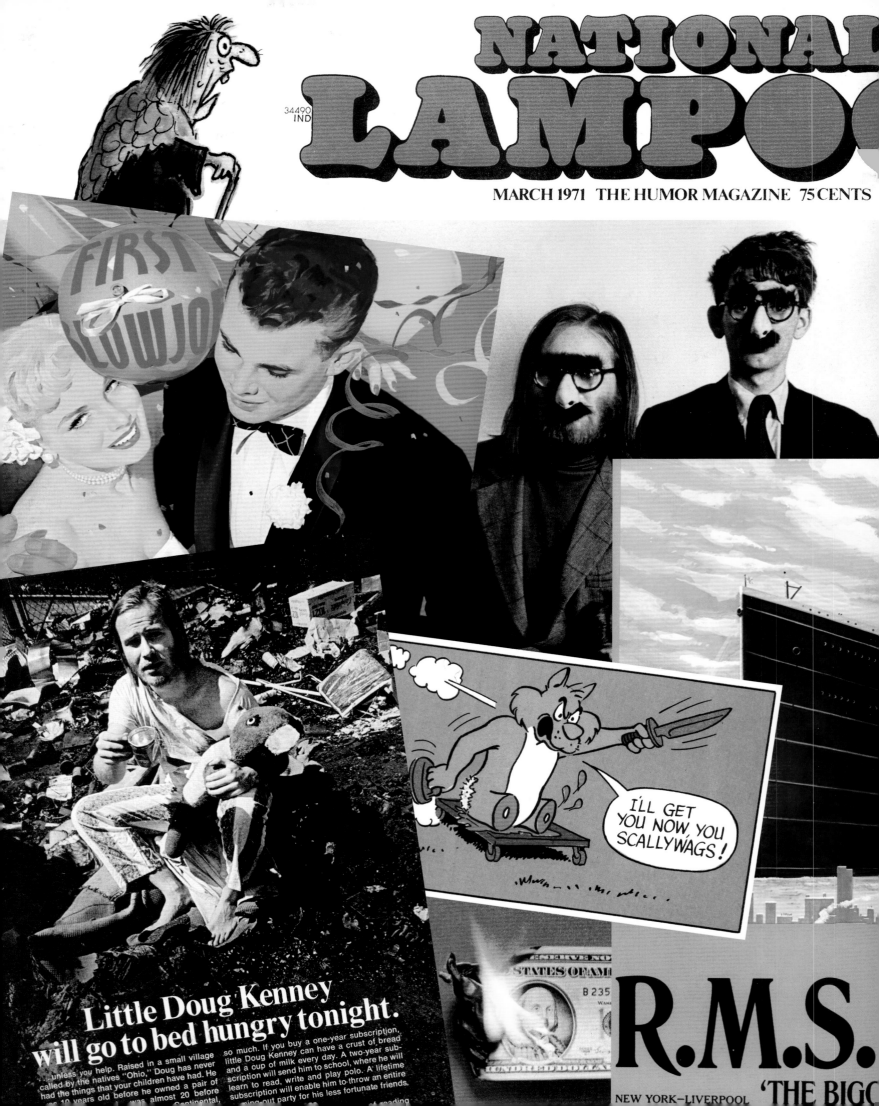

NATIONAL LAMPOO

MARCH 1971   THE HUMOR MAGAZINE   75 CENTS

I'LL GET YOU NOW YOU SCALLYWAGS!

Little Doug Kenney will go to bed hungry tonight.

...unless you help. Raised in a small village called by the natives "Ohio," Doug has never had the things that your children have had. He ~~~ 10 years old before he owned a pair of ~~~ was almost 20 before ~~~ Continental,

so much. If you buy a one-year subscription, little Doug Kenney can have a crust of bread and a cup of milk every day. A two-year subscription will send him to school, where he will learn to read, write and play polo. A lifetime subscription will enable him to throw an entire ~~~ing-out party for his less fortunate friends.

R.M.S.

NEW YORK–LIVERPOOL   'THE BIGG

DRUNK STONED BRILLIANT DEAD

THE WRITERS AND ARTISTS WHO MADE THE NATIONAL LAMPOON INSANELY GREAT

BY RICK MEYEROWITZ

ABRAMS, NEW YORK

CONTENTS

Humanity has unquestionably one really effective
weapon—laughter. Power, money, persuasion,
supplication, persecution—these can lift at a colossal
humbug—push it a little—weaken it a little, century
by century; but only laughter can blow it to rags and
atoms at a blast. Against the assault of laughter
nothing can stand.

—Mark Twain

Making people laugh is the lowest form of humor.

—Michael O'Donoghue

Left to right: Michael O'Donoghue, Brian McConnachie, Barbara Atti, Len Mogul, Henry Beard, Michael Gross, Matty Simmons, and David Kaestle

Sirs:

It says here that you're starting some sort of funny magazine. All I can say is that you people have a lot of nerve. Haven't you looked outside your own selfish egos long enough to see that people are being wronged and oppressed all over the world? Take the fascist military regimes which grow in number every year. In these stricken countries, you can't even look cross-eyed without the secret police writing your name down in their little notebooks. It may be even years later that one night you are roused from your sleep by the terrifying sound of rifle butts breaking down your flimsy rattan door. The brutal thugs drag you, heedless of your piteous cries, deep, deep into the jungle. Never to return. And you, with your funny magazine.

Viola da Gamba
South Orange, N.J.

Sirs:

As I wa

First letter to the editor from the first issue of the *National Lampoon*, April 1970, written by Doug Kenney

INTRODUCTION

In July of 1969 NASA launched three men to the moon, and Messrs. Henry Beard, Doug Kenney, and Rob Hoffman of Harvard arrived in New York to launch a national humor magazine. And why not? They were prodigies of the kind that made other prodigies appear incompetent. At the *Harvard Lampoon* they had edited parodies of *Time* and *Life* magazines, and Beard and Kenney had written *Bored of the Rings*, which had been a best seller. They brought with them a dazzling talent for wordplay and vocabularies of a size not seen in these parts since S. J. Perelman decamped to London.

The three formed a partnership with Twenty-First Century Communications, whose owners, Matty Simmons and Len Mogul, were the publishers of *Weight Watchers* and *Signature*, the Diner's Club magazine. Simmons and Mogul had arranged advertising, printing, and distribution for the *Time* parody.

"The boys," as Simmons called them, consulted experts and were advised to drop the whole enterprise. They conferred with mentors who counseled caution, they drank themselves into comas, acquired a mad commune of underground art directors, hired a staff, smoked odd substances, and drew to them like-minded, almost equally brilliant writers and artists who all wanted to change the world—or blow it up, or both. And somehow, in April of 1970, they published the first issue of a magazine called *National Lampoon*.

Highlights from that issue include "Normal Rockwall's Erotic Engravings," a mock ad; "White House Romance," a comic book in which Richard Nixon and his family are mercilessly lampooned; and a pitch-perfect Dr. Seuss story mated with the dinner scene from *Titus Andronicus*. It was a hodgepodge of ideas and confusing graphics, but it was smarter than anything else out there, and it boldly proclaimed that this magazine would be totally, gleefully, perversely, socially, politically, infamously, every way possibly, incorrect. This was not going to be your old *MAD* magazine; this would be something new. It took a few issues, but the *National Lampoon* caught fire. Not from the sweating sticks of dynamite an admirer once mailed to an editor (causing the evacuation of the entire office building), but from its own intense heat.

Doug Kenney and Rob Hoffman

PHOTO BY MICHAEL GOLD

It was an electric place to work. It had the feel of a rogue enterprise, and competition to top each other was fierce. You could feel the energy in the air, and I swear you could hear the synapses of some of the funniest minds of that generation firing like broadsides from a pirate ship. Visiting the office anytime, or attending editorial meetings with the crew, was never less than exhilarating. Along with Doug and Henry, a typical group might consist of Christopher Cerf, George Trow, Michael O'Donoghue, Sean Kelly, Tony Hendra, Gerry Sussman, John Weidman, Brian McConnachie, P. J. O'Rourke, Ted Mann, the art director Michael Gross, and artist contributors such as Bruce McCall and me. If it had been organized in advance, Henry or Doug would lead the meeting at a huge oval table. If it hadn't been organized, and was, as often happened, disorganized, the meeting would take place on the run from office to office, and resemble a crowd of drunken guests at a barbecue having a yelling contest. It was a comedy slam/insult fest/humor decathlon that energized everyone who played a part in it.

It was unforgettable, and for those of us who lived it, remains unequalled since. The experience was one we felt as a group—a creative energy level—as if a giant electric cable thrumming with juice was running through everything we did. We were comic commandos, and the *National Lampoon* was where the action was.

That kind of thing can wear you out. After five years, Doug and Henry were no longer young; they were, instead, twenty-eight years old. So they cashed out, took their scads of money, and ran. Doug went to Hollywood, where he made *Animal House* and *Caddyshack*, but he thought the town was lame, and the work bored him. The money he made seemed to him to be ill gained. He spent a fortune on powders to inhale but he was still unhappy. So he traveled to Hawaii, and all alone on a high cliff, on a rainy morning in 1980, only ten years after the *Lampoon* published its first issue, he slipped out of sight forever.

Henry took up carpentry for a while. Over the years he published many short, funny books, including best sellers on Latin and French for cats. But he keeps a profile so low he's slipped from sight—in a different way than Doug did, but the effect is the same. The scuttlebutt is he spends his days alone, golfing—even in the rain—maybe especially in the rain—and he never keeps score.

As for the *National Lampoon*, with the arrival of *Saturday Night Live* in 1975—staffed with *Lampoon* alumni—the magazine began to lose its grip on its audience. *Animal House*, which appeared in 1978, was the *Lampoon*'s last real contribution to our culture. Bright and talented editors and contributors kept the magazine afloat for another few years. But they met with diminishing results. During the 1980s, busty babes became the magazine's stock-in-trade, until finally, by the early 1990s, the whole lackluster enterprise capsized—the funniest thing they'd done in years—and unnoticed, sank out of sight.

The magazine's writers and artists dispersed to the ends of the comedy earth, but mainly to television. They went to Broadway, to Hollywood, and to publishing, too. They wrote books and worked for other magazines. They taught, blogged, Twittered, and created apps. They grew older, but not duller. Yet, aside from the founders, their names are not well known. Those fortunate enough to still be alive will tell you the work they did for the *National Lampoon* was the work they are most proud of, and that it is largely unknown.

Until now.

Four years ago, Eric Himmel of Harry N. Abrams asked me to create a book about the *National Lampoon*. Eric seemed to think I had a unique insight into the subject; I thought I was woefully inadequate to such a task. But I was intrigued, and in a moment of sheer hubris, I said I would. In the forty years since it was first published, the *Lampoon* has become a legend whose best pieces are now obscure even to those who once read them, and whose most important contributors are, in many cases, now forgotten. Who remembers the writer and editor Gerry Sussman? When Gerry died in 1989, he left behind seventeen years of *Lampoon* articles and a group of colleagues who thought he was the funniest man on Earth. Who remembers the cartoonist Charles Rodrigues? Charlie created, in twenty years of cartoons, a unique body of *Lampoon* work. He died in 2004, leaving behind a lifetime of brilliant drawings to molder in plastic bins in a shed on the Massachusetts coast.

I have not written the story of the *National Lampoon*. That's been done, first in Tony Hendra's excellent book, *Going Too Far*, published in 1987, and again in Josh Karp's 2004 book, *A Futile and Stupid Gesture*. If you want to know about the history, politics, and all about the business side of the *Lampoon* and its place within our culture, consult one or both of those. I have something else in mind.

Henry Beard

PHOTO BY MICHAEL GOLD

Drunk Stoned Brilliant Dead illuminates the contributions of contributors such as Gerry and Charlie, who made the magazine so unforgettable, and who I think were the best and funniest of the editors, writers, and artists at the *Lampoon*. Those I've chosen each have their own chapters. My choices were based on how funny I thought the writing was, or how good the art was, or how a piece would define each of those individuals I wanted to devote a chapter to. Those were my only criteria. In a few cases, a work had to be abridged or transcribed and newly typeset so that it would fit a given space, or so it would read and look better than the yellowed or poorly printed original. Some articles have been newly laid out for this book. The art or photography has been reshot and the type reset. Many artists made their original art available to me so that it could benefit from digital reproduction and up-to-date printing on good paper. These works now sparkle and look even better than when they first appeared in the magazine.

My memory of what was said among friends forty years ago tends to be a bit fuzzy. Nonetheless, this hasn't stopped me from writing about those featured here as if I knew what I was talking about. Often, when the truth was not available, a good story was, and I made use of it. Many former writers and artists had great stories to tell about other writers and artists. I've included as many of those as I could without skimping on the actual work of the individual whose chapter it is. Because this is not a "best of" collection, some classic or infamous *Lampoon* articles have been left out, and a number of very funny writers and artists are not represented in this book. I regret I didn't have another five hundred pages to fit them all in. *The National Lampoon Radio Hour*, the record albums, the two stage shows, and *Animal House* are also not included. Sadly, neither are the "Funny Pages," which rightly deserve their own book.

Reminiscing about his days as a member of *Monty Python*, Michael Palin said, "I was the Spanish Inquisition, I was one half of the fish-slapping dance. I look at myself and think that may be the most important thing I've ever done." He's right, of course. The hundreds of illustrations I drew for the magazine, my painting of the *Mona Gorilla*, and the posters I did for *Animal House* will probably turn out to be my most enduring contribution to whatever culture will have them. I was lucky to have been part of such a funny and exhilarating enterprise. As silly as it was sometimes, as serious a business as it could be, it was still, for many of us, the best work we've ever done.

—Rick Meyerowitz

DOUG KENNEY

"I don't deserve this. I don't know how to take care of it." Doug handed me the painting I had given him a year earlier. The glass was fractured and the wood frame was split at the corners. I asked him what happened. "I'm not good with nails," he told me. I couldn't help myself. I had to laugh at the way he said it. Looking around, I could see he was not good with a lot of things. His apartment on Bank Street was an incredible mess— almost empty of furniture except for a motorcycle he, or someone else, had dragged up the stairs. It was sitting in the living room covered with clothes: a 300-horsepower valet. Doug didn't live in this apartment, he camped in it. I don't think he ever really learned how to live anywhere. He didn't even know what to do with his clothes once he wore them. There were piles all over the house. It looked like a collection point for clothing being sent to poor folks in a third world country, to address their unfortunate lack of Brooks Brothers finery.

I often called him "Dougie." As in, "Dougie, you really shouldn't be doing this." I should've said it to him more often, but he wasn't a child, and anyway, it was sometimes intimidating to give him advice. After all, he was the smartest guy in whatever room he was in, and he was so damn likable, so effortlessly charming and funny—not just funny, but deeply, brilliantly funny in unexpected ways. What advice would you give? He, like his friend Henry, had always been the smartest boy in his class and, in Doug's case, the most subversive. On leaving Harvard, instead of harnessing that Rolls Royce of a brain to win a Nobel Prize, he chose to drive it through every plate glass window of the establishment—any establishment—and wreck the joint.

Years later, I visited him in Los Angeles. He was a star now, but still charmingly—and, if you thought about it, alarmingly—unable to manage the basics. We were in his room at the Chateau Marmont getting ready to go out. Doug couldn't find the keys to the new house he wanted to show me. He'd had them in his hand a minute before, but somehow they'd

PHOTO BY MICHAEL GOLD

vanished and he didn't know where to look. For Doug, logical wasn't necessarily an option. He would've looked on the ceiling for them. Maybe it was the drugs. (He'd just shown me a drawer full of powder that I told him to dump.) I found the keys where he'd dropped them—along with some papers—in the wastebasket.

We drove up Mulholland Drive in his Porsche and stopped at one of those scenic lookouts so I could see the view of Los Angeles spreading out below. "One day," I said, tossing an old cliché at him, "all this will be yours." Doug smiled. "I wouldn't bet on it," he said.

The new house was a nicely landscaped place with a pool and more furniture than an Ethan Allen. We hadn't been there five minutes before Doug lost his wallet in the living room. At the Chateau Marmont, I'd noticed it on a table. It was the size of a grapefruit. Losing it in a modest-sized room was an accomplishment. While he wandered around gazing up at the valances and drapes, I walked over to the couch where he'd been sitting and pulled the thing out from between the cushions. Inside of an hour he'd lost his keys and his wallet.

We went out to dinner afterward. And that was fine. His wit, as always, crackled with energy and left me breathless. But around the edges, anyone who cared about this man could see he was losing himself. When he died later that year, slipping or sliding off that wet cliff face on Kauai, we mourned as a group. Doug was the first of the *National Lampoon*'s inner core to die. At his funeral, among the friends and the stars, many let some anger show with the tears. He had an epic carelessness about his own person. His body had been on that cliff, but his head was in never-never land. How could he throw himself away? How could he leave us when we loved him so? And, damnit, he was only thirty-three years old.

—Rick Meyerowitz

LETTER FROM THE EDITOR, JANUARY 1971

The time has come for us to set straight certain wild-eyed individuals who have publicly accused the *National Lampoon* of harboring chauvinist pigs, sexist dogs, female-exploiting jackals and other unfashionable quadrupeds in its editorial kennels. Nothing could be further from the truth. However, to allay the fears of the 27% of our readership who happen to be Female (68% Male, 5% Undecided), we hereby openly admit that certain female staff members of the *National Lampoon* have grown restive of late (under the inflammatory goadings of a certain Managing Editor Marshmallow, no doubt).

The Editors were recently presented with a list of demands by these shrill individuals which included the following outrageous ultimatums: 1) all female staff members' salaries are to be paid in real money or its equivalent in edible produce, 2) a permanent cessation of corporal punishment for lateness or general editorial pique, and 3) exemption from the *National Lampoon*'s Weekly Purification and Fertility Ritual.

Needless to say, these preposterous prattles of a too-long-pampered platoon of pusillanimous panhandlers were rejected out of hand. Nevertheless, our crack team of negotiators responded immediately with what we, the management, feel was a reasonable, perhaps even over-generous counterproposal that included 1) free dimes for the executive washroom, 2) free track shoes and uniforms for the morning wake-up jog around the Editor's desk, and 3) free medical consultation following any injury resulting from the Weekly Purification and Fertility Ritual.

We are unhappy to report that these magnanimous counter-offers were unceremoniously hooted at by our strikers, not all of whom, we must add, have been a credit to their sex. However, after long sessions with strike representatives and days of haggling, whining, and the stamping of stacked heels, an equitable compromise was finally hammered out, and we are pleased, ladies, that we have arrived at a happy solution.

You're fired. —DCK

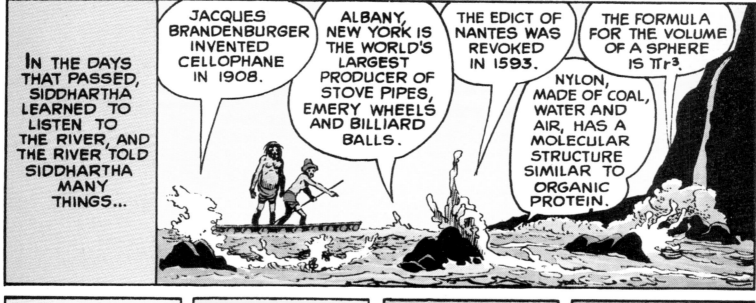

"Siddhartha," from *Classy Comics Illustrated*, February 1971

MRS. AGNEW'S DIARY
TRAVELS WITH JUDY, MAY 1970

Dear Diary,

Sorry I haven't had time for my usual "jottings," but I've been worried sick over Kim, our youngest, and I hardly know what to think. As you know, dear Diary, Kim has always been the "rebel" in our brood. In Annapolis, we caught her and some of her good-for-nothing friends (none of whom I have ever liked the looks) in the rec room with the air full of a funny smell. Sure enough, Spiggy hunted around and found a whole package of that illegal pot drug stuck in one of the holes of the pool table!

Well, as you remember, Spiggy gave her the hiding of her life and called up the parents of all her dirty-looking friends. As Spiggy always says, parental discipline is the gateway to knowledge, and I must say, I couldn't agree more. I mean, if the family can't provide the bedrock security of the soul, then who *can???* Maybe Spiggy was a little hard on her. She *so* loved her record collection, even if Spiggy didn't.

Well, anyway, I was going through some of Kim's things this morning to see if she had an extra ankle bracelet and I came across a little box full of *more of that pot drug!* Well, let me tell you, I marched right into the bathroom and flushed the pot drug, along with a lot of those nasty little papers, right down the johnny! She had some little pink things wrapped in tin foil too. And after all Spiggy and I had told her about between-meal treats. The junk kids put in their stomachs. They tasted just awful—no wonder she never has any appetite at dinner.

Spiggy will be so angry when he gets home. He'll have to know. As he says, it'll hurt him more than it will hurt her. I've only majored in marriage, but—oops, there's the phone. Be right back.

That was Spiggy. He'll be working late tonight. I just couldn't tell him yet. I'll make a nice meat loaf first. In fact, I should be helping Juanita with the marketing, but I'm feeling a little, I don't know, funny. I feel a little queasy in my tum. I think I'll just sit here for awhile and chat, dear Diary. It gets so lonely here sometimes.

Something very funny is going on. Things look sort of blurry. The table keeps wobbling. (Well, I don't mean it's actually wobbling, but it sort of looks that way.) And there's a ringing sound in my ears. Dring dring dring. Just like that. Dringdringdring. What on earth is happening? My, I feel woozy all over. I think I'd better sit down. Oh, I *am* sitting down. Well, then, maybe I'll just stand up for awhile awhile. (Isn't that silly? Writing "awhile" twice twice?) Gracious, I can't seem to write cclearly. I really do feel . . . odd. I wonder wonder (now isn't that the absolute limimimit?) oh, there's the fone again. .

It wasn't the fone ad all. iSn't tHat sTRangE???? i mean, aren'T tHOse VIoletts loovely? All thoSe PInks and gOldz and gReens and polKadOts. PolKADots??? Ohhh, thEre's thatt ffone—

nO FOne nofone what is that thing crawling in the corner??? AND THE WALLS!! LIKE LEATHERN WINGS of sssome GIGANTIC BATT sssoaring ovver ccaverns of lllimitless VOID VOID VOID Oh! the emptiness of SPACE and the unthinkable lonlinesses . . . oh the pure thrilling pain—the agony and the bliss of self-knowledge that is a a a SOUNDLESS SCREAM!!! LOOK OUT! It's growing!!! IT'S GETTING BIGGER AND BBBIGGGERRRRR!!!! ohgod ohgod ohgod ohgod ohgod ohgod ohgod ohgod ohgod ohgod ohgod OHGOD OHGOD OHGOD STOP STOP STOP STOP STOP STOP STOP STOP STOP STOP STOP STOP STOP STOP STOP ETAOINSHRDLU ETAOINSHRDLU ETAOINSHRDLU ETAOINSHRDLU ETAOINSHRDLU SHOOTOFFEUCLIDIANS SHOESIN E U C A L Y P T I C A L S H R E D D E D WHEAT . . . ohgod . . . h ere they come again. AAAAAAAAAAAAAAAAAAAAAAAA AAAAAAAAAAAAAAAAAAAAAAAAA AAAAAAAAAAAAAAAAAAAAAAAAA AAAAAAAAAAAAAAAAAAAAAAAAA RRRRRRRRRRRRRRRRRRRRRRRR RRRRRRRRRRRRRRRRRRRRRRRRR RRRRRRRRRRRRRRRRRRRRRRRRR GGGGGGGGGGGGGGGGGGGGGGGG GGGGGGGGGGGGGGGGGGGGGGGGG GGGGGGGGGGGGGGGGGGGGGGGGG HHHHHHHHHHHHHHHHHHHHHHHH HHHHHHHHHHHHHHHHHHHHHHHHH HHHHHHHHHHHHHHHHHHHHHHHHH HHHHHHHHHHHHHHHHHHHHHH HH H HHHHH H HH HHH HH H H HH H H H HH HHH H H H HH HH H H HH H H HH H HH HHH H HH HHHHHH H H HH H H HHHH HH H H H H H! HHHHHHHHHHHHHHHHHHHHHHHHH ooh, look at the pretty sky through the window. it seems to glow with bright points of light, now static, now pulsing with what seem to be the flames of a hundred white-hot novas! a noiseless explosion and a hot wind following, scattering the stars in their tragic loveliness, as if (though maybe I'm just being silly) a sophoclean lament for an entire younger generation obsessed with the futile need to excorcize a manichaean daemon.

oh! hear the song of the bonerock, the granite harmonics whitman may have glimpsed but could never penetrate. i wish to plunge deeper into that crystalline matrix and pierce it through to the core. take, take me to your nether worlds, fly me to the moon and let me play among the stars, enfold me with your cold fires and cleanse me with that purifying flame!

oh god, here they come! look at them! millions of them! so horrible, yet so beautiful! aaahhh! leave me, leave me! their colors are so brilliant, but so evil! their millions of tiny feet scuttling with the sound of dry leaves their

tiny

sharp

teeth white and their

tiny

red-flickering   tongues

i must be strong

i

must be strong   !!!
ohgodohgodohgodohgodohgod-
ohgod!!!!!!!

i can see it! i can see it! like the breaking of the sun over the lip of the sea. an answer. an answer to the questions asked since the beginning of man! thousands of years of asking and relentless seeking ended in this final, powerful and awakening of the human spirit. is it not a false dawn . . . ? no! it's it's—ohgod, that ringing! it *is* the phone. persons from porlock who—

Tthat wass Spiggy. Ssaid he'll be coming home on time after all. Isn't tthat nnice? For a minute, I felt almost like I was speaking to a total stranger . . . ? And I just looked at the time! Must have been napping. Isn't that the oddest thing? I'd better talk to Juanita about the meat loaf. Spiggy certainly works up an appetite after a long day at work. Must run.

Bye for now,

Judy

P.S. I don't think I'll tell Spiggy about Kim and her you-know-what, after all.

The Undiscovered Notebook of Leonardo Da Vinci

compiled by Doug Kenney   reconstructed by Daniel Maffia

Scientist, painter, engineer, architect — Leonardo Da Vinci was undoubtedly the greatest thinker of Western Civilization. Although born in 1454, his voluminous notebooks predicted not only the airplane and helicopter but many other modern day miracles. Thinkers through the ages have gleaned from these notebooks great insights ("Gravity is what makes birds fall down when they have heart attacks"), as well as a wealth of fascinating biographical data ("Four pairs stretch tights . . . six doublets . . . no starch . . ."). Thus, the *National Lampoon* is honored to be able to present portions of one of Da Vinci's notebooks that has never been discovered. We hope that you will be as awed as we were at the genius and vision revealed in this remarkable and priceless document. . . .

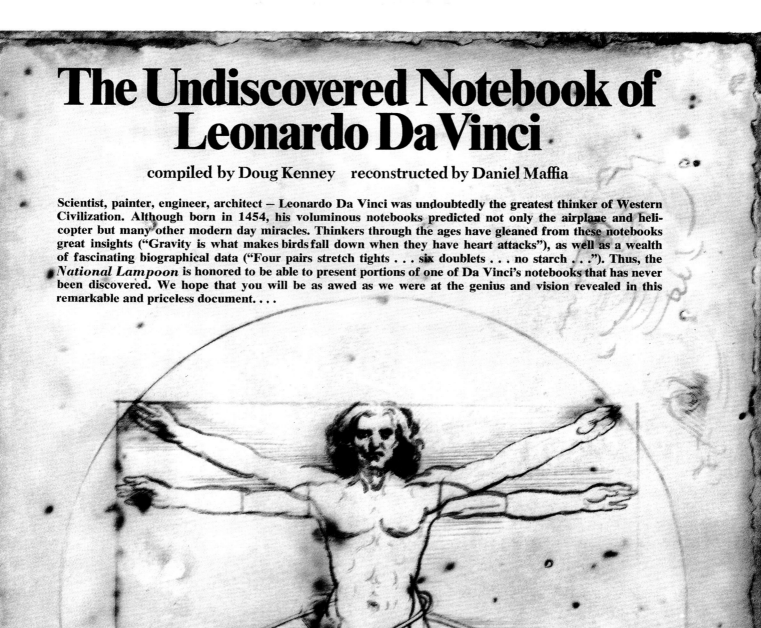

"Rota-
Reducione?"
"Circula Magica?"
"Hulus Hoopus?")

Ingenuo Mechanismo Per Reducione
L'Eccesso Obesito Del Grosso Stomacchi .
Questo mechanismo semplice e inexspensivo
enablo le personni con molto crisco in la banza
transformi a slendare personni. Pronto e facile
impresso la bella feminas!

March 1971

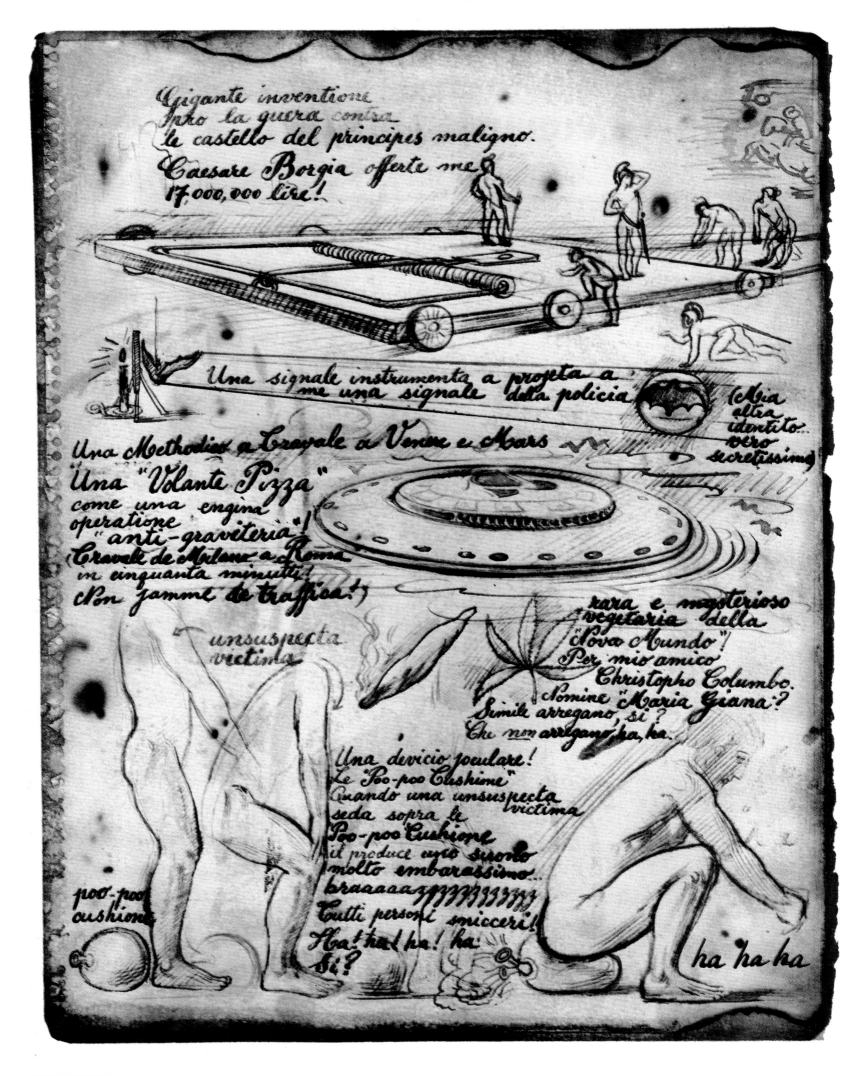

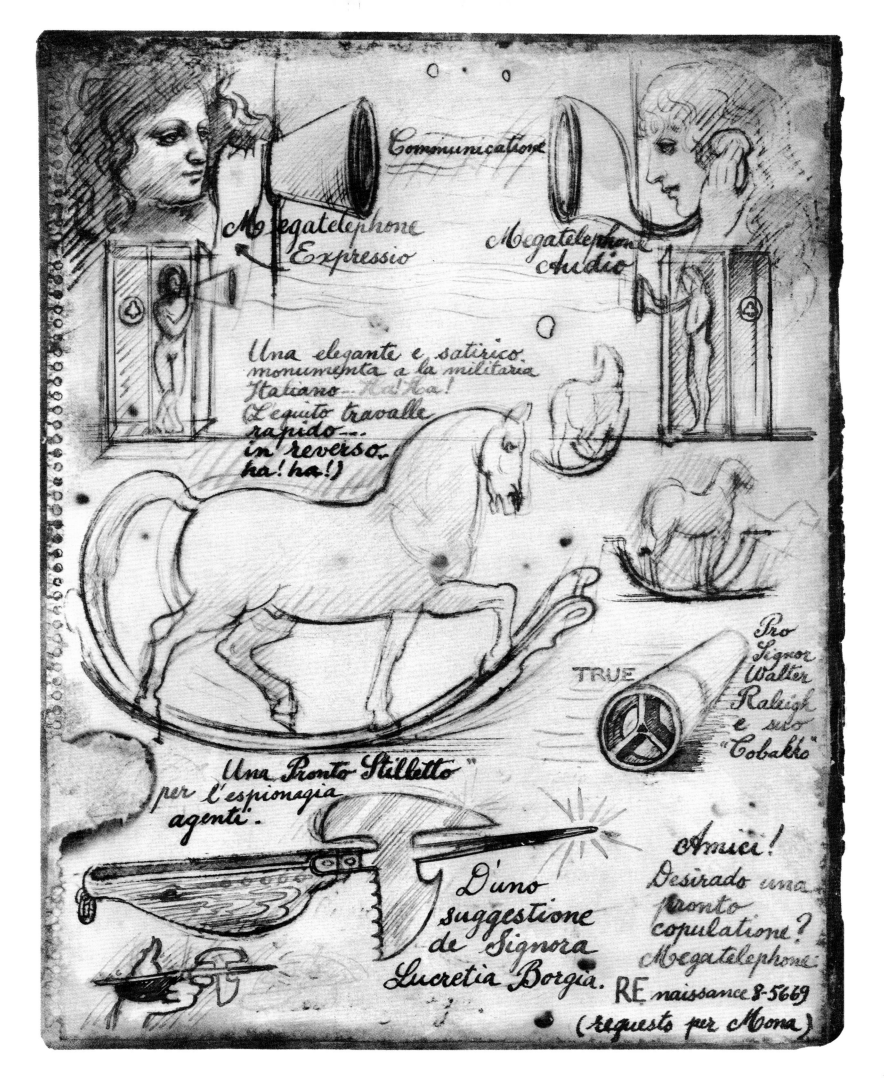

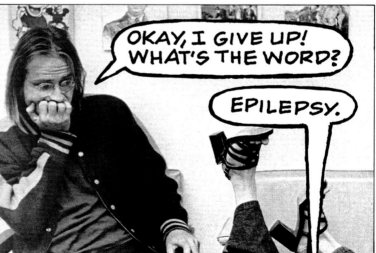

December 1971

Che Guevara's Bolivian Diaries

(Editor's note: Following the world-wide shock and mourning over the reported death of Ernesto "Che" Guevara by a Bolivian Army firing squad, the personal diaries of the revolutionary's tragic and abortive attempt to overthrow the oppressive Barrientos regime quickly became a classic text on guerilla warfare. However, recent chemical analysis of these documents have revealed minute traces of ketchup and A.1. Sauce ingrained in the paper, two substances Che himself denounced in an article on field kitchen maintenance for the Chinese news magazine Ping An as "reactionary and counterrevolutionary condiments fit only for bourgeois pigs and their revisionist cookouts." Other telltale clues belie the authenticity of the "diaries" as well, specifically the close attention given to spelling and grammar. Simultaneously with the discovery of this cruel hoax, Nat-LampCo News Service Latin American correspondent Douglas Kenney recently discovered the authentic manuscript outside the La Paz airport, where its pages were being employed as wrappers by an illiterate taco vendor. Craftily obtaining the documents from the simple peasant in return for some beads, hand mirrors, and assorted trinkets, newshound Kenney returned stateside immediately with the diaries, only then realizing that his wallet was missing. NatLampCo is proud to publish these historic footnotes to the brave rebelde's work, and hopes that they may fan the flames of global indignation against tyranny, oppression, and greaser pickpockets.)

Noviembre 7
At long last, our little band has touched Bolivian soil! The flight from Havana was uneventful, although every one of us stretched our revolutionary discipline to the limit fighting down the urge to jump out of our seats, rush to the cockpit and stick a *pistola* in the pilot's ear. In fact, Marcos, my hot-blooded second-in-command, did, at one point, lose control and leap from his seat shouting, "¡Prende ce avion o Cuba!" Luckily Marcos' seat belt was still fastened and his attention diverted by a double hernia long enough for Tanya, our East German *compañera*, to whisper that the plane was still *in* Havana and stuff an air-sickness bag in his mouth.

Marcos and I supervised the unloading of our baggage. We are posing as a Mexican mariachi band, our tools of war cloaked in the guise of musical instruments. Unfortunately, one of the customs officials discovered that our bass-fiddle case contained a Russian-made YD-47 heavy mortar. Thinking quickly, I put my mouth to the barrel and, with no little difficulty, improvised a few bars of "Beso Me Mucho" until his suspicions were allayed. There was, in addition, a tense moment when a porter accidentally pulled the pin on one of our maracas, but, as fate would have it, the device was of Bulgarian manufacture and failed to explode.

After breaking our fast (and one of my fillings) with tacos bought from a little peasant vendor outside the airport, Tanya, Marcos, Pombo, Camba, and I hailed taxis and directed them to our secret hideout in the trackless jungles of Nancahuazu. As we drive, Marcos, a swaggering adventurer who even apes the way I curl my beard, looks over my shoulder as I write in my diary, hoping to steal some good lines for his own. You are an idiot, Marcos, and it is no wonder that your publisher wouldn't give you an advance.

Noviembre 8
We have arrived at Nancahuazu, a forbidding jungle valley in the Cono Sur region. There is much to be done here. I have sent Pombo and Camba out in search of game, and Marcos out in search of them both to make sure they do not break discipline and bring the animal back unfit to eat. Men without women—an old story. I have also sent Tanya back to La Paz in search of my wallet, which I *know* I had before we ate those tacos.

Noviembre 9
Tanya has already done much to make the old farmhouse comfortable. She has set up an elaborate wire clothesline in the surrounding palms and amuses herself by sitting under it prattling to her vanity case in that husky baritone I have come to love. When she tires of this game, she will adjust her wig (an early illness has left her with a permanent crew-cut) and lumber off to her pet pigeons, first attaching shiny metal capsules to their feet for ballast. This morning, in a burst of feminine exuberance, she climbed hand over hand to the top of our hideout with a bucket of red paint in her teeth and decorated the roof with a gay bull's-eye.

At least there is one in whom I can have confidence.

Noviembre 10
Our first contact with the peasant population. Pombo was roasting a jaguar and Camba was occupied trying to kill it, when the noise attracted a passing worker returning from the distant tin mines. I ordered him to stop and fired over his head, barely creasing the scalp. With that, four others who had been watching shyly behind some acacias ran toward us in joyful recognition, shouting, "¡Non fuere, non nos muertos, por favor señor!" ["All hail the glorious revolution!"—Ed.] Now that we had won the confidence of these ragged but plucky recruits, I told them that they would be the nucleus of a people's army which would one day overthrow the corrupt Barrientos dictatorship and free its victims from conditions of exploitation indistinguishable from the Middle Ages. Childlike, they stood dumbly at first, too overwhelmed with pride to speak. I triggered a volley high over their knees to loosen their tongues, and, as one man, they raised their hands over their heads in agreement and enthusiastically emptied their pockets.

Now we are ten.

Noviembre 13
Excellent news has come in a coded newscast from Radio Havana. Fidel tells us that Bertrand Russell and Jean-Paul Sartre have espoused our cause and will marshal support for us throughout the European Left. Not only will this shower us with arms
continued

continued

and followers, but, if they agree to coauthor the introduction, my diary sales should be boosted by easily fifty thousand copies. Perhaps we can get out another printing of my other book as well (*One Hundred and Fifty Questions to a Guerilla*, People's Press, Havana, Cuba. Seventy pesos, hard-cover, thirty pesos, soft-cover.)

There is bad news as well. The peasants grow restive, making unreasonable and petty demands for food and water. The jaguar is gone, and has taken most of our rations with him. All that is left are open-face iguana sandwiches and pineapple soup. Even I found myself forcing down a bottle of Coca-Cola, the vile *maté* of *yanqui* imperialists. Although the foul liquid made me gag, I noticed an odd aftertaste that I could not dispel. A half hour later I found myself having another, and yet another. This is foolish counterrevolutionary weakness on my part, and I will steel myself against it.

But I suppose it can't hurt to kill the six-pack.

Noviembre 28
A visitor. Regis Debray, the famous French war groupie, has come with more happy news. *L'Express* has finally agreed to my price for the prepublication rights, and there is talk of a series based on our adventures for French television. But this matter must rest until more important tasks are completed—negotiations are stalled with Marboro for my poster, and Gomez, my agent, says Timex is still sitting on the wristwatch. Accordingly, I have radioed Gomez that they can make my arms go backwards and use "It's Counterrevolutionary!" as the sales gimmick.

¡Viva la revolución!

Diciembre 1
Dissension. Again the men complain about the lack of food, and the seasonal rains have begun causing widespread diarrhea, making our movements plain to the enemy. Ha ha, a joke, *si*? As Mao has written, "In times of hunger, one jest can be worth a hundred bowls of rice, particularly if you have no bowls of rice anyway." The men have taken to routinely disobeying orders, and frequently have to be disciplined for pillow-fighting after lights-out. If this seems harsh, it must be remembered that for pillows, true guerrillas use logs.

Marcos' patrol has returned with word of an enemy encampment not five kilometers from where we stand. Tonight we meet to plan an ambush and vote on whether or not to eat Tanya's pigeons.

Marcos reports the enemy has Coca-Cola!

Diciembre 2
The euphoria of victory! The ambush is a success despite a minor tactical blunder that decimated our forces. This morning, before our column advanced on the enemy, I told Gamba to (1) scout the trail ahead, (2) set up the ambush down river, and (3) organize a perimeter defense. Misunderstanding my orders, he (1) wandered aimlessly into the jungle, (2) became hopelessly lost, and (3) fell asleep. Nevertheless, Gamba's piece accidentally discharged as he collapsed, and the enemy was wiped out to a man in the ensuing, pointless crossfire. The dead were stripped of their uniforms and equipment, but little in the way of weapons were recovered save a few pocketknives and BB pistols. However, we managed to salvage a portable cooler full of Coca-Cola, a beverage I am finding more and more to my liking.

¡Hasta la Victoria Siempre!

Diciembre 4
Radio La Paz reports that a search party is being organized to locate a troop of Eagle Scouts that has failed to return from an overnight camping trip in the Nancahuazu region.

¡Oops!

Diciembre 10
The rains have begun again, and there is much wheezing and sniffling. Not to mention whining. We have run out of Contac. The men are hungry and are reduced to boiled hand-grenades. Tanya still refuses to let us at the pigeons and spends most of her time talking to her vanity case. Neither will she sleep with me, although I have pursued her for these many weeks. Do all East German women have such long periods? It is very strange. Perhaps that is why so many of their men jump over the Wall.

Also, the mosquitoes plague us by night. They are of immense size and their constant buzzing robs us of our sleep. So used are we to their continual presence that it was not until an hour ago that I realized via Radio La Paz that our positions are being bombed and strafed nightly by Bolivian helicopters.

There is no more Coca-Cola and I notice my hands are trembling.

Diciembre 15
Rain.

Diciembre 16
Rain.

Diciembre 17
Rain.

Diciembre 18
Our first loss. Camba, as usual, fell asleep on guard duty with his mouth open and drowned.

Diciembre 22
Marcos relates a wonderful dream he had last night. He dreamt that in three weeks we will march triumphantly into the capital leading ten thousand soldiers. The gates open before us without a shot being fired, and in the plaza we are greeted by throngs of delirious well-wishers. Little children stringing garlands around our gun mounts dance beside our armored cars, and the old ones weep with joy, singing the old songs again, shrieking the old shrieks. At the top step of the palace, Barrientos himself is standing meekly. Head lowered, he offers his sword, but, in the tradition of the great *generals,* I refuse it and shoot off his kneecaps. Then, arm in arm, Marcos, Pombo, Tanya, and I walk into the palace, where we are given champagne, caviar, cigars and certificates good for ten rubdowns at the Nogales Health Spa. We get unlimited room service. We can put our feet up on the desks. No one cares if we don't make the bed. The phone rings and it's Fidel congratulating us and asking us if we can spare a fiver. We live happily ever after, and our story is made into a major motion picture starring John Wayne, Omar Sharif, Steve McQueen, and Candy Bergen. We get 10 percent of the gross.

This is a good dream.

Diciembre 23
Marcos has had another dream. Harold Stassen is sworn in as President of the United States aboard the S.S. *Titanic*, while overhead floats the Hindenburg piloted by Amelia Earhart and Wiley Post, who are being married by Judge Crater and about to embark on a two-week honeymoon in Atlantis.

We must always be on guard against such idle, bourgeois fantasy.

Enero 2
More bad news from Havana. Sartre's and Russell's appeal to Europe's revolutionary youth has brought little gold to our war chest. However, Fidel has cheered us by forwarding a petition of support from the fifth-grade class of the People's Primary School in East Berlin containing twenty-eight signatures and a pledge of two weeks' milk money. In addition, we have, to date, received thirty-six inquiries from Sorbonne PolySci majors requesting information for their doctoral theses.

Also, Gomez writes that the watch gimmick didn't go over and Debray has received a letter from the French television network rejecting the series idea. They claim it wouldn't stand a chance against "Hogan's Heroes."

This afternoon, as a demonstration of their affection for their liberators, the peasants have deserted.

Enero 5

More rain today. Once again the men are racked with diarrhea and our patrols are frequently halted, as marching is difficult with everyone's pants down around his ankles. Our situation is desperate. We have also run out of air freshener.

Enero 6

The diarrhea grows worse. We have run out of corks as well.

Enero 14

The extremity of our need has driven us to reckless adventurism. Last evening, under the cover of a moonless night and some captured Airwicks, we stole into the little town of Palamos and attacked the local *farmacia*. Suddenly, many guns opened up on us and we were caught in an ambush of Bolivian soldiers before we could get to the Kaopectate. How could they have known? Luckily, we escaped with our lives, although several of us have suffered flesh wounds from kamikaze pigeons. The men begin to grumble and, in their rush to blame others for their own tactical mistakes, cast suspicious eyes towards Tanya, who, by the way, says her period will soon be over and we can begin heavy petting.

Nevertheless, the men must be pacified, and our now-routine diet of stuffed mortar rounds has been supplemented with squab.

Enero 17

No Cokes for three days. My hands are shaky and my knees are weak. I am itching like a man on a fuzzy tree. Delirious. I cannot go on unless I have another. Soon. A peasant in the village will deal with me—one rifle, one six-pack.

Soon the sentries will be sleeping.

Enero 18

The camp is in an uproar. Someone slipped past the guards last night and stole six rifles. No one is above suspicion, and as an example to the rest, I shot Pombo through the foot with the remaining rifle.

Marcos has been stirring up trouble again. He is jealous of my deal with *Playboy* for the "Che" tie clips and billfolds. If we take the capital by spring, I tease him, the *norteamericanos* will be forced to recognize Cuba and I can plug my book on the Juannie Carson show. This is another of those jests I have previously described. But Marcos persists in disobeying my orders, and was absent for bed check. I was forced to discipline Marcos and order him to stand in the corner for three hours. However, there was another helicopter raid last night and there are no corners left in the camp. I made him stand in the latrine instead. Barefoot.

Enero 19

Today we planned the major thrust of our campaign. The time is ripe for decisive action, for the men grow listless waiting around to be picked off by snipers. Marcos, impetuous romantic that he is, foolishly proposed striking at the U.S.-owned oil refineries at Camari, while the rest of our dwindling brotherhood wished to march on the United Fruit Company complex in Fuelga, in the hopes of cadging some bananas from the Fruits. Another jest. One of Mao's favorites.

After several hours of democratic discussion, I rapped my rifle butt (which serves in this rough-and-ready forum as a gavel) on Marcos' head and settled the matter. Tomorrow we set out for La Nosa, the industrial nerve-center of *yanqui* colonialism in Bolivia. Also, the largest Coca-Cola bottling plant in the southern hemisphere.

Onward!

Enero 20

A black day.

It began well enough. The men who had not been carried off by the jaguar were roused from their trees at dawn, and by noon we were gliding stealthily down Highway 42 to La Nosa, stopping only to eat, sleep or loot an occasional *cantina*. My brave *compañeros* were in high spirits, and several times I reprimanded them for exuberantly singing what has become our song of battle, the "Bataan Death March." When we neared La Nosa, I divided our force into three squads —Pombo was to move his men around to the left flank and pretend to scavenge for 2-cent-deposit bottles, and Marcos was assigned to assault the main gate under the cover of the guardhouse searchlights. It fell to me and Tanya to wait behind a granite outcropping and shout hearty advice and encouragement.

We waited until dusk, and at precisely 0800 hours I gave the signal to move out. At 0810 I gave the signal to shoot anyone still cringing behind the trees, and the attack was underway. As Pombo's unit moved into the clearing, a company of Bolivian infantry opened fire, chopping Pombo and his men into *paella*. Immediately, I sensed that something had gone wrong. As if to confirm my suspicions, Marcos' men advanced to the gate and were cut to ribbons. Marcos himself barely escaped with his life, shielding his body with a Coca-Cola cooler, and scrambled back to our position covered with thick, sticky fluid. Despite my hopes, it was not his blood, but the sight of a five-foot-two-inch, 120-pound Cuban running at breakneck speed with a quarter-ton vending machine under his arm did, at least, distract General Orvando's soldiers long enough to make good our escape.

As we struggled back to our base, it became obvious that we were being observed, because whoever lead our column was periodically shot between the eyes. This obstacle to our progress led to an animated debate among the survivors as to who next was to become the first, or "point man," for the remainder of our withdrawal. Marcos, unwilling to obey both my orders that he lead *and* continue to carry the Coke machine on his back, suggested that we confuse them by walking backwards.

And this man, I tell you, was not only free to walk the streets of Havana, but to drive an automobile.

Enero 21

All hope has vanished. They surrounded us as we slept. We are out of ammo, the men are threatening to eat Debray and Pombo is acting suspiciously despite his death in my previous entry. I think I, too, am feeling weary of the chase. Poor Tanya. So deranged is she by the rout that she now only croons to her case, even while the artillery rounds, as if by magic, slowly find the range on our positions. They are coming for Che. The noose is tightened, and soon, the fascists think, Che will be captured, shot against a peasant wall and dragged through the muddy streets like a slaughtered goat.

I look at Marcos, sleeping peacefully now that I have clubbed him into insensibility, and I think of how many dreams we shared together during the Cuban revolution, how he looked up to me like an older brother, copying everything about me, and how proud he would be, were he conscious, to know that I have just traded identity papers with him, shaved, and covered my head with one of Tanya's shawls, which she soon will no longer be needing, I can personally assure you. Then, over the river and through the woods, who knows? Maybe my cousin in Buenos Aires who works at the you-know-what factory will hide me.

Che *must* live, for wherever the people are ground under the heel of *yanqui* imperialism, my spirit must be with them, whether it be in Rio de Janeiro, Tahiti or Acapulco. Soon, a new dawn, a red dawn, will give light to the world, and perhaps these few small things I have done to hasten that day will be remembered, particularly if Dalton Trumbo (*Spartacus, Viva Zapata*) agrees to rough out the shooting script. *Che Lives*? . . . *The Che Guevara Story*? . . . *A Che for All Seasons*? . . . *I Remember Che*? . . . *Viva Che*? . . . *A Che Is Born*? . . . □

THE CODE OF HAMMURABI
TRANSLATED BY DOUG KENNEY

I Hammurabi the Just, true son of King Zestab-pez-necco and conqueror of the evil tyrant Ashur-du-smelbad, by this stela set in the marketplace do set down my Code. Let it be known throughout all Mesopotamia, both to Assyria and Babylonia, that these laws will make the flesh of the people glad, and are not to be leaned on.

* * *

◆ If two oxcarts meet at a crossroad, the oxcart on the right has the right-of-way.
◆ If an oxcart meets a war chariot at a crossroad, the vehicle equipped with bows, arrows, spears, slings, and scythe-blade hubs has the right-of-way.
◆ If traveling in congested cities, charioteers shall set melons on the points of their scythes.

* * *

◆ If a man split the ear of his wife, the ear of his favorite dog shall be split.
◆ If a man split the ear of his slave girl, his first and second wife shall split the sewing.
◆ If a man deflower another's slave girl, he shall pay one-half mina of silver and the cost of new sheets.
◆ If a woman in a quarrel damages the testicles of a man, her testicles shall be damaged.
◆ If a man damages the testicles of a eunuch, he shall inform the eunuch.
◆ If a man flog his wife, pluck out her hair, or smite and damage her nose, she shall have been flogged, had her hair plucked out, been smote, and had her nose damaged.

* * *

◆ If a temple prostitute refuses the silver coin of an undiseased freeman, she shall be made to lie with his ox in the square, and miniature bas-reliefs of the event may be sold to adult males above the age of fourteen.
◆ If a slave strikes his master's son, the slave's hand shall be cut off.
◆ If a son kills his father's slave, his allowance shall be cut off.
◆ If a son says to his father, "You are not my father," he shall be sent upstairs without supper and smothered.

* * *

◆ If a freeman kills a tax collector of the King, he shall be sent on in his place, swordless, to Palestine.
◆ If a house of mud brick collapses, killing the owner, the mason shall be pressed under every tablet relating to building codes.

August 1975

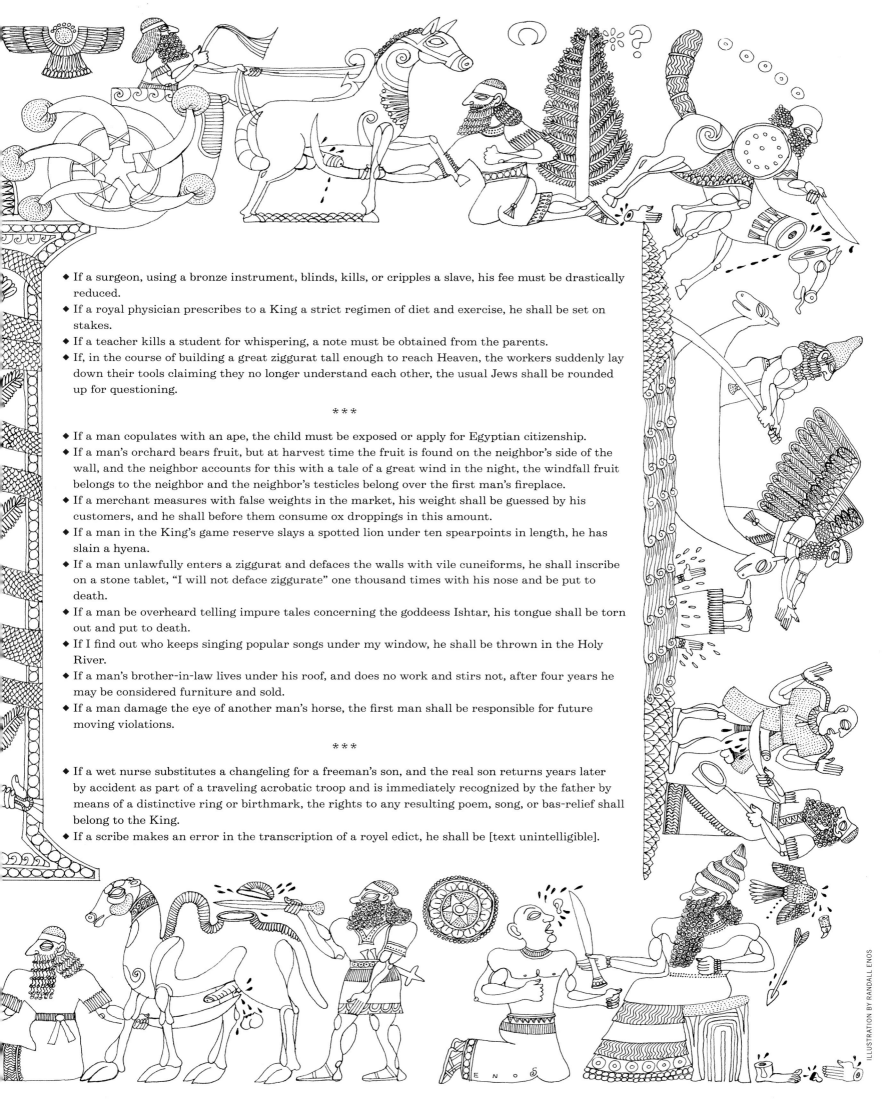

- If a surgeon, using a bronze instrument, blinds, kills, or cripples a slave, his fee must be drastically reduced.
- If a royal physician prescribes to a King a strict regimen of diet and exercise, he shall be set on stakes.
- If a teacher kills a student for whispering, a note must be obtained from the parents.
- If, in the course of building a great ziggurat tall enough to reach Heaven, the workers suddenly lay down their tools claiming they no longer understand each other, the usual Jews shall be rounded up for questioning.

* * *

- If a man copulates with an ape, the child must be exposed or apply for Egyptian citizenship.
- If a man's orchard bears fruit, but at harvest time the fruit is found on the neighbor's side of the wall, and the neighbor accounts for this with a tale of a great wind in the night, the windfall fruit belongs to the neighbor and the neighbor's testicles belong over the first man's fireplace.
- If a merchant measures with false weights in the market, his weight shall be guessed by his customers, and he shall before them consume ox droppings in this amount.
- If a man in the King's game reserve slays a spotted lion under ten spearpoints in length, he has slain a hyena.
- If a man unlawfully enters a ziggurat and defaces the walls with vile cuneiforms, he shall inscribe on a stone tablet, "I will not deface ziggurate" one thousand times with his nose and be put to death.
- If a man be overheard telling impure tales concerning the goddeess Ishtar, his tongue shall be torn out and put to death.
- If I find out who keeps singing popular songs under my window, he shall be thrown in the Holy River.
- If a man's brother-in-law lives under his roof, and does no work and stirs not, after four years he may be considered furniture and sold.
- If a man damage the eye of another man's horse, the first man shall be responsible for future moving violations.

* * *

- If a wet nurse substitutes a changeling for a freeman's son, and the real son returns years later by accident as part of a traveling acrobatic troop and is immediately recognized by the father by means of a distinctive ring or birthmark, the rights to any resulting poem, song, or bas-relief shall belong to the King.
- If a scribe makes an error in the transcription of a royel edict, he shall be [text unintelligible].

June 1971

JOE COLLEGE
Tony Hendra on Doug Kenney

Doug Kenney had Joe College good looks and shoulder-blade-length blond hair. He would've been the natural leader of the *National Lampoon*'s group of writers and artists, except that this group, including him, was the kind of group that wanted all natural leaders dead. And he was a terrible editor, given to remarks like, "This sucks, but I don't know why." In the first moments after I met Kenney he informed me that all British humor was totally unfunny. Moments later, he was improvising flawlessly in the manner of Thackeray—and I mean Thackeray, not Trollope, or Mrs. Gaskell, or Dickens—and moments after that, he was demonstrating that he could put his entire fist into his own mouth.

PHOTO BY MICHAEL GOLD

HEAD-ON
P. J. O'Rourke on Doug Kenney

Unfortunately, I'm not much help with Doug Kenney anecdotes. I just don't have any amusing stories to tell about Doug. He was, I think, the funniest person I've ever met, but he was too good at it. Whenever he said or did anything hilarious, it was always so perfectly in context that to take the act or the saying out of context and recount it would be to fail to do him justice. And his writing, of course, stands on its own. But there's another problem: Doug was not primarily funny. Doug was primarily smart. And there's such a thing as being too damn smart. In order to make sense of life, it's necessary to be oblivious to a lot of things or to ignore them or to twist them around so they fit with your perceptions of everything else. Doug was unable to do this. He saw too vividly and understood too acutely everything that happened around him, everything that happened to him, and everything that he caused to happen. Existence is grotesque. Doug had no blind eye to turn on it. This made his life uncomfortable at best and sometimes an agony. At least he was able to harness his perception of absurdity in a way that brought fun to others. He didn't wind up as a mental patient or a boring old crank like Sartre. However, I'd need to be a genius to make a charming tale out of Doug's head-on collision with the universe. I'm not one. As to what else I remember about Doug, mostly I remember the kind things he did for people. Alas, there's nothing funny about that. And the kindest thing he ever did for me was to make me happy to be not too damn smart.

Sirs:

Life is an unending river that flows from the snowcapped mountains to the fishy seas, never pausing on its journey, not even for a Dr Pepper or a bag of tasty Fritos. This thing we call Life is a long, lonesome highway along which the weary traveler may happen upon Adversity and Annoyance, and, at other times, a large quantity of very useful Truth and Beauty, or maybe even a lost transistor radio that will still work if you get some fresh batteries.

Life, then, is an enigmatic puzzle, although others find it a puzzling enigma, revealing her secrets only to the Pure, the Good, or the Highly Influential.

Wise Ones have sometimes likened Life to a pile of Turds, but Others have not. Personally, I tend to side with the Turds theory.

> K. Gibran
> Mt. Vernon, Iowa

Sirs:

Turning and turning in a widening gyre the falcon cannot hear the falconer; things fall apart; the center cannot hold.

> Ralph Nader
> New York, N.Y.

Sirs:

The best lack all conviction, while the worst are full of passionate intensity.

> Martha Mitchell
> Washington, D.C.

Sirs:

And what rough beast, its hour come round at last, slouches toward Bethlehem to be born?

> S. Agnew
> Washington, D.C.

Sirs:

Burma-Shave!

> Rod McKuen
> Los Angeles, Calif.

Sirs:

I know this really isn't your line, but I wondered if you could help me interpret this weird dream I keep getting night after night. I'm walking toward the Washington Monument arm in arm with this giant hot dog who's smoking a big cigar when all of a sudden I'm kidnapped by these telephone poles and tossed onto this long train that goes into a tunnel and falls into a deep, dark pit while a Tootsie Roll screams dirty words in my ear.

Any ideas?

> Paulus Sixtus
> The Vatican, Italy

Sirs:

Listen, you bunch of f--king homos, last night I caught that c--ks--king son-of-a-b--ch kid of mine reading your s--t-eating magazine again. I grabbed the little pr--k by his cr--h and beat the c--p out of the little c--thead until he about p--d in his pants. The *next* time I catch that little m----rf--ker with it, I'm going to ream his s---y little r---g with a can opener and take his h---ing p--g and make him g---y f-----m it until the tr--d runs out of his dr---p and his r--k t--bs j-ks revolve like a rusty crankshaft.

> Noah Webster

Sirs:

Maryland, the seventh state to join the Union, has an area of 10,577 square miles. It is nearly three times as large as Delaware, and would fit nicely into Kentucky if you chopped off some of Wicomico County and sort of squashed it up into the Chesapeake Bay. Its largest city is Baltimore. The most abundant natural resources are water and Little Tavern hamburgers. Major industries: horse racing, seborrhea, karate. State Bird: pink flamingo. State Flag: yellow and black quadrangles on dark rye with cole slaw.

> Spiro Agnew
> Baltimore, Maryland

Dear Sirs,

Congratulations (gratulations, felicitations, blessings, compliments, good wishes, best wishes) on your excellent (bueno, bon, bonzer, bonny, fine, nice, goodly, splendid, capital, braw, estimably, virtuous) magazine (journal, gazette, periodical, serial, ephemeris, pulp, slick, bulletin, daybook)! It certainly is funny (humorous, amusing, witty, droll, whimsical, risible, rich, priceless, farcical)!

> Peter Roget
> West Malvern, England

Dear Sir,

Your rare publication certainly is well done. (That's a jape!) I laughed so hard I almost forgot to add the ¼ cup bread crumbs to the mixture of 1 cup ground ham, 1 egg, ½ cup milk, Worcestershire, and chopped parsley (to taste), which after being shaped into patties, browned on both sides in bacon fat, and served with mustard sauce, makes my famous Ham Patties! (Serves two or three.)

> Fanny Farmer
> Boston, Mass.

Dear Sir,

As long as you are filling up space with letters made up, in your apparent desperation, for the most part of gleanings from reference works (which no doubt were the first thing that came to hand as you sat down to the typewriter at the last possible moment to write a long overdue column), might I suggest the following quotation, chosen at random, from my exhaustive compendium? "Let those with racquets give chase to the ball; for my part, I shall find sport enough pursuing, with a walking stick, the evanescent favors of the Devon countryside."

> —Thomas Porfsby, 1823–1884.
> John Bartlett
> Chicago, Ill.

Dear Sir,

I enjoyed that Roget-Fanny Farmer-Bartlett bit in your current issue, but although you gave the correct *Thesaurus* synonyms and the actual recipe for Ham Patties, you seem to have invented the Bartlett quotation, since I can find no "Thomas Porfsby" in my *Familiar Quotations*. Was it a misspelling, or am I right in assuming that you wanted a Bartlett's quote but had left your copy at the office, and so composed an appropriate quote, and then being so pleased with yourself at having come up with that wonderful fake one, you wrote this letter so everyone would know how clever you were?

Jermyn Smith-Corona
New York, N.Y.

Sirs:

I get no kick from cocaine. I'm sure that if I took even one sniff, it would bore me terrifically, too.

But I get a kick out of you.

Cole Porter
New York, N.Y.

Sirs:

Once, at a Holl7wood party, the famed Tallulah Bankhead overhe@rd an impudent young starlet prOcla?m tha½ most Hol&ywoo# stars were "just a bunch %f ¢heap tramps," and that sh3 hersel* was prob5bly the "onlE girl in H(llyw//d who still has her ch&rry."

To whi7h Miss Ban¼he@d replied, "Thxt's very nic¢, dahlin&, but doesn't it get in the way when you f#*k?"

Buster Hyman
Hayforth, Calif.

Sirs:

My name is Timothy Leary.

Timothy Leary
Zurich, Switzerland

Sirs:

My name is Timothy Leary.

Timothy Leary
Zurich, Switzerland

sRRis#

myi Nmmea stxa tmitthhe lllreeryy

tmitthhe llreeryy
zoork, zwiszszirlnd

Sirs:

Taxi! Taxi! Hey, over here, you prick! Taxi! Christ, the law says you gotta have your off-duty sign on, you're not gonna pick me up! Taxi! Hey! Over here! Shit, fuck, none of the bastards will stop!

Martin Scorseesee
Belmore Cafeteria, N.Y.

Sirs:

Things aren't bad enough. I send my emissary to your country with $300,000 to buy rifles. The shipment comes, but, instead of rifles, the idiots send us handcuffs. Now my troops, who aren't exactly Phi Beta Kappa candidates, get a hold of these and within two days, to a man, have locked themselves to beds, cabs, toilets, each other, tourists, garbage cans, churches, ice-cream trucks, cattle, and every other large, difficult-to-move object you can think of. And, of course, there are no keys. Could you see if you could find the keys? And for God's sake, don't tell Argentina or those CIA bastards of yours.

Salvador Allende

My Dearest Son Richard:

Don't eat muffins that seem to evidence foot tracks. Be considerate and thoughtful of persons of high station. Don't comment idly or act unduly impressed at seasonal changes. Cover your eyes and face in the sight of God. Walk with a brisk rhythmic pace swinging your right arm forward as your left leg extends and your left arm forward with your right leg. Never bathe with men who know Latin. If you should grow a boil, be neither ashamed nor proud. Shun the company of barrel makers and fletchers. Never place paper in your mouth. Only subtract numbers you feel comfortable with. Shift your weight if you witness yourself out of balance. Be evasive with Chinamen. Don't attempt to sing while lying down. Avoid intoxicants distilled from pitted fruits. Don't tie large copper pots to your legs or feet. Sleep twixt good stout sheets, for those of satin are the Devil's putwillies. Know a man by the heft of his stallion and the cut of his hankie. Be slow to judge the motives of animals smaller than your ear. Count to yourself while you dance. Disdain from men who would scratch at their nether parts—for they are louts. Attend all this I have said to you and you will soon be a

proper man. And don't forget to wish the *National Lampoon* a happy anniversary.

Lord Chesterfield
Dublin, Ireland

Sirs:

You want to know what really cracks me up? It's the little *pttt* sound that cans of Tab make when you pull off the pop top. I think it's terrific.

Andy Warhol
New York, New York

Sirs:

A few issues back I told you about my little ol' forty acres called the Slough of Despair. I'm now quite proud to announce the opening of Woe World—thanks to a hefty loan from the Emir of Jockrashi, I have converted my private gloom into a six-million-dollar Xanadu of hopelessness. Don't expect to see Goofy or Pluto at the gates of Woe World; you will instead be greeted by the boatman Charon and his grouchy mutt, Cerberus. They will grumpily escort you to various rides like Bleak House, the Sealed Tomb (Aida's Scream), and the Cramped Roman Galley. If that doesn't wilt your spirits, you can slink over to the Woe World Repertory Playhouse and watch my latest play, *Savage God, Part II*, wherein the hero (Job Schopenhauer) is subjected to the green-apple trots and a travelogue on Bolivia. Our entire staff is agog with torment. Name me one other park where you can cast your grin to the wind.

C.S. Lewis
Gnash-on-Teeth, England

Sirs:

I've noticed that the *National Lampoon* writes to itself rather than printing comments from its readers. I think this is a wonderfully novel idea, and your delightful "Letters" column is consistently the funniest part of the issue.

However, one thing has been puzzling me for months. Don't you ever simply "run dry" of ideas? It must be pretty grueling coming up with this great stuff month after month. Don't you ever get the urge to just say "Fuck it," turn off the typewriter, smoke some dope, and see what's on the tube? I don't know how you do it, but I really envy your self-contr

HENRY BEARD

The first thing I must tell you is that in 1975 Henry Beard told me he would never speak or write about his experiences during the five years he edited the *National Lampoon*. That book is closed for him. Philip Nolan–like, Henry would sail through the rest of his life wishing never to see or hear the name of the *National Lampoon* again. He might still have a country, but he's become the man without a magazine.

His friends, and I am one, respect his wishes—to a point, because he also told me he'd never grow a beard. "I'd be a walking joke." He must have decided he liked the joke. Henry

PHOTO BY MICHAEL GOLD

Beard has had a beard for 35 years. So perhaps there's an opportunity for a change of heart about his history at the *Lampoon*. I hope so, but it won't happen here. Henry is quite divorced from this endeavor, and while I like to think he wishes it well, I also believe he couldn't care less.

The Office
Standing in the hallway just outside their offices, looking through adjacent doorways, you can see both of them. On the left, Doug is talking on the phone. He's typing something and speaking with Rob Hoffman, who sits on a sofa, examining proofs with David Kaestle. A young art assistant stands next to Doug, her hand resting on his shoulder. She laughs at everything he says.

Henry is alone. He's bent over a manuscript, editing. He grimaces, runs his hand through his unruly hair and unleashes a squall of dandruff. He holds his head, chews his pipe, and works quickly with a pencil, scribbling notes all over the thing. Warp speed. He finishes a page every few seconds. I can't look away. It's mesmerizing.

Riding Shotgun
Henry, Tony, and I are walking along a perimeter fence on Tony's farm in New Jersey. We've got a big old double-barreled shotgun. Our pockets are stuffed with ammo. The three of

us, many beers ago, decided we needed to rid the landscape of gypsy-moth nests. We are convinced the best way to handle the situation is to keep drinking and then blow the little bastards to bits. We come to an oak with about ten big, webby nests. Henry shouts, "Get down before they see us!" It occurs to me he's serious. Henry's on his back loading the gun. He drops a shell on his chest and curses. Then he gets to his feet and shouts, "Okay, men, LET'S GO!" Tony yells, "For England! And Saint George!" We follow as Henry charges the tree, stops, and empties both barrels at it. The recoil knocks him on his ass.

Later, we discuss how a shotgun blast will definitely remove large gypsy moth nests from trees. Not a trace left! The downside is the amount of tree removed from the tree. We fired about thirty shells that afternoon. Tony's trees looked like Swiss cheese when we were done.

Water in the Hole
Wherever he is now, Henry plays golf more than he writes. How is it, one former editor asked, he hasn't written the great American comic novel, the one he was born to write? "You write that," Henry might say. "I've got another few holes to play."

At Inverness or at Pebble Beach, there's a bearded man in tweeds. He's alone long after the other duffers have left for the day. He fishes a wet ball out of the cup and wipes it on his jacket. Peering into the fog, he sees nothing but the mist that's settled onto the lenses of his thick glasses. The world in swirling grays. He places the ball on the tee, sets himself, and swings. There is no sound, only the slap of water and air mixing as the ball describes a high arc into the fog and silently evanesces.

There is joy in Mudville.

—Rick Meyerowitz

McGOVERN WINS NOMINATION!

Henry Beard created "News of the Month" and wrote most of it
for two years. Collected here are some of his fiercest and funniest pieces.

NEWS OF THE MONTH

MARCH 1971

The Union Chemical Co. has announced that a shipment of 5,000 gallons of ultra-pure mercury, destined for its giant petro-chemical facility in Stumfton, Ind., was spoiled when a worker, during a routine inspection, inadvertently dropped a tuna fish sandwich into the tank car in which it was being transported. Company spokesmen said the mercury was found to contain .5 parts per million of tuna and is considered totally unfit for industrial use.

AUGUST 1971

The U.S. Coast Guard has reported sighting a twenty-six-mile-long water slick several miles off Santa Barbara, California. The transparent and slightly salty fluid—which one observer described as "greenish-blue with occasional flecks of white"— apparently welled up from a subterranean spring on the sea floor, possibly as the result of a minor earthquake. Coast Guard officials feel that unless there is a sudden change of wind, the giant slick poses no danger to the delicate rust-prone machinery commonly found along the coast, and at present they do not plan to try to break it up with detergents or other chemicals.

THE CHOICE OF THE CENTURY

VOTE FOR ME! I'LL FINISH PACKING THE SUPREME COURT WITH NARROW-MINDED NEBBISHES, I'LL REPEAL THE REST OF THE BILL OF RIGHTS, AND I'LL MAKE INDOCHINA LOOK LIKE THE BOTTOM OF A SHAKE-'N-BAKE BAG.

VOTE FOR ME! I HAVE THE ECONOMIC KNOW-HOW OF A BULGARIAN SHOE-FACTORY MANAGER, THE GRASP OF WORLD AFFAIRS OF A BOLIVIAN CIVICS TEACHER, AND THE DECISIVENESS OF A BED OF KELP!

JUNE 1972

The Pentagon, the world's largest warmaker, announced last week that the recall of more than 500,000 soldiers begun three years ago is nearing completion. The callback, which was initiated as the result of widespread complaints of "bogging down" and high operating costs from individuals who had bought the heavily advertised war when it came out in 1965, involves virtually every model soldier in the line, including the high-performance Marine, the sporty Greet Beret, the rear-echelon Officer, and, accounting for over half of the total recall, the stripped-down Draftee, which had no options and came in black and white, with a red interior. Although there has been no official admission from the Pentagon, it is known that many, if not all, of the soldiers involved were inadvertently sent out without a rational purpose, a "minor oversight" according to Defense Department officials who refused to be identified and would not confirm or deny the claim. The absence of this component has apparently caused "hesitation," the annoying delay between the time an order is given and it is obeyed, "fragging," "mainlining," and a momentary loss of ideals. A large number of soldiers recalled also have missing parts, shot body work, and other major defects, and estimates of the number that ended up in the "graveyard" range as high as fifty thousand, but Pentagon officials said they could not be liable for repairs of accidents that occurred as the result of normal service. They did say, however, that they would provide, free of charge, a whitewash and a Vietnamize job.

SEPTEMBER 1972

Recently completed studies of aerial photography have led to intensive speculation in the scientific community that there may be life in northern South Vietnam. In between the huge craters and in portions of the wide, vast areas of coastal plain, which is so empty it seems to have been scraped by giant bulldozers, researchers have discovered small, dark patches of what a few optimistic biologists think may be a stunted, bushlike growth that somehow manages to exist in the poisonous soil. Unlike the moon, the Quang Tri region of Vietnam does have natural groundwater and an atmosphere, and it has long been theorized that a crude kind of pond scum could thrive in the shallow pools of water that fill some of the larger craters, but the purported discovery of a more sophisticated form of vegetation is certain to be as rich a source of controversy and excitement as the celebrated episode in 1970 when an overeager seismologist mistook the detonation of a series of delayed-action bombs for signs of geological activity similar to those found by Apollo 14 in the lunar highlands. A final determination of the matter will have to depend on higher-quality photographs, since members of the scientific community are extremely reluctant to participate in any manned explorations of the area. As one put it, "I'd rather make a space walk in a raincoat."

SEPTEMBER 1972

Last week, with its 3,457th consecutive day, the perennially smash war *Vietnam!* edged past the lesser-known British hit of the fifties, *The Malayan Counterinsurgency*, to become the longest-running military conflict of the century. *Vietnam!*, which opened to mixed, but generally favorable, reviews more than ten years ago, has spawned a number of imitators during its phenomenally lengthy engagement, including *Cambodia!* and the poorly publicized underground belligerency *Laos!*, and yet another, *Thailand!*, has reportedly been optioned and is scheduled to begin casting next spring, but none of them seems likely to approach the attendance figures of the original, whose magic nearly two million Americans journeyed to the old Pacific Theatre to be a part of. A money-waster bigger even than unforgettable *South Korea!*, *Vietnam!* is likely to be the last of the elaborately staged American shows of force that some trace back to the 1898 comic operetta *Remember the Maine!* "The day of the big, brassy wars is over," lamented one old-timer. "No one's got twenty or thirty billion to sink into a brush-fire production that might close in the U.N. after nine months. And there's no talent. Why, a lot of these kids, they just get out there

ONE OTHER THING I PROBABLY SHOULD TELL YOU, BECAUSE IF I DON'T THEY'LL PROBABLY BE SAYING THIS ABOUT ME TOO, WE DID GET SOMETHING! A GIFT BEFORE THE ELECTION. A MAN DOWN IN TEXAS REMEMBERED MY MENTIONING THAT ALL PAT HAD WAS A RESPECTABLE CLOTH COAT. AND BELIEVE IT OR NOT, THE DAY BEFORE THE NEW CAMPAIGN LAW WENT INTO EFFECT, WE GOT A MESSAGE SAYING THERE WAS A PACKAGE FOR US. YOU KNOW WHAT IT WAS? IT WAS TWO MILLION DOLLARS IN ONE HUNDRED DOLLAR BILLS, SENT ALL THE WAY FROM MEXICO. NICE AND GREEN AND CRISP. AND I JUST WANT TO SAY THIS RIGHT NOW, THAT REGARDLESS OF WHAT THEY SAY ABOUT IT, WE'RE GOING TO KEEP IT.

and die, they've just got no stuff. The lure of the light at the end of the tunnel, the smell of the napalm, the roar of the shells, that old 'the slaughter must go on' spirit, they just don't have it in their blood." There are rumors that *Vietnam!* will officially close late this summer, but, according to Pentagon Productions, it is expected to continue "for several more years" with an all-Vietnamese cast.

DECEMBER 1972

The Air Force has announced that the accidental bombing of the French mission in Hanoi was the result of "stupid bombs." According to Air Force sources, the older, less intelligent bombs are being replaced on an accelerated schedule with the new "smart bombs," but the huge increase in the number of sorties flown over the North has made it necessary to use more of the relatively simple explosive devices than had been anticipated. "Let's face it, those babies are dummies," commented one senior Air Force pilot, referring to the type of outdated bomb that allegedly caused the damage. "They've got nothing in their warheads but TNT, and they don't know their tail fins from a hole in the ground. They make those naval mines that can tell the difference between a freighter and a school of tuna look like Einsteins. You'll be over your target and you'll say, 'Railyard, get that railyard,' and those bombs will drop off the racks mumbling 'choochoo' and go blast an orphanage.

Yes, we have no bombing raids today
NIXON NOMINATED FOR NOBEL WAR PRIZE

The pilot probably said 'trenches,' and one of those dodo blockbusters thought he said 'Frenchies.' You ask any one of those foreign correspondents who was there. Five'll get you ten there was a big loud 'Duh!' when the damn thing went off."

MARCH 1973

In view of demands by a number of religious groups in California that science textbooks explaining the Darwinian theory of evolution give equal space to the Biblical view that the earth and life were created in six days, it seems only fair to provide space in basic-science texts for other equally important contributions to scientific thought by the Christian religion, including the following: the theory that the sun revolves around the earth; the body of thought that holds that lunacy is the result of infestation by devils; an interpretation of the noted "torture" cure; a list of roman-numeral multiplication tables; a good, clear statement of the flat-earth theory; a thorough study of the angel-pinhead problem; and a detailed explanation, preferably with diagrams, of the fascinating mechanisms involved in virgin birth. Similarly, it seems equally fair to require that all Bibles printed in the United States include a chapter, immediately following Genesis, explaining the DNA molecule, natural selection, genetic mutation, paleontology, continental drift, carbon-14 dating, and the Big Bang and solid-state theories of the formation of the universe.

I DIDN'T WRITE "LAW OF THE JUNGLE"
John Weidman

In 1973, or maybe it was 1974 (there's a lot about the early seventies that was a little blurry, even then), I was a second- or maybe a third-year law student at Yale Law School. I had graduated from Harvard with Doug in 1968, had been a regular contributor to the *National Lampoon* since its inception, and had continued to contribute to the magazine while I was learning about torts and contracts.

One day Henry called, asking me if I wanted to write a piece called "Law of the Jungle." This seemed like an entertaining idea, and it was obvious why Henry thought I was the right person to write it, so I agreed and proceeded to knock out what I thought was an amusing little article about jurisdictional grazing rights among wildebeest, the Constitutionally protected freedom to screech, and stuff like that.

Several days after I turned it in, I got a call from Henry saying that he liked it, but would I mind if he tinkered with it a little bit. "Not at all," I said, and I promptly forgot about the piece until it was published.

As you can see, "Law of the Jungle" is credited to the two of us. It was generous of Henry to leave my name on it, but, in fact, by the time Henry had finished tinkering, "Law of the Jungle" was entirely his creation.

It was also as pure an expression of one particular facet of Henry's genius as anything that he ever published in the *Lampoon*. Dense—beyond dense—the piece takes the idea articulated in the title and explores it with an exhaustive, one might almost say exhausting, wit, intelligence, and intensity. Never once violating the stylistic imperatives of the thing which it lampoons—arch, but never too arch—"Law of the Jungle" spins its premise out over the course of some twelve thousand words, not one of which is wasted. Answers.com, which I have just consulted online, defines *tour de force* as "a feat requiring great virtuosity . . . often deliberately undertaken for its difficulty."

"Law of the Jungle" is a tour de force.

SHOOT THIS COPY EDITOR
Louise Gikow

Copyediting is like Zeno's paradox. You aim to correct all of the mistakes in a manuscript before it goes to print. First read you catch about half. Next read, the other half. Next read, another . . . and so on. But you never catch that last mistake.

Especially on a piece like the first one I read as copy editor of the *National Lampoon*. It was for the January 1974 issue. The theme was "Animals." The lynchpin piece was Henry Beard's astounding and elephantine, twelve-thousand-word "Law of the Jungle," written with John Weidman.

It was typed, of course, single spaced and a bit smudgy, with almost no corrections, as if it had emerged full-blown from Henry's imagination. And there were footnotes . . . miles and miles of them.

It was twenty-plus pages of pure intellectual muscle. Not a single joke was left untold in two languages—English and Latin. Well, three, if you count the language of the law.

I knew no law. I knew no Latin. By the time I'd finished "Law of the Jungle" for the first time (and I'd be reading it again and again), I wasn't sure if I knew any English. I certainly hadn't read any quite like Henry's.

He demonstrated a breathtaking knowledge of jurisprudence, human nature, the arts, biology, botany, history, and words of more than three syllables.

He hadn't missed a joke . . . every word and phrase seemed to have been twisted, turned, analyzed, and wrung dry of its comic potential.

And the whole thing seemed effortless.

In certain ways, it's almost unreadable, at least in one sitting—like trying to eat ten gallons of butter pecan ice cream in a half hour.

I think of it as one of the most brilliant pieces Henry has ever written—which means one of the most brilliant pieces ever.

Law of the Jungle

by Henry Beard and John Weidman

(Opposite: A somewhat romanticized portrayal of the landmark restraint of evolution case, Unicorns v. Animal Kingdom *(26 Mamm. 244). In the celebrated legal action, seven unicorns, the entire number still in existence at the time, brought a Doe suit against all animals, claiming unfair competition and conspiracy to render extinct, and asked that a writ of vivo vivantur, literally, "live and let live," be issued, permanently enjoining all living creatures from encroaching upon the habitats and domains of the unicorn. Although the principle of the right of an animal to the perpetuation of its species was well established, the action was an unusually sweeping one, and by ill chance, the jury, which was composed, according to the custom in extinction cases, by members of the plaintiff, rather than the defendant animal's order (in this case the horned mammals), was distinctly unfriendly. In any case, the ruling went against the unicorn, and although an appeal was brought charging that fabulous and mythical beasts, particularly basilisks, cockatrices, and phoenixes, had been systematically excluded from the jury, to the prejudice of the unicorn's interests, the case became moot when the last unicorn died during the taking of depositions in a related lawsuit.)*

I

INTRODUCTION

It is generally thought that the law of the jungle, or lex biologica, as it is properly known, can be reduced to a pair of simple catch phrases: "kill or be killed" and "survival of the fittest." This is, of course, no more true than the proposition that all human law can be expressed in the single solomonic principle of "an eye for an eye and a tooth for a tooth," but a number of commentators, Charles Darwin, the Huxleys, Robert Ardrey, Konrad Lorenz, and Rudyard Kipling, to name a few, have been responsible for spreading within the last century a considerable amount of misinformation about animal law which has significantly contributed to the erroneous idea already well rooted in popular belief, that animal jurisprudence consists primarily of the simple feudal concept of trial by combat. A flood of "nature films" depicting animals tearing each other to pieces which are regularly shown to children as education as well as entertainment have tended to reinforce at a very early age an image of animals behaving in a wild and lawless manner. Needless to say, films which show the aftermath of the bombings of Dresden or Hiroshima, or the liberation of Buchenwald, or even daily life on one of the poorer streets of our great cities, should logically be equally damaging evidence of the absence of a body of law among men, but the very fact that the word "animal" has come to be accepted as synonymous with uncivilized behavior is sufficient proof of the deep prejudice which exists.[1]

In fact, so inaccurate a notion represents a serious oversimplification of a highly complex and sophisticated legal code, one which compares very favorably with the great Western legal traditions—Roman law, English common law, and the French Napoleonic Code.[2]

Like human law, the lex biologica evolved over a long period of time, and it isn't difficult to find periods in animal history when the sum of legal niceties was "bite makes right," but countless examples of human legal concepts at an immature stage of development can be cited to show that animals have no monopoly as far as having a background of legal crudity goes. Less than a thousand years ago, trial by fire and water, the Inquisition, the common infliction of the death penalty for petty theft, and the regular use of torture to obtain confessions, were common practice throughout Europe. By comparison, even in Jurassic times,[3] animals had the rudiments of a legal structure. One of the first recorded cases, *Brontosaurus v. Tyrannosaurus Rex* (7 Fossils 3446), a fairly routine waterhole case in which a dispute arose following the closing of a traditional easement by a volcanic eruption, indicated that the beginnings of an awareness among animals of a need for an orderly means of settling disagreements without bloodshed existed long before parallel developments in human law.[4]

Unfortunately, the larger reptiles, particularly the dinosaurs, behaved like Norman knights, refusing in many cases to accept unfavorable verdicts, and almost invariably resorting to the ancient custom of trial by eating. Needless to say, this was a far more critical factor in their catastrophic decline than the Ice Age.[5]

Nevertheless, the development of legal institutions in the animal kingdom has for the most part been a steady and inevitable one, sometimes making huge jumps forward (for example, the adoption of the Universal Genetic Code), sometimes suffering setbacks, yet always moving towards greater detail, more precision, and, on the whole, an ever-widening recognition of animal rights. The remarkably exact and voluminous body of law which began to be introduced with the advent of warm-blooded animals and their eventual domination of the animal kingdom is a far cry (literally) from the stay-out-of-my-territory-or-I'll-bite-off-your-proboscis mentality that spawned it, but the process by which animal law grew,

---

[1] Another example of this attitude is the oft-quoted line from Dickens, "The law is an ass." To set the record straight, it should be noted that a number of asses have been very distinguished jurists. For example, an ass, sitting as judge in the famous migration case, *Vertebratae Americanae v. Alaska Land Bridge,* established the principle of the right of unlimited evolutionary spread. In another instance, an ass wrote the celebrated dissent in *Goldfinch*

v. Bluejay (12 Ornith. 148), holding that a search of a bluejay's nest for evidence of its having eaten the eggs of the plaintiff goldfinch, a search which, as it developed, did yield incriminating evidence of several other similar crimes, violated the defendant bluejay's rights since it was based not on specific probable cause but on the general knowledge that bluejays traditionally raid other birds' nests. The principle was later accepted.

[2] In terms of complexity and overall fairness, most observers put the lex biologica on an equal plane with German law, with which it shares surprising similarities.

[3] The word Jurassic, incidentally, comes from the Latin root juris, or "having to do with law," and refers to the period in which animals first developed legal institutions. Sadly, many people do not know this.

[4] For a fascinating glimpse of this birth period of animal law, see *Equus on Reptiles.* Interestingly, all three major branches of the lex fauna, land law, aquatic law, and aerial law, developed from the codex reptilia, since this extraordinarily numerous and varied class counted swimming, walking, and flying specimens among its members.

[5] See *Tyrannosaurus Rex v. Canadian Ice Sheet,* and other similar cases.

NATIONAL LAMPOON

and still grows, is direct, logical, and quite methodical. Alas, there simply isn't space here to describe it,[6] nor is there room to give any but the most sweeping introduction to basic animal law. As an example of the task involved in gaining a working knowledge of the lex fauna alone, it usually requires anywhere from seven to ten years for an animal to be admitted to the stump and allowed to practice law, a fact which, unfortunately, permanently prohibits a large number of short-lived species from pursuing legal careers.

Basically, the so-called "law of the jungle" (or more accurately, the lex biologica, or "law of living things"), falls into two categories, plant law (lex flora) and animal law (lex fauna). We won't concern ourselves except in passing with plant law. Actually, it is quite simple, and apart from a rather large and tedious body of case material on root rights of way, leaf easements, water rights, and the inevitable entanglement suits brought by trees against various species of ivy —a caseload which always threatens to strangle the courts—plant law is very sedate and straightforward.[7] There are, of course, numerous areas of overlap between plant law and animal law, for example, pollination cases, in which various flowering plants bring suit for breach of contract against bees, and property law, an instance of which is the implied lease which a bird enters into when it places its nest in a tree.[8]

Animal law, as has been suggested, is usually divided into the law of the sea or aquatic law (corpus juris maris); the law of the air or aerial law (jus aeris), which is really just a subdivision of the law of the land rather than a separate division, like aquatic law, since birds and insects actually spend a majority of their time on the ground; and the law of the land (jus terrestris) itself. (Unfortunately, since the lex fauna developed in much the same way as English common law, that is, by fits and starts, according to no specific plan, and incorporating every oddity and phase of evolution along the way, it is mind-bendingly complex, with intertwining jurisdictions and separate codes, a fact which is probably becoming clear just about now, and which explains why this discourse can only serve as an introduction.) Within land animal law as a whole, and occasionally overlapping aquatic law, are herbivore and carnivore law, each with its own separate courts. Generally speaking, carnivore courts end up handling criminal cases and herbivore courts civil cases, not because of any sensible legal reason, but simply because, traditionally, a carnivore convicted in a herbivore court got off lightly or ate the court. However, because of the confusion, an animal, let us say a mountain lion involved in a territoriality dispute with another mountain lion in which he accidentally killed the other mountain lion during a fight over a cave, and was hence charged with animalslaughter, and tried for that crime in carnivore court, might also be charged with a civil breach arising out of the same act, such as simple trespass, and tried in a herbivore court, without protection from double jeopardy. Admittedly, it happens rarely, and most of the civil penalties, at least, are fairly minor by comparison with the criminal ones, but it is arguably a flaw in animal law.

Within both the lex flora and the lex fauna, there is microbe law, including the codex bacteria, the lex protozoa, virus law, and a few others, and together they represent the most stupefyingly difficult imaginable legal structure. Fortunately, the obvious problem of size difference renders it, of necessity, beyond our concern, but out of sight is not quite entirely out of mind. First of all, as elsewhere in the overall lex biologica, many cases occur between jurisdictions. For example, in the junction between microbe law and plant law, there are an incalculably large number of nitrogen-fixing cases, a criminal matter taken very seriously by most vegetation. But the largest impact of microbe law by far is in its relation to animal law, for the very good reason that, as is well known, viruses and bacteria particularly play an immensely large role in animal life, and although an obscure trial of an influenza virus on a criminal trespass charge may seem the height of triviality, it takes on considerable importance if the jurisdiction turns out to be the Superior Court for the Lower Intestine in your own body. Similarly, a summary judgment granted in favor of a streptococcus bacteria seeking under the provisions of the Genetic Code to alter its cell wall to render it immune to the effects of penicillin mold on the grounds of tortious conduct on the part of the penicillin mold, to wit, reckless interference with reproduction, may be the beginning of a major epidemic. Along the same lines, in plant law, a judgment ruling in favor of a contention on the part of a tobacco mosaic virus that the xylem of a tobacco plant represents a legal right of way could result in the bankruptcy of a farmer.[9]

Of course, within animal law, there are a vast number of jurisdictions, generally, but not always, corresponding to the major natural divisions of living things. A few of the most common are the Vertebrate Courts, the Reptilian Courts, the Invertebrate Courts, the Rodent Courts (administering the special codex rodenta), and, in a quirk produced by the early separation of the Australian land mass from the rest of the continental agglomeration, the Marsupial Courts. Marsupial cases, incidentally, are unique to the extent that, in criminal prosecutions, evidence by the young, if they are in the pouch at the time of the commission of the alleged

[6] The best source still is the classic *Cherrystone's Commentaries*.

[7] There are a few more colorful cases in plant law, as for example, *Bluebottle v. Venus Fly Trap* (49 Botan. 236), a complex entrapment case, in which the principle of the right of an animal to sue in a botanical court was upheld. It is something of a curiosity, because most actions brought to protest ingestions go the other way—plant to animal, as would be the case, say, if a genus of plains grass sued a buffalo herd for overgrazing. In practice, of course, there are practically no interjurisdictional suits, because very few animals have the patience to sit through interminable botanical proceedings. Most evidence is taken by osmosis, the courts adjourn in the fall and don't reconvene again until spring, and a careless footstep of a large animal not even involved in the case can completely wipe out several months of hearings.

[8] *Hazelnut v. Gypsy Moth* (2 Arb. 361), is an intriguing instance of overlap, with a wild card thrown in. The case, which is still in adjudication and is likely to be so almost indefinitely, revolves around a very tricky legal point, itself unresolved. The gypsy moth begins its life as a worm, at which point it erects huge tentlike structures in the branches of trees and proceeds to eat them bare. This suit was brought by the tree in question under the principle of trop mange,

literally, "you're eating too much," a long-established concept in both plant and animal law, which holds that if there is a reasonable alternative source of essentially the same foodstuff in another neighboring locality, it is the obligation of the predator animal not to completely eliminate any given subject species, an act which would of course infringe on its right not to be rendered extinct. In animal law, a lion is thus prohibited from eating all the members of an antelope herd, or even confining its diet merely to antelopes, when gazelles or impalas are equally available. In plant law, the principle is generally taken, in the case of large vegetable growth, like trees, to refer to single specimens—that is, a giraffe would, under plant law, be enjoined from completely stripping one tree, thus dooming it, and leaving another nearby untouched. *Hazelnut v. Gypsy Moth* would thus be a prima proboscis, or open-jaw-and-shut case of trop mange, except for one thing. Once the tent caterpillar has finished its life as a worm, it changes into a moth and flies away. This, of course, is exactly what the defendants in *Hazelnut* and all similar suits have done. One would think that the case could be resolved by bringing an action against the creature in its moth phase, but even presuming that the time problem could be overcome (the moths generally live no longer than a day or two), there is no legal basis for a suit, since the moth has no chewing apparatus, does not in any way damage the tree, and immediately leaves the tree once it can fly. It is cases like this that make the law of the jungle so fascinating.

[9] Microbe law is so impossibly convoluted, and, for obvious reasons, so difficult to get any hard information on, it is really worth forgetting about, if only for your own peace of mind. No one likes the idea that some inept coliform bacteria, sitting as judge in his gall bladder, is going to let off a cancer virus on a technicality. We apologize for bringing this up in the first place.

crime, is not admissable, and cannot be compelled.

In aerial law, there are the Courts of Ovivipary and Vivipary, and the Nest Assizes, and in insect law, itself an unimaginably large jurisdiction, the Court of Common Stings and the Ant Military Courts. These, and those courts mentioned above, are all in addition to the more or less standard interspecies courts, and there are endless jurisdictional disputes.[10] Incidentally, while we're on the subject of insects, it's worth mentioning that when you hear the characteristic high-pitched noise which cicadas make on a summer day, the odds are you are hearing a Court of Small Crawls being called to order.

The minutiae of all this is admittedly bewildering. Of course, nothing mentioned thus far begins to compare in complexity and sheer orneriness with aquatic law. Virtually every species from mammals, birds, and reptiles, down through saltwater fish[11] to more or less fixed creatures, some of which, like the hydra, spend half their lives subject to the lex fauna and half subject to the lex flora, are represented. In addition, any breach, civil or criminal, committed in the sea or above it by an animal normally subject to the jus terrestris falls automatically under the jurisdiction of the corpus juris maris. This can have problematical implications. In a famous case, *Seagull v. Mollusk* (187 Atlan. 30), a gull which had taken a clam from among some rocks near the seashore normally covered by high tide and had dropped it from a considerable height to break its shell, found itself charged with unlawful breaking and entering under the corpus juris maris for an act which under the jus terrestris and the jus aeris is not a crime if committed in the course of a lawful search for food. The critical point was that the clam had been seized in an aquatic jurisdiction, and when it fell, it fell into an aquatic jurisdiction, namely, on a rock covered at high tide. Thanks to a very smart lawyer indeed (a cormorant, not surprisingly), the seagull was eventually acquitted on a technicality. (The cormorant argued successfully that the case fell properly into the jurisdiction of the jus aeris and the jus terrestris, jointly, because at

the instant of the commission of the act held to be a crime under the corpus juris maris, namely, the moment the seagull released the mollusk from its beak with the intent that it should fall on a rock, thus breaking its shell, the seagull was in the air over dry land, a contention he was able to produce witnesses, in the form of an albatross and a pelican, to support.)

Another famous case in aquatic law, one which is still continuing, and at 17,567 years, is surely the longest litigation in any jurisdiction, is *Great Barrier Reef v. Starfish* (2 Pacif. 412). First entered in the Court of the Lower Depths, and after 3,416 years, transferred to the Marine Court for the Western District of the Lower Pacific when through statute that court gained jurisdiction, the case has been carried on by successive individual polyps against all members of the species *Asterias vulgaris* engaged in feeding off said plaintiff polyps along the eastern coast of Australia. On the face of it, it was a very ordinary case, a malicious predation suit, charging the starfish with deliberately limiting their diet to the easy-to-locate polyps, and thus endangering the predated species and its habitat. It was a little unusual, because by eating the polyps, the starfish were inhibiting the growth of coral—actually, the skeletons of dead polyps of previous generations—and in some cases destroying it, thus, in one act, violating two very basic rights: the right of perpetuation of a species, and the right of preservation of its habitat. A key decision, which the court probably came quickly to regret, was to allow new members of the coral polyp species to take up the suit when previous plaintiffs died. The resulting suit has forced several other species, involved by an accident of jury selection at the beginning of the suit, to move their habitats to the coral reefs and adapt themselves to life there so as to be able to continue hearing the suit. Several original participant species have since become extinct, and as an odd side effect, the reefs have grown immensely, partially because it is in the reefs that the inconceivably voluminous transcripts are stored.

Of course, the overwhelming majority of aquatic cases are a good deal less exotic, and in its fundamentals, the corpus juris maris does not differ greatly from the jus terrestris. Most of aquatic plant law is covered by the codex algae, and as with land animal law, the distinction between carnivore and herbivore courts, that is, their division of responsibilities into criminal and civil cases, is followed. The few mammals, like the whale and the dolphin, which returned to the sea, are entirely within the jurisdic-

tion of the corpus juris maris, and on the whole, relations between the aquatic and land courts have been surprisingly free of acrimony.

There are still more divisions and subdivisions, including the process of appeals up through various levels of jurisdiction, and their complexity is numbing. Basically, under the lex flora and the lex fauna, appeals are permitted to the Supreme Court in each of the geographical areas in the plant and animal kingdoms, but appeals from aquatic cases end with the Marine Supreme Court, and appeals in aerial cases can only be heard by the appropriate land Supreme Court if there is a significant question under the jus terrestris. Decisions and precedents differ enormously from place to place. For example, the African courts, particularly the Supreme Court of the Serengeti Plain, have tended to favor carnivores. By comparison, the laws regarding predation in North American districts are exceptionally strict. Jurisdictional disputes between geographical areas are many and vituperative.[12]

This brief description, which has probably confused and enlightened in equal measure, was intended to give some notion of the complexity of the law of the jungle, and it is really only prefatory to an enumeration of the basic legal principles which govern the conduct of affairs in the animal kingdom (some of them also apply in the plant kingdom, but obviously, plants, with their lack of mobility, are usually involved in far fewer litigations, civil or criminal). Again, since the lex fauna evolved piecemeal, it simply isn't possible to organize these principles in any truly logical fashion, and the presentation here, which is only one of a number of satisfactory possibilities, is somewhat arbitrary.

II

"UNWRITTEN" RIGHTS

As is the case in the British legal system, the key individual rights enjoyed and claimed by animals are "unwritten"—that is, they are not specifically enumerated in some document or legal instrument like the Bill

---

[10] These jurisdictional disputes often lead to flagrant miscarriages of justice. See *Porpoise v. Porpoise* (505 Aqua. 44), a felonious assault case. The defendant porpoise, quite clearly guilty, evaded punishment on a technicality, because the prosecutor made the fatal jurisdictional mistake of bringing the case on the Fish and Crustacean, rather than the Sea Mammal, side of the Magistrate's Court for the Bermuda Triangle.

[11] Fresh water fish in streams and lakes are subject to the codex flumen and the corpus laccus, or to pond law, depending on their habitat. All of these jurisdictions fall within the jus terrestris.

[12] A good example is *Old World Monkey v. New World Monkey* (220 Amaz. 45), a relatively routine unfair competition case which exploded into a nasty slanging match between the Supreme Court of Serengeti and the Superior Court of the Lower Amazon Basin. Considering that the courts involved coerced two species of birds who normally migrate between South America and Africa into carrying insults back and forth, and that in so doing the birds may have violated portions of the jus aeris by being party to the communication of a libel, the whole matter was disgraceful. Not surprisingly, at the root of it was man, who brought the Old World monkey to South America in the first place.

of Rights of the United States Constitution, but are instead expressed in a number of roundabout fashions, sometimes hidden in convoluted language in a relatively minor statute, sometimes implied by precedent and tradition, sometimes accepted by long practice, and so forth. This relative imprecision of statement should by no means be read as an indication that these rights are taken lightly by animals or are likely to be easily dismissed by them.

In this regard, there are a number of important rights and freedoms which together form the underlying basis of all of the laws of the animal and plant kingdoms, including the lex fauna, the lex flora, and all subsidiary codes. It should be noted that these rights apply equally to all creatures, regardless of jursidiction, and except to the extent that they are specifically limited or qualified by statute, these rights are absolute.

A. The Right to Eat

Also known as freedom of predation, the right to eat guarantees to every living creature the right to sustenance, without criminal penalty, regardless of whether ingestion consistent with this right leads directly or indirectly to the death of another animal or plant, provided that the predator, if challenged, can demonstrate beyond a reasonable doubt that its consumption of said animal or plant was purely and solely for the purposes of survival and continued existence and not for any lesser purpose. This fundamental right has been discussed and restated on a number of occasions and in a variety of forums, but it is certainly best expressed in Title 76 of the Carnivore Code of the lex fauna: "Any creature bearing fur or fin or feather who shall, in the pursuit of its rightful desire to prosper within the confines of its habitat and according to the manner of its species, devour, feed upon, or otherwise ingest another living thing, have it blood or sap, provided that said living thing shall not be of the same species, shall not be held culpable of a felony, nor of eating nor of animalslaughter, and any action for retrieval of damages, and any charge under the criminal code shall fail, nor shall any injunction issue, save that it be demonstrated that said devourment, feeding, or ingestion was willful or malicious, lacking of necessity for survival, or not arising out of hunger, and the burden of the proof of improper predation shall rest with the plant or animal fed upon, for otherwise than that it be proven that the intent of the predator was in the first instance to kill, and not to feed, this right, as enumerated, shall be absolute."

Needless to say, the distinction between killing to kill and killing to obtain food is paramount throughout animal law. One of the most famous and important statements of the right to eat resulted from the case of *Gazelle v. Lion* (245 Mamm. 198), in the Court of Carnivore Appeals for the Northern Veldt. The plaintiff gazelle prayed for the issuance of a writ of habeas carcasse, the so-called "Great Writ" which, when issued, demands the return of the remains of a preyed-upon animal and its release ex mandibilia, literally, "from the jaws," pending determination of the legality of the predator's actions. (It was the plaintiff gazelle's temporary good fortune that an officer of the court happened to be in the neighborhood during the disputed attack—normally, writs of habeas carcasse are issued post mortem.)

Following the issuance of the writ, the gazelle presented evidence that the defendant lion had within twenty minutes of the attack upon itself, killed and left uneaten an antelope, and that therefore any further attacks which the lion made prior to the ingestion of the prey it had already killed could not be rationalized as motivated by legitimate hunger, since if hunger were the prime motivation, as required by the statute, the lion would eat what it killed before it killed again, and if it killed again, before it ate what it killed, then, it must follow, the lion's prime motivation, regardless of its nature, could not be hunger. In a judgment nullifying the writ of habeas carcasse, the court, presided over by a notorious "feeding judge," it must be noted, answered this somewhat sophist argument with one of its own, finding that the lion's legitimate and protected right to eat remained intact, for at the time it killed the antelope, it could not be argued that it was not hungry, since it had not eaten the antelope it had previously killed, and, having not eaten the antelope, it could hardly be argued that at the time of its attack on the gazelle its hunger was any the less.

This case is far from being the most shining example of animal jurisprudence, but it serves to underscore the reluctance which all of the animal courts have displayed in reducing or limiting the right to eat, recognizing as they have its integral and essential relationship to the right of survival. In practice, the only animalslaughter or felony eating (Eating One, Eating Two, etc.) cases which are ever adjudicated are those in which killings within species are involved or in a few extraordinary cases where killings which cannot be rationalized as consistent with hunger, because of the

impossibility of the predator devouring its prey, occur.[13]

B. The Right to Breed

The statement of this freedom often seems redundant to observers of animal law, probably because in fairly recent human experience, direct interference with human reproductive processes has rarely if ever characterized the actions of even the worst tyrant, and the most passing familiarity with police records indicates that it is rape, and not the prevention of intercourse, which is the leading sex crime. All of this, of course, is to miss the point. It is very rare in the animal kingdom (somewhat less rare in the plant kingdom)[14] that mating processes of one species are interfered with by another, but the statement of the right to breed is nevertheless important because of the critical protections which emanate from it.

The first of these key protections is the "not guilty by reason of instinct" defense.[15] Since there is no explicit right to individual survival—this is often puzzling to persons whose notion of animal life is limited to a high school level introduction to Darwin's unbelievably myopic observations[16]—the "instinct" defense, a very useful and common one, can be legally based only on an animal's natural desire to perpetuate the species.

[13] This principle has become known as the Boa Test, the name having come from a freakish negligent animalslaughter case which resulted from the accidental killing of an elephant by a boa constrictor. The large snake—made logy by the heat—had entwined itself around the leg of a grazing elephant, thinking it was a tree trunk. The elephant failed to notice the snake and eventually it moved on, with the snake still around its leg. As luck would have it, the boa awoke with a start just as the elephant was negotiating a tricky path along a rocky escarpment; the elephant was startled, tripped over the boa, and fell to its death. The charge of negligent animalslaughter was a little extreme, but the boa managed to achieve acquittal by actually eating the remains of the elephant during the seven month period of the trial, thus both disposing of the evidence, and, more importantly, moving the killing of the elephant into the area of legitimate predation.

[14] The complexity of some botanical reproductive processes, and the implied involvement of third parties, such as bees, complicates matters in the plant kingdom. In addition, direct collisions between the right of birds to eat seeds and the right of the plants which produce the seeds to breed new plants are very common. If you have noticed that birds rarely if ever establish nests in fruit trees, it is for the very good reason that fruit trees simply won't grant leases, even on a season-by-season basis, to the creatures with whom they are perpetually involved in unpleasant litigation.

[15] There is also a "not guilty by reason of rabies" defense, which is self-explanatory.

[16] Darwin based his concept of the law of the jungle on the Galapagos Islands, a very odd and unrepresentative jurisdiction. (It would be analogous, and equally unconstructive, to base a sweeping study of human law on the legal processes of the Scilly Isles, where feudal law remains in effect.) Because it was settled almost entirely by birds, who obtained unusually sweeping evolutionary charters in the absence of competing claims, the jus aeris obtains through-

Species have an implied right of survival; individuals within a species, because of the limitations which result from the need to permit the free exercise of the right to eat on the part of other animals, do not have an implied right of survival.

For example, the female of a species may not be charged with any criminal act while guarding its young.[17] Similarly, a male of a species who kills another male of the same species in a fight over a female of the same species cannot be charged with animalslaughter. Generally speaking, the fact that a crime of violence occurred during mating season is usually a sufficient defense. (An almost identical principle exists in human law. Crimes committed while the mistral is blowing in southern France traditionally are treated with less severity because of the long-noted effect this hot, dry wind appears to have on people's tempers.)

Incidentally, there is a rather large body of mating law, and the Mating Courts tend to be quite busy, particularly in the spring, settling cases ranging from abandonment of the nest to eating one's own young (an ugly occurrence, but it does happen).[18] As is the case with Family Courts in human law, the Mating Courts are dreary places, and it must be wearing indeed to have to listen to the endless cases of brutal peckings and stompings, to trumpeting matches between a pair of estranged elks, or to an accusation by a sturgeon that its mate fertilized someone else's roe. Alas, animals often turn out to be very human.

C. Freedom to Cry, Howl, Bay, and Hoot

This is a straightforward, well-established freedom, and except for a few very specific limitations, it grants to all living creatures the right to any form of expression they may choose.

The most notable limitation is contained in the hoary phrase, "The free-dom to cry is not so unlimited as to permit an animal to bellow 'Fire!' in a crowded herd." Some jurisdictions also have enacted statutes prohibiting "breach of the peaceable kingdom" and have attempted to establish cur-cris during various hours of the night, but such laws are rarely left undisturbed by higher courts on appeals, because they challenge not only the freedom to cry, but also the right to eat, since many animals seek food at night, and of these, a large percentage—most notably, bats—depend on various sorts of noises to assist them in their search for food.

D. The Right to Bare Claws

This right, which is quite special and which rarely is cited in contemporary cases, arose out of an extremely long controversy over the wide disparity in the distribution of antlers, horns, fangs, poison sacs, and the like among species in the animal kingdom. A number of species charged unfair competition in a series of cases, but not surprisingly, the plaintiff species often became extinct before a final determination was made in their cases, and the question was rendered moot. The net result was the establishment, by default, of the right of species to develop any offensive appendages they might wish, consistent with the Genetic Code.

E. The Right to Assemble in Herds, Migrate, and Stampede

This is a case of another right which became part of the package of unwritten freedoms in the lex fauna through a process of evolution. The first animals which organized themselves into large herds gained an instant and quite terrifying advantage over other species, and a number of unfair competition and restraint of evolution suits were brought. It was most commonly charged that herds tended to monopolize huge habitats, making continued survival for other species virtually impossible. Attempts at regulation were made from time to time[19] but the courts ultimately found themselves powerless to enforce the break-up of even moderately sized herds, flocks, or schools.

In any case, the herd concept led to the recognition of the absolute right of animals to free movement, an essential development. Actually, herd activity is not entirely unregulated. There are a number of migratory courts which are responsible for the management of flyways, heavily used passes, key ocean currents, and so forth, and the growth and increasing sophistication of herd law has removed most of the worst abuses.[20]

F. The Right to a Speedy Trial by Jury

The jury concept is very deeply rooted in animal law. Invariably, animals are given the opportunity to be tried by a jury composed of animals in their class, order, phylum, or other appropriate division—for example, a flat worm's jury would be limited to the *Platyhelminthes*—and, for obvious reasons, members of its own individual species would not be included in its jury because of their easily demonstrable prejudice.

The concept of "speedy" varies greatly. Under the jus aeris, for example, a moth charged with a capital or infamous crime must be brought to trial within twenty minutes. Under the codex botanica, a plant charged, say, with choking off the sunlight of a neighboring plant, must be brought to trial within five years.[21]

G. The Right of All Animals to Be Secure in Their Nests

This is an ancient right, neatly summed up in the phrase "an animal's dwelling is its nest." Interestingly, this right is so deeply ingrained in the lex fauna that it even supersedes the right to eat, at least in theory. An animal which invades another animal's nest and eats it cannot be convicted of a felony eating charge presuming it is able to demonstrate that it acted out of hunger, but it can be charged with criminal trespass and breaking and entering. In practice,

out the islands. Even the famed Galapagos sea turtles are subject to aerial law, and are said to be "flying in the salt sky" when swimming, a legal fiction which was undoubtedly invented by some hair-splitting avarian "legal eagle" to rationalize the primacy of the jus aeris.

[17] Once again, the Australian jurisdiction provides a quirky exception. Female kangaroos carrying their young in pouches tended to abuse this blanket immunity from prosecution, often going on rampages for which they could not be charged. It is now limited in marsupial courts to the period immediately following the birth of the young.

[18] Another unpleasant area is the growing number of sterility and infertile egg cases, a result of the use of insecticides. This is as good a place as any to mention that at last count, there were over seventy-eight million subpoenas pending against *Homo sapiens*, charging everything from reckless extinction to malicious destruction of habitats. Not one has ever been answered.

[19] *Coyotes v. Buffalo Herd* (2 Quadrupeds 66), brought in the Court of Appeals for the Northern Great Plains, was a landmark case. The coyotes argued, unsuccessfully, that the domination of the plains by the buffalos, some of whose herds numbered in the millions, rendered an immense area uninhabitable, and asked that the buffalo species be broken up into several subspecies. However, even though the coyotes lost the case, an important principle was established: the right of individual members of one species to sue an entire herd as a whole, rather than attempting the impossible task of suing its individual members one by one.

[20] Some still remain. The locusts, who rather shrewdly registered as a swarm under the notoriously weak herd laws of the Arabian Peninsula, have managed thus far to evade prosecution for their indisputably illegal activities. And two species of army ants have refused to answer subpoenas issued by several of the African courts, claiming that they are subject only to their own Courts Martial. In one case, a War Crimes Tribunal was actually convened following a particularly catastrophic ant rampage, and found 750,000 ants guilty of crimes against animality. In spite of their insistence that they were only following their instincts, they were executed. The gesture was somewhat pointless. An average ant horde numbers in the billions; eradicating what amounted to a single platoon achieved nothing.

[21] Once again, the Galapagos provides a curious legal example, in this case the problem of definition involved in the word "speedy." Because the jus aeris is the only code in use, turtles are subject to the requirement that defendants be brought to trial within five days of the commission of an alleged crime. The usual practice is to hold the proceedings on the back of the turtle as it makes its way to the court. When it arrives, it is either sentenced or acquitted, depending upon the outcome.

this fact does little to deter the constant habit of many species of preying on other species' nests, but it at least indicates a revulsion on the part of a great many animals for the unlimited savagery which all animals are widely supposed to engage in.

As weak a bulwark as it has proved to attacks by other animals, this right does provide protection against searches of an animal's nest for the gathering of evidence in criminal cases, an area of the lex fauna which is better covered as a part of procedure.

III

STATUTES, CASE LAW, AND PROCEDURE

Once again, the complex structure and accidental nature of the lex fauna and the lex flora make it impossible to proceed through a description of the workings of the law of the jungle in everyday practice in any logical fashion. But it is possible to give some feeling of the way the law operates, as it permits, prohibits, and regulates all conduct within the animal and plant kindoms. Our concern here will be only with the most important and common areas of the law, and for the most part we will pretend that legal practice is more or less the same throughout geographical jurisdictions and among the various codes, an assumption which, unfortunately, is far from true.

A. Contracts

Contracts play as large and essential a role in serving to regulate and formalize relationships and obligations within the plant and animal kingdoms as they do in human affairs. There are myriad examples of contractual arrangements which animals and plants enter into on a regular basis and to a considerable degree, contracts form the absolute foundation for much of what is thought of as "life in a natural state." In point of fact, much of what is generally taken for granted as occurring "naturally" is the result of a complex, interconnected web of promissory covenants and explicit commitments between and among vast numbers of living creatures and things whom one would not at first glance think of as being even aware of, let alone vaguely concerned with, one anothers' existence. Conservationists who speak of the delicate ecological balance and the interrelationship of living things are, whether they know it or not, describing a legal, as much as a biological, structure.

One or two of these legal relationships have been described in preceding sections, but in our earlier discussion, we made no attempt to convey the sheer magnitude of this area of non-human law. To illustrate the situation which prevails in the animal kingdom today, it is only necessary to examine a very small, representative slice of the biosphere and point out only a few of the more obvious legal agreements which provide the essential stability which, paradoxically, is so crucial to life in "the wild."

Apart from pollination and seed transportation covenants with a variety of insects and animals, most plants, from ferns to trees, are linked by contract to any of a thousand or so genera of fungi for long-term processing of decaying vegetable matter into usable phosphates, nitrates, and other nutrients. In return, the standard fungus contracts call for the provision of a certain stated weight of dead leaves, sloughed-off bark, acorn husks, or whatever, in a given season, and in the case of most of the mosses, a certain square footage of trunk space with a northern exposure.

In addition, most plants have root-service contracts with worms, calling for a specified number of linear feet of soil aeration annually, and where applicable, grub-control contracts with woodpeckers. Most of the grazing animals, particularly horses, cows, sheep, and deer, have specific short-term arrangements with any number of common field grasses for the supply of agreed upon amounts of soil-enriching dung (whether in cake or pellet form) in return for forage rights.

The success of the contract as a regulatory device is evidenced by the rather remarkable "balance" which exists in nature, and the impressive extent to which properly executed legal instruments are honored throughout the various plant and animal jurisdictions is a testament to the respect which the law enjoys. This wasn't always the case, and the gradual development of the concept of the sanctity of contracts is one of the most significant events in the history of the lex biologica.

The first really important case involving contracts, *Root v. Frond* (14 Fossils 56), concerned a suit brought by the root structure of a Jurassic giant fern against its fronds, charging a breach of contract to supply vitally needed dextrose to the lower portion of the plant, thus threatening to "willfully stunt, inhibit, and otherwise cause to be halted, proper root growth as would reasonably be expected and anticipated were such sugars, as specified in a valid agreement, supplied and made available." The root structure further pointed out that it had honored its part of the covenant and supplied nutrients to the fronds, and asked the court to order recision—the breaking up of the fern into its constituent parts.

In a key decision that was to mark a watershed in evolution, the court promulgated what became known as the Fern Rule, that no portion of any multicellular plant has standing in any court to sue any other portion of the same plant, in an action for recovery of damages, for assessment of penalties, for redress of loss, or for any other reason.[22] The organization of large numbers of formerly separated microorganisms into vast, highly differentiated superorganisms, was, on the scale of things, a fairly recent occurrence, and the ruling was an unusually courageous and far-seeing one. Certainly, it spared the law of contracts what would surely have been an extremely regressive and potentially fatal role as a mechanism for evolutionary stagnation.

In a considerably more recent, but equally precedent-setting case, an obscure African herbivore court, the Civil Court of Pleas and Cries, established in *Hippopotomi v. Tick-Birds* (14 Herb. 44), the principle that the courts will not look into the sufficiency of consideration in an otherwise valid contract. Plaintiff hippos brought suit for specific performance of a contract, wherein the hippos were to provide defendant tick-birds with transportation and sustenance in exchange for which said tick-birds were to expend their best efforts to keep plaintiff hippos' teeth clean and free of decaying vegetable matter.

Plaintiff hippos also sued for damages resulting from the loss of molars, bicuspids, etc., due to defendant tick-birds' failure to honor a freely-entered-into covenant.

What had transpired was that several weeks after this rather standard interspecies symbiosis contract had been "pawed and clawed," the defendant tick-birds, a species not noted for its shrewdness, recollected that they had wings, and could very easily transport themselves "hither and thither" and locate their own food without the assistance of plaintiff hippos and promptly took wing en

[22] Not long after the same principle was voiced in a proceeding under the lex fauna. In *Pedes Anterior Dexter v. Stegasaurus* (26 Fossils 3), the left rear foot of a dinosaur of an unusually large and slow moving species brought suit against the rest of the creature for having negligently permitted it to become seriously gnawed during a fight with another dinosaur. What almost certainly happened was that the stegosaur, which had a brain the size of a partially devoured cashew, simply forgot it had that particular foot. The Reptilian Court made a parallel decision, and in a gesture almost as significant as the decision itself, it cited the *Fern* decision in the botanical courts as a precedent, the first time that kind of courtesy had been exchanged between courts in floral and faunal jurisdictions.

masse,[23] after somewhat noisily accusing plaintiff hippos of having roared them into a bad deal.[24] The hippos brought suit, and the Court held: "Said contract as between plaintiff hippopotami and defendant tick-birds is a legitimate bargain and accord, and is enforceable under the lex fauna, notwithstanding any representation or determinations, made here or elsewhere, at the time said agreement was entered into or at a later date by the parties concerned regarding the fairness, rightness, or judiciousness of said bargain or accord, such a determination being outside the proper scope and purlieu of a court of law."

It is a measure of the prestige and the respect which the law enjoys among animals that, in spite of their dissatisfaction with the terms they had negotiated, the tick-birds abided by the decision of the court and to this day continue to honor the original covenant.

Another key case affecting contract law was the famous case, *Beaver Dam v. Upper Sturgeon River Authority* (9 Rivers 41), and the subsequent appeal. A group of beavers, plaintiffs in this case, had formed one of their usual dam-building companies and obtained from the Upper Sturgeon River Authority (a quasi-public body composed of representatives of all the major animal species inhabiting this particular Canadian river and its immediate riparian environs, including embankments, estuaries, and tributaries), an exclusive permit for dam construction. The dam was built, and proved to be very popular, particularly among waterfowl, who tend to dominate the river authorities in northern jurisdictions, at least in the summer sessions, and when another beaver dam company appeared, it was immediately granted a permit to construct a second dam.

The original beaver dam company immediately sued, charging that the second dam, which was to be situated a short distance upstream, would seriously lower the level of the pond which they had created, depriving them of their livelihood, and reminded the Upper Sturgeon River Authority that it had granted them an exclusive permit, quite clearly a contractual obligation which was not being honored.

The lower court ruled in favor of the original beaver dam company on the grounds of the sanctity of contracts, but on appeal, the decision was reversed, 3–2, by the Northern Woods District Court,[25] which held that the public interest, in this case "the clearly demonstrated desire on the part of the denizens of this waterway" to have additional pond areas, held precedence over any prior contract. It was quite a revolutionary decision, and it led, indirectly, to the establishment somewhat later of the principle of eminent animal domain, that is, the right of properly constituted bodies, acting inter animalia, to set aside contracts and regulate habitats, a matter of some importance in property law.

B. Property or Territory Law

The basic legal control of land in the animal kingdom is many times more complex than the simple concept of ownership prevalent in human law,[26] for the obvious reason that only in rare cases does a species, subspecies, herd, or individual have exclusive use of any given habitat. The principle of territoriality, probably the oldest concept in animal law, is exceedingly well-rooted, but from the very beginning it presupposed the sharing of territorial control among a large number of species, both competing and non-competing. For instance, the territory of an individual family of bobcats, itself a minute portion of the overall range of the bobcat species, will contain within it the nesting grounds (usually under a freehold or lease) of hundreds of birds; subterranean easements held by moles; forage areas populated by elk; pond frontage belonging to frogs; and possibly even a bat cave (most of these are condominiums). In turn, it may be included, in whole or part, in the hunting territory of an eagle.

This does not mean that the bobcat family, or any of the other species mentioned, are trespassers: typically, they will have valid territoriality deeds, leases, a grant of subsoil rights, or whatever.[27] Nor does it mean that there are constant squabbles over ownership leading to endless litigation. To a large degree, the species which share a given habitat are unaware, or at least uninterested, in

each others' existence; when this is not the case, it is usually because one species, say the bobcats, are preying on another, say field mice, and an attempt on the part of a field mouse to serve papers on a bobcat for some imagined trespass would be a particularly dangerous and unrewarding form of folly.

The key precept in territory law, and the main reason why the courts are not constantly occupied with territoriality cases, is that a given species or individual within it must be able to demonstrate "reasonable use" of a given habitat or portion thereof and "a preponderance of duplication of use" likely to result from the entry of a competing species before he can bring a motion for the eviction of the new species.[28] Thus, for example, should our bobcat wake up one morning and discover that a species of mountain goat hitherto not present in his territory was grazing in a rocky area in one corner of it, he would have to show *both* that he made reasonable use of that area in his search for food and that the newcomer species was also likely to use it in its search for essentially the same food. He might be able to demonstrate the first point, possibly by getting an uninterested outsider, perhaps an osprey, to testify that he, the bobcat, used those rocks to sun himself, or perhaps he might offer into evidence the branch of a briar bush from that area containing tufts of his fur as proof he visited it regularly. But he could hardly argue that the mountain goat, a ruminant, was likely to compete with him for his food supply. Case dismissed.

Territory law, however, is not confined to simple trespass cases, as a glance at the docket of a representative court in a typical session indicates, in this case the period following the mating season recess of the general session of the Supreme Court for the Southern Congo Basin, Mr. Justice Baboon presiding. The calendar is quite a full one, and includes a number

[23] It's worth noting here, just in passing, that under the jus aeris, by far the most common felony charge is flight to avoid prosecution. This particular case was civil, rather than criminal, and the tick-birds incurred no penalty, other than the likelihood that in their absence a judgment would be entered by default for the plaintiff.
[24] Thus risking a libel action on top of the original breach of contract suit. This didn't happen, but for a fascinating introduction to animal libel law, see *Gazelle v. Hyena* (33 Herb. 22), and *Redwing Blackbird v. Mockingbird* (198 Ornith. 20).

[25] The matter was eventually settled amicably enough with the original beaver dam company being granted a veto over future site-awards and a perch on the authority board.
[26] None of this complexity exists in the plant kingdom. Almost all plants obtain a straightforward deed, registered in Seed Court, and the majority of the disagreements are over air rights.
[27] Title search in the animal kingdom is a nightmare. It is often necessary to sift through thousands of pounds of bones, teeth, and fossils to settle the simplest territoriality

case. As a general rule, in most northern jurisdictions, no claims arising out of territorial titles in existence before the last Ice Age are accepted, but even so, the task of clearing a title is unbelievably difficult. An animal about to enter the practice of law, who has a high threshold of boredom, can count on not having to do much grubbing for roots and berries during his natural life if he should choose to specialize in property cases.
[28] A lot hangs on the definition of "reasonable" and "preponderance." Depending on the jurisdiction, these have been taken to mean anything from one visit per season and deprivation of any foodstuff eaten by any animal on which the complaining animals ever preyed, respectively, to weekly visits and sharing "predatory interest" in over half of the animals the complaining animal preys on. This kind of problem of definition, which is common throughout animal law, represents either excessive vagueness or laudable flexibility, depending on your point of view.

HENRY BEARD 43

NATIONAL LAMPOON

of territory cases, for example: A challenge to a decision by the Inner Jungle Council of the Booratoola rain forest to rezone portions of the forest to exclude nocturnal predators of over three hundred pounds gross weight and winged predators having a claw length in excess of two inches (ruled for the plaintiff, a panther, on the grounds of incomplete representation on the zoning board by members of carnivore species); an appeal of a decision in a landlord-tenant dispute between a giant lake trout and a fresh water remora, in which plaintiff trout was held to have proved parasitism and defendant remora was ordered to disgorge (affirmed—note, incidentally, that this case, which was tried originally in a lake court, falls as a freshwater litigation under the jus terrestris, not the corpus juris maris); an attack on a restrictive covenant which had the effect of excluding certain members of the heron family, chiefly flamingoes, from occupying nesting grounds in a large wetland area (returned to lower court for a determination of competitive impact); a suit brought on an appeal by a group of tapirs to enforce their affirmative easement over defendant tiger's territory to the Pungaree waterhole (let decision in favor of plaintiffs stand); and a negligent migration suit, brought by a herd of antelope against a herd of elephant, which in the course of migrating south, were found by a lower court to have "trod, trampled, and caused to be tread upon plaintiff's habitat, to wit, the plain herein referred to as 'antelope's grazing ground' to such a degree as to cause plaintiff antelope irreparable loss of forage and grazeage" (affirmed).

This last case was one of eminent animal domain, by now a well-established principle in the lex fauna, with a sizable body of precedent and case law behind it, and, as mentioned earlier, an important development in territory law. The clearest statement of it is in the classic case, *Smelts v. Anchovies* (49 Fish 908), and it is noteworthy that the concept is recognized throughout the animal kingdom.[29] In the smelts case, a school of anchovies sought to bar a school of smelts from entering their traditional feeding grounds, which, due to a slight shift in a major north-south current, were suddenly astride the smelts' most natural migratory route. The anchovies had a good case: they could easily prove "reasonable use" of the territory, since they occupied it to a density of about one anchovy per square meter, and "preponderant duplication of use" was equally easy to demonstrate, since both smelts and anchovies feed on precisely the same diatomic plankton. However, the local Department of Migration had ruled that the new current, like the previous

one, was a regular migratory route, and had offered to compensate the anchovies with a different feeding ground, and every court from the local Court of Underwater Appeals to the Supreme Court of the Pacific upheld the right of the smelts to migrate through the traditional territory of the anchovies.[30]

C. Torts

Torts, in animal as in human law, are best defined as "non-contractual civil wrongs," that is, an action of some sort by one animal other than a failure to live up to the terms of a contract, actual or implied,[31] which leads to the suffering of some demonstrable damage, hurt, or harm by another animal. As a practical matter, torts are far easier to recognize than to define, but generally speaking, most tort cases go off on the question of alleged negligence on the part of the given defendant animal.

A good example is the case of *Spider Monkey v. Giraffe* (26 Mamm. 44), in which plaintiff monkey accused defendant giraffe of negligent nibbling in the branches of the tree in which he was sleeping, defendant giraffe having not taken reasonable precaution to ensure that another creature, one not the object of any permissable predation, would not be harmed by his action.

The damages which the monkey claimed (damages are the key to all tort actions, since if no harm can be shown, no wrong is held to have occurred), were temporary loss of locomotion caused by bites on his legs and permanent loss of the ability to swing, occasioned by his tail having been bitten off. In one of the larger pain and suffering judgments recorded, the jury found for the plaintiff monkey and awarded him sixteen thousand bananas, to be fetched for him at his

[29] It is not recognized in the plant kingdom. In fact, it is specifically rejected, for the very good reason that historically, the establishment of migration routes, trails, paths, etc., have been very much at the expense of the vegetation which formerly occupied them, and since very few plants are able to respond in any meaningful way to an eviction notice, there is a good deal of bitterness about the fairness of the principle as it applies to plants. See Eminent Animal Domain: Freedom of Movement or License to Trample?, 24 Gymnosperm Law Review 467.

[30] The right of eminent animal domain, as against specific territorial rights, is far from absolute. Nothing prevented the anchovies from eating the smelts when they came through. This important reservation is stated best in *Salmon v. Bears* (34 Alask. 877), in which plaintiff salmon argued that by eating them as they moved upstream to spawn along a riverbed which had been established as a salmon migratory route by eminent animal domain in previous times, the bears were in fact closing a right of way and frustrating the original intent of its appropriation, namely, to make available a spawning route to the salmon. The court rejected the argument in unusually explicit language.

[31] It should be noted that there are practically no crimes of omission in the lex biologica, except those arising out of some sort of contract. Even in cases where an animal could reasonably be expected to have come to rely on another animal's affirmative action, say, one beaver on another's slapping its tail to warn of the approach of a predator, the failure of the beaver to do so is not actionable, even as negligence, because no action, in a legal sense, took place. Of course, if the second beaver had been serving as a sentry, and had accepted an appointment to do so, that would be a different matter, since a contract is implied.

"Maybe he can't swim."

request by defendant giraffe.

Briefly, then, tortious conduct, a civil matter, occurs whenever an animal negligently harms another animal. In almost every case, an animal who deliberately harms another animal, presuming that his actions are not covered by the right to eat, is guilty of a criminal act, a felony rather than a tort.

As an example of a tortious act committed more or less knowingly, the animal who cried "Fire!" in a crowded herd (an instance cited in the discussion of the freedom to cry), could be sued by an animal injured in the resultant stampede.[32] The critical difference here is whether the animal cried "Fire!" without really considering the consequences or whether he did it deliberately to cause the herd harm.

D. Classification Law

Somewhat analogous to corporation law, classification law deals with the activities of groupings of animals, classes, orders, phylums, species, herds, schools, flocks, and so forth, and their internal legal relationships, as well as their relationships with other groupings of animals. Classification law covers a very large legal area, everything from the issuance of grazing stock when herds are formed and the registration of new species to extinction cases and the divestiture of vestigial organs.

However, by far the most important part of classification law is anti-domination law, a rough parallel to anti-trust law. Anti-domination law, which is divisible into unfair competition and restraint of evolution, grew in response to the challenge presented by highly successful species to the natural order and the threat of monopolization of the animal kingdom by a handful of species to the exclusion of all others.

The first great anti-domination case was *Animal Kingdom v. Reptiles* (19 Fossils 409), and the finding by the court that the reptiles had acted to restrain the evolution of all other species by so crowding the landscape with members of its class that no other animal forms could successfully enter into competition was one of the great landmark rulings in the lex biologica. The decision led to the break-up of the reptiles into birds,

amphibians, snakes, lizards, and several kinds of fish, and eventually resulted in the rise of the rodents and the mammals, among others.[33]

Another crucial anti-domination case, brought under the unfair competition portion of the statutes, was *Five Australian Finches et al. v. Kiwi* (109 Ornith. 476). Plaintiff finches in this case maintained a "class action"[34] on behalf of themselves and all other Australian birds, of whatever species, similarly situated. The finches alleged that defendant kiwis weighed anywhere from ten to eighty times as much as any other winged creature to be found at that time on the Australian land mass, an advantage which, taken together with the tremendous speed and maneuverability which the kiwis exhibited when airborne, gave the kiwis a virtual monopoly of all available food supplies and permitted them to dominate the air to the exclusion of all other birds. Plaintiff finches prayed the court for, and were eventually granted, a permanent injunction prohibiting the kiwis from engaging in any flight greater than that caused by a high hop, and the court ordered the kiwis to divest themselves of portions of their wings, an order which after considerable litigation, several appeals, and a pair of counter suits brought under the Genetic Code, they reluctantly obeyed, in yet another remarkable tribute to the position of respect the law holds in the minds of all animals.

Restraint of evolution cases are most typically brought by a species on the brink of extinction, and, indeed, the courts have often been criticized for refusing to hear such cases promptly enough to give plaintiff species a reasonable chance for survival and for scheduling hearings with little attention to the desperate plight of some of the plaintiffs, for whom meaningful legal relief usually comes too late to be of any use. The problem, however, is not as cut and dried as it

might appear, for the courts argue, quite logically, that it isn't possible to hear extinction cases under the doctrine of unfair competition or restraint of evolution until they are "ripe," that is, until extinction, the damage being charged, is actually imminent. In other words, if a species is about to become extinct, it has a case, but it is probably too late, given the time even the most expeditious litigation requires, to save the species; if a species brings an action before it is demonstrably in danger of extinction, then presumably, it hasn't got a case. Unfortunately, as of now, the discussion is rendered somewhat moot, since every single pending extinction case names *Homo sapiens* as defendant, and the jurisdictional problems mentioned earlier make any resolution of the matter unlikely.

Extinctions themselves fall under classification law, since they represent an important legal question involving a grouping of animals. Extinction, to continue the analogy offered earlier, is generally comparable to bankruptcy, and when a species or subspecies files for extinction under Section 118 of the Competitive Code, the court involved appoints an arbitrator,[35] and an attempt is made to divide up the species' habitat among its major predator.[36] It is an orderly, if a sad, process.[37]

IV

TRUSTS AND ESTATES

Animals occasionally execute testamentary instruments providing for the division of their possessions and effects, at the time of their death, to their offspring, mates, perhaps close associates in a herd, or even some creature with whom they have had a long symbiotic relationship. In practice, very few animals do so, since with few exceptions, they usually have very little in the way of real property to pass on except possibly some freshly-killed food or recently gathered forage, and estates are almost always eaten up (literally) by the lawyers handling the probate.

Turtles, snails, clams, conches, and similar creatures have somewhat more

[32] If one of the barnyard creatures whom Chicken Little alarmed with her announcement of impending aerial catastrophe suffered a heart attack or harmed himself in seeking shelter, he would have a very good case indeed against Chicken Little, regardless of whether Chicken Little genuinely thought the sky was falling. It would have been an interesting case, since Chicken Little, though flightless, would have been tried under the jus aeris, in a Court of Vivipary, and she could have gotten off if she proved she was molting at the time.

[33] Needless to say, as mentioned earlier in passing, a number of suits are pending against *Homo sapiens* under this same statute, but the jurisdictional question is an effective bar to any action in the foreseeable future. Flies and mosquitoes, the traditional process servers of the animal kingdom, have been serving subpoenas to every member of the species *Homo sapiens* they have been able to locate for literally centuries in this and other cases. Alas, the painful welts have consistently been ignored, or misinterpreted.

[34] Class actions, phylum actions, species actions, etc., are suits brought by one or more members of a class, phylum, species, etc., on behalf of a much larger group of individuals, all of whom have a similar complaint. It is a highly equalizing legal technique, in that it permits relatively unorganized and unimportant creatures to challenge in court the mightiest of animal groupings. For a very lively and interesting discussion of this kind of group litigation, see Species Actions, Genus Actions, Phylum and Subphylum Actions: Plaintiff's Right to Be a Herd, 48 Phylum Cordata Law Review 2880.

[35] The most distinguished arbitrator in recent times was the exceptionally gifted cormorant who handled the extinction of both the dodo and the passenger pigeon. A remarkable lawyer, he served as a chief counsel for the invertebrates for several years, and was eventually appointed an Associate Justice of the Supreme Court of the Northern Flyways.

[36] Obviously, it is the animals which were accustomed to prey on the extinct species who have the first claim on that species' assets.

[37] It is also a costly one. The lemmings, who often file for elimination of the herd, a special form of local extinction, might well be driven to rush in suicidal fashion off the cliffs by the thought of the legal bills they have incurred.

real property to dispose of, but their shells are of little actual value, except to humans, which in practical terms means they are worthless (if there has ever been a case of a clam or conches' heirs ever receiving anything from a *Homo sapiens* who snatched its inheritance right out of its psuedopods, tendrils, or whatever, there is no record of it). As a result, most mollusks who are left shells in the wills of fellow mollusks usually donate them to the sea floor, take the inorganic matter deduction, and forget the whole damn thing.

V

COPYRIGHTS AND PATENTS

From earliest times, animal courts have recognized an absolute right which resides in individual species to the uniqueness of their plumage, their distinctive coloration, their trademarkings, the arrangement of their key features, the characteristic patterns of their fur, scales, or feathers, and so on, and the necessity of granting to various species exclusive use of physiological improvements they have developed through the patenting of mutations. These are far more essential protections than would appear at first glance, for they provide an atmosphere of regulation and stability in which the natural play of competition between species is allowed to operate without any species being able to gain a significant advantage over another species through the piracy or unauthorized appropriation of trademarkings, survival secrets, or evolutionary developments.

In animal copyright law, mimicry, the deliberate copying of one species' highly recognizable appearance by another, invariably to take advantage of some defense against predation which the first species evolved, is the most common and the most serious statutory violation. In the well-known case of *Mayfly v. Mayfly* (34 Bugs 989), a subspecies of mayfly which was the object of continual predation by a number of bird species, particularly starlings, undertook to duplicate, over a number of generations, the characteristic wing design of a subspecies of mayfly which had developed, and held a patent on, a technique for excreting a powerful hormone that made the subspecies so unappetizing to birds that they usually regurgitated any mayfly of that subspecies within five minutes of ingesting it, and consequently more or less left them alone. The defendant mayfly subspecies had not infringed upon its patented method of discouraging predation, and argued that no harm had been done, since the only demonstrable damage was to the various species of predator birds, who had been fooled into thinking that an edible subspecies of mayfly was in fact inedible.[38] The plaintiff mayfly species insisted, however, that a very real damage had been done, since the mimicry carried out by the defendant mayfly subspecies had had the effect of diluting the effectiveness of both the patented bird-repelling hormone and the special wing design, a copyrightable trademarking, which signalled its presence to potential predators. Sooner or later, the plaintiff mayflies argued, a starling, acting in desperation or confusion, would eat one of the mimicking mayflies, and finding, contrary to its belief and expectation, that it was quite tasty, spread the word that all mayflies having that wing design were edible. The result would inevitably be countless attacks on the subspecies of mayfly, which, through its own efforts and ingenuity, had formerly managed to protect itself, and the consequent destruction of their long and carefully established reputation as being foul-tasting, with resultant loss of life for untold members of the subspecies.

The court agreed and promulgated the principle that demonstration of a clear intent to confuse, in essence, "to fob itself off," on the part of a mimicking species—what is now known as the Mayfly Test—rendered the mimicry an actionable offense under copyright law.

Under the provisions of the Genetic Code, animals can apply for, and, depending on the merits of their application (determinations of merit are usually made on the basis of originality), are awarded patents for mutations which represent a significant new technique, an improved organ, a novel appendage, and the like, for example, night vision, retractable claws, the multiple stomach, an improved lymphatic system, etc. Generally, patents are granted for a specific period of time, usually thirty to fifty generations, after which the improvements they represent become part of the public animal domain and other species can, for an agreed upon consideration, obtain licenses to employ them. By contrast, morphological copyrights are awarded in perpetuity.

Of course, there are limitations on both copyrights and patents. For instance, no animal can copyright, say, the color red or the idea of spots, only a specific shade of red or a particular arrangement of spots. Nor can a species, for example, the cats, with a copyright on a certain pattern of facial whiskers, sue a leopard for adopt-ing it, because the likelihood of confusion is so remote. Obviously, any animal who can't tell a leopard from an ordinary cat isn't going to be around long enough to be on hand to testify in a copyright infringement suit that he was confused by the similarity of the whiskers between the two.

The courts have also held, most notably in *Crocodile v. Alligator* (114 Amphib. 47), that similarity itself, where there is no intent to confuse and no damages are demonstrated, is not improper, and that further, copyrights are not unlimited geographically. Plaintiff crocodiles held that defendant alligators had copied their characteristic scale design and snout, a fact which defendant alligators did not contest. In responding, defendant alligators argued, and the court agreed, that the copying was not motivated by an intent to confuse and that no possible unfair competitive advantage had been gained by it, since any creature with reason to fear and avoid a crocodile should likewise fear and avoid an alligator, even if it had feathers and antlers.

The court ruled further that since the two species were at the time occupying widely separated habitats, they were not in actual competition in a legal sense and established the principle that a species must be actively competing in the same habitat to secure its copyright in that habitat, and that if two species adopt more or less identical copyrighted forms in two different habitats, each will be enjoined from entering and competing in the other's habitat.

Patents are granted only for significant morphological changes, not minor refinements of existing ones. Articulated legs are patentable, but the technique of using a large number of them in a series is not.[39] In addition, no species can patent an idea for an evolutionary improvement and then sue a species that actually develops it.[40] The species must be in

---

[38] The starlings brought suit later against the mimicking mayfly subspecies claiming fraudulent mismarking, an offense under the Competitive Code.

[39] See *Centipedes v. Millipedes* (556 Pests 49).

[40] In *Acanthodia v. Crossopterygians* (16 Fossils 119), plaintiff species, a primitive fish, sued to enjoin defendant from using his fins as legs and developing an apparatus for breathing the atmosphere, ideas which the plaintiff species had had many generations earlier, as testified to by a number of third parties. In what turned out to be a decision unusually far-reaching in its effects on the animal kingdom (it is not rare that fairly obscure cases are responsible for vast changes, such is the power of the law), the court ruled against the plaintiff species, on the grounds that to permit copyrighting of an idea would hinder, rather than promote, evolutionary progress, contrary to the spirit of the relevant statutes in the Genetic and Competitive Codes. See also *Lemur v. Anthropoid Apes* (16 Primates 66), the famous "opposable thumb" case. The court held that the apes had improved upon the original arrangement of appendages to such an extent that their use of it constituted a new, and itself patentable, development.

current possession of the mutation before it can claim protection. Equally, if a species undergoes a major and permanent morphological change or an organ or limb on which it holds a patent becomes vestigial, the right which it had to its exclusive use are held to have lapsed.

Certain forms of animal expression —birdsongs, mating cries, the sonar squeaks of bats, to name a few examples—are also copyrightable, and over 400 million cries, hoots, murmurs, grunts, growls, etc., have been registered.[41] It should be very obvious why species must be permitted to enjoy exclusive use of their characteristic cries, since distinctive forms of oral communication play such a large role in the process by which they attract mates. It would be well-nigh impossible for, say, an elk to find a female elk if half the creatures in the woods were using his mating call for warbling, boasting, threatening, warning, or whatever.[42]

VI

DOMESTIC RELATIONS

Apart from the portions of mating law described earlier, there is really very little in the way of statutory law regulating the sexual (or asexual) relations among members of a species. The courts have wisely abdicated any responsibility they may have felt from time to time to interfere in reproductory matters, having decided a very long time ago that "the law has no business in the nest."[43]

The paramount position which the right to breed holds in the lex biologica invariably makes prosecutions for any wrong, civil or criminal, impossible if even the vaguest connection to the process by which species replicate can be shown. As an instance of the enormous area of protection involved, no insect court has ever issued a writ of habeas carcasse, or even enchrysalised a grand jury to consider an indictment, in any of the thousands upon thousands of cases brought by male praying mantises who have been mortally bitten by the female during the reproductory act.

The courts will, if pressed, grant separations, most often in cell division and budding cases, but they prefer to keep out of the entire area, and most animals oblige by conducting their mating affairs ex curia. A few legalisms exist, such as the process by which an animal informs other animals in his habitat that a mate "has left his nest and nibble" and hence he will not be bound by any contractual obligations she may undertake, and in the case of a few species, the process of precedent has made reproduction subject to some legal restraint. (Such is the case among the bees, where a form of swarm law, a division of classification law, covers mating. See *Queen Bee v. Drones* [45 Bees 222], an action brought by a queen bee in Hive Court to compel specific performance of an insemination contract.)

VII

CRIMINAL LAW: STATUTES AND PROCEDURES

This is just too wide an area to get into in any depth. The various criminal codes, like the competitive codes, cover such a variety of offenses, and vary so greatly from floral to faunal law, and among the major subdivisions of each, that only the most cursory examination is possible. In addition, the codes are being constantly updated, and through the process of precedent, reinterpreted, and even learned judges have a good deal of difficulty keeping up to date.

Basically, most aggressive acts not specifically entered into as part of the right to eat, the right to breed, or motivated by self-defense, are proscribed. What this leaves may seem like a very small area, but, in practice, it is not, and includes such disparate offenses as stampeding to endanger, possession of a deadly substance (excretion of certain poisons is forbidden), negligent animalcide, eat-and-run, conspiracy to peck to death (see *The Animals v. Twenty-two Chickens* [550 Poultry 11]), purr-jury, howljury, etc., and various forms of larceny and nest-breaking.

The statutes are usually lengthy and precise, as this example from the lex fauna, a section covering felonious assault, suggests: "Any creature subject to the law, be he a bird of the air, a beast of the field, a fish of the sea, and anything which does crawl, swim, wriggle, burrow, lope, jump, slither, or fly, upon the ground or under it, upon the sea or in it, in the air or through it, have it lungs, have it gills, have it fur, fin, feather, fleece, or fuzz, who shall bite upon, gobble, gnaw, or nibble, or cause to be bit upon, gobbled, gnawed, or nibbled, any other creature subject to these laws, whether

it be by horn or by claw, by tooth or by tusk, by fang or by pincer, if he have not cause to breed or to feed, shall be guilty of a felonious act under this Law and shall be subject to such penalties and forfeitures as may be prescribed by the lesser Codes to which his species is subject and shall answer for his crime in a Court having jurisdiction over the place of the act or the person of the accused, as shall be determined."

Even in this statute, some of the debilitating jurisdictional problems which plague animal law are apparent, but we'll dispense with any further inquiry into those. Let us instead follow a representative animal, charged with the crime involved as his case is heard. In this mythical case, we'll assume that a badger bit another badger in some dispute not connected with mating.[44]

Like all animals, the badger enjoys the right to be tried by a jury of his order, in his own habitat, and according to the laws which govern his species, in this case a combination of the jus terrestris and the Varmint Code. He has further the right to counsel, to hear the evidence against him, and to confront and cross-examine witnesses, and to have compulsory service to obtain the testimony of witnesses in his favor, that is, to subpoena other animals who might be reluctant to testify in his behalf but whose testimony might be exculpatory (likely to prove his innocence).

Animals who have any interest in the case are excluded from the jury (another badger with whom our badger was having a territorial or mating dispute might be prejudiced against him). The trial itself goes according to a very strict procedure, under which certain types of activity are permissible and others are not (badgering a witness isn't, a fact which could put our theoretical defendant at something of a disadvantage when his accuser testifies); and certain kinds of evidence are admissible, and others are not. Since evidence is an essential part of procedure, in both civil and criminal cases, the question of its admissibility is worth going into here if only in passing.

There is a considerable array of rules governing the allowability of evidence in trials and litigations, and the legal propriety of using certain sources to obtain it, and means of
continued

[41] The crows are still paying royalties to the heirs of an obscure, long extinct reptile, for their use of their "caw-caw" cry. Interestingly, the heirs are a subspecies of flounder, who are, of course, mute. Animal law is full of such fascinating arrangements.

[42] Deliberately mimicking another species' cry, even without any criminal intent, is a serious matter, usually a major tort. See *Bird of Paradise v. Parrot* (15 Ornith. 23), and *Wren v. Jackdaw* (146 Vivip. 20).

[43] This decision came very early on. After hearing something like the billionth mitosis case, the Court of Unicellular Appeals decided in *Paramecium 1 v. Paramecium 2* 1339 Chromosomes 55), that what went on inter mura (between the cell walls) was none of its business, and declared that it would hear no more cases of a similar nature. This example was speedily followed in other jurisdictions.

[44] We were going to cite instead a more common case, that of a cow which negligently bit a small field rodent, perhaps a squirrel, in the process of grazing, but the question of whether forcing a cow to regurgitate evidence of the act and gaining access to its cud leads to some complex and unsettled legal areas involving unreasonable self-incrimination, illegal search, and compulsion of testimony.

gathering it. For the most part, searches of animals' nests to gather evidence of a crime are allowed only for the purpose of locating evidence specifically named in a warrant, and not for "fishing expeditions." Thus, if a legal search of the badger's nest yielded no evidence of its having assaulted another badger, such as bits of fur, or whatever, but did yield evidence of another crime, say, a cache of acorns pointing to a possible misappropriation of food from a squirrel, that evidence would not be admissible in the original trial, as an indication of the defendant's character, or in a later trial for misappropriation of food.

There is also a rather touchy question, one which falls into the area of self-incrimination, of whether an animal's fur, or claws, or other portions of its body can be searched for traces of blood or other indications of the commission of a crime. Generally, the courts have held that this kind of search is permissible if carefully limited, but there are some curious qualifications. For example, a turtle's shell is held to have some of the same aura of inviolability that nests possess, and in several cases, the introduction of skins sloughed off by snakes and a few insects into evidence has been successfully challenged on the grounds that it in essence represented an attempt to force a large, albeit no longer contiguous, portion of the creature to testify against itself.

Another rule covers so-called heargrowl testimony (or hearchirrup, hearsnort, hearcry, hearsing, hearwarble, heargrunt, etc.). Invariably, out of court roars, chatters, trumpets, and calls are inadmissible for the truth of their contents—what an animal claims to have heard hooted about on "the jungle telegraph" regarding a legal matter cannot be offered into evidence, only what it has heard or observed firstpaw.[45] Other rules require the authentication of "real" evidence (including such tangible objects as fangs, feathers, furballs and fumets, hoofprints and materials bearing identifiable odors, and the like) before such evidence may be admitted, and the proper qualification of expert witnesses before they may testify in court as to the identification of clawmarks, mauling scars, indications of parasitism, etc.[46]

Once all the admissible evidence

has been heard, the witnesses cross-examined, and all statements by involved parties made, the jury is reminded that an animal is innocent until proven guilty, and retires to deliberate. Depending on its decision, the badger will go free, or, if found guilty, he may be ordered to pay a fine of a given amount of forage (little more than a slap on the paw) or, if the crime is serious, he could end up in a zoo. If he is found guilty, he has the right of appeal, sometimes several appeals, and if he has an able defense attorney, and his species is not noted for its longevity, he may evade punishment entirely.

VIII

DERIVATIVE SUITS AND CONSUMER PROTECTION

In recent years, the number of litigations by individual members of herds, flocks, schools, and other animal groupings against the leading animal in the pack, pride, gaggle, etc., have increased enormously, a reflection, no doubt, of the gradually widening awareness in the animal kingdom of the inherently exploitative nature of the domination of food supply, females, waterholes, and so forth, by the strongest member of the herd.

Derivative suits brought by herd members typically involve an allegation by the herd member that the leader or leaders of that particular grouping are not acting in the best interest of all of its members. More and more, the traditional fight to the death between a herd member who wishes to challenge the herd leader is being replaced by litigation, a healthy development very much in the best tradition of the rule of the law superseding force majeure and the droit de plus fort.[47]

There have also been a number of suits aimed at breaking the power of the so-called "mammalian-invertebrate complex," the near-total domination of the upper portions of the predation chain by a small number of species, to the detriment of the average animal.[48]

Consumer protection suits are a very recent development and one whose outcome from the point of view of the evolution of animal law it is too early to predict. They have been brought in several jurisdictions by a number of animals of quite different species in an attempt to limit the incredible number of poisons and injurious substances which many thousands of species, both plant and animal, secrete, and to force unusually dangerous species to restrict their activities.[49]

IX

CONCLUSION

There are countless areas of the lex biologica which, in this brief introduction, it has proved not feasible to cover except in passing, if at all. The diversity of the law of the jungle is extraordinary, and it rewards all who have the patience to study it with a glimpse of a structure unimaginably more complex than that of the DNA molecule, which Watson and Crick spent so long unraveling. (The lowliest sea slug is better acquainted with the Genetic Code.)

It is sad indeed that legal biology has failed to gain the attention it so clearly deserves, and it is mankind, surely, who is the loser. Think, for example, of how convenient it would be to be able to swear out a writ of nolo pestare in Insect Court against every mosquito on your property, or of how many lives could be saved if the sharks along our coasts were hit with a succession of beach warrants and cease-and-desist-eating orders!

It is equally sad that our notion of animal behavior, shaped as it is by the narrow context of the legal codes of our own species, Homo sapiens, is characterized chiefly by the picture of animals loitering, with no visible means of support, universally guilty of bestiality, and regularly committing nameless acts in dark places. It is true that animal law is not perfect, that many species still take matters into their own paws, and that the ancient principle, "ingestion is nine-tenths of the law," still infects much of the legal atmosphere in the animal kingdom, but to dismiss the law of the jungle as little more than a code of survival and a rationalization for the rule of brute force is to do a grave injustice to the legal standards which animals have evolved along with the wings, nervous systems, carapaces, etc., which are the more visible evidence of the increasing sophistication of life in "a state of nature." □

---

[45] Basically, what "the little bird" tells one is not admissible.

[46] Speaking of parasitism, the courts recognize several protected relationships, and thus, one mate may not be compelled to testify against another mate. Interestingly, parasitical relationships (and symbiotic ones as well) enjoy a similar protection against the compulsion of testimony. See *The Fish v. Pike* (90 Streams 404), in which the testimony of a lamprey was ruled inadmissible.

[47] See *Pride of Lions v. The Lion Known as "Simba"* (43 Carniv. 58). The court ordered Simba deposed. In a similar suit, *Gnat v. Cloud of Gnats* (88 Bugs 577), the court ruled in a case brought by a gnat who had formerly been deposed in a derivative suit and now complained of discrimination in awarding of swarming space by the new leader that the gnat had no standing in court because of the long-established doctrine of "unclean paws." Under this doctrine, an animal who has clearly been committing a given wrong cannot sue another animal for the same wrong.

[48] A similar situation has also arisen in the plant kingdom. See *Conifers v. Deciduous Trees* (119 Leaves 414), a restriction of sunlight case. These and other public interest suits will be interesting to watch, particularly if they lead to the establishment of a principle limiting in any way the right to eat.

[49] See *Dogs et al. v. Porcupines* (4490 Quadrupeds 81). As of now, the basic principle is still caveat predator, or, "let the eater beware."

CARL THE CREAMER
Sean Kelly on Henry Beard

In 1964, I fell in love with *Candy*, a novel co-written by Terry Southern and Mason Hoffenberg. High on my list of literary touchstones (I was an English teacher at the time) was chapter 11, in which the beautiful, innocent Miss Christian encounters two randy, potty-mouth poets, an unscrupulous gynecologist, and the outraged manager of a Greenwich Village bar, who, as the police raid his establishment, shouts at the now-naked heroine, *"You are barred from the Riviera!"*

Cut to 1974. After a lengthy, bibulous *Lampoon* editorial meeting somewhere downtown, we—Henry Beard among us—were beyond the first phase of drunkenness, Witty and Charming, had moved past the Fuck Dinner stage, and were approaching Bulletproof. Since the evening was a balmy one, we repaired to the nearest outdoor café for a cocktail.

Henry in those days was of a reserved and taciturn disposition, but when overserved, could become surprisingly playful. At such times it was his wont to perform a tabletop puppet show starring one "Carl the Creamer."

On this occasion, Carl (whose lid mouth Henry manipulated with his thumb) was in Don Rickles mode, interacting with those seated near us—for the most part young couples from the outer boroughs, now getting a little more bohemian Village atmosphere than they'd anticipated.

Of course, this caused the rest of us to snort and weep and howl with mirth, and to order more Heinekens, the elixir fueling Henry's—and Carl's—brilliant routine.

One or more of the adjacent tourists must have complained to management, for a substantial chap in an unfortunate necktie now approached and suggested we keep it down. We all mumbled in a chastened manner—except Carl, who called the man an offensive name and threw up on his shoes.

This was our cue to arise and go, and I only realized the identity of the establishment we were departing when the bouncer with cream on his feet screamed after us, "You are barred from the Riviera!"

MICHAEL O'DONOGHUE

"Why is it," Michael O'Donoghue once asked me, "that we writers never think we can draw, but you artists always think you can write?"

Well, here goes. It was January 1969: We were in Rappoport's, an East Village dairy restaurant, on a freezing night. Michael ordered split pea soup. When it arrived, he dropped a whole bialy (similar to a bagel, but better) into the soup. It floated magnificently on a green sea, accompanied by crouton icebergs. "I think we can teach it to swim," he said.

We'd met earlier that afternoon at Grove Press. We were both regular contributors to *Evergreen Review.* I illustrated articles. He wrote *The Adventures of Phoebe Zeitgeist*, an astoundingly offbeat parody of adventure stories: part Flash Gordon, part Henry Miller, and part SCUM Manifesto. There had never been anything like it before, because there had never been anyone like Michael O'Donoghue before. It was as if he'd sprung, fully formed, from the head of some fierce and demented Zeus. And suddenly there he was, blazing away at the universe.

We left Grove together and walked to Michael's Spring Street loft. Nixon's inauguration was just days away, and we were all holding our breaths, which we could see. The loft was freezing. The cold, like the memories of the year just ended, seeped in everywhere. 1968 had been filled with staggering events, beginning with Vietnam, then the assassinations, the Chicago riots, and Nixon's election. It ended with Apollo 8 circling the moon and the astronauts reading from Genesis. When they were done, we still had Vietnam.

Michael's loft seemed like some grisly adjunct to the times. It was a cabinet of curiosities, filled with peculiar collections

and tiny horrors. He had an obsessive love of macabre detail and collected everything from shrunken heads—"They say this was Disraeli"—to, later, cans of Bon Vivant vichyssoise bloated with botulism toxins. "Creepy" was the best thing you could say about them, and Michael reveled in the revulsion they caused. I fell in love with a basket of rubber rhinoceroses he kept so visitors like me would ask, "What's that?" and he could answer, "Oh, that? That's a basket of rhinoceroses." I talked him into giving me one. He did, but reluctantly so and made me promise he could have it back if he ever needed it.

His conversation dazzled and sparkled. Talking with Michael felt like having cold seltzer poured on my brain. I must have enjoyed the feeling: We became friends. In September 1969, he phoned to ask me to meet him and two guys from Harvard who were starting a new magazine. That meeting would eventually lead to this book.

At the *National Lampoon* he was genius in residence, and resident enfant terrible. His temper was legendary; he made enemies as easily as he made friends. By the time he left the *Lampoon* in 1974, he'd stopped talking to almost everyone.

Years later, I ran into him at an art fair. He was friendly and almost sweet. He was about to leave for Ireland, where he had a house in County Mayo. "I'm Lord of the Manor, old boy, I must show up from time to time to cudgel my serfs." He looked around at the tasteful art on the walls. "God-awful dreck," he said, and we laughed.

—Rick Meyerowitz

KODAK TRI X PAN FILM

UNDERWEAR for the DEAF

BY MICHAEL O'DONOGHUE

Michael Doret

PURCHASE ONLY NAME BRANDS BACKED BY REPUTABLE MANUFACTURERS.

JEEPERS, NAN! EVEN THOUGH THESE *DEAF-O PANTIES* I ORDERED FROM THAT MAIL ORDER SUPPLY HOUSE THAT STUCK THEIR MIMEOED FLIER UNDER MY WINDSHIELD WIPER ONLY COST 67¢ PER PAIR, ALREADY THE COLORS HAVE FADED AND THE ELASTIC HAS LOST ITS SNAP!

I'M AFRAID YOU'VE LEARNED THE HARD WAY THAT SO-CALLED "BARGAINS" OFTEN COST MORE IN THE LONG RUN! NEXT TIME, STICK TO *KLEER-TONES, GREEN CROSS, AUDIO-TEX,* AND OTHER NAME BRANDS BACKED BY REPUTABLE MANUFACTURERS!

YOU'LL HAVE TO SPEAK UP!

I SAID, "I'M AFRAID YOU'VE

ALL TOO SOON...

DOESN'T THAT TAKE THE CAKE! TWO WEEKS OLD AND READY FOR THE TRASH BASKET! DARN IT ALL ANYWAY!

photographs by David Kaestle, graphics by Alan Rose

National Lampoon Encyclopedia of Humor, 1973

The Dink Patrol and the Love Slaves of Xuyan Tan Phu

**He sprayed the crazed killer-kids,
knocking them over like dominoes...
All that stood between him and certain
death was his M16 and a handful of bubble gum...**

By Mike O'Donoghue (US Army Ret.)

A twig snapped. Reacting with all the speed and precision of a coiled spring, I spun around and let loose with a burst from my M16. It caught the dink in the neck. She stood there, her face a curious mixture of shock and surprise. Then, as a last vicious act, like a marlin that still snaps after it's in the boat, she threw her doll at me . . . and crumbled. But I hit the dirt before she did. The seconds ticked by like years . . . 8 . . . 9 . . . 10 . . . 11 . . . 12 . . . Nothing happened. The doll must have been a dud. I got up slowly, dusted myself off and remarked, to no one in particular, "Scratch another slant-eye!"

We were out on dink patrol. As part of a Special Forces S&K (Search and Kill) team, the Hueys had dropped us at a clearing in the U Minh forest near the southern tip of the Mekong Delta. We had orders to investigate Xuyan Tan Phu, a town G-2 had reason to believe was a Class I Viet Cong outpost in control of the dread Ta Doi (Dragon) Division. This report was based on information obtained from a VC prisoner minutes before they'd chucked him from a chopper hovering 800 feet over Yu'Chiang. He had also confessed to kidnapping the Lindbergh baby and promised us a secret cure for cancer if we let him live.

The company commander gave us the dope on the mission before we shoved off. When he was done, he paused briefly and added, "You're going into 'no-man's-land,' that is to say, a village run by savage women and children. Anybody who wants to pull out can do so right now and no one will think the less of him!" We stared at him with unblinking eyes. Nobody moved. Nobody spoke a word. He put on his helmet and, flashing a look of grim determination, hollered, "Let's get this show on the road!" His name was Captain Lockport. He was tough, he was flashy, he threw away the rule book. And every

man-jack of us would follow the crazy sonofabitch into hell without batting an eyelash.

Moving through the dense underbrush, the relentless Vietnamese sun broiling my back, the leech-infested mud tearing at my boots, my mind went back over the three years I had spent in this squalid country. I recalled the countless times the shifty, unprincipled natives had taken me for a chump. I was 9,000 miles away from home, laying my life on the line to protect their freedom, and the slimy little yellow bastards screwed me every chance they got. There was the street urchin who burned me for a sawbuck on a dope deal. Once I was stopped by a kid who said, "Hey, dog-face! You want make rub-rub with my mama? She plenty good! She virgin!" "What the hell!" I thought to myself and followed him down the narrow, twisting alleys of Saigon until he finally indicated a doorway. I threw open the door. Inside sat a girl, not more than 15, wearing only a pair of sheer, lace panties, which she slipped off as soon as I entered. Pale moonlight splashed through a window and bathed her nakedness She was beautiful, as wogs go. I took her in my arms. Her face was alive with passion and desire. Her warmth was reaching me. I lifted her until our lips met. She clung to me, her firm, ripe breasts heaving with the ecstacy of the moment, her moist lips making promises and delivering. "Take me!" she pleaded. "Take me now!" I threw her to the floor, flung off my clothes and fell on her. Rapture had its way. The next morning, after shoving a fistful of piasters into her grateful hands that still trembled from excitement, I left, never to return. All in all, it cost me a little under three dollars. A few days later, I began to itch. The crummy broad had given me the crabs.

The eerie cry of a chicken jolted me back to reality. We had reached the

town. I went in first, alone, cautiously advancing down the road with my rifle at the ready. The joint looked deserted. Maybe the Commies had seen us coming and decided to take a powder. But then a zipper-eye came out from a hut. Then another. And another. Within scant seconds, the road was swarming with them. The mob had encircled me. I was cut off.

There I was, surrounded by women and children. Raw hate gleamed in their eyes like cold steel. "Yankee go home!" was written all over their cruel, Mongol faces. They started to come at me, hands outstretched, clutching, grasping, clawing. Without warning, one of them screamed, "You give chew gum, Joe!" My blood froze. My heart hammered against my rib cage like a pneumatic drill. Knowing that one slip would be my last, I swung my automatic weapon up to gut level and barked, "Freeze, Jocko! One more peep outta you and—" But he kept coming, demanding Hershey bars and powdered milk. Holding my ground, I squeezed off a warning shot that caught him squarely in the right temple. He dropped in his tracks.

As if triggered by a secret signal, the villagers immediately ducked for cover, playing the old Asian game of attack and retreat. A few, in an obvious diversionary tactic, threw themselves at my feet, begging, "No shoot . . . please . . . we give up, boss!" But they weren't getting off that easy. They asked for a fight and now they were going to get it. "Eat lead, heathen gooks!" I shouted and swung into action, sending a hail of hot slugs slashing into the quivering Orientals that knelt before me. If there's one thing I can't stand, it's a coward.

By now my buddies had joined in, raking the Reds with a withering barrage of flying steel, hacking them apart with everything we had, from a blistering rain of small-arms fire to a howling mortar barrage. Not one shot was re-

(continued)

ILLUSTRATION BY RUSS HEATH

turned. It was apparent that we'd caught them off guard.

Covered by riveting machine guns that fed belt after belt into the bamboo huts, I pressed our advantage by leading a charge into the main village. "Okay, you meatballs!" I snarled. "Let's go get 'em!" Counting a two-second delay, I lobbed a sputtering, phosphorous incendiary grenade into a group of so-called "civilians" huddled outside the church, undoubtedly plotting some ruthless counter-assault. It clobbered them like a bowling ball hitting the one-three pocket.

I hurled myself through the church door. Inside, pressed against the floor, lay half a dozen curvaceous young girls. They wore only scraps of clothing that revealed their nubile bodies and jutting breasts. I'd read in one of those men's magazines about how the VC's keep love slaves who cater to their every whim, shameless sluts who give themselves to any man who asks. This bevy of buxom beauties who lay panting before me, wantonly displaying their charms, were probably the love slaves of Xuyan Tan Phu. They began jabbering at me in their weird lingo, trying to lure me into some deadly trap. "Kee-ripes! That mumbo-jumbo's enough to give a guy the willies!", I thought to myself as I slammed in another banana clip and opened up. "Die, moon-face!" I growled as the spitting lead ripped into one of them. The rest made for the door, but I cut them down before they could take two steps.

Only one was left. She knew the game was up. But a cornered rat will try anything. When I raised my rifle to finish the job, she cried, "What are you doing? Why are you slaughtering innocent women, children and infants? We are not NLF sympathizers! We are just harmless peasants! The mission fathers who taught me your language also taught me that Americans were kind!

They said — " I hosed her down with my M16, watching the bullets walk across her chest and chew her up. She had betrayed herself as a trained agent, ready to infiltrate and sell us out to the Commies. Her Chink masters had taken great pains to teach her English. They'd shown her how to flatter and how to play upon a GI's innate compassion and goodwill. But they forgot one thing — they forgot that it takes more than a pretty face and a few rosary beads to bamboozle an old combat-happy vet like me.

Outside, the battle had erupted into a blasting hell. Chattering M60s underscored the scorching salvos of the 105s tearing the town to shreds. The villagers now realized that their ambush had failed, that this was the end of the line. There was no hiding from the United States Army. I saw a shavetail send a spray of bullets crashing into a party of Vietnamese who foolishly assumed that they could cheat the undertaker by merely raising their hands and waving a white flag. Some mothers cradled babies in their arms, as if using their very children as a human shield would thwart their own deaths. No such luck.

From the corner of my eye, I spotted one of the enemy making a break for the jungle. Since he stood no more than two feet tall, he was going to be hard to hit. It's a common Cong trick to deploy small soldiers who make bad targets. As he toddled toward the foliage, I knew I'd only have one chance to plug him. Taking careful aim, I fired and...bingo! He spun as the steel-jacketed slugs struck home and went down like a canvas-back duck that just stopped a load of No. 5½ buckshot. "Bite dust, slopehead!" I hollered, riddling his body until the clip ran out.

Pulling back to the perimeter of the village, we radioed HQ to send in the "zoomies" to blow it. The tree-skimming bombers arrived tense moments

later and let fly with the works—HEs, APs, incendiaries. Flames licked the sky. Occasionally, a dazed survivor would stagger from the inferno, only to be stitched by a sizzling cross fire. It looked like we had it on ice when suddenly the swirling smoke parted and there stood the man that every GI fears the most — *the Geneva Conference Observer!*

Whipping out my .45, I darted after him, but he was gone before I could get off a shot. Half choking on cordite fumes, I raced into the blazing village, knowing that if I didn't bag him, he'd blab to all those nelly Congressmen, homo non-combatants, kooky eggheads and assorted fruitcakes who would love to raise a stink just because the dinks we zapped may have worn the wrong color pajamas. Needless to say, he'd neglect to mention the cache of jagged scythes, pointed hoes, sharpened digging sticks and all the other tools of terror we had uncovered. This much was dead certain — I had to shoot his mouth off before he did.

I caught sight of him cowering behind a frangi bush. As soon as he saw me, he bolted. I emptied my .45 at the fleeing figure, cursed and took out after him. I chased him up hills, across rivers, through rice paddies. We ran for miles. Then it happened. I tripped over a vine and went down. I was stunned. Pain ignited my head and swept down my spine. My mouth was filled with the salty taste of blood. Somehow, I managed to stumble to my feet. I could hardly walk. I was exhausted. Sheer guts was the only thing driving me on. Sheer guts, and the terrible knowledge that the whole ball game was riding on one man — me!

Finally, I cornered him. "You butchering swine!" he screamed dementedly. "You've violated international agreements, treaties, pacts—" "Nuts to you, buster!" I replied, lashing out with a sledgehammer blow to the crotch. He toppled over with a groan. These Swiss talk big, but they're not so tough when you get them alone. He tried crawling away, but I soon put an end to that with a lightning-fast kick to the head that laid him out for the count. I leapt on him and then pummeled him with pile-driving fury, each dull thud turning his face to hamburger. "You maniac . . ." he managed to mutter, and croaked. Just to make certain, I cut off his head.

By the time I got back to the village, it was nearly twilight. The dying sun shot its last rays through the smoldering trees. As I stood at the outskirts, watching our guys silently sifting the ruins for souvenirs to send home to their sweethearts, a medic rushed up to me and asked, "Are you okay, Chaplain?"

"It's nothing," I replied, "only a flesh wound." □

" . . . Replace a hymen for 6 o'clock? NO WAY, Mr. Burns! That's an all-day job—
I gotta drop the pelvis, disconnect the uterus, pull out the bladder, unscrew the peritoneum . . ."

CARTOON BY CHARLES RODRIGUES September 1985

Take a minute and read over these

21 DANGER SIGNS OF CANCER

It could save your life!

YOU HAVE CANCER IF:

1. Your gums bleed.
2. Your teeth tarnish quickly.
3. Your warts or birthmarks take on an unhealthy brown color.
4. The veins in your arms are becoming more apparent.
5. You are unduly startled by loud noises.
6. Your fingernails grow too rapidly.
7. You yawn frequently and tend to nap in the afternoon.
8. High-speed elevators make you dizzy.
9. You are troubled by canker sores that last longer than three days.
10. Your neck itches.
11. You feel a pressing need to urinate upon arising in the morning.
12. Hosiery and undergarments leave curious red marks on your skin.
13. You are often edgy and irritable.
14. Your lips chap excessively.
15. Hair grows immoderately in your nostrils.
16. Your feet "fall asleep" more than twice a week.
17. Headaches are inclined to localize at the base of the brain.
18. You are subject to recurrent attacks of hiccups.
19. You bruise easily.
20. You find it difficult to salivate properly.
21. A thick yellow wax collects in your ears.

If you have one or two of the above symptoms, act swiftly and there is a *slim, remote possiblilty* that you can be saved. If you have three or more symptoms, don't bother consulting a physician because it's *too late*. You've reached what we of the medical profession call "the point of no return." In the few weeks left to you (*sometimes as much as four months!*), put your affairs in order, say a last goodbye to loved ones, and prepare for the Eternal Darkness that lies ahead. . . .

Send for your free copy of *A **Grave** Situation*, the informative 24-page booklet that lists over 500 foods, cosmetics, and common household products that have been linked to cancer. You'll be surprised by many entries, including such familiar articles as fabric softeners, margarine, cork-lined bottle caps, oven cleaner, feminine hygiene deodorants, chives, and freeze-dried coffee.

O'DONOGHUE

Brought to you as a public service by The National Cancer Institute
The National Cancer Institute, P.O. Box 2294, Washington, D.C. 00106

by Michael O'Donoghue, August 1970

DUEL IN THE SUBWAY
Tony Hendra on Michael O'Donoghue

His stringy chestnut ringlets surrounded a fierce white face with bloodred lip, death cell of countless Virginia Slims. Michael O'Donoghue wrote with incredible precision, each perfect word set in its perfect place like a razor blade concealed in mouthwatering *amuse-gueule*. He had a unique gift for drawing humor from things that normally make people recoil, without ever cheapening them. He was the funniest of the group; laughter followed him everywhere. But yucks didn't do it for O'Donoghue; making people laugh, he said, "is the lowest form of humor."

To my surprise we hit it off. We began collaborating on the first issue I edited and collecting stuff for the *Lampoon*'s first comedy album, to be called *Radio Dinner*. Since my family was ensconced in an ancient stone house near the Delaware Valley—a bus ride of several hours—he offered me a couch in his vast, drafty SoHo loft. It was filled with weird bits of late Victoriana: a gout stool; mannequin limbs; a silver grape peeler; things that might be shrunken heads or long-dead rodents; sinister, dog-eared daguerreotypes; and, everywhere, card files, each card containing a comic haiku of exquisite horribleness.

He had a small-town background and a similarly humdrum education, but he soaked up crucial phrases and ideas from countless sources—Kafka, matchbook covers, old copies of *Life*, the original *Nosferatu*, *The Book of Common Prayer*—making amazing connections between them to produce a kind of poetry of humor.

What he saw in me I wasn't sure. I was a great rarity in his circle, the downtown Velvet Underground crowd: a man his age with kids. Kids and parents intrigued O'Donoghue mightily, a fascination that drove his strongest work. For my first issue, he concocted "The Vietnamese Baby Book": a saccharin-sweet pale blue memento of baby's first year, except that baby was one of those machine-gunned at My Lai. Later, in his *Saturday Night Live* character Mr. Mike, he was the ultimate loco in loco parentis.

The winter of 1971 was a hard one, but neither of us noticed much. By night the loft seemed like a dark, satanic vessel sailing the trackless wastes of SoHo, from which we'd launch the destruction of our enemies. Given the *Lampoon*'s felonious salaries, there was often little food, so our bohemian vices had to be cost-effective. My preferred drug that winter was port (the Portuguese rather than the brown paper bag kind so popular a few blocks east). O'Donoghue went for pot of an affordable some-seeds-and-sticks grade. We expended much genius debating the merits of these substances: the old sixties doper-juicer schism in more eloquent form. To buck cliché it became necessary for each to try the other's poison. So was born the great Port-Pot challenge: O'Donoghue would drink a bottle of port. I would smoke two "substantial" joints. We would keep track of our reactions. We would offer the results to *The Journal of the American Medical Association*.

The night of The Challenge I am terrified, having smoked pot only once, the longest and most suicidal night of my life. O'Donoghue, who almost never touches alcohol, is unduly quiet. Promptly at 8:00 P.M. he sips, I suck. He looks pleasantly surprised. I am already getting the familiar sensation of flying loop-the-loops upside down in a rickety biplane. I beg for port to even me out. He refuses. He is honor-bound to drink it all. He suggests fresh air. Outside, it is arctic and I straighten up some. I manage to ditch the remains of the first joint, but there is still the second. Plenty of time, says O'Donoghue heartily, beginning to assume a vaguely Anglophone port persona.

O'Donoghue carries himself well; he does not throw up. He does not sway. He feels, he says, like Fernando Rey in *The Discreet Charm of the Bourgeoisie*. I feel okay but have a paralyzing fear of returning to the loft. I'm convinced muggers are at large and it will be curtains for us. What we need, says O'Donoghue, is a sword stick. Some mugger messes with us, we'll run the fucker through. This seems to me an entirely natural and excellent idea. O'Donoghue knows a bric-a-brac store on Christopher Street where there's a sword stick. We get it on credit from the owner, a friend. The sword stick's thin, vicious blade slides out of its cane sheath with the ease of a samurai weapon. OK! We stride arm-in-arm to the subway, buoyed by our magnificent weapon and waling aid, and take the train to Spring Street.

O'Donoghue is reeling, his Augustan phase having passed. I am shivering with paranoia. Out of the gloom a cop appears. "What ya got there?" "A walking stick," I say nonchalantly. "Looks like a sword stick," he snaps. "Gimme." I'm about to obey when O'Donoghue, with a remarkably deft move, draws the sword from the cane in my hand and slashes it through the air a few times. In the twilight of the subway, it looks incredibly lethal. "I said gimme the fuckin' sword, OK?"

"You'll have to prize it from my cold, dead fingers," snarls O'Donoghue and turns toward him. This is 1972, and with an enemy of the state on every corner the cops are extra trigger-happy. There's about a second left before a very drunk O'Donoghue menaces a nervous New York City cop with a three-foot-long shiv and gets shot dead.

I cross his sword with the cane. From my mouth come the words, "For the love of God, Montresor!" I have no idea what this means or where it came from. O'Donoghue's eyes sparkle. "You would disarm me, scum?!" He expertly fences the cane away and gets the sword point in my Adam's apple. "Hey hey hey!" yells the cop. "Kill me then," the voice in my mouth yells, "but God save King Louis!" O'Donoghue collapses in cackles. The cop grabs the sword. We stagger up the subway steps and away. And so to bed. O'Donoghue later claimed this to be a hands-down victory for pot. I didn't see it.

Portions of this story were first published in Harper's Magazine, *June 2002.*

THE OTHER SERVICES SOON LEARN NOT TO TANGLE WITH THE TWIN-FISTED DENTAL CORPS....

HEL-LO, DREAMBOAT! HOWZABOUT YOU AN' YER GALFRIEND DITCHIN' THESE CREAMPUFFS AN' JOININ' US?

WHAT SAY WE DRILL A LITTLE SENSE INTO THEIR HEADS, MEL?

YOU MUGS JUST BIT OFF MORE THAN YOU CAN CHEW!

SECONDS LATER...

The Blue Boar

HOLY MOSES! SOME NUMBSKULL MUSTA RILED THEM CRAZY DENTISTS AGAIN! WON'T THEY EVER LEARN?

THIS SAME FIGHTING SPIRIT MAKES THEM A BATTLE-FIELD LEGEND, FROM THE STEAMING JUNGLES OF BATAAN...

TAKKA! TAKKA!

THE TINFOIL FROM THIS CHEWING-GUM WRAPPER SHOULD SERVE AS A TEMPORARY FILLING UNTIL WE CAN GET YOU BACK TO THE BASE, SON!

DUB DUB DUB

...TO THE BULLET-RAKED BEACHES OF ANZIO....

HMMMMMMM! WELL, IT APPEARS AS IF YOU NEED SOME WORK ON THE UPPER RIGHT MOLAR AND...LET'S SEE...

BUDDA BUDDA

SOME WON'T BE COMING HOME....

AND REMEMBER, BRUSH REGULARLY AFTER EVERY ME—

PHLUUUUUEEEE

MONDO MIKE IN NIRVANA
Emily Prager on Michael O'Donoghue

Michael O'Donoghue was a tall, reedy man with a foxlike Irish face, delicate little hands and feet, and brown, squinty, glittering eyes. His shoulders hunched over in the manner of someone skulking, he darted about like a wraith, and he smoked long, skinny, brown cigarettes whose smoke he sucked in so hard that his intake of breath was an audible gasp. When I was first introduced to him by Doug Kenney, in 1973, he was not yet sporting the 1930s round-frame sunglasses behind which he intimidated the less talented and garnered privacy to craft his persona. He was still an older guy (thirty-two) from upstate New York with a mind and tongue so sharp and quick and a temperament so unreliable, it was sometimes hard to tell if he was gifted or cursed.

He was very funny. His métier was black humor, gallows humor, but he liked all kinds of humor. Once, in 1976, he and I were walking down a path on a Greek island and we bumped into a young man who had been out shooting pigeons but who was carrying a large melon. Michael stopped and mimed to him, "Did you shoot this?" and the guy fell on the ground laughing.

Mike loved two things in life best: messing with taboos like cancer and death, and the graceful, little-bunny world of the 1930s children's nursery, both of which chimed together in what I think was his greatest prose piece, *The Vietnamese Baby Book*. He also loved women, loved dressing them up and giving them presents and treats, and he put so much of his whole heart into his girlfriends that when he had a breakup, he got terribly low. "Love," he muttered once, lying in the fetal position on his brass bed where, like Colette, he did all of his writing, "love is a death camp in a costume."

I spent a lot of time in editing rooms with Michael, both for the radio show and later for *Mr. Mike's Mondo Video*, where every second of comic timing was meticulously tapped out while we played an ancient Egyptian game that he liked called "TUT." But my favorite memory of Mike is when we were filming *The Cat Swimming School of Amsterdam, Holland*, one of Mike's more arcane ideas. Mike had discovered that cats do swim, and so we had a lot of cat actors in a pool on top of a building in Manhattan and they would swim from one end of the pool to the other and then hoist themselves out in the most amazing way, and we had handlers to blow them dry. It was going well. We almost had all the footage when, suddenly, an ASPCA squad burst into the pool area with drawn guns. Terrified, I turned to look at Mike and never have I seen a man so happy. It was the culmination of everything he stood for. He was beaming like a man who had reached Nirvana.

From "Our Sunday Comics," December 1973

ILLUSTRATION BY WARREN SATTLER

From Michael O'Donoghue's "How to Write Good," March 1971

GEORGE WILLIAM SWIFT TROW

The last time I saw George Trow was in 1974. We bumped into each other on the corner of Park Avenue and Sixty-second Street. George was wearing a tuxedo and a white Borsalino. We talked awkwardly for a few minutes, because we always talked awkwardly when we talked. He seemed to me to be from another world: a very suave fellow, all Ivy League. I can only speculate on what I seemed like to him, but Piltdown Man comes to mind.

What I did know is that he was immensely charming, had effortless personal style, and he wrote like a dream. At the *Lampoon*, he worked the midway between the irreverent hilarity of Doug Kenney and the rapier-edged wordplay of Henry Beard. Everything George wrote sparkled with wit and style and was suffused with his mordant incredulity about how truly stupid we all are. Dashing, brilliant, smoking, drinking George was the *Lampoon*'s Noël Coward.

I believe he lost something when he moved over to *The New Yorker* full-time. A logical step for him to be sure: mature work, it paid better and allowed him to take on serious subjects. But in doing so, he lost some of his sense of play.

"Within the Context of No-Context," his most well-known work, filled a full issue of *The New Yorker* in November 1980. It was a mind-bending dissection of our American way of life, beautifully written in a gorgeous, flowing prose that entertains as it excavates and polishes some of the most disconcerting

PHOTO BY ANNE HALL

aspects of our modern culture. It is highly regarded among those who claim to have read it, and it secured George's reputation as a serious man.

But by then, he was running out of whatever it was that powered him. His heart wasn't in his work. In a way, he'd become a bit like one of his professed idols, Jayne Mansfield: his head was at *The New Yorker*, but he'd left the rest of himself at the *National Lampoon*.

This dichotomy may have caused his later derailment. He was a lonely man, prone to depression and disappearances. By the nineties, he'd perfected a vanishing act that unnerved his friends. He lived the last few years of his life in a walk-up flat in Naples, unreachable and incognito. And he died there, in 2006, alone with his troubled soul. My guess is he didn't battle his own demons—he wouldn't have thought it was worth the trouble. Within that context, there was no contest.

On Park Avenue that evening in 1974, George said he was going to a "function." "You know," he said, "rubber quail and people who make the heart cluck." I told him I was on my way home to my family. "Lucky boy," said George.

—Rick Meyerowitz

Four Ways to Avoid Unpleasantness

by George W. S. Trow

ESCAPE the ugly consequences of Straightforward Speech

Learn EUPHEMISM*
(*reg. trademark)
The Language of Evasion

Do you need Euphemism? Read these sentences:

1. You're a Jew aren't you, Mary?
2. Thank God I'm rich.
3. I'd like to take you out, Alice, but frankly, I'm a homosexual.
4. So many people of your age seem to be dead.

Did you spot the treacherous Straightforward Words (evocative of painful *reality*) in these simple sample sentences? If you didn't, you can expect endless difficulty and embarrassment in your pathetic little life. Let's *review* the FIVE MOST TREACHEROUS WORDS IN OUR MOTHER TONGUE, the words that cry out for translation into Euphemism, the language of evasion. They are (and, if you play your cards right, you need never face them again): "JEW," "RICH," "HOMO-SEXUAL," "DEAD," and "FRANKLY." Learn Euphemism, the only language endorsed by the Department of Health, Education, and Welfare (as well as three leading Midwestern universities), and we'll tell you how to avoid these dread words, EVEN WHEN TALK-ING TO OR ABOUT MARCEL PROUST!*

*Our booklet, "The Lore of Euphemism," available for a nom-inal fee, tells the moving story of Euphemscholar Nancy Tmolin, who translated the sentence "Frankly, Marcel, you're a rich, dead, homosexual Jew" into Euphemism in ten sec-onds flat.

NOW LOOK AT THE SUBTLE PROBLEMS POSED BY THIS SECOND GROUP OF SAMPLE SENTENCES:

1. How come you don't have any children?
2. I have plenty of time, Mother, and I would come to see you more often, but actually I find you depressing.
3. I guess you're in the hospital for good this time.
4. How many toes do you have, anyway?

We'll teach you to defuse even these problem sentences.

1. You will learn ten ways to discuss the Middle Eastern Situational Conflict without ever mentioning the ugly word "Jew."
2. You will discuss *without blushing* people who are no longer alive!
3. You will learn the language secrets of the Carolinas (North and South), where absolutely nothing is said!
4. You will wear the miracle Eu-pho-phone (yew-foe-foe-nn), which automatically bleeps out offensive words in the speech of others.

Send coupon today:

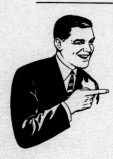

I'm tired of saying what I mean.
I want to escape.
Help me learn Euphemism, the language of evasion.

Name_____

Address_____

LADY SINGS THE SCALES

by George W. S. Trow

First Lady of Song: When Kate sang, she touched something special in white people everywhere, making even the humblest branch manager and the lowliest shareholder proud of their Euro-American ancestry.

More Than a Foolish Fatty: The producers of *Lady Sings the Scales* go out of their way to depict Kate as a hopeless eater. Relentlessly, they show the things Kate shoveled down her throat, but they seem to forget the beautiful things that came out.

They're cashing in on Kate. On her suffering. There's a movie now, *Lady Sings the Scales*, and it's supposed to be about Kate. Mama Cass plays Kate in that movie, and Mama Cass is fat, just like Kate was fat; and she gets fatter, just like Kate got fatter, but Christ, she's not playing the lady I knew. Kate Smith wasn't just a fatty stashing pecan pies in her dressing room—she was an authentic white voice sending out a screech of protest against three centuries of involuntary pulchritude. Kate Smith is the woman who sang "God Bless America" and made us proud to be white, but the exploiters pass over that so they can sensationalize Kate's addiction to food. Scene after scene. Kate hiding Mallomars in her garter belt. Kate gobbling the leavings off her neighbor's plate. Kate throwing away her fork and shoveling in the mashed potatoes with her pudgy fingers. It's true. Kate ate more than was good for her. Like many White Americans, she was oppressed by abundance and took it out at the dinner table. But that's not what Kate was really about, and it's time to set the story straight.

Kate, like most girls in the white community, learned about dessert early. The legend has grown up that her own mother introduced her to cookies and milk, but Kate's cousin Lois (who, incredibly enough, was never consulted by the producers

Ivory magazine, April 1973

God Bless America: Kate hits a high note in the hearts of her countrymen.

of *Lady Sings the Scales*) denies the story. "Kate's mama, my Aunt Charlotte, was very opposed to sweets, and I remember once when Uncle Willie bought lollipops for all us kids she threw him out of the house. Aunt Charlotte wore false choppers and was a real bug on tooth decay. Anyone who knew Aunt Charlotte at all would know that she would never have initiated Kate into dessert." The fact is, of course, that dessert was rampant within the white community and that Kate could have picked some up in any number of places. Indeed, the standards of the society Kate grew up in were such that it would have been very unusual for Kate *not* to have experienced "sweets" by a very early age. The point is that, unlike the other white kids who popped a candy bar now and then, Kate couldn't handle her food. By the time her singing career was under way, worldly musicians had introduced her to cream tarts, cheesecake, cherry cobbler, and double cream. Soon she was wearing tentlike dresses to

The Long Way Down: Eager for publicity, forced to exploit her own misery, Kate, in later days, sometimes posed with food.

hide her weight. At first she was thin enough to get into billowing chiffon outfits, but later it is true she wrapped herself in army-surplus parachutes. There *were* snickers, and Kate had to give up singing food-reference songs like "You're the Cream in My Coffee" for fear of mirthful audience reactions. But again, those who were closest to Kate maintain that her food addiction was peripheral to her life and that she has been done a grave injustice by her film biographers.

"Actually, what her trouble was," says Kate's cousin Lois, "was painful corns and calluses. That's what did *her* in. Sometimes her dogs hurt so much she couldn't get a note out. Nobody knows but me how she suffered from corns and calluses. That food stuff they always play up wasn't nothing in comparison to what she suffered from her feet."

Let me tell you what it was like growing up in Grosse Point, Detroit's white ghetto, during the forties and fifties. And what Kate meant to us white kids then. The heat of summer would drive us out of the house (it was before the days of air conditioning), and we'd hang around together on the bridle paths and fairways. We were a pretty rough bunch, I guess, and at least some of the guys ended up fencing golf balls, but I can remember that when we listened to Kate, when we heard her unexampled throaty whine, the voice that clung to the upper register like chewing gum to a drugstore counter, something in our whiteness was touched. That was the forties, and we hadn't learned to articulate our whiteness. No one shouted "I'm blanc and I'm proud." But when we heard Kate screech "God Bless America," we were, somewhere deep in our epidermis, complete. And we began to know who we were. Thanks a lot, Kate.

TheStupidGroup

> "A world where yesterday's aspirations take a leap into tomorrow's greed, right now!"
> W. Hawley Smoot, Chairman, The Stupid Group.

Who are we?

**Who are we?
We're the anytime spend-lure!**
We're **Stupidcard**—the revolutionary new *total credit system* that lets you spend money you'll never have—right now! An intriguing cyclical charge feature allows us to charge you over and over again—even if you never made the purchase to begin with! A "limited liability" feature insures that, should your Stupidcard fall into the wrong hands, you'll be charged for every single penny the malefactor runs up! Right now! In advance! And you can use your Stupidcard in so many ways! If, for instance, you are forced into receivership, or if (when we take you to court), you face a stiff fine, just shout, "Charge it!" We'll be happy to bill you right now!
Stupidcard stands behind you.
And we stand behind Stupidcard.

TheStupidGroup
stupidcard
6328 8079 302 845
1075 VALID 0-3-74 THRU 0-2-75
YOUR STUPID NAME

**Who are we?
We're a step-out meal-lure!**
We're **Tower of Pepper**, the country's fastest-growing slow-food franchise chain. You've seen them —on trashy highways and in blighted urban areas—the tall, distinctive, papier-mâché pepper mills where irresponsible families just like yours queue up for our famous pepper treats. Black, white, or costly cayenne, it makes no difference what you order, because the secret is in the incredibly slow service! You'd think, considering how long it takes, that we'd be serving high-quality, fresh-ground pepper, but the joke's on you! It's low-cost flavored silt!

Tower of Pepper stands behind you.
And we stand behind Tower of Pepper.

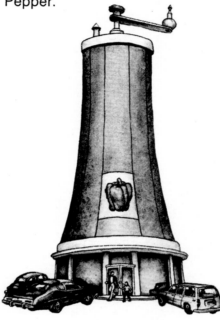

**Who are we?
We're a whole new way to keep medicine out of the hands of your children.**
We're **No AdmitTins**, the safety-time pill tin. No AdmitTins has developed a sturdy, dependable lucite container *without a top* so that potentially harmful medicine stays inside, where it belongs, *away* from precious baby. No AdmitTins comes in five striking colors to match the decor of any layette and costs just as much as accessible medicine.
No AdmitTins stands behind you.
And we stand behind No AdmitTins.

**Who are we?
We're an artificial leg-lure.**
We're **P'eggs**, the exciting pantyhose designed for the gal with "problem" legs. How do our P'eggs fit your pegs? Exactly!
P'eggs stand behind you.
And we stand behind P'eggs.

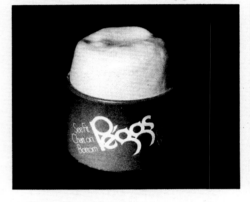

**Who are we?
We're a leisure-time fun-lure.**
Our Bureaucrackers division makes **Ennuitos**, the nasty little snack treat that bites you back.
. . . A unique blend of fibrous fillers woven into crunchy morsels the size of an airmail stamp, Ennuitos have the famous "morning after" aftertaste that makes them the only crackers especially designed for boring cocktail parties.
Ennuitos stand behind you.
Bureaucrackers stands behind Ennuitos.
And we stand behind Bureaucrackers.

TheStupidGroup

Who are we?
We're a treat-time sweet-lure!
We're **Dumbwhip**, the loathsome dessert topping you can use to inflate your tires. Dumbwhip takes the "dairy" out of nondairy dessert treats. There is nothing in Dumbwhip that even faintly resembles anything occurring (organically or inorganically) in nature. Isn't that reassuring? And while every harmful nutrient has been scientifically removed from Dumbwhip, it's loaded with the artificial fatteners you crave! And expensive! Dumbwhip costs two or three times as much as cream!

Dumbwhip stands behind you. And we stand behind Dumbwhip.

Who are we?
We're a travel-time trip-lure.
We're **Lug-A-Round bulky luggage**, the weighted luggage with the patented "pop-open" lock (guaranteed to make even the smallest thief giggle with contempt), and the famous "give-way" handle—the handle scientifically patterned after a test-pilot's ejection seat. Lug-A-Round luggage features "non-retentive memory" construction so that when you dent the sides of a piece of Lug-A-Round luggage, it *stays* dented. And, of course, our famous weight makes Lug-A-Round the luggage that makes *you* want to stay home. Lug-A-Round weighted luggage stands behind you.

And we stand behind Lug-A-Round.

Who are we?
We're a party-time dress-up!
We're **Jejeuna©** and **Blandon©**, the lemon-flavored fabrics from Saturn that make you glad to be here on Earth! Jejeuna©—with the subtle texture of linoleum, but none of the upkeep—gives your hostess gown all the sparkle of a spanking new bathroom floor! More and more, you'll find Jejeuna© in everything you wear—and everything you wear out, too, because Jejeuna© has the life-span of a mayfly! And don't forget Blandon©, the rubbery substance that's perfect as a house-paint or a raincoat. Blandon© pops up everywhere—from pot roasts to golf mittens—because its uniquely unstable molecular structure keeps on changing its mind!

Jejeuna© and Blandon© stand behind you.

And we stand behind Jejeuna© and Blandon©.

Who are we?
There's so much more!
We're a highway rest-lure! We're *Crasscourts*, the coast-to-coast chain of appalling motels. . . . We're a death-time tomb-lure. We're *Crasscourts Gardens*—the cemetery franchise chain with a motel-like atmosphere. . . . We're media—we're *Stupid News and World Report*, we're *Stupid Hairdo Magazine*, we're *Stupidités* (the most beautiful stupid magazine in the world), we're *Stupid Homes and Gardens*, we're *Stupid Stories*, *Stupid Screen*, *Stupid Detective*. We're *Stupidity Today*. We're *Stupid Digest* and *Selections del Stupid Digest*.

And that's not all. We're *Daft* brand comfort tissue. We're sugar-slathered *Corn-Duds*, the nutritionless breakfast sensation. We're *Imbecil*, the semi-suppressant cough-remedy-like medicine. And we're the exclusive importers of *Kakka*, the Greek olive liqueur, *Repulznaya*, the fabled vodka of the Polish Corridor, and *Aneurin Bevin Old Backbench* scotch whiskey.

We're new gray *Tepid*, the gritty, sudsless detergent that gives your clothes a once-over wishy-wash in penny-saving lukewarm water. . . . We're *Shop Steward—Labor Union in a Drum* household products—thirty-six separate cleansers in individual containers. A specially formulated cleaning compound for every cleaning chore around your house, from bathroom bowl to messy dog dish. Each one does the clean-up job it's meant for! And nothing else!

For the man of the house, we're the Merv Griffin wardrobe, featuring wash-and-weary Permawrinkle suits made of quintuple-knit Banalon, and *Hackney* slacks. We're also *Twit* brand men's toiletries, and *Old Stilton*, the aftershave with a fresh hint of cheese.

For milady, we're *Plain Janes*, the fabulous collection of custom-mass-produced clothes designed by Walter Gropius, and Andy Granatelli signature scarves. We're also *Nondescriptique* cosmetics, *Drab Lash* eye makeup, and *Furtiv* feminine hygiene spray, with a fresh hint of cheese.

We're *Cloyettes*, the purse and pocket-sized breath freshener that looks like a poker chip, tastes like a mothball.

We're *Ashtré* sachets, the closet and drawer odorizer with just a whiff of old cigarette smoke.

We're *Jeez*, the industrial strength cheese dip, and *R.S.V.P.* reusable crackers.

For the kitchen, we're *Dip 'n' Flip*, the gravy-like caulking mixture that turns roasts into conversation pieces, and the whole host of handy *Cook 'n' Eat* canned goods. We're *Deadpan*, the greaseless, silicone-based cooking substance. And we're *Atomrange Gammaray* ovens—the frankly terrifying stove that cooks foods in just seconds and gives them a festive party glow.

TheStupidGroup
Where stupidity gets down to business.

I'm a defense minister.

My salary is tiny for the job I do. Do you have any idea how hard it is to push people around for twenty years and still come off as the underdog? Sometimes I wonder how I do it. And this year the crucial raw material I need to create the webs of self-justification people expect is just about to run out. Even with careful hoarding of World War II guilt, even taking advantage of the stupidity of our neighbors, this year self-righteous fervor may not be enough. What happens when people begin to take a hard look at my questionable real estate deals? I don't know, but this year, more than ever, I'm relying on the Middle East Appeal. Time and time again the Middle East Appeal has been able to supply the distorted vision, false loyalty, and meretricious morality we need to get the job done!

Keep The Peculiar Promise

Give to the

Middle East Appeal

mea

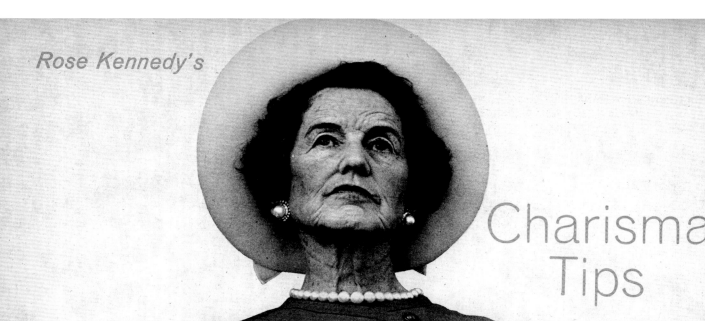

Rose Kennedy's

Charisma Tips

So many candidates these days are conscious of the importance of charisma but just don't know didilly squat, if you'll pardon my French, about what it is or how to get it. They all think it's some important quality of leadership you have to be born with, like good judgment, common sense, or $100,000,000, and that someone who hasn't got it is doomed to live out his days in backwoods caucuses, holding down a desk in the Department of Public Works and waiting for the day when he can be County Comptroller.

Well, you can take it from me, that's just a lot of hooey and I put one son through Electoral College and my youngest is about ready to make it two, so I should know what I'm talking about. Charisma is easy once you understand what it's all about—getting the voter to look at you and not your record. Let's face it, you could be congressman from the Black Lagoon and you'd still be better off if old John Q. is eyeballing your mug and not your brag sheet.

Now the first thing to remember is that there are only three Winning Images: Lincolnesque, Camelot (my personal favorite), and Mr. Smith Goes to Washington. Your first job is to pick the one that fits you best. For example, if your face looks like an old couch and your voice sounds like a postoperative laryngectomy patient talking over an army public-address system, go right for the Lincolnesque. You don't have to overdo it (one candidate I know of used to smoke Lincoln logs), but remember, it's the total image that counts. You mustn't confuse the voter: when he gets into that booth, he's ready to vote for only three people: Abe Lincoln, John F. Kennedy (it makes a mother proud), and Jimmy Stewart, and if you don't come to mind in one of those Key Charisma Categories, forget it!

How do you know which category you're best for? Here's a simple rule of thumb: if you're ugly, stupid, old, Southern, or have recently suffered a stroke—Lincolnesque; good examples of the Lincolnesque style are Karl Mundt, Lyndon Johnson, and Everett Dirksen. If you're young, rich, handsome, and have perfect teeth and good speechwriters, it's Camelot. But don't flatter yourself: it's the easiest category to blow, and if you don't believe me, just ask John Lindsay, Chuck Percy, or James Roosevelt to draw you a floor plan of the White House.

Now most of you are Mr. Smiths (no need to be ashamed —you count the current President among your number!), and this is really the most reliable image. It's the lawyer who made good but didn't forget his roots (or the train whistle in the night or whatever), who's shocked to find that when Senator Blowhard crumples up a "carefully prepared speech," it's nothing but a blank piece of paper! For you, I recommend off-the-rack suits during campaigns, a little pancake makeup for those bad wrinkles (let's not confuse Mr. Voter—he isn't going to give the nod to Jimmy Lincoln), shirtsleeves if that's your style, and at least six anecdotes of the hardware business during the Depression (or pharmacy business).

A quick note on TV appearances: You Lincolns, gargle with Clorox and pat about a half pound of naval jelly into your face and jowls—TV tends to exaggerate those little arroyos, grottoes, cisterns, mesas, etc., and too many reruns of <u>The Mummy</u> have spoiled that overly weathered look; Camelots, put Murine in your eyes to make them twinkle; Smiths, make sure you have an American-flag pin in your lapel and send an aide into the studio before the taping to break all the closeup lenses with a ball peen hammer.

One last point: charisma isn't looks alone. Keep those speeches, unfair assaults, and so forth in character. Let's take the bussing issue. Lincolnesque: speak slowly. "You ask me where I stand on bussing, and this is my answer: let reason triumph, let cooler heads prevail, let no man ever have to say, "They put their destiny on the bus of hope and it was struck by the train of hate on the poorly marked grade-crossing of the future."

Camelot: resounding. "But in a larger sense, it is for us to whom the hope of free men everywhere is entrusted to take up the challenge of the times, and now more than ever we must, as John F. Kennedy so eloquently put it, 'Ask not what our country can do for us, but what we can do for our country.'"

Mr. Smith: loud and sharp. "My opponent wants to send your children across state lines on flatbed trucks, packed like smelts, their tiny heads crushed together, only to be dumped like so much human landfill in the marijuana-choked yards of trade schools, where their gaily painted lunch boxes will be ripped from their grasp by savage Ubangis packing automatics."

Well, that's all for now.

Rose

August 1972

INTERIOR DECORATION

*I*n your heart of hearts, you know. Others, even those closest to you, find you tiresome. Pathetic old booby that you are, you no doubt hide the truth from yourself, get drunk on cough syrup, and wait to be asked for Thanksgiving. All the while, you *could* use your *natural penchant for the pedestrian* to carve a niche for yourself in the INTERIOR DECORATING FIELD. In today's decorating field, as never before, there is a crying need for those with a taste for the trite. Hospital waiting rooms, collegiate art centers, corporate conference rooms, Beef & Beer restaurants, and *millions of private homes* must be decorated in accordance with prevailing standards of poor taste in the years ahead.

ARE YOU RIGHT for the prestigious Interior Decorating Field?

Frankly, it isn't likely. Only a tiny, tiny percentage of the adult population can make the grade. BUT, if you pass the test below, WE'LL TAKE A CHANCE and start you on your first lesson. If you fail, however, we must ask you to go on with the rest of the magazine, and try to forget we ever mentioned that success and popularity were briefly within your grasp. Yes, you'll just have to go on with the rest of your unrewarding life until you die.

WHAT FATAL ERROR IN JUDGMENT DID
THE DECORATOR OF THIS ROOM MAKE?

1. Too many mirrors
2. No Barcalounger
3. Insufficient space given to personalized hobby collections and other family needs
4. Too la-dee-dah

Rate your score by turning page upside down.

CONGRATULATIONS! You are qualified to be an INTERIOR DECORATOR.

From "Our Sunday Comics," December 1973

ILLUSTRATION BY WARREN SATTLER

CHRISTOPHER CERF

C hris Cerf: *Harvard Lampoon.* Random House. *Sesame Street. National Lampoon.* Muppets. *Not The New York Times. Between the Lions. Lomax.* Emmies.

Grammies. Books. Records. Television Producer. Record Producer. Songwriter. Author. Editor.

Henry Beard called him "The Switchboard" because he knew everyone and was generous in his willingness to connect people he thought might mutually benefit.

I met Henry through Chris. I met P.J. O'Rourke through Chris. I met Abbie Hoffman, Rick Meyerowitz, and George Plimpton through Chris. I met Jim Henson through Chris. I could fill the rest of this book with the names of people I met through Chris.

But Chris's real talent is that he knows how to work with talent. He is tireless, often working sixteen to eighteen hours a day, every day. Much of it is grinding work for which he gets no credit and earns nothing except the pleasure of helping create great stuff. Not the easiest thing in the world, but he is an absolute master at it.

Chris and Henry were an amazing team. Henry, of course,

PHOTO BY JONATHAN BECKER

knew everything. And whatever idea they had, Chris either knew it already, or he'd learn it—fast. To Henry, Chris was mentor and friend, and the only one whose opinion mattered. Together, they shaped some of the most subversively funny work the *Lampoon* ever published. Their faux anti-Dutch screed, "Let's Get America Out of Dutch," was ferociously, hilariously, off-the-wall. As was *Constitutional Comics*, which told the story of the political machinations of Nixon and Ford's Transportation Secretary, Claude Brinegar, whose plan to rise to the presidency from his position of twelfth in line provided an absurd text outlining the Machiavellian potential for mischief built into the U.S. Constitution.

Some had higher profiles at the *Lampoon*, but no one had the behind-the-scenes influence Chris had. Whenever Henry ran into a problem, he knew he could count on The Switchboard to connect him with a solution.

—Bill Effros

From "Dutch Treachery redux," May 1974

ILLUSTRATION BY DON PERLIN

Henry Beard and I decided to produce a parody of hate literature for the April 1973 "Prejudice" issue. We had in mind the type distributed by groups such as the National White People's Party to warn unsuspecting Americans that Jews, Blacks, Communists and/ or Catholics (to name just a few) were relentlessly conspiring to overthrow Western civilization. In order to avoid the appearance of defaming those groups the hatemongers had targeted in the first place, we would select the most benign and unthreatening national group we could find and outline, in searing and vitriolic detail, the heinous threat they represented to "all we hold dear."

In those days, Henry and I loved to bat around ideas for *Lampoon* pieces at Original Joe's, a restaurant in the East Sixties. We went to Joe's to figure out who should be the target of our screed. It wasn't as simple as we'd expected. The Belgians? Other than fattening us up with their waffles, what could we accuse them of doing to us? Finally, we hit upon the Dutch. "They're cutting all our doors in half," I noted. "God knows what they bake in those ovens of theirs," Henry responded. And so it went for the next couple of hours until, fortified by numerous glasses of Heineken (or "Dutch swill," as we had already come to call it), we stumbled out onto Second Avenue with more than enough material to fill the inaugural issue of the Americans United to Beat the Dutch (A.U.T.B.D.) newsletter. Our parody might not win awards for its subtlety and restraint, we realized, but we were confident that it could make our readers laugh without being offended.

Unfortunately, we were wrong about the "offended" part. Publisher Jerry Taylor, a man of great skill and graciousness, had been courting *Time* magazine's advertising manager for months and had finally convinced him to place a series of ads in the *Lampoon*. But, as luck would have it, *Time*'s media buyer was Dutch, and when he received his copy of the "Prejudice" issue, complete with Henry's and my A.U.T.B.D. article, he was anything but amused. "They called my queen a *dike*!" he sputtered at Jerry, and he promptly cancelled his entire *Lampoon* campaign.

The story doesn't end there. Week after week, phone call after phone call, Jerry worked patiently on getting *Time*'s ads back into the *Lampoon*, and finally the media buyer relented.

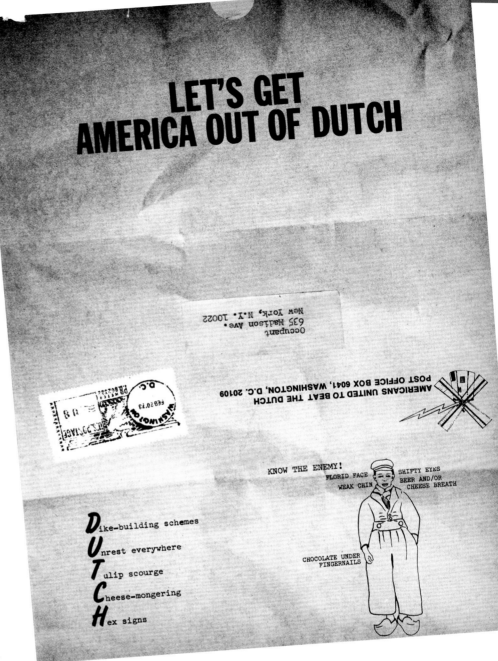

"Perhaps I *did* overreact," he allowed, and he agreed to begin advertising again in the next available issue. But unbeknownst to Jerry, Henry and I had been shamelessly shaping the leftovers of our seemingly infinite supply of anti-Dutch material into a second A.U.T.B.D. newsletter (see cartoon on the page to your left). In May 1974, only days after *Time* had returned to the fold, our sequel hit the stands. Needless to say, the newsweekly immediately withdrew its ads once again. And that time, alas, they never returned.

—Chris Cerf

The A.U.T.B.D. Newsletter

PRICE--50 CENTS

ACTION!

*

We're happy to welcome all you new tile-smashers to the fight against Dutch subterfuge. Our movement is growing by leaps and bounds every day, and although we cannot disclose the exact number of our members to prevent infiltration from certain persons who feel more at home in footwear made out of trees, we can say that it is very large indeed and getting larger! Politicians be warned!

You will ignore this aroused brotherhood of true Americans at your peril! And if you don't believe us, take a wishy-washy position on Government-supported elm-seeding programs and stiff tariffs to protect our razor-makers, breweries, dairies, diamond mines, and chocolate manufacturers next Election Day and SEE WHAT HAPPENS!

****

by Henry Beard and Christopher Cerf

I regret to say that I must begin this month's issue of the A.U.T.B.D. newsletter with an important piece of unfinished--and unpleasant--business.

I am referring, of course, to Mijnheer Duane Van Der Vincent and his band of Soestdijk Palace hirelings who lick the hollandaise from the wooden jackboots of Prince Bernhard while pretending to be fighting the Bane of the Benelux! All of us true Americans at A.U.T.B.D. had him and his cheese-loving crew spotted from the moment they tried to infiltrate the organization three years ago, and we were just playing along with them, waiting for them to try their power grab. Now that they've shown their chocolate-smeared hands by forming their transparent front group at the bidding of the Big Burgher in an effort to confuse and divide American opposition to the Low Country's highjinks, we can expose them for the delft double-crossers they are! Do not be fooled by their claims of militancy against the Nederlander menace! They are not true opponents of the nemesis of the North Sea! They are in the pay of the Bandit Prince! They loll in their plush offices, eating grilled-cheese sandwiches, swilling creme de cacao, and reading Dutch pornography! We must unite to oppose these vicious upstarts! Ignore their crude propaganda and laughable attacks on real foes of the tyrants of Rotterdam! They are beneath contempt! They stink of Edam and Gouda! The lewd litanies of the Dutch Reformed Church are ever on their lips! SHUN THESE SINISTER IMPOSTERS! REPUDIATE THEIR BASE LIES! THE INFECTED ELM MUST BE CUT DOWN TO SPARE THE HEALTHY TREES!

--Leading Dike-buster Raymond Petri

xxxxxxxxxxxxxxxxxxxxxxxxxxxxxxxxxxxxxxxxxx

Tulips Take Lead

WILL HE FALL FOR IT?

FORT WAYNE, IND., Aug. 14 (UPI) —According to statistics released here by the National Flower Growers' Association Convention, tulips are the nation's number-one Easter gift-flower, with sales of over 14,000,000 individual blooms last year alone.

Lilies, which used to be the favored holiday flower, are now in second place in the potted-plant category. The popularity of the distinctive Dutch import, long a familiar part of the Easter scene, has been growing steadily for years, in spite of the fact that it has practically no scent.

No scent? No, just the odor of conspiracy and the foul smell of deceit!

xxxxxxxxxxxxxxxxxx

The Bandit Prince and his evil Queen, the Grand Dike Juliana, enlist more willing dupes into their vicious drainage schemes.

xxxxxxxxxxxxxxxxxx

sab·o·tage \'sab-ə-ˌtäzh\ *n* (fr. *saboter* to trample on with sabots, the wooden shoes worn in European countries, chiefly Holland) **1:** destruction of property or hindering of manufacture by discontented workmen **2:** destructive or obstructive action carried on by a civilian or enemy agent designed to hinder a nation's war effort **3:** an act or process tending to hamper or hurt.

—Webster's American Dictionary

Sabot

Thanks, Mr. Webster--that's all we needed to know!

A big vote of thanks is due to the staunch zee-protectors who braved the rain to picket the notorious Concertgebouw Orchestra during its appearance at the Bushnell Auditorium in Hartford, Connecticut. In spite of the inclement weather--and it's no accident we've been getting so much bad weather, either, since the natural process of evaporation has been thrown out of kilter by the Bandit Prince's relentless drainage projects carried out behind wraps on supersecret "wildlife preserves"--more than half a dozen loyal Americans were on hand to alert the audience to the insidious manhood-robbing melodies scheduled by Mijnheer Joachim Ruyter and his "musicians." As usual, the police had been bought off with boxes of Dutch Slavemasters cigars from Mijnheer Fidel Van Der Castro's plantations, and they prevented the hardy band of cheese-grillers from greeting the Maestro of Maastricht backstage with a good old-fashioned American "review" of his performance.

Still and all, a good day's work, and a potent reminder to some people who shine their shoes with shellac that this country isn't about to be sweet-talked into swallowing the Soestdijk Palace line with a few phony low-country lullabies!

illustrations by Celia Bau

While we're at it, it's high time to blow the whistle on the whole sly scheme of the gnomes of Zeeland for world economic domination. With the help of the Stuyvesants, the VanDerBilts, the Roojkefellers, and other double-dealing Dutch cousins who are big cheeses in Nieuw York banking circles, these guilder-grubbers use promises of diamonds—and shares in the vast profits from their perfidious trade in narcotics made from Flanders poppies and opium tulips—to woo greedy Wall Street tycoons into backing their plan to put the financial world onto the discredited cheese standard. At the same time, they labor long and hard to ruin confidence in gold by flooding the Free World with gold coins that on close inspection turn out to contain nothing but chocolate. And every time some money-hungry fat cat, his brain fuddled by their flourine-laced liqueurs, falls for one of their dirty Dutch deals, millions more pour into the coffers of the Bandit Prince and his robber-burghers. And where does it go from there? It goes to finance Royal Dutch Shell, which at this very minute, under the ridiculous pretense of drilling for oil in the North Sea, is actually pumping dry this vital ocean highway, sending billions of gallons of water into the already dangerously swollen English Channel.

The Dutch timetable for conquest is clear. It's the eleventh hour on the flower clocks of the Hague. Yet while good Americans loll in their bone-crushing van der Rohe chairs, unknowingly allowing their bodies to be poisoned by radioactive Dutch Boy paints and foolishly subjecting their delicate facial follicles to the same deadly Phillips razors used by Mijnheer van Gogh to cut off his ear when he flew into a fury after learning that his plan to foist off forgeries of his work as his own had been discovered, our politicians are being seduced by buxom milkmaids at wild cheese-tasting parties at the Dutch embassy and bought off by promises of huge estates in the New Holland they'll build once the Great Lakes are drained!

*

```
XXXXXXXXXXXXXXXXXXXXXXXXXXXX
X                          X
X    KEEP OUT OF THE REACH  X
X                          X
X       OF CHILDREN         X
X                          X
X   AVOID CONTACT WITH EYES X
X                          X
XXXXXXXXXXXXXXXXXXXXXXXXXXXX
```

This label was reproduced from the side of a can of Old Dutch Cleanser. The Surgeon General obviously considers this product too hazardous to be used by America's youngsters, and, apparently, the things it can do to your eyes are just too horrible to describe! And yet in the name of "good sportsmanship" our snivelling, vote-seeking politicians make no move to take Old Dutch Cleanser off the market. We say, "To hell with Old Dutch Cleanser! To hell with Juliana and Bernhard and their treacherous American puppets! The spirit of Leopold I of Saxe-Coburg-Gotha will prevail!"

Dutch Gets Boost

UNITED NATIONS, N.Y., Feb. 12 (AP)—A report issued by the U.N. Information Office shows that Dutch has moved from 14th to 13th on the list of the world's most commonly spoken languages.

The shift puts it just ahead of Malay and behind Tamil, a Hindu dialect. U.N. officials attributed the change to a previous error rather than to any significant growth in the number of people speaking the oddly lilting European tongue.

The only "error" is on the part of our leaders, who are so blinded by promises of chocolate-covered diamonds and other Hollander gewgaws that they can't—or won't—see the handwriting on the dike!

****

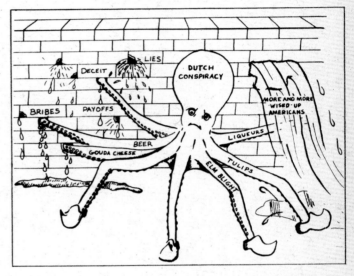

"A touch. A smile. A shared memory of a special time. That look that says more than a volume of poetry. The kiss that says you are a dream come true.

Diamonds are more than a promise. Diamonds are forever."

—De Beers Consolidated Mines ad

Just another of the many open invitations to adultery and lustful behavior planted in our popular publications by the Bandit Prince and his greedy gem-lords to weaken our will, so that when we hear the sound of a chain saw cutting our doors in half in the middle of the night, we'll be too sated with sickening pleasures to resist!

Here's a poem from a little girl in Buffalo, New York, which should give us all a lot of hope for the future!

Roses are red,
Tulips are bad,
I hope Prince Bernhard
Chokes on a shad.

(Shad are a kind of fish they have in Holland which I read about in geography class and we couldn't find the Frisian Islands on the map, either.)

ILLUSTRATED BY RUSS HEATH

November 1974

Christopher Cerf and Henry Beard produced the ten-page "Constitutional Comics," in which Claude Brinegar, Nixon's secretary of Transportation, schemes to succeed the president. Chris and Henry use the real-life firings and misfirings of the Nixon years to give plausibility to his risible plans of succession.

This lengthy, carefully researched piece lay in peaceful obscurity until a few days after Claude Brinegar died in 2009, when his daughter reached out to Chris via the internet. "You and Henry Beard wrote a brilliant piece on my dad, Claude Brinegar, plotting to move up the line of succession. He loved the piece. When he died last week we dug up the magazine and enjoyed it all over again. I want to thank you on behalf of my dad and the family, your work brought us joy at an otherwise sad time."

Very touching, but what kind of book do you think we are? Let's end with Henry's comment on hearing the news. "Ah, Claudie, we hardly knew ye. But then, practically no one knew ye. As fine a native-born American as one could ask for, and now a fine native-deceased American."

Ah Chrissy! Ah, Henry! Such work you did.

—Rick Meyerowitz

JOHN WEIDMAN

That John Weidman left the *National Lampoon* to become a successful playwright and librettist comes as no surprise to those who know him. And despite George

Kaufman having said, in one of those annoying little aperçus that can be discussed forever, "satire is what closes on Saturday night," many of John's shows outlasted their Saturday expiration dates. This may have had something to do with Stephen Sondheim, but let's not sell our boy short; he's done pretty well on his own. At Harvard, he had been an Asian studies major whose focus was Japan (*Pacific Overtures*). He went to Yale Law School to become a comedy writer (*Anything Goes*). And recently he spent ten years as president of the Dramatists Guild (*Assassins*).

white man, became 'Good Indians.' Each of these handsome platters will be as vividly painted as the faces of the dead braves depicted, as beautifully fired as the Indian villages themselves."

When he took aim at a target, he skewered it perfectly. His writing is always crisp, always funny, and sometimes remarkably profane. He has a unique and recognizable voice, yet he partnered often and easily with many other writers. Tony Hendra told me, "I laughed with a lot of people while working with them but I never laughed as hard as I did with John. He is intoxicatingly silly for someone so intimidatingly smart." John was a team player in a sport that was a kind of cross-country ego-demolition derby whose players despised teams. I loved working with John. It wasn't work. It was plain old fun. And anyway, I always thought of him as The Beatles of the *Lampoon*: he was the smart one, the quiet one, the cute one, and the funny one all rolled up in one guy.

John was one of the sharpest political political pens at the *Lampoon*. At the same time he was winning Emmys writing for *Sesame Street*. (The right wing is right! Burt and Ernie *are* Commies!)

Here's John, from an article he and I did called "America Celebrates: Triumph of the Swill," celebrating the *100th anniversary of the Massacre at Wounded Knee*. "Two hundred unarmed Indians—including over fifty women and children—pursued through the snow by the U.S. Cavalry and gunned down in their tracks! To help celebrate this milestone in American genocide, the Franklin Mint will issue a series of commemorative plates dedicated to the Sioux, the Cherokee, and all the other Native Americans who, with the help of the

P.S.: *The Bunker*, which appears here, is set in what may be the best location of any play ever written by anybody, anywhere. It is one of several plays John wrote for the magazine over the years. The man knew where he was going.

—Rick Meyerowitz

BAR ASSOCIATION OF THE STATE OF NEW YORK

1975

EXAMINATION
FOR ADMISSION TO THE BAR
JULY 21, 1975

This examination is designed to test knowledge of the laws of the State of New York.

Time allotted: Eight hours. All questions must be answered.

STOP! Do not turn page until instructed to do so by the examiner. Your examination paper has been assigned the following code number. Do not write your name anywhere on this booklet.

A68045

August 1975

The legal profession was going through a difficult period in the mid-1970s. The most famous lawyer of the day was White House Counsel John Dean, who memorably remarked, "There's a cancer growing on the presidency," and made sure he said it loud enough to be clearly audible on the Oval Office taping system.

I attended Yale Law School in the early 1970s. It was a great institution, roiling with provocative debate on the most important social issues of the day, where I once found myself sitting in class with Bill Clinton on one side of me and Clarence Thomas on the other. Between my second and third years, I took the then obligatory summer job with a New York law firm and got a feeling for how the "law business" actually worked. That feeling, accurate or not, gave birth to the following piece.

—John Weidman

Congratulations, *John "Jake" Sussman, Esq.* !!!!!!

You have just passed the New York State Bar Exam. You are now privy to one of the best-kept secrets in the nation. You're in. You're it. You're one of us.

Do not look up. Do not cheer. Keep quiet and keep reading.

For the last three years, we have been following with satisfaction your progress at *Yale Law School*. You have shown yourself to be amply qualified to practice law in this, the best of all possible states. Needless to say, it would be superfluous to force you to take another examination now, *or at any time in your career.*

Sssshhhhh.

Sixty-three percent of the people in this room are reading what you are reading. Thirty-seven percent are attempting to answer intricate questions covering points of law which, as we and now you know, are insoluble. Rest assured that the Negroes in this room are among that 37 percent (except for the tall buck in the corner, whose father was Commissioner of Sanitation under Governor Harriman. And you don't have to worry about him because he's slated for Legal Aid).

Don't worry. Keep your head down. We will tell you when it is safe to look up.

Perhaps you are wondering how we arrived at this percentage.

Each year, the Board of Examiners gathers at a small country club outside of Albany to determine the number of new lawyers the state can absorb without disturbing the economics of the prevailing attorney-client ratio. And, irrespective of qualification, *you made it!!* Perhaps you are also wondering, given all of the above, why this charade is necessary. As we and now you realize, this organization must preserve its public image of screening would-be entrants to the profession in order to ensure that the finest legal assistance is provided for the good people of the great state of New York.

Don't laugh!

Now then. In order to maintain the fiction that you are, in fact, undergoing a grueling examination of your legal expertise, you must stay in the room for the next eight hours. During this time, you will have to display various forms of emotion: frustration, elation, anxiety, determination, fear, etc. We leave the delineation of these emotional pyrotechnics in your already capable hands, as a prospective courtroom lawyer.

Go on, give it a try. Try frustration. How did it go?

We and now you realize that this kind of silliness is not going to get you through the next eight hours. (You can fool the jury but you can't fool yourself.) So we've put together a few time-consuming tidbits to help you through. Remember one thing, however. You're in. You're it. You're one of us. Nothing you do on these diversions will make any difference in the way we feel about you.

Have fun.

¹H	O	L	²D	S	U	³P
O			E			E
⁴R	⁵R		⁶F	A	⁷I	⁸R
⁹R	O	¹⁰M	E	V	N	J
¹¹O	N	A	N		¹²N	U
R			S			R
¹³S	H	E	E	N	E	Y

Across

1. What your client does to the corner candy store.
4. If you defend one of these, remember: The attorney gets paid before any of the creditors.
6. *My_____Lawyer:* Harvard Law School Revue of 1966.
9. Little-known 1932 case upholding compulsory Hail Marys.
11. The first man to handle his own case.
12. What 13 across completed all his opinions with.
13. Mr. Justice_____: Brandeis, Frankfurter, Goldberg, Fortas, and probably a few others.

Down

1. What Daniel Webster got the morning after.
2. What you sit on if you're the prosecution.
3. Everybody's doin' it, doin' it, doin' it.
5. _____Rico: Wasn't he the lawyer who defended Trujillo?
7. Association of Ventriloquists (abbr.)
8. Stupid American lawyers traveling in London try to book a room at Lincoln's _____.
10. What you yell when you fry.

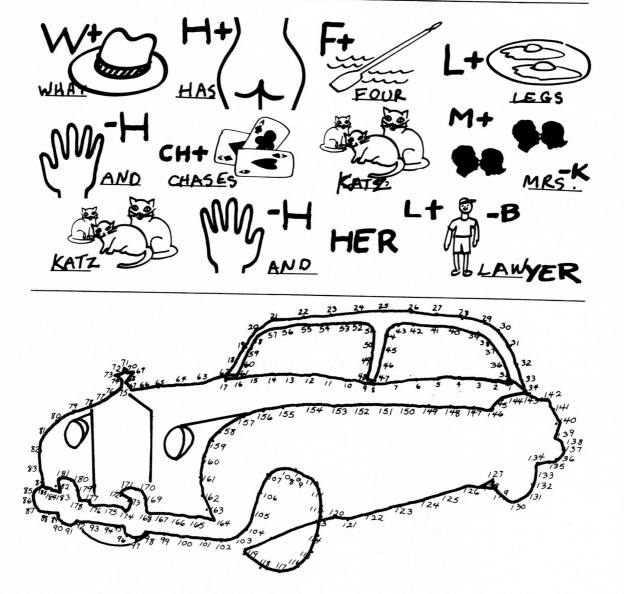

In order to get you started, here is a case for you to work on. We do not mean that you are being examined on this case. This is a real case. You can make money on this case—lots of it—the minute the exam is over.

A, a welfare mother who has just won the New York State Lottery, is on her way to the corner of a busy midtown intersection. When she reaches the corner, she calls across the street to her child *B*, who is begging on the opposite corner of the intersection, to inform him of this fact. *B* puts down his cup and crutch and runs across the street towards *A*. A car driven by *C* is approaching the intersection. Fearing that the car will strike *B*, *A* screams a warning. *C*, startled by the sudden noise, loses control of his automobile and mounts the sidewalk, striking *D*, President and Chairman of the Board of the Chase Manhattan Bank, in the ankle. Simultaneously, another car driven by *E*, a film star, strikes and kills *B*. *D* had been informed by his physician a week previously that he was slightly overweight, and had been advised to play polo at least three times a week, which he is unable to do due to his ankle injury. This results in an additional weight gain on *D*'s part, which in turn results in the appearance of an editorial cartoon depicting *D* and titled, "Inflated interest rates or what?" in a local newspaper. *D* alleges severe mental distress and professional anguish, and seeks to recover damages in the amount of $250,000.

As you remember from your days in law school, *A*'s scream is clearly the "but-for" cause of the injury sustained by *D*. Coincidentally, the amount of money won by *A* on the day in question was $250,000. *D* is looking for a lawyer. His number is 555-4070.

Warning!

Although it has never yet happened, it is possible that you may be tempted to share this privileged information with unauthorized persons. Needless to say, this indiscretion would work a hardship on all past, present, and future members of the New York State Bar Association. If you shoot your mouth off:
1. Your estate will be immediately probated.
2. Your personal property will be attached, liens will be slapped on your real property, and you can kiss your chattels good-bye.
3. We will hound you to death.

O.K., that's it. You can raise your head. Have a nice practice, and remember—one hand watches the other.

This examination has been a service of the New York State Bar Association.

A Play in One, Last Act

by John Weidman

The Time: The first and last day of World War III. The End of Life on Earth As We Have Come to Know It. Armageddon.

The Setting: A cramped, claustrophobic space, dank and dimly lit. The walls are vague and ill-defined, covered with odd patches of glistening ooze and pulsing bumps. The atmosphere is steamy; an acrid haze hangs in the air. *We are inside Ronald Reagan's asshole.* Stage left is the entrance to his upper colon. Stage right is his anus.

As the curtain rises, the walls are shaking and the air is filled with the muffled sounds of huge explosions. The room is a beehive of furious activity.

GEORGE SHULTZ, the secretary of state, is perched on a ladder, stage left, trying frantically to shore the ceiling up with odd bits of planking.

CASPAR WEINBERGER, the secretary of defense, sits at a small desk downstage surrounded by a tangled array of telephones, "hot lines," and radio receivers. He wears a headset, listens intently, and desperately spins dials on the radio set.

RONALD REAGAN, the president of the United States, sits in an easy chair, stage right, opening his mail and occasionally glancing at a highlights film of Super Bowl XIV which plays on a TV in the corner.

As the lights come up, there is a tremendous explosion. The room rocks, and a slab of semi-digested jelly beans falls off the ceiling and knocks Shultz off his ladder. On the TV screen, Lynn Swann leaps for a pass, grabs it, then drops it as he's upended by a Rams defender.

SHULTZ:
Shit!

WEINBERGER:
Christ, that was close!

REAGAN:
(*chuckling*) They can jump like monkeys, but they hate to get hit.

SHULTZ:
I thought Star Wars was supposed to knock those bastards out!

WEINBERGER:
It was. It *will*. The boys at General Dynamics have a few more kinks to iron out, then— (*reacting to his headset*) Incoming! Get down! *Get down!*

(**SHULTZ** *and* **WEINBERGER** *jump for cover as another enormous explosion rocks the room.* **REAGAN** *frowns and adjusts the vertical hold on the TV.*)

SHULTZ:
What the hell was *that?!*

WEINBERGER:
Judging by the impact, I'd say it was an SS-20, Malenkov class, launched from Vladivostok.

SHULTZ:
I thought they offered to dismantle those.

WEINBERGER:
They offered, but we turned them down. Cheap Commie trick.

(*Another thundering explosion. Sparks shoot from the TV and the picture tube blows up.* REAGAN *smiles.*)

REAGAN:
Must be halftime....So! How're we doing?

WEINBERGER:
Mr. President, the tide of battle has begun to turn our way. The forces of international communism are in disarray. It's true, of course, that every American city larger than St. Augustine has been destroyed. It's true that France and Britain are no more. It's true our gallant allies in Japan have sunk beneath the waves. It's true—

REAGAN:
How 'bout Qaddafi—did we get him yet?

WEINBERGER:
(*smugly*) The line of death now runs right through his bathtub, sir.

REAGAN:
And the Sandinistas?

WEINBERGER:
Gone. Completely wiped out.

REAGAN:
(*triumphantly*) Wait till Tip O'Neill hears *that!* Say, can I get a call through to the contras? Do they have a locker room?

WEINBERGER:
I'm afraid that they've been wiped out too.

REAGAN:
No!

WEINBERGER:
Yes. Apparently we overshot Havana with our first wave of Minutemen.

REAGAN:
What did we hit?

WEINBERGER:
A little bit of everything.

SHULTZ:
Iowa now shares a common border with Brazil.

REAGAN:
(*thoughtfully*) That puts Brazil in the Big Ten. I wonder—

(**WEINBERGER**'s *radio begins to buzz and click.*)

WEINBERGER:
Hang on, there's something coming through! (*He listens intently, then pounds the desk triumphantly.*) We've done it! We've stripped them bare! The last flight of Soviet ICBMs has been knocked out! The bastards are defenseless!

SHULTZ:
Now *that's* what I call disarmament!

(**WEINBERGER** *rises and holds out a box with a big red button on it.*)

WEINBERGER:
Mr. President, you stand at this moment on the very threshold of the future. With one bold stroke you have it in your power to eradicate forever the pernicious threat of Marxist tyranny and Soviet expansionism. By pressing this button, you can unleash one last barrage of Titan missiles, which will destroy the Soviet Union now and forever more.

(*A momentous pause.*)

REAGAN:
What does "pernicious" mean?

WEINBERGER:
Just push the button, sir.

(**REAGAN** *reaches for it.*)

SHULTZ:
Wait! I've got a better idea! They don't have any missiles left? Let's sell them some of ours! (**WEINBERGER** *looks at him as though he's lost his mind.*) Don't you see? They're desperate! We can charge them anything we want!

(**REAGAN** *beams and shakes his head with admiration.* **WEINBERGER** *pumps* **SHULTZ**'s *hand.*)

WEINBERGER:
You can take the boy out of Bechtel, but you can't take the Bechtel out of the boy!

(*They laugh, embrace, and crack open a bottle of Old Grand-Dad. They are passing it around, sucking down enormous slugs of bourbon, when the "hot line" phone rings.* **WEINBERGER** *answers it.*)

WEINBERGER:
Boom Boom Room! This is your Cap speaking.... Oh, hiya, George! (*to* **REAGAN** *and* **SHULTZ**) It's Bush. (*back into the phone*) Where are you, pal? I can hardly hear you...Oh, yeah? Hey, that's great! (*to* **REAGAN** *and* **SHULTZ** *again*) He's in Saudi Arabia. He says the sheikhs are shitting bricks, they'll cut back production, increase production, they'll stabilize oil prices anywhere we want 'em, just stop the goddamn bombs.

(**REAGAN** *chuckles,* **SHULTZ** *whoops with glee and grabs the phone.*)

SHULTZ:
(*into the phone*) George? This is Shultzi. Yeah. Tell 'em we gotta think it over. Tell

May 1970

"... Never mind the thmart remarkths, mithter, just thwow down that bokth of gold ..."

'em we're gonna put a bunch of dish towels on our heads and eat a bowl of camel shit with our bare hands while we discuss it. Tell 'em— (*Through the receiver comes the sound of a distant, muffled "boom." SHULTZ winces and holds the phone away from his ear, then speaks back into the receiver*) George? …George, are you there?…Hello? (*He turns solemnly to WEINBERGER and REAGAN*) Gentlemen, the vice president is dead.

REAGAN:

Does that mean I'm president?

WEINBERGER:

(*shaking his head with awe*) Incredible. Saudi Arabia is gone. The greatest oil-producing nation in the world is no more.

REAGAN:

(*chuckling again*) Well now, I guess that makes us number one.

(*They all consider this, then…*)

WEINBERGER:

Christ, the price of Texaco is going to go through the roof! (*He lunges for the "hot line" and barks into the phone*) Quick! Get me Merrill Lynch!

SHULTZ:

(*grabs at the receiver*) Gimme that! Hello, Lehman Brothers?!

REAGAN:

How 'bout me?!

(**REAGAN** *pulls the phone away from* **WEINBERGER**, *who grabs it back.* **SHULTZ** *shoves him away and the three men fall to the floor, struggling for the phone, punching and kicking in a Dagwood Bumstead-style fight. The men shout and snarl, then offstage right, from* **REAGAN***'s lower colon, comes a rhythmic, thumping thud. The sound grows louder. The walls begin to pulse. The men stop fighting and cock their ears.*)

SHULTZ:

What's that?

REAGAN:

Sounds like it's coming from my lower colon.

(*The sound grows louder, as if it— whatever "it" is—were coming closer.* **WEINBERGER** *crawls over and peers into the murky tunnel.*)

SHULTZ:

Can you see anything?

WEINBERGER:

I can't.…It's too dark, it…Oh, my God!

SHULTZ:

What is it? (*peers over* **WEINBERGER***'s shoulder*) My God, it's horrible!

WEINBERGER:

The *stench!*

SHULTZ:

It's *grotesque!*

REAGAN:

Nancy, is that you? (*He crawls over next to them and takes a look. He frowns, then beams.*) My tumor…It's my tumor!

WEINBERGER:

It must have been irradiated by the bombs! It's *glowing!*

REAGAN:

Look at the *size of it.*

SHULTZ:

It's getting *bigger!*

WEINBERGER:

And it's coming toward us! It's *alive!*

SHULTZ:

No! *No!*

(*The pulsing sound becomes deafening; the walls begin to buckle inward; an orange glow shines from the tunnel.*)

REAGAN, WEINBERGER and SHULTZ:

Aarrgghh!!!

BLACKOUT

JOHN WEIDMAN 85

RICK MEYEROWITZ

In December 1970 Doug Kenney and Henry Beard visited me in my Chinatown loft. We opened a few beers, sat on my old velvet-covered couch, and talked about

possible projects we could do together. I'd been a steady contributor to the *National Lampoon* during its first year, and the three of us had become friends. It is rare in anyone's life that he finds himself alone in a room with two geniuses at the same time, but there I was.

Doug told me he was writing a parody, in ersatz Italian, of the notebooks of Leonardo da Vinci. He asked if I could come up with something "Leonardo-like" for the cover.

PHOTO BY M. BLOOM

tears were running down his cheeks.

I had never had that kind of reaction to anything I'd ever said in my life. I tried, but I couldn't talk them out of it. I accepted the assignment as a challenge, and we walked around the corner to have dinner at Hong Wah on the Bowery. We were all in a good mood. I think we laughed until we choked, or maybe that was the food.

I did the painting soon after that and was surprised that it turned out so well.

I don't know where it came from—I was pouring a beer and reaching for some pretzels—but I answered, "how about the *Mona Lisa* as a gorilla?" Still talking to myself, I said, "Nah, too sophomoric." When I looked up, Henry was laughing and choking on his pipe; little bursts of ragged smoke surrounded his head. Doug stood up and raised both hands in the air. He plopped down on the arm of my couch and the entire thing collapsed to the left, shredding wood, ripping velvet, and landing in a pile on the floor with Doug on top. He was laughing so hard,

I believe some of the credit may have to go to Leonardo, but I don't think he needs any more credit than he already has, so I'll keep what I get. My worries about being pegged as a sophomoric artist never materialized; at least, they never materialized because of that painting. The cover was a huge success. *The Mona Gorilla* became the magazine's mascot. She has been widely reproduced and ripped off. One critic said it was "the best Mona Lisa parody ever"; another called it "one of the enduring icons of American humor." How could I argue with that?

—Rick Meyerowitz

From "The Dick and Spiro Show," October 1970

The Mona Gorilla, March 1971

Rick Meyerowitz

A Guide to the Little-Known Art Treasures of Italy

by Rick Meyerowitz
Curator, Museo Molto Grosso, Venezia

Rape of the Sabine Men
Giovanni Battista Tiepolo, 1720

This magnificent oil sketch came to light recently when the last heir of the Deviante family of Perniccia passed away and the contents of the estate came up for auction. It depicts the events of AD 426 when the Liberacci, a brutal tribe from the island of Carcinoginia, purportedly in search of wives, raided Sabinia and abducted all the men between six and sixty, leaving only the women, who in turn were then taken in a raid by the Romans.

To this day there is confusion over the true purpose of the Liberacci. Did they know they were taking men? Perhaps they were just trying to protect the Sabines from another fierce tribe of raiders, the Brucci. And how did they cross the Mediterranean without boats? These answers lie lost in antiquity, along with the Liberacci, the Sabines, and fortunately, the Brucci.

September 1985

Reliquary—Middle Finger of Cardinal Fonghool
Chiesa d'Intolleranza, Rome

The cardinal, 1454–1616, was chief inquisitor in Sub-umbria for over a century. He thought himself a great wit, and had a ready answer for all those who would question his authority—the Holy Finger!

It is said that when he ordered the population of the village of Mammamia, and its animals, burned at the stake, he culled the twelve-year-old girls and had them brought to his residence, Castello Reptilli, for safekeeping. "After all," he explained, "without charity I wouldn't be in business."

Lorenzo il Incredibile
Michelangelo Buonarroti, 1530

Everyone has heard of the Medicis: Cosimo the Elder, Lorezo il Magnifico, and his son, Lorenzo il Incredibile. The Medici's effect on every aspect of Italian life is, well, history.

Michelangelo considered this his greatest sculpture. His *David* paled by comparison. Every detail of this enormous work, carved from one block of the finest Carrara marble, was accurate and lifelike. Alas, in 1533 a mob of Austro-Hungarian castrati, acting under orders from Emperor Penus I, mutilated the statue and carried its marble member away with them. Its whereabouts remain a mystery to this day. Michelangelo was heartbroken. He never worked in marble again. He drank heavily and went to work for a Florentine caterer. From then on, his most delicate sculptures were devoured by hungry celebrants as they munched on chopped-liver Pietàs and Crucifixions.

As for Lorenzo il Incredibile, life imitates art. While attending a party in honor of Leonardo's newest invention, "il elevatore," he was killed when the doors suddenly closed, trapping the largest part of him outside, and the whole thing dropped into the basement.

ON CARICATURE

What recourse do we really have to affect the flow of events? We are, all of us, swept from one annus horribilis to the next like flotsam in the surf. Our leaders are frequently awful and there's not a thing we as individuals can do about it beyond casting our quadrennial vote.

The *National Lampoon* gave me a big soapbox to stand on, and I used it to draw dozens of caricatures of those in power. My goal was to get the attention of my subject by publishing an image they, or their aides, would see, and to make them wince with recognition. If I couldn't change the course of events, I could at least give them a virtual smack in the nose. It was incredibly satisfying. I always begin with what I feel about the person. Just how much can't I stand him? I want to capture his personality, not exaggerate his features. When I draw someone, I want the reader to look deep into his eyes (below), or in the case of the ayatollah on the opposite page, into his mouth, and shudder as something of the inner corruption of the man is revealed.

And that's all there is to it. Well, except for a lot of talent. I leave it to you, dear reader, to decide what is revealed in each piece. I just painted what I saw.

—Rick Meyerowitz

From "The Birds of Washington" by Rick Meyerowitz and Sean Kelly, October 1987

Although they migrate with astonishing frequency to the California coast, we see here the **Imperial Wattle-throated Noddy** and his mate, the **Shrieking Virago**, upon the banks of the Potomac. The Noddy (with its distinctive tall orange head feathers) is apparently nocturnal—it has never been observed awake during daylight hours. Notice, in the background, an example of a species native to the capital, the **Bullet-headed Hawk**.

Opposite: From "Bye-Bye Bozo," November 1988

Readers! Did you know that President Bozo is not the only senile old crackpot ideologue who panders to fundamentalists, has little regard for the truth, naps during office hours, and is about to pass from the scene? There is another. Say hello and goodbye to the ayatollah. We feel a great sadness that he cannot enjoy the same martyrdom that he created for the one million nine-year-olds he sent to be gassed at the front.

SPECIAL REPORT

REPORT OF THE CONGRESSIONAL COMMITTEES INVESTIGATING THE

IRAN-CONTRA AFFAIR

IRAN

RICK MEYEROWITZ'S BELIEVE IT OR NOT GUIDE TO LITTLE-KNOWN SEXUAL PRACTICES OF FARAWAY PLACES; Or, What to Do in Ouagadougou When You Want to Do What the Ouagadougons Do

Depicted here, the ancient Japanese practice of **Wow-za**: the adjustment of sexual desire by manipulation with chopsticks. The greatest living practitioner of the art is Zowiyaki-san, who at 119 years old is a living national treasure of Japan. He works deftly with silver chopsticks to prepare couples for intercourse. With imperceptible movements he can make pudendas sing and testicles dance. But he has an unpredictable streak. In June 1941 Adolf Hitler made a secret visit to him for an adjustment. On seeing Zowiyaki-san, a nervous Führer let out a gigantic fart. Zowiyaki-san was stunned! How impolite! Take that! And with one quick twist, he took his revenge. The chastened tyrant rushed back to Germany. After that, everything he did ended in disaster, including the Third Reich!

January 1986

The Schwarzwalderkuckoofucher, or Black Forest Kuckoo Festival, takes place every spring in the Bavarian town of Oberammergau. The town was made famous as the site of Wagner's opera *Die Nibbler*. The festival is the most picturesque event of the year in this picturesque and quaint country. Happy fräuleins (Klock Teasers) try to coax the kuckoo from its little house exactly on the hour. Points are awarded for the size of the kuckoo, presentation, and punctuality. Circumcised kuckoos are taken away and never heard from again. Kuckoos that spit are disqualified. Winners are given large cars and allowed to drive two hundred miles per hour on the Autobahn. The losers are shot.

Szechuan Hot-Taste. The two lovers consume large amounts of No Fun, a potent hot pepper. When their mouths are sufficiently spiced they perform Tung Lo and Dong Lick on each other. The resulting male orgasm is sweet'n'sour and female orgasm is sweet'n'lo. Together they are so satisfying that oral sex is the only kind desired by the participants, thus reducing the population by curtailing copulation, and at the same time, defeating the nefarious plots of the Gang of Four!

In the ancient Persian city of Rugallah, where a holy man may have many wives and a large sexual appetite, there has arisen a sect of Big Baghdaddies called **Mullah Fu-Q'ers.** For the wives of these potent holy men it's no more Ramadan-and-thank-you-ma'am. Sex has taken a more interesting turn. The Mullah Fu-Q'er lines up his women in a wife kabob, not forgetting a sheikh (for every wise man wears a sheikh), and, chanting whole chapters from Jimmy Carter's book *Why Not the Best?*, in a delirium of religious ecstasy, services all his wives and Allah at the same time.

THE BALLAD OF PULP AND PAPER

by Sean Kelly

Of the great Northwest where brave men quest
For power and pulp and gold
Where the tales are all like the timber tall
There are many sagas told
Of the lumberjacks with the singing ax
And the wolf that learned to swear
But the strangest tale on the sawdust trail
Is of Paul and the Crazy Bear.
Now the trees that grow in the Land of Snow
Were put there by You-Know-Who
To be scaled and topped and sawed and chopped
And ground to a mushy goo
Which becomes the stuff to make paper enough
For wrappers for bubble gum
And almanacs and paperbacks
And paper to wipe your bum.
Big Paul was the best in the whole Northwest
At ridding the land of trees
Of all shapes and kinds to enrich young minds
And the paper companies.
But one winter's day as he hacked away
Beside Babe, his big blue ox,
This hideous bear roared out of his lair
And challenged Paul to box.
"You're stupid and bad and money-mad
And your harvest is rack and ruin,
But you'll deal with me before your next tree!"
Cried the ecocrazy bruin.
They fought to the death, and with Paul's last breath
He howled, and the mountains chorused
The touching plea of the industry:
"Only *you* can prevent a forest!"

I have always loved American tall tales. My favorite is Paul Bunyan, who was originally conceived as a shill for the lumber industry—Paul existed to cut down the forests. I wondered what would happen if he ran into Smokey the Bear, who was born to save the forests. I made this painting of our two heroes ripping each other to shreds. The wickedness of what I'd done made me giddy. So I brought it to Sean Kelly, who shared my love of folklore. His laughter on seeing it, a gleeful "Hee, hee, hee!" told me he knew what was needed to make the painting into something more. That something more is what you see here, and it is something else.

—Rick Meyerowitz

December 1976

Plate I: Birds of Israel
by Rick Meyerowitz

National Lampoon Encyclopedia of Humor, 1973

1. BLUEBERG
2. SIX-DAY WARBLER
3. ASWAN
4. RUBIN REDBREAST
5. GOLDBERG
6. VOODPECKER
7. SIEGEL
8. ORTHODOX PENGUIN

ANIMAL HOUSE: THE POSTER

Early in 1978 Doug Kenney and Chris Miller came to my studio with the script for *Animal House*, the first *National Lampoon* movie. Doug, Chris, and Harold Ramis had written a great screen comedy, but all I knew was that Doug wanted me to do the poster. He gave me the script and an envelope of photos from the shoot, then we went to lunch at a Tex-Mex place around the corner where I roughed out some ideas for them on napkins.

A week later, I was sitting in a Park Avenue screening room between Doug and John Belushi. During the screening, Belushi fell asleep. His head rolled forward onto his chest and he began to snore loudly. We watched a twelve-minute selection of scenes from *Animal House*. It was incredibly funny. Afterward I said to Doug, "So these are all the funny parts, right?"

"Nope," he told me. "The whole film is like this." He wasn't kidding.

I began work in late March. The art was due on the twenty-ninth. On the twenty-seventh my wife went into labor. I phoned the producer and told him that art would be delivered late because we were delivering a baby. He was magnanimous. "That's great," he told me. "Take 'til Thursday." My daughter, Molly, was born Tuesday, March 28, and somehow, despite the craziness of the next few days, I managed to get the painting done, turning it in on Friday, March 31.

Belushi was in the office when I arrived with the art. Everyone loved it. John pulled me aside to tell me he wanted his face to be drawn a little more angular so he didn't look like "some asshole in a cartoon." "Look at my profile," he said, turning his head sideways and raising his chin. "John Barrymore!" I didn't know what he was talking about, but I did a few touchups and everyone was happy.

Animal House was screened for the first time at the big book convention in Atlanta in late May. It was a huge theater, and it was jammed. Just before the screening I went out back with John and a few others. We stood behind a Dumpster and enhanced our moods for the show. By the time we wandered into the theater, the only seats left were in the front row.

So that's how I finally saw *Animal House*: neck craned upward, mood enhanced, Belushi snoring away next to me, and the audience behind me screaming with laughter. It was something else.

Afterward, John and I stopped in the lobby in front of a huge reproduction of the poster. We were both staring holes in it. I was thinking I was a lucky guy; I'd managed, somehow, to capture the whole damn thing in one piece of art without having seen the entire movie first. John, as if reading my thoughts, said to me, "You nailed it, maaannn. You really fuckin' nailed it." It is the best compliment I have ever received about my work on *Animal House*.

—Rick M.

MICHEL CHOQUETTE

I t is, I think, the world's most orderly storage unit. Everything is labeled beautifully and put away in exactly the right place. We sit at a long central table and examine

original art, sketches, notebooks, documents, and photos from the life and work of Michel Choquette, whom I've flown to Montreal to visit. We're looking at the photos I've come to see, and I am overwhelmed. A lifetime ago (thirty-eight years!), Michel had this idea, and he pursued it the way he pursues everything he's interested in: with an all-consuming passion until it is completed. In this case, Michel's passion led him to create one of the best set pieces ever to appear in the *National Lampoon*, "Stranger in Paradise."

Michel spent much of the 1960s traveling the United States and Canada as part of the comedy duo The Times Square Two. Why this descendant of tough French settlers who arrived in Quebec to fight the Iroquois in 1665, this polymath and speaker of several languages, was in show business in the first place is a puzzle. But in 1969, when the act broke up and his singing and clowning days were over, Michel introduced himself to that group of intellectual Olympians who were founding the *National Lampoon*, and he found himself a home.

Michel had a profound effect on the new magazine. The *Lampoon*'s founders were Harvard boys who only knew other Harvard boys. Michel had many friends, and within months of his arrival, he'd recruited Sean Kelly, a professor of English and history; Anne Beatts, an advertising copywriter; and Tony Hendra, another showbiz veteran whom Michel had known on the comedy-club circuit. They and Michael O'Donoghue were the un-Harvard: two Canadians, an Englishman, a woman,

PHOTO BY ANNE BEATTS

Michel sur le site en Martinique.

and a guy from Rochester, who, together, brought a darkly mutinous anti-establishment sensibility to the new magazine.

In January 1972, in an issue appropriately themed "Is Nothing Sacred?" Michel partnered with Kelly to create the inflammatory "Son-O'-God Comics." The blasphemy exploded off the page. Myocardial infarctions were rampant in dioceses all over the country. The article registered on seismographs as far away as the Vatican and resulted in an epic shit storm of cancelled subscriptions. It was just the sign our boys were looking for. They did a sequel—twice! There's not enough space for "Son-O'-God" here. But these days you can look anything up.

This chapter is devoted to the reason I went to Montreal: Michel Choquette's magnificent "Stranger in Paradise," which he conceived, photographed, wrote (with Anne Beatts), and believed in so strongly that he made it happen by waiving any fee for his work on it.

The Michel I remember from those days had hair down to his waist, was as lean and sharp as a lightning rod, and just as electric. So it's not shocking that he found other fish to fry and left the *Lampoon* in 1974 to tackle a lifetime of creative projects. These days, he teaches at Concordia University in Montreal. Michel's hair is somewhat shorter now, but he's still lean and sharp, and he still has the capacity to shock. Anyone that electric would.

—Rick Meyerowitz

SHOOTING THE STRANGER IN PARADISE

Michel Choquette

Chaplin once said he would not have made *The Great Dictator* in 1940 if he had known what was going on in the camps. But perhaps by 1972 he would have, though differently. As for me, when I saw a filmmaker friend's photos of the Swiss Hitler impersonator Billy Frick, I knew immediately I wanted to do a *Lampoon* piece with him in full Hitler regalia, but in an incongruous setting.

Before I opted for the sometime-after-the-war tropical paradise, I had many ideas, including Hitler as a volunteer fireman in Ohio, Hitler as a hippie peacenik in San Francisco, and even Hitler slicing pastrami at the Second Avenue Deli. In the end, I chose to shoot him among the palm trees rather than the pastrami, because this juxtaposition appealed to me more than any other. The soft, dreamy, picture-book backgrounds were timeless and would be an ideal contrast to the hard-edged uniformed figure. And to be honest, the idea of spending ten days on the beach in Martinique did influence my decision.

Any depiction of Hitler out of his 1940s Nazi context will be seen as a Hitler survival tale. Even though I had not set out to create one, I realized as I was shooting that this is exactly what I was, in fact, doing. As for the shape of the article, I imagined it would end up as a spoof of a tabloid scoop. The idea of doing it as a travel parody came to me back in New York when Michael Gross and I were looking at the slides. A shot of a particularly beautiful sunset came up on-screen, and Mike and I both said, "*Holiday* magazine."

My concept for the text was to have my imaginary travel writers so absorbed in the task of packaging the piece that they'd ignore the contents. They couldn't see the Führer for the palm trees. I thought it would be too blatant to acknowledge the fact that Hitler was *Hitler*. The text, which Anne Beatts helped me draft, could apply to any old man who has mellowed, learned to relax, but still is hanging on to his old character traits. It could apply to, say, an old railroad man who has retired to Naples, Florida (where, in fact, Billy Frick *had* retired to), but still lives by the clock when it comes to mealtimes, putting out the trash, checking if the mailman is on time, etc. The fact that the subject of the piece is Adolf Hitler is, of course, what makes it funny.

I don't recall having been told of any letters or telephone calls complaining about the article after its publication, but I do know that one of our printers in Ohio, who was Jewish, told me that when he showed the article to his elderly mother, who didn't know it was a parody, she simply shrugged and said, "So? They found him."

STRANGER IN PARADISE

PHOTOSTORY BY MICHEL CHOQUETTE,
WRITTEN BY MICHEL CHOQUETTE, WITH ANNE BEATTS

All of us dream of a return to paradise,

of an escape from the hustle and bustle of everyday life. But few of us

are fortunate enough to find paradise on earth.

One man has.

In the peace and seclusion of a small, uncharted tropical island a

modern-day Robinson Crusoe has elected to spend the winter of his years.

He leads a simple life of simple pleasures. His wants are few and the climate

is warm. He keeps himself in top physical condition by taking a refreshing

dip in the ocean each day, while his faithful native companion,

whom he has christened Freitag,

waits on the beach.

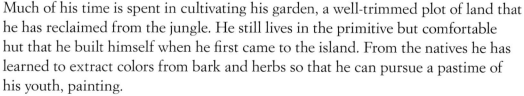

Much of his time is spent in cultivating his garden, a well-trimmed plot of land that he has reclaimed from the jungle. He still lives in the primitive but comfortable hut that he built himself when he first came to the island. From the natives he has learned to extract colors from bark and herbs so that he can pursue a pastime of his youth, painting.

The aboriginal inhabitants love and revere this friendly white man, one of the few they have ever seen. Native tradition has it he came from the sea in a great silver fish many years ago.

Although this self-exiled hermit lives a life of leisure, he is no believer in indolence. He is an early riser, getting up at dawn to join in the hunt for edible snakes.

Later, from his cliff-top eyrie, he looks on while Freitag leads a select group of natives in calisthenics. It is his philosophy that the island's young men should channel their energy into worthwhile pursuits.

He himself is a stickler for neatness and never neglects his household chores. He washes his clothes in the stream, using the age-old method of pounding them with the rocks. He has become an expert at darning and mending.

Each day he gives the roof of his hut a going over with a handmade rake. He likes to set an example of cleanliness and order. He has trained Freitag in the tonsorial arts so that he may be kept well groomed, and regularly inspects the other young men of the island to ensure that they adhere to the proper dress code.

Wild fruits hang from the branches, waiting to be plucked, and the waters of the lagoon are full of fish. The natives are happy to share this bounty with the gentle recluse.

Like old men everywhere, he is a great storyteller and delights in recounting tales of his faraway homeland.

The fervent idealism of youth has mellowed with the passing years. He has stopped trying to save the world and now he cares only for his peace of mind. Hidden away in his little Eden, he has his thoughts and his memories to fall back on.

Occasionally he looks up at the migratory birds flying overhead. But he finds in himself no longing to leave with them. It would seem that this stranger in paradise is, by now, very much at home. ❧

ARNOLD ROTH

From "Bad Taste Is Where It's At," July 1970

Arnie Roth greets his muse.

By the time we boys, overeducated and otherwise, were creating the *National Lampoon*, Arnold Roth had been a star for more than a decade.

He wrote and drew sophisticated lines, laying them down like the swinging saxophonist he still is, in a cool, jazzy style, with maybe a touch of yiddishkeit, for the *New Yorker*, *Punch*, *Playboy*, *Trump* (*Playboy*'s short-lived attempt at a humor magazine), and the much mourned and truly brilliant *Humbug*, a magazine he invested in, and on which he didn't lose all his shirts, only most of them.

He came to the *Lampoon* early enough to do the cover of the third issue, which was appropriately themed "Blight." Whether *blight* described the magazine itself or was an editorial comment on the world at large is debatable. Arnie's contribution to the magazine is not. He immediately raised the level from awful/stoned-all-the-time/amateurish to stylish/cocktails-after-work/professional. We were in awe of him.

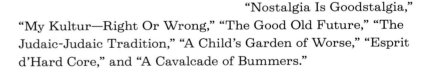

102 MOORE STREET
PRINCETON
NEW JERSEY 08540
609 921 2348

ARNOLD ROTH

Arnie's business card, circa 1970

ing them down like the swinging saxophonist he still is, in a cool, jazzy style, with maybe a touch of yiddishkeit, for the *New Yorker*, *Punch*, *Playboy*, *Trump* (*Playboy*'s short-lived attempt at

Arnie created the paradigm of the *National Lampoon* artist-writer. He came up with his own ideas, and he wrote and drew his own articles. He was so effortlessly professional that just having his work in the magazine raised the level of the whole enterprise. For two years he was a regular, creating pieces with titles such as "Bad Taste Is Where It's At," "Nostalgia Is Goodstalgia," "My Kultur—Right Or Wrong," "The Good Old Future," "The Judaic-Judaic Tradition," "A Child's Garden of Worse," "Esprit d'Hard Core," and "A Cavalcade of Bummers."

And then that was it. Arnie and the *Lampoon* parted ways after only two years. No hard feelings are held, and no one, including Arnie, can recall why he never worked for the magazine again.

Arnie isn't retired. No way he'll be sitting on some golf course under a palm tree. He's working hard, the way he always did. He's still the funniest guy with the best stories in town. He's still producing amazing art, and he's still lugging that saxophone around town, playing his heart out at every gig.

—Rick Meyerowitz

My Kultur-Right or Wrong

by Arnold Roth

Kultur is easily identified by the fact that the only enjoyment one gets from it is a sense of superiority over those who are enjoying life, instead. These pictures will help with visual identification — in case you ever bump into any Kultur surrounded by ink lines and filled in with water color. In such a case, notify your local Kultural attaché case worker.

A CAVALCADE OF BUMMERS

As cavalcades go, this one's a bummer.

Henry David Thoreau had the makings of a bummer.

HISTORICAL BIBLIOGRAPHY—The Jews are the Chosen People—which is no great honor when you think of the competition.

Top: from "A Cavalcade of Bummers," August 1971; bottom: from "The Judaic-Judaic Tradition," June 1971

Top left: from "The Good Old Future," May 1971; top right: from "Adventures in Everyday Living," April 1971; bottom right: from "Nostalgia Is Goodstalgia," November 1970

Childish Physiology:
The inside dope—or, a map of uncharted wastes

Childish Afterplay:
Children are honest, loyal, trustworthy, and generally insensitive, except the ones who are sloppy, dopey, mean, selfish, and terrible bowlers—which is most of them. Their universal failing is that they degenerate into adults.

From "A Child's Garden of Worse," September 1971

From "A Christmas Story," December 1971

TONY HENDRA

W e staggered out of the Colonnades bar at 1 A.M. It was a weeknight in the winter of '76, and warm for February. My brains felt like pretzels. I couldn't believe

I was standing up. Roger Law, my friend from London, Tony Hendra, and I had been inside drinking since 9 P.M. I had introduced two Englishmen to each other, and the explosion of alcohol and singing at our table eventually produced a tsunami of empty glasses that over- whelmed our waitress, poor thing, who disappeared around midnight. Roger, fifteen beers sloshing around under his belt, wobbled away on foot. Tony, incredibly, after fifteen glasses of wine, mounted his bicycle and pedaled home, singing at the top of his lungs some- thing that sounded to me like "Amazing Grease."

Tony Hendra is one of those editors we are referring to when we say they were over- educated and brilliant. More than that, singing or writing, Tony had the most distinctive voice at the *National Lampoon*. Often, reading the magazine, you can't tell who wrote what, but Tony's prose has a specific gravity. You can feel its weight

PHOTO BY MICHAEL GOLD

on the page. His sentences, like shiny steel, fit together with a metallic sound, like the business parts of a Gatling gun lock- ing in place. And his words ring like bullet casings hitting a steel deck after being fired. Somehow this is apt for a man brought up during the Blitz, who claims his first toy was a piece of shrapnel.

He came to the magazine via stand-up comedy and writing for television—both censorious realms. The *Lampoon* gave him permission to unleash his natural voice and blast away at anyone in official or corporate or cultural power. And so

he did: sticking it to the upper crust, making sure "the bas- tards didn't get away with it." ("It" meaning anything). I loved working with Hendra. There was a gleeful bad-boyishness to his work. I found his desire to attack hypocrisy fit in with my wish to attack everything. And the bloody-minded boy in me was thrilled with his love of meat and viscera, the blood and guts of humor.

In October 1976, we did a bloody antiwar parody of a children's book we called *Sher- man the Tank*. Sherman gradu- ates war school and joins a war firm Tony named "Mud, Blood, Guts, and Corruption." Sher- man is sent into battle, and in one of those "whaddaya know about that?" moments, finds himself shooting at a tank from another war firm, that of his older brother Herman! Of course, our hero Sherman wins—it's his story—by blowing his own brother to bits. Tony has their mother, Mom Tank, justify the fratricide with a simple "You did your bit, and that's all one tank can do."

We've traveled some years down the road, fallen into some ruts now and then. We meet a few times a year to share sto- ries or work on projects together. Tony will arrive on his bike, wearing the chain as an accessory. He can still drink me under the table—he can drink the table under the table! And there's that voice again, ready for the hunt; ready to challenge author- ity: still a strong voice, still distinct in its sound, still ready to lock and load.

—Rick Meyerowitz

The Joys of Wife-Tasting

by Anthony Hendra

God created wife to make merry the heart of man, says the good book, and in truth nothing complements a fine meal, warms a winter evening, cools a soft summer day, or turns a casual moment into a memory more exquisitely than a few rich-red mouthfuls of wife. Beyond the simple pleasures of refreshment, however, lies a panoply of further delights for the discriminating palate, subtleties of flavour, colour, age, and bouquet whose appreciation constitutes nothing less than a fine art, and for a fortunate few, a life's work. Who can wet his lips, as once the Roman legions did, upon the great wives of Burgundy without rhapsodizing over that inimitable flavor that packs the mouth with its classic fragrance? Who can resist the hint of sun-soaked soil the dainty wives of Moselle offer, somewhat sweet to the palate but nectar to the nose? And who in all conscience can much longer remain a member of that dwindling clique to whom the smooth, fruity, sea-breeze savour of the Napa Valley wives is anything but sublime? These are not pleasures, as the wag once remarked, to be sniffed at.

An opportunity to indulge in such epicurean delights presented itself in the most appealing fashion recently when the Société Internationale des Grand Maîtres de Tastefemme foregathered at the sumptuous Hotel Sheraton-Sonesta-Marriot in downtown Chicago for its annual tasting. The occasion brought together the fine old classics of France, Italy, and Germany, the relative newcomers from California, and for the first time the robust if somewhat tangy wives of Australia. In short, all the major wife-producing areas of the world were represented, with the exception of New York State and Spain, whose wives I must confess my palate still finds somewhat raucous. More than two dozen wives were tasted by the Société during the course of the evening, ranging from the stately '41s to the new crops of '54 and '55, many of which, to our surprise, we found extraordinarily mature. As in previous years, however, we were disappointed to find that some of the domestic wives had been the victims of sprays and other chemical additives, so much so in one or two cases as to completely obliterate the original flavour. Happily, the incidence of this deplorable practice was noticeably less than before; one feels certain that the Californians, with their uncanny ability to assimilate in years what others have taken centuries to learn, will soon master the innermost secrets, so long an exclusively French province, of wife husbandry.

The theory and practice of wife-tasting has been enshrined elsewhere in far clearer words than my humble mind can conjure. Nonetheless, a brief recapitulation might be useful for the neophytes amongst my readers.

Wives are, of course, as myriad as the regions which produce them, some dark, some light, some pink, some deep red, some lusty and full-bodied yet gentle withal, some unassuming and dainty yet with a flavor to make Bacchus blush. Notwithstanding the width of their range, however, the manner in which a great wife is brought to the lips of a *connoisseur* is generally uniform. The wife must proceed through three stages—seeding, aging, and maturing—and no matter what the idiosyncracies of a given area,* all three of these must be observed for the wife to be palatable.

Many profess to enjoy if not prefer young wives before they are aged; however, while unusually vigorous and effervescent at this point, they have little flavour and always lack depth. I have never found the tasting of young wives, necessary as it occasionally is when one has to buy early on a bumper crop, anything but a disagreeable task.

A wife is generally seeded in the spring—although this is not a rigid rule—and is up the next morning. Once the bloom of youth has disappeared, the wife usually goes

---

*In southern France, for instance, during the maturing stage, wives are often left open for weeks at a time—an unconscionable process to the wifemasters of Northern France but which nonetheless gives them a quite inimitable tang.

continued

continued

through a hollow period, during which she has little or no flavour, no body, and no colour. An inexperienced wifemaster might despair at this point, but happily the great wives are in the hands of those who know that this is when stupendous flavours and bouquets are building up, only waiting for release through the magic of *maturation.*

Maturing is the most critical process for the wifemaster, for he must bring out two of the most important aspects of his wives—their bouquet and their colour. The bouquet will have already established itself, so all that he has to do is make sure that it regulates itself at all times and in all places, even after traveling.

The colour, however, is a very different matter. The process of maturation involves constant opening and tasting, and according to climactic conditions, the wifemaster must not only be wary of overexposure to the elements and hence of oxidation—lest the wife become *tuillée* or brown round the edges—he must also protect the delicate flavour and bouquet from foreign bodies which can easily enter the wife at this point. During maturation, a number of other dangers beset the wife, due primarily to constant uncorking and recorking, but if the wifemaster is circumspect—and I have yet to meet many who are not—the labourious journey should end in triumph.

As regards the actual tasting itself, this time-honoured activity is of course attended by a number of distinct rules. Wives are considered in four main categories and graded accordingly: *colour, bouquet, flavour,* and what the Americans rather unromantically refer to as *aftertaste,* but which I prefer to designate *finish.* Wives are uncorked about half an hour prior to actual tasting to give them time to breathe, and are sampled at room temperature. There is a school that prefers the lighter wives somewhat chilled, but I prefer them if anything rather warmer than their heavier, richer counterparts in order to bring out their subtleties more fully. The deplorable practice of chilling all Californian wives prior to tasting needs no further condemnation in so knowledgeable a body as the Société Internationale. I might point out for my own satisfaction, however, that I consider this practice little more than an overt attempt to disguise their abominable flavor.

Properly, the wife is first held up to the light in order to ascertain the depth and texture of colour, although in some cases mere exposure to light, such as a candle, suffices for the expert. Personal preferences aside, there are no connections made between quality and colour—who could honestly claim that the light translucent pinks of the *femmes blondes d'Alsace* are any better or worse than the cardinalatial reds and episcopal purples of the stately wives of Tuscany? No, here comparison is made on the perfection, uniformity, and depth of colour, the lustre and sparkle that the wife displays. Too little 'glisten' may indicate a wife that will be disappointing to the nose; too much may indicate a wife who finishes poorly.

Second, the *bouquet,* or, for the uninitiated, the smell of the wife is tested. For some, a wife's 'nose' may be quite sufficient to discern all that need be known regarding quality, origin, and flavour; indeed, for many epicures it is the supreme pleasure of which the actual tasting is but a confirmation. The taster passes his nose lightly back and forth over the wife at a distance of a few inches, inhaling profoundly so that the full fragrance is taken deep into his nostrils. It is hard to convey any precise guidelines for assessing bouquet, so subtly and yet so distinctly do wives differ. Suffice it to say that a certain yeastiness will usually mean the wife is not yet fully matured, while acridity, whether of notorious 'fishy' kind or of some less identifiable scent, will usually mean the wife is past her prime. On the other hand, both these qualities, when correctly combined with other savours, are actually sought after in some regions (e.g., Sicily).

At last, the supreme moment—the actual tasting. Here, the years of preparation and work, the endless hours of tending and trimming, the arduous process of maturation, finally come to fruition. The wife is taken into the mouth—anything less than a generous mouthful is an insult to her quality—and rolled slowly round and round the tongue. The full force of flavour, skin, and juice is thus unleashed upon the palate, filling the mouth with ambrosia. If the taster is not completely certain at this point, he may proceed to roll the wife somewhat more around his mouth in order to allow the flavour to pass back and forth over his tastebuds. Of critical importance here is the proportion of skin to juice. The perfect wife will juice just enough to blend all the flavours into one delicious whole; a tendency to overjuice usually indicates immaturity, although if the juice is full-bodied this bodes well for the future, since juice is, after all, the beginning and end of a wife's flavour.

It is of interest to note that during blindfold tastings —such as this was—the actual tasting will convey to the expert a veritable wealth of information concerning age, maturation, and, of course, origin. Some experts can, from a single tasting, discern the origin of a wife down to village, street, and even box number.

Immediately after this, the wife is, of course, expelled from the mouth (I prefer *expelled* to the hideously graphic *spit*), and the aftertaste, or *finish,* is savoured. The taste of a truly fine wife may linger delightfully in the mouth for as long as five minutes, and such a period is a true testament to the skill of the wifemaster's art. It should hardly be necessary to add that a wife must *never, never* be swallowed, since this may severely damage her for future gustation, although— horreur!—such an occasion did occur at the Société's tasting when one of our older members, carried away by her excellence, attempted to swallow a fine young wife of the Loire. Happily, aside from his perpetual expulsion, little damage was done beyond a pair of broken glasses.

Three sumptuous *femmes de Bordeaux* await the arrival of the Grands Maîtres and the opportunity to warm a discerning palate.

The Ratings

Femmes de Bourgogne

Jeanne-Paul Musigny Première Crue ('49) A superb wife of incomparable depth and body, sprightly yet with a hidden hauteur, beautiful full nose, just the right amount of breeding to balance the weight. 18/20

Gervaise-Chambertin les Cazetières Grande Crue ('53) Medium colour, delicate nose, has fruit but is still somewhat closed up. A little more time to counteract acidity should guarantee this wife an excellent future. 14/20

Cloë des Ruchottes-Chambertin Première Crue ('53) Another splendid wife that fairly explodes in the mouth! Nose as smooth as velvet, bashful yet demanding, a superb tribute when compared with her north-slope relative above, of what regular exposure to the sun can accomplish. 19/20

Cloë de Vougeot Première Crue ('54) Good, full, fruity demeanour with a certain sauciness of bouquet, but displaying some unfortunate oxidation despite youth, hence considerable browning around the edges. 12/20

Alexis Corton Grande Crue ('51) '51 was not considered a good year for Burgundy due primarily to an extraordinary influx of Algerian wives, forcing a small crop and not a good one at that. Nonetheless this great family has once again produced a superlative wife, very deep, full, and round with plenty of nose, though perhaps a little too much skin in proportion to juice. 15/20

Yvonne Romanée Première Grande Crue ('50) A joy! A blessing! Fabulous nose, staggering earthy full-fruit flavour, finishes like a thoroughbred. The kind of wife, as they say, that tastes you back. 19/20

Femmes de Bordeaux

Madame Venus de Mons (Medoc) Première Grande Crue ('41) Alas, how can one express it without doing an injustice? This grand old wife, which I have tasted several times previously (notably at Dijon in '66 and Canterbury in '68), has still the same inimitable depth and nose, the same wit and verve, the same *insouciance*. And yet something has gone. Perhaps it comes from being laid down too long, perhaps it is simple age, but the finish was thin and a trifle bitter. 14/20

Madame "Pêche" Evelle (Saint Julien) Deuxième Cuvee ('55) *Quelle surprise!* This comparative newcomer has amazing colour, "glisten," and full, round, flavourful finish for one so young and—dare one say it—so cocky! A treasure indeed. 18/20

Madame Rosanne Ségla Première Crue ('53) A product of *fillerandage*, this small fruity wife has an attractive bouquet and an unexceptionable finish. The sweetness, however, like that of some Californian wives, seems to me more suited to a feminine palate. 13/20

Madame Margot Première Grande Crue ('50) Superb, as usual. What can one say? Depth sublime, nose without compare, finish olympian! I have never come across a Margot that did not stun my palate with her superlative qualities, so much so that if there is not a dud soon, tasting them will become quite a bore! 19/20

Madame Gloria (Medoc) Première Crue ('55) While exhibiting all of the breeding of this great and ancient line, the '55, incredibly enough, appears to have undergone some incorrect care in the early stages. I noticed definite signs of *pourriture* ("staining with earth or sand") that quite corrupted an otherwise luscious flavor and rich nose. 12/20

Madame Magdelaine (Saint-Emilion) Première Cuvée ('49) Though a poor year for this region, this is big, special wife with a fine earthy flavour that is tasting particularly well. 17/20

Rosie d'Anjou ('58) Although exceptionally young and apparently still in the stage of maturation, this wife must be singled out as having a quite singular capacity to please. Light of nose, daintily fruity, lacking depth but amply compensating with vivacity and *joie de vivre*, Rosie is undoubtedly a wife that will go with anything (or anyone). 20/20

A brief tasting of the wives of Italy, although celebrated by some members of the Société with more powerful palates than this author, was as always somewhat disappointing. One has the feeling that these wives are consistently pressed too hard to develop a really true flavour. Nonetheless, one young '57 Veronese seemed to be perfect for those who seek an inexpensive wife for everyday use.

The few German wives that were tasted exhibited as usual an exceptionally delicate if not pale colour and that almost transparent nose and flavour so typical of the softer reaches of the Moselle.

Gretchen Himmelreich Kabinett ('55) An amazing translucent colour and a fresh, flowery bouquet, both very tentative, surprising one with a mouth-blowing flavour, not quite of the sea, not quite of the marshes, but indubitably typical of a culture to whom herring is a staple. 15/20

Needless to say, the world-famous *eisfrau* (of which there were several examples available for tasting), left this humble Francophile cold.

The Wives of California

Barbara (Martini) ('55) An impressively dark colour, and fine rich bouquet, indeed almost stifling, and sumptuous flavour reminding one of incense. I found this wife quite exhausting even though the tasting was brief. 9/20

Joanne Berger (Heitz) Grande Crue (?) ('45) Truly Californian wives are distinctive! A curious colour, light yet cloudy, a somewhat vinegary bouquet. Though well aged, this wife displayed definite greenness and the flavour, while full and rich, reminded one unmistakably of pickles. 5/20

Blonde de Blondes (Schramsberg) ('55) Otherwise unnamed, this wife displayed a superb colour, light, subtle, and with a glisten to make the best wives of the Loire jealous beyond endurance. This, coupled with a strong and distinctive nose, should have resulted in a flavour to match its appearance, yet a deep, prolonged (if rather puzzled) tasting left the inescapable impression that this wife had been heavily sprayed. 7/20

The Wives of Australia

Several of the best wives of our Southern friends were available but all exhibited much the same characteristics. One rating should suffice.

Sheila Kookaburra (Wallaby Wines and Spirits) ('54) Absolutely devastating colour of deep purple (almost black) and a nose that practically burned the olfactory nerves to a cinder. Flavour indescribable—buffalo? rabbit stew? ham and eggs? This is a powerful, florid wife not for the shrinking palate. 0/20

DETERIORATA

GO PLACIDLY AMID THE NOISE & WASTE, & REMEMBER WHAT COMFORT THERE MAY BE IN OWNING A PIECE THEREOF. AVOID quiet & passive persons unless you are in need of sleep. Rotate your tires. ❧ Speak glowingly of those greater than yourself and heed well their advice even though they be turkeys; know what to kiss and when. ❧ Consider that two wrongs never make a right but that three do. Wherever possible, put people on hold. Be comforted that in the face of all aridity & disillusionment and despite the changing fortunes of time, there is always a big fortune in computer maintenance. ❧ Remember the Pueblo. Strive at all times to bend, fold, spindle, & mutilate. Know yourself; if you need help, call the FBI. Exercise caution in your daily affairs, especially with those persons closest to you. That lemon on your left, for instance. Be assured that a walk through the ocean of most souls would scarcely get your feet wet. Fall not in love therefore; it will stick to your face. ❧ Gracefully surrender the things of youth, birds, clean air, tuna, Taiwan; and let not the sands of time get in your lunch. ❧ Hire people with hooks. ❧ For a good time, call 606-4311; ask for Ken. Take heart amid the deepening gloom that your dog is finally getting enough cheese; and reflect that whatever misfortune may be your lot, it could only be worse in Milwaukee. ❧ You are a fluke of the universe; you have no right to be here, and whether you can hear it or not, the universe is laughing behind your back. ❧ Therefore make peace with your God whatever you conceive Him to be: Hairy Thunderer or Cosmic Muffin. ❧ With all its hopes, dreams, promises, & urban renewal, the world continues to deteriorate. ❧ Give up. ❧ ❧

BY TONY HENDRA

FOUND IN AN OLD NATIONAL LAMPOON: DATED 1972

WRITING WITH TONY
John Weidman on Tony Hendra

Tony Hendra and I wrote a considerable number of pieces together. We liked each other and our comic sensibilities overlapped, although I'm not sure I could tell you what those comic sensibilities were. In any case, when we did collaborate, we almost always did it in the same way. At the end of what passed for a work day at the *Lampoon* offices, Tony would go out and buy a bottle of port. (In a pinch, Tony would drink anything, but his preference was for what he called "fortified wines.") We would then repair to his office, Tony would sit at the typewriter, I would wander around the room, and we would write. And we would continue writing until we had either finished the piece or Tony had finished the port—events which, in most cases, coincided.

I'm told that when Eugene O'Neill was writing *Long Day's Journey Into Night*, he would take a typewriter and a bottle of bourbon up to the hay loft in the barn behind his house and only come down when the bottle was empty.

It worked for him and it worked for us.

Above: "Deteriorata" was a *Lampoon* poster. It was first printed in the magazine in November–December 1990.

The cultural exchange program that traded Jerry Lewis to France for Marcel Marceau also entailed the swap of Topo Gigio for Clint Eastwood. The spaghetti western became popular. The rest is history—Gibbon, to be exact.

LA SERA, IL VIENE.
CERCANDO LA VENDETTA...

IL SHOWDOWN A RIO JAWBONE

REALIZZATO DA ALFREDO DENTE

...IL COWHAND PIÙ FURIOSO DEL WEST, UN DUDE CHI FA TREMBLARE I CUORI DI TUTT'ALTRI, GOODGUYS O BADGUYS...

...O'MAC HUGGINS!

CINQUE ANNI CHE SU FRATELLO È HUMILIATO NEL TUMBLEWEED DI OKLAHOMA, HUMILIATO A MORTE. CINQUE ANNI LA SUA VENDETTA. ADESSO ARRIVE... IL SHOWDOWN!

SI, SIGNORE?

GALLIANO!

From National Lampoon's Very Large Book of Comical Funnies, 1975

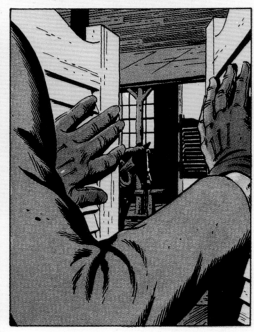

FROM THE WEATHER BUREAU

**They looked from pig to man, and from man to pig, and from pig to man again;
but already it was impossible to say which was which.**
—George Orwell, *Animal Farm*

The time has come for us all to face up to the facts and take the right remedy. We are all of us, black and white, brothers and sisters, pigs; and if we have any sense of cosmic rightness left in our bodies, we owe it to humanity to off ourselves.

You know this. You just don't want to face up to it. But if you need some prodding, just remember a couple of these stools from my stool-box:

- If you live *anywhere* in the North American continent, even if you poison nothing, kill nothing, contribute nothing, commune, meditate, you're living on land ripped off from the Indians. You're a pig.
- If you exhale *any* breath, it's mostly carbon dioxide, and if you don't think that's a No. 1 boss poison, try putting a plastic bag over your head sometime and see how long you last, pig.
- If you shit or piss *anywhere* on Earth you're dumping a load of ureic acid on Mother Earth, and ureic acid is one of the basic ingredients of friendly old Mr. PolyUrethane. You pig.

- If your body gives off *any* heat, it contributes to thermal pollution, which in turn is a basic energy degradation that is killing the universe. Goddamn motherfucking pig.
- You're reading this on the corpse of a tree, pig. A cow died to make your fucking belt.

Remember: if you're not part of the final solution, you're part of the problem. But don't go offing yourself half-cocked: if you take poison, it goes right into the environment; I won't even talk about guns; and there's enough gunk in the ocean without you adding to it by jumping off a bridge. I recommend hanging, with hemp, NOT NYLON, rope, over a four-foot-deep hole half-filled with active compost. If you must leave a note, write it on bark.

Of course, suicide is the ultimate ego trip. With my Sufi training I have reduced my ego to the size of the Blessed Peanut and cast it into the Lake of Denial. I am powerless to act.

What's your excuse, pig?

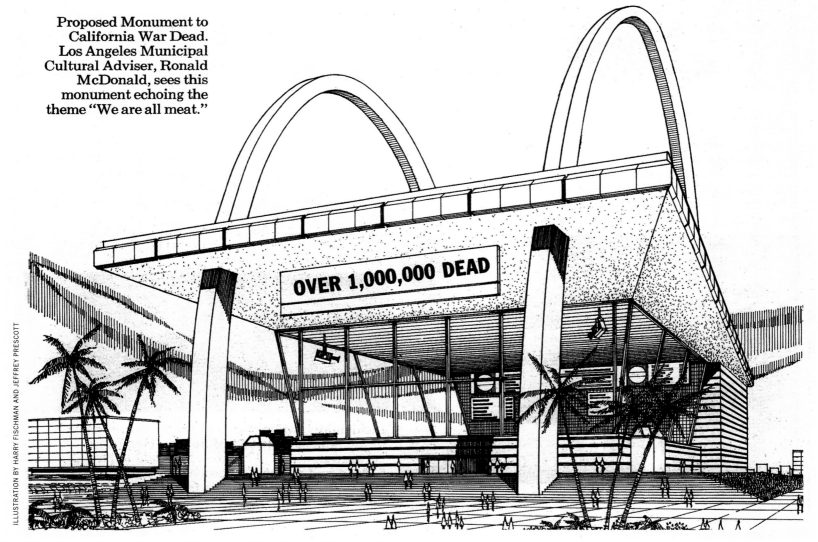

Proposed Monument to California War Dead. Los Angeles Municipal Cultural Adviser, Ronald McDonald, sees this monument echoing the theme "We are all meat."

OVER 1,000,000 DEAD

ILLUSTRATION BY HARRY FISCHMAN AND JEFFREY PRESCOTT

Top: "The Weather Bureau," January 1972; bottom: "War Memorial," March 1972

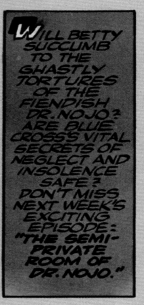

ILLUSTRATION BY FRANK THORNE

THE SOCRATIC MONOLOGUE

by Hendra and Kelly

Thank you very much, ladies and gentlemen. • It's great to be back here playing the wonderful Athens Gymnasium. • I just got back from spending a month in Sparta over the weekend. • Boy, they don't call them Spartans for nothing. They sure live simple in Sparta. My room there was so spare, it was a spare room! • That's what I call a minor premises. • The kids there are so tough they steal the horses off moving chariots. • But they're boring. A good time on Saturday night in Sparta is going downtown to watch somebody get a haircut. • No, but seriously, we only kid the Spartans 'cause we hate them so much. I kid my family, too. Take my wife, Xanthippe. • To Macedon! • I don't want to say she henpecks me, but when I get home from a night out with the boys, she's just like all women. Completely illogical. Whatever that means. • Really, it's enough to turn you into a cynic, right? You know the difference between a stoic and a cynic? A stoic is what brings the babies, and a cynic is what you wash 'em in! • But take Diogenes, the cynic. Just don't take him to lunch. • That guy is dirty! He just got married in that tub he lives in. • They called it a double ring ceremony. • But philosophers today, though, I tell ya…in my day, we were all peripatetics. I was a peripatetic before I could pronounce it. • My teacher was Zeno. I was his pet—he couldn't afford a dog. • Actually, I was one of his two personal physicians. He called us Zeno's pair o' docs. • Seriously, the whole cosmos is irrational. Whatever that means. • Take the Persians. By storm. • You know how the Persians got here? The first one swam across, and the others walked over on the scum. • We renamed the whole country after them. Grease. • We implored the gods to protect us, so Zeus threw a thunderbolt at Persia. It slid off! • No, but I love the gods. When I was a kid, I thought I'd be an atheist, but then I found out you don't get no feast days. • I remember the first time I saw the gods. I was with my father. He pointed to them and said, "Mount Olympus." I said, "Okay, which one is he?" • Now, my favorite goddess is Pallas Athena. They say she sprang full-grown from the brow of Zeus. Which means he gives great head, right? • Whoops! Gotta watch that impiety stuff! You never know when Anytus might be listening. You know it was Anytus who first called me a gadfly? I said, whaddaya mean, gadfly? Of course, I *do* bug him. • And he *is* a horse's ass! • No, I kid Anytus, but really he's a great governor. He's in the audience here tonight. No! No applause, please! You'll only encourage him. • Seriously, Anytus, you're doing a great job with Athens. First we had the Golden Age, then the Silver Age, now we've got the Mortg Age! • If only Anytus would go back to doing to his catamite what he's been doing to this city, Athens would be a republic! • And while we're on the subject, lemme tell you what I mean by a republic…hey! What's this? A drink from the audience? Thanks, Anytus! You're a prince! Well, as Zeus said to Ganymede, bottom's up! Jesus Christ! What is this stuff? Tastes like Persian aftershave! You drink it? No wonder your mouth looks like a southern view of Pegasus flying north! This stuff tastes like hemlock! Anyway, about that Republic, I…*aargh!*

Henny Youngman. Photograph By Phil Koneig

SAM GROSS

Sam tells me, "My cousin Larry is the world's foremost authority on the pancreas of the salamander." He tells me this while we're having lunch in a Denny's.

We are in Rhode Island on our way to visit Lorraine Rodrigues, Charlie's widow, at her home near Cape Cod.

In the car Sam says that he has done 26,453 cartoons in his career. This is a formidable number, and I do not doubt it. I cannot recall ever seeing an unfunny cartoon by Sam Gross. His drawings and captions work perfectly together. In my book, Sam is the funniest, hardest-working, most knowledgeable star in the cartoon universe. If there is anything Sam does not know about the cartoon business, you can bet nobody will know it.

Sam did hundreds of cartoons for the *National Lampoon*. There isn't a clunker in the bunch. To be consistently funny is not a given. Sam's recurring themes, such as little match girls, gingerbread houses, people (or frogs) in little wheeled carts, and, occasionally, a nice enema-bag or tampon cartoon, were the laugh-out-loud leavening embedded in every issue of the magazine. Sam also edited the magazine's cartoon collections, and he became their cartoon editor, which gave him the opportunity to loudly advise any tin-eyed editor where he could stick any poorly drawn, unfunny cartoons he was thinking of printing.

PHOTO BY ANNE HALL

At the Seaport Cafe in Mattapoisett, we have breakfast with Lorraine and her friends. How did Charlie Rodrigues produce such demented work while living his life in this quiet, conservative little town? I think how odd it is for one of the most irascible and famous cartoonists in the world to be sitting at this vinyl-covered table watching me eat a second doughnut as he chats amiably with these women, who, as soon as they finish their coffees, will be going to mass at St. Anthony's or to Our Lady of Purgatory in New Bedford to play bingo.

I thought this road trip with Sam would give me material to write this little essay, but it's Sam who's gathering the material. And it dawns on me that one of these days I'm going to turn up in a cartoon signed *S. Gross*. He'll probably draw me in one of those little Porgy carts. After having donated my pancreas to a salamander, I'll be doing something improper with a doughnut, while one of the nice old ladies from breakfast belts me over the head with an enema bag.

And I bet the caption will be even funnier than the drawing.

—Rick Meyerowitz

"They're 'tits.'"

December 1970

Sam's frog is the _National Lampoon_'s ur-cartoon. We've been enjoying this frog's legs since December 1970.

August 1976

"Well then, for God's sake, what have you done with your tea bag?"

circa 1975

"We *know* it was the gingerbread boy! We found crumbs in her vagina."

June 1983

"I say let's do it. We've never had a lemonade enema before."

I don't know why, but I find Sam's gingerbread cartoons to be irresistible. The irreverence with which he takes on classic fairy tales, adding crumbs, Nazis, and enemas is, well, classic.

July 1981

"Mein Gott! It never occurred to me Hansel and Gretel might be Hitler Youth!"

May 1971

"They got me, Lennie—I'm wounded."

September 1983

"He followed me home, Mom. Can I keep him?"

Sam explores our relationships to our adorable animal friends by giving vent to paranoia (a possible penguin conspiracy), criminality (a goldfish gangster), and scatology (a proctological event featuring a mythical beast).

January 1975

"Who's behind this?"

CARTOONISTS DON'T DO NO STINKIN' PENCILS

Larry "Ratso" Sloman on Sam Gross

I first met Sam shortly after I had joined the *National Lampoon* as executive editor in early 1985. He was coming in to show me cartoons for a spread in our fifteenth anniversary issue, but first he had a meeting to discuss merchandising his famous frog cartoon with the owner of the company, Matty Simmons.

"You cocksucker! You son of a bitch. I'm not going to let you rip me off like that," a heavy Bronx accent thundered down the hall. The commotion was coming from Matty's office. A few of us rushed over and huddled by the door. A steady stream of invectives continued, aimed at Matty and whoever else was in there. Finally, the cursing and carrying on subsided. There was a moment's silence; then we heard the voice of Julian

Weber, the *National Lampoon*'s eloquent lawyer: "See, Matty, I told you Sam wouldn't go for it."

A few minutes later Sam was in my office, laying out the cartoons for the spread, still muttering under his breath about being "ripped off" by these "assholes." But there was a huge disjuncture between his appearance and his verbiage. Sam was older than us, married, with a child. He was wearing a natty tweed jacket and a plush turtleneck sweater underneath. His neatly trimmed salt-and-pepper beard gave him the gravitas of a college professor. Then he opened his mouth again. "Here's the fucking spread."

I picked up the first cartoon. It was a biblical scene. There was a stiff-as-a-board naked woman propped up in the corner of a bedroom and two handmaidens changing the bed of an important Israelite. "Lot still keeps her around," one woman told the other. "He says she tastes like pussy." Right there, I fell in love with S. Gross.

What wasn't there to love? Sam had the single-mindedness of the Mahatma. He knew he was going to become a cartoonist when he was six years old in Mrs. Levy's first-grade class in the Bronx. Back then, Sam inked his cartoons right onto his wooden school desk. Mrs. Levy summoned Sam's mother, who came

February 1972

S. GROSS

"Hey, what exposure are you using?"

to school armed with a bar of Kirkman's, an industrial soap. The two of them had to wipe away the offending cartoons. "My first fucking editor," Sam remembers fondly.

For years Sam toiled as an accountant. In 1962 he and his wife, Isabelle, saved eight thousand dollars, quit their jobs, and took off to Europe for a year. By the end of that year, Sam knew all he wanted to do was draw. He returned home and sold his cartoons everywhere from the *New Yorker* to the *Realist*.

Sam became our go-to guy. Unlike some cartoonists, Sam knew how to tell a joke, and he never missed a deadline. His work was topical and surrealistic, and he was consistently hilarious. About a year into my tenure, I realized that we were understaffed and that I had my hands full with our creative but wacky writers, so I had the brilliant idea of making Sam our cartoon editor. I had implicit trust in Sam's judgment. With the comic pages and the spreads and the cartoons, I knew he was good for twenty pages an issue.

He'd amble into my office.

"M.K. Brown just got back from the dentist and she had a horrific time."

"Five pages," I'd say, without even looking up. and Sam would shuffle off to deal with her and Rodrigues and Gahan Wilson and Meyerowitz and the rest of them. Better him than me.

After five years, I left the *Lampoon* and a new executive editor took over. He called Sam into his office.

"From now on, I want

pencil sketches from all the artists before they do anything," he told Sam.

"Pencils! Cartoonists don't do no stinkin' pencils. Rodrigues will tell you to go fuck yourself rather than show you a pencil." Sam said. "Oh, and by the way, you *can* go fuck yourself." His tenure as cartoon editor was finished. But the funny thing is, Sam was still selling cartoons to the *Lampoon* long after that editor had been penciled out of his own job.

June 1972

S. GROSS

SEAN KELLY

On Achill Island in County Mayo, in the lobby of the Amethyst Hotel, on a table made from the bones of some ancient beast dragged out of the bog, there stood a sign meant for guests: "May the road rise to meet you, but pay your bill before you leave. The Mgmt."

Himself, Sean Kelly, as Irish a boy as was ever born in Montreal, was an editor and writer at the *National Lampoon*. He contributed a coruscating variety of work that blew the synapses of readers and colleagues alike for twenty years. Drunk, stoned, and dead don't apply to Sean Kelly, but brilliant fits him like a ski mask. As does erudite, flinty-eyed, cheerful, cynical, amiable, and ferocious when aroused or on the trail of an argument. He's a man who sees the barbarity of our culture, the dubious folktales we genuflect to, and the great bureaucracies that overwhelm us, and who isn't afraid to raise his voice against them.

He was godfather to the Irish gaggle that dominated the *National Lampoon* during the 1970s. Occasionally he'd be done dirty and lose his place in the *Lampoon* hierarchy. Then, like Benny David, the nebbishy hero of his, and Michel Choquette's provocative and heretical "Son O' God Comics," he'd rise and

PHOTO BY STATELY, PLUMP BUCK MULLIGAN

return again to the magazine, where he held the position of poet-parodist, and where he'd mentor another generation of comedy writers.

Husband and father many times over and putative master of one yappy terrier, Sean, who was teaching classical literature at Loyola when he first arrived at the magazine, now teaches the same at Pratt Institute, sharing his vast learning with bubbleheaded Twitterers whose parents nervously shell out a pirate king's ransom for the privilege of what is called an education. With Sean Kelly, they get their money's worth. He delivers the most memorable lectures in Brooklyn, but whether, like the Irish monks who saved civilization, Sean can save their children is not clear.

Himself has other things on his mind. "Just breathing," he says, is a privilege. School day over, Sean collects his paycheck, pays all bills when due, feels the sun shine warm upon his back, turns to face into the wind, and whichever way his road home dips and turns, he always rises to meet it.

—Rick Meyerowitz

December 1973

THE BEAR
Fred Graver on Sean Kelly

First time we go out for drinks, Sean tells me this joke: Guy hears there's this massive black bear, deep in the woods, that no one's ever been able to hunt down. Guy says, "I'm gonna get the bear." He takes his rifle, hides behind a rock outside the bear's cave, and waits. Days and days go by. . . . Suddenly, the bear appears behind the guy, seizes him, and has him. It mauls him: tears the flesh from his body, sodomizes him, leaves him for dead, thinks about it, comes back, and beats and sodomizes him again.

When I heard this joke it was the early 1980s. I'd arrived at the *Lampoon* courtesy of Mike Reiss and Al Jean, who'd been working there and gotten a call from a producer to work on a movie called *Airplane* . . . well, technically, *Airplane 2*. They'd done what every writer fantasizes about doing—they literally left the piece they were working on in their typewriter, announced their departure, and departed. I was one of two people hired to replace them. Warning sign: editors at this magazine were replaceable.

The *National Lampoon* had given America a totally new sense of humor—ten years before. We were beyond *Airplane 2*; we were like *Lampoon 16: DOA*. Just my luck to hop on the bus just as the gas tank was reading empty.

Oh, so back to the joke: Guy is half-dead, the bear's had his way with him, but he crawls back to civilization. Recovers after eight months in the hospital. Gets out, says "I'm goin' back for the bear." Grabs his rifle, camps behind the rock and waits . . . and waits. . . . Days and days later, the bear appears, grabs him from behind, mauls him, tears him apart, sodomizes him, sodomizes him again, tears him apart, leaves him for dead. Again.

So why, with all the old hunters gone, with the gas running out of the tank, was Sean still at the *Lampoon*? It was my great fortune to become his friend then, to sit and listen to him parse everything from Flann O'Brien to fart jokes. Satire should, Sean believed, leave the bear bleeding. Sean believed in the joke that sent its victim home to cry, keening to the fates for his cursed, dismal nature. At Sean's table, you got points for speaking the unspeakable. It's the first place I heard the rumor about Keith Hernandez, the one that made an episode of *Seinfeld* ten years later. It's the first place I heard anyone mutter the words, "Someone should take that fucking Mother Teresa down a peg or two."

The other thing I learned from Sean was the writer's way of life. He introduced me to an endless circle of agents and producers, packagers, and promoters, all of whom had a quick check ready for a funny idea. He introduced me to the idea of Canadian dentist money—the money a hapless guy with a little extra pocket change would pay to be close to show business. When asked why he was still at the *Lampoon*, he'd shrug and say, "Baby needs a new pair of shoes!" I tagged along as Sean, the Ginger Man of Manhattan, navigated through children's television networks and soft-core cable channels, making jokes so mean and wonderful that everyone in the room laughed and no one in the room trusted him. You could see it in their eyes: "What will he say about me?"

Speaking of bleeding: so the guy in the woods gets left for dead a second time. A second time, he crawls his way back to civilization, spends two months in the hospital, finally walks out the door, and the first thing he says is, "I'm gettin' that bear!" Grabs his rifle, goes back, sits behind the rock, and waits.

One day, the boss called us into his office and closed the place. I think Canadian dentists own it now. My last glimpse of the *Lampoon* was Sean on the phone, talking to an agent, pitching another book idea: "Baby needs a new pair of shoes."

OK, OK. The guy is in the woods. It's his third time back, he's waiting behind the rock with his rifle, day after day. One day, he feels a tap on his shoulder. He spins around, sees the bear.

Bear looks at the guy and says:

"You're not here for the hunting, are you?"

KĀ·SI ATTA BAT

BY SEAN KELLY AND RICK MEYEROWITZ

Not brilliant was the outlook for the Yokohama Prawn—
The score stood four to two, with eight and one-half
     innings gone.
But the fans loved *basa boru*, and so in the stands they sat,
And hoped for one more chance to watch Kā-Si-*san* come to
     bat.
Go, Nagasaki Goldfish! Yokohama Prawn, hurrah!
Hot saki here! Cold Kirin! Sushi, get it while
     it's raw!
With stoic calm they watched two
     hitters pop to shallow short.
Of scorn they gave no raspberry, nor
     of disgust a snort,
Although they knew Frin (who
     was small) and Burake (who
     was fat)
Would have to stay alive to bring
     Kā-Si-*san* to the bat.
But with Zen patience Frin just
     stood, and somehow drew a
     walk,
And after Burake and the third-
     base coach had had a talk
Concerning kamikaze, Bushido, and
     loss of face,
The fat man caught a fastball in the ear,
     and took his base.
Now the Kabuki cheerleader, a white-faced acrobat,
Leapt up and led a chorus of "Kā-Si-*san* atta bat!"
You may well wonder (while they give their neat,
     preprogrammed cheer)
Just how that diamond superstar came to be playing here:
Men's motives may be many, but the yen to win is why
The vaunted slugger had become a Rent-a-Samurai.
The Mudville owners wouldn't pay the wages he was worth,
So Casey took his glove and bat halfway around the earth.
By geishas he was entertained, and on tempura dined,
He was honored, he was worshipped, and eventually signed,
To play his nation's pastime in the nation of Nippon,
As the round-eyed gate attraction of the Yokohama Prawn,
Where the scoreboards and the stadiums and the bullpens
     look the same,
But just a little *smaller*—a scale model of The Game.

He strode out of the dugout, swinging half a dozen bats,
Through a blizzard of kimono belts and meditation mats.
His muscles flexed, his knuckles white, his visage set and grim,
He dug in with his cleats, and then—the umpire *bowed* to him!
A pause. The umpire bowed again. How formal. How discreet.
Our hero sent a gob of Red Man splashing at his feet.
     "Ah, so!" the umpire murmured, and he signaled to
          the mound.
     The pitcher nodded, stooped, and rolled the
          ball along the ground!
     While Casey watched, amazed, it
          reached the plate, and there
          stopped dead.
          "Hey, what the hell . . ." said Casey.
               "Stlike one!" the umpire said.
          Now Casey stepped out of the box,
               and looked up at the stands.
          Not a single soul was shouting.
               They were sitting on their
               hands.
          The players in the dugout, the
               coaches down the lines
     Were quiet as the bodhisattvas in
          their roadside shrines.
     Once more the umpire smiled and bowed,
          and once more Casey spat.
          He grabbed his crotch and crouched and sneered
               and twitched his mighty bat. . . .
This time the pitcher lobbed the ball somewhere not far from
     third.
And Casey shook his head, because the only thing he heard
Was the umpire saying, "Stlike two!" and no other sound
     at all,
For the silence was so perfect, you could hear a lotus fall.
Now Casey threw his helmet. Now Casey lost his cool.
He called the ump a dog's child, out of wedlock born, a fool;
Set out upon a stomping, spitting, shouting, swearing spree;
And stopped to catch his breath, and heard the umpire say,
     "Stlike thlee!"
Two hits. Two left. No runs. O shame! O terrible disgrace!
O awful loss of ball game! More awful loss of face!
Now, Casey thinks, "Can't win 'em all . . . wait 'til next . . . *what
     the hay?!*"

July 1982

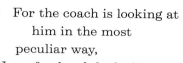

For the coach is looking at
 him in the most
 peculiar way,
Not a fan has left the bleachers,
 and his teammates gather 'round,
Looking sad and kinda solemn, and
 nobody makes a sound....
And just now Casey notices the batboy coming toward
Home plate, where Casey's still standing, and ... he's carrying
 a *sword!*
It's raining in the Favored Land. They've had to call the game.
But there's joy in Yokohama, where they honor Kā-Si-'s name,
For there's nothing more exciting to the fans of old Nippon
Than an executed sacrifice, when the suicide squeeze is on!

132,000 PC. ROMAN CATHOLICS SET

ONLY $198

Fight again the Albigensian Crusade—Catholic against Christian! Mount your own brave defense of Beziers, where, on July 22, 1209, TWENTY THOUSAND men, women, and children, innocent Cathar "heretics"—the first Protestants—were raped, slaughtered, and burned!

HERE IS WHAT YOU GET:

12 Bishops—Fully armed and mounted
10 Papal Legates—Complete with catapults & dispensations
10,000 Bloodthirsty Basque mercenaries
5,000 Fanatic Dominican priests
20,000 land-grabbing French knights
Stakes, racks, thumbscrews, and 1 Piece of the True Cross

PLUS

A magnificent scale model of the Citadel of Beziers, moat, houses and Cathedral. All highly flammable. Streets specially constructed to RUN WITH BLOOD!

RUSH COUPON TODAY

Gentlemen: Here's my $1.98. Rush my ROMAN CATHOLICS set to me. If not convinced of the perfidy of the RC Church by this atrocity, I must be mad and/or a Dominican.

NAME ....
ADDRESS ....
CITY .... STATE .... ZIP ....

ILLUSTRATION BY RUSS HEATH

A CHILD'S CHRISTMAS IN ULSTER

BY SEAN KELLY

with woodcuts by Randall Enos

One Christmas was so like another in those years around Waterside now, that I can never remember whether there were twelve Papish killed on the twenty-fourth or twenty-four Papish killed on the twelfth.

All the Christmases roll like an armoured patrol down Shakhill Road, ricochet round my brain like rubber bullets in a bogside boxcar, and into the Donneybrook I dash to salvage whatever I can find. Into the gas cloud bottle bomb melee of Belfast memories I scramble, and out I come with Mrs. Shaughnessy, and the Tommies.

It was in the aftermath of the day of Christmas Eve, and I was in Mrs. Shaughnessy's back alley, waiting for Catholics, with her son Tim. Patient, cold, and callous, our faces covered with nylon stockings, we waited to clobber the Catholics. Wild-eyed and drunk as lords and horribly whiskied, they would stagger or slink, saying Aves and Paters and rattling their beads down the cobblestones, and the sharp-eyed gunners, Tim and I, King Billy's dragoons from the battle of the Boyne, off Crumlin Road, would fire our deadly dumdums at the red of their eyes. The wise Catholics never appeared. We were so still, black and tan marksmen lying in ambush for the Mayo Flying Column, that we never heard Mrs. Shaughnessy's first scream. Or, if we heard it at all, it was, to us, the far-off lament of a Sinn Fein banshee over the smoking ruins of Cork. But soon the cry grew louder. "I.R.A.!"

cried Mrs. Shaughnessy. And we ran down the alley, our guns in our hands, toward the house; and glass indeed was shattering out the windows, and automatics were rattling, and Mrs. Shaughnessy was howling bloody murder as was appropriate to the time and place.

This was better than all the Catholics in Ulster with targets pinned to their greatcoats standing in a row. We crawled to the threshhold, cradling our rifles, and peered into the door of the pitchblack room.

It was pitchblack with reason, and so was Mrs. Shaughnessy, who was rumored to be very high up in the Women's Auxiliary of the local Orange Lodge. She was sitting in the middle of the room, saying, "A fine Christmas," and clawing away at the smouldering tar with which she was smeared top to toe. "Call the Constabulary!" she bellowed, a surprisingly talkative tar baby.

"They won't be here," said Mr. Shaughnessy. "It's Christmas."

Opposite: May 1974; above: December 1974

There were no I.R.A. men to be seen, only Mr. and Mrs. Shaughnessy, and she black as sin and scrubbing away at herself like Aunt Jemima playing Lady Macbeth.

"Do something," she said.

We let go a round or so out the back door—I think we missed Mr. Shaughnessy—and ran out of the house to the telephone box.

"Let's call the army as well," Tim said.

"And the B Specials."

"And Ian Paisley, he likes riots."

But we only called the Royal Ulster Constabulary, and soon the paddy wagon came and the tall men in helmets rushed into the house with Thompson guns and Mr. Shaughnessy got out just in time before they opened fire.

Nobody could have had a noisier Christmas. And when the policemen ran out of ammunition and were standing in the destroyed and bloody room, Tim's aunt, Miss Shaughnessy, came downstairs and peered in. Tim and I waited, very quietly, to hear what she would say to them. She had the gift of the gab, for sure.

She looked at the three tall policemen in their brass and helmets, standing among the smoke and rubble and her expiring sister-in-law, and she said: "Would yez care for a drop o' the crayture, at all, at all?"

Just yesterday, just yesterday, when I was a boy, when there was trouble in Ulster, and the night sky was bright orange as a twelfth of July flag, we ran riot day and night down streets that reeked of fear and pee, and we chased with tins of petrol the superstitious nuns and leprechauns through the wassailing streets of Christmas in the North, when it rains. And rains.

But here a small boy says: "It rained last year, too. It washed my whitewash slogans off the walls, and I cried."

"But that was not the same rain. Our Christmas cloudbuster rain was wet as martyrs' blood, our rain roared down the gutter like beer from a blown-up public house, our rain glistened on the mackintoshes of the patrolling B Specials till they glittered like Christmas trees in the flare light, and it swept the bits of bodies and such down the true blue sewers out to the Protestant sea."

"Tell about the presents."

"Ah, the presents. After the dour and sour smelling service, the presents. There were Useless Presents: toys and dolls and King James Bibles, crayons in various shades of orange, red, white, and blue; never, of course, green; and a pair of socks or some candy..."

"Go on to the Useful Presents."

"Plastique bombs and ammo belts, spring knives and knuckle-dusters, blackjacks and cherry bombs, ski masks for tugging over your mug till your own mum wouldn't know you at a mugging, toy guns that looked realer than real ones, and a shrill whistle to summon your friends to call the Tommies to save your hide; and a booklet that warned in big bold type NOT to make incendiary devices out of the accompanying batteries, blasting caps, wires, bottles, rags, petrol, and powder, with instructions and detailed diagrams, oh! easy for little guerrillas!"

And on Christmas morning I would walk the rain-wet streets with Tommy, conjuring whistle and a bundle of weapons under my coat, scouring the town for mass-happy Catholics, saluting the local patrols as they slithered by on the slippery streets, till I rounded a corner and out of a rain-veiled lane would come a boy, the spit of myself but a Dogan for certain, misshapen and grim as a Galway spud. I hated him on sight and sound, and reached for my gun to blow him off the face of Christmas when suddenly he reached into his coat, whipped out his revolver, and we sprayed the street with a volley of shots so quick, and so exquisitely wild, that tinseled windows shattered all down the block and a half-dozen goose-gobbling citizens fell face forward into their Christmas dinners, instantly concocting a traditional Ulster recipe, brain stuffing. The young gunmen, he and I, unharmed, ducked and were gone before the echoes were.

And when I got home, as often as not, there was a crater where the dining room had been, and Uncles like burst balloons and Aunts like broken teacups would be festooning the ruins of the feast. And I would squat amidst the rubble and nibble bits of what I hoped was the turkey, carefully following the instructions for little guerrillas, and produce what might be mistaken for a battery-powered nuclear device.

Or I would go out, my shiny new pistol cocked, into the Bogside, with Tim and Dan and Mike, and prowl the still streets, leaving little bullet holes in the fences and people.

"I bet people will think there's been provos."

"What would you do if you saw a provo coming down our street?"

"I'd go like this, bang! I'd throw him over the railings and roll him down the embankment and then I'd kick him behind the ear and he'd pack it in."

"What would you do if you saw two provos?"

Trenchcoated and terrible provos strode and strove through the sputtering snow toward us as we passed Mr. Grogan's house.

"Let's post Mr. Grogan a fire bomb through his letter box."

"Let's write things on his walls."

"Let's write Mr. Grogan looks like a Dogan all over his front door."

Or we walked by the freshgrave patchwork cemetery.

"Do the corpses know it's snowing?"

A bogside cabbage-smell fog drifted in from the docks. Now we were crack troops of Cromwell, scouring the fens of Fermanagh, eagle-eyed and English armour-plated, and cowering Catholics fled before us to hell or Connacht. And we returned home through the poor streets where only a few children scrawled Free Derry on the charred walls and fired a few aimless rounds at us as we scampered across the bridge above the troopship bobbing docks. And then, at home, the Uncles would be solemn, and toast the Queen and absent friends which in this case meant half the family and most of the neighbors, now deceased, for the old cause.

Bring out the tall tales now that we told while the peat fire made fairy pictures of King Billy, his white horse like a ghost of flame, and the blazing battle of the Burning Boyne. And the gory ghosts of slaughtered Sinn Feiners listened at the blacked-out windows and the Tommygun spirit of Michael Collins lay in ambush under the bed I must climb to trembling in the dark.

And I remember we went out terrorizing once when there wasn't by chance a building burning to light the terrifying streets. Flush to the cobbles was a big brick house. And we stood before its black bulk with our safeties off, just in case, and all of us too brave to say a word. The wind came round stone corners, cold and sharp as the blades of invisible pikes.

"What shall we give them? The Protestant Boys?"

"No," Mike said, "The Auld Orange Flute. I'll count three."

One, two, three, and we began to sing, our voices high in the darkness round the house full of baby-eating Catholics maybe.

In the County Tyrone in the town of Dungannon Where many eruptions meself had a hand in . . ."

Then a big red roar, like the sound of a muzzle loader that has not been fired for a long time, slammed against the door; a loud, old Gaelic gun blew shot through the keyhole. And when we stopped running, we were outside *our* house; the parlor was lit for Christmas and everything was bright and clean and Protestant again.

"Perhaps it was a priest," Tim said.

"Perhaps it was the College of Cardinals," Dan said, who was always reading.

"Let's go in and see if there's any gelignite left," Mike said. And we did that. □

BARBAR AND HIS ENEMIES

by Sean Kelly and Tony Hendra
illustrated by Peter Kleinman

There is great sadness in the country of the elephants, for the Old Lady is dead. Barbar the King orders all his subjects to feel sorry, and pay their respects three times a day, on their knees.

"Barbar and His Enemies" appeared in the March 1975 issue. Sean's introduction (below) is a clear indication that he had other things on his mind than making people laugh.

Jean de Brunhoff's 1931 *Histoire de Babar* is an anti-imperialist satire; a "beast fable" in the tradition of the medieval fabliaux, Anatole France's *L'ile des Pingouins* (1908), *Animal Farm*, and *Maus*. Consider the illustration of the colorful, pastoral jungle when it is transformed by "civilization" into the drab, prisonlike Celesteville.

But the many Babar books that followed became little more than marketing devices for plush toys, meriting the accusation—by Ariel Dorfman, in *The Empire's Old Clothes* (1996)—that they "anticipate the theory of neocolonialism."

Hence the inevitable uprising. *Venceremos!*

—Sean Kelly

That naughty monkey Zephyr won't pay his respects, and stays at home in Monkeyville, reading bad books.

The pranks of Zephyr and his friends get even naughtier! Zephyr hurts old Caligula, while he is asleep with one of his friends. This all makes King Barbar very tired, and he decides to take his family for a holiday in Switzerland. Alas, the monkeys stop him before he can get away.

Mischievous Zephyr goes down into King Barbar's gold and diamond mine, and keeps everyone from doing their work. What a troublemaker he is! Soon some of the monkeys decide to be like him, and be lazy. They even say unkind things about King Barbar and their Queen.

What is this? Those silly monkeys have moved into the palace, and strung up Barbar and the Queen on meat hooks! And all the other elephants are being sent back to France. Where will they live, now the Old Lady is dead? They will have to join a circus! Long live President Zephyr!

March 1975

JOHN BELUSHI: AN EDITORIAL, JULY 1982

You know how sometimes you're really wrapped up in watching a life-and-death situation on a real great TV show like *Knots Landing* or something, and just at the most gripping, exciting, realistic moment, you see a boom shadow, or somebody muffs a line, and it spoils everything? It really wrecks the illusion.

Well, this editorial, appearing in the July 1982 issue of the magazine, wasn't written in July. It was written, right against deadline, in early March.

You're taking the shock really well.

What that means is five whole months will have passed between the time we all heard about John and the time you read this.

By the time you read this . . .

Søren Kierkegaard, the late Danish humorist, used to wonder at the absurd optimism implied in making assumptions about the future. How dare we accept a dinner invitation? Mightn't a tile have fallen off a roof and totaled us by dinnertime?

Five months. More than enough time for the mother of Hamlet (another late Danish humorist) to dry her tears and happily remarry . . .

In five months, John may actually have dropped off the front pages, after they've counted the molecules in his poor cells, and interviewed the dozens of creeps he was alone with at the end, and all the old friends he never met, who tried to warn him . . .

In late '72, John left the Second City company in Chicago and came to New York to star in a *National Lampoon* off-Broadway show called *Lemmings*. He didn't much want to come. But the audiences helped convince him he'd made the right career move. It was love at first take.

Lemmings was a sort of musical, about rock music, drugs, and death at an early age. Those things all seemed pretty funny, at the time . . .

The character John played in *Lemmings*—or, to be accurate, the character John *brought* to *Lemmings*—was a homicidal, suicidal, totally out-of-control teddy bear. He stayed with the show a year. He kept the part for life.

Which is not meant to diminish his skill as an actor. He was a witty, brilliant improviser, with the added and unusual ability to work away at a gesture, a pause, a take, until he

had it perfect—and then freeze it, leave it alone, execute it the same every time. He never undercut his material, or went baroque with it, joking on the joke, breaking up the band. He was a pro, as they say. But *powering* the skill and hard work and stage smarts was John, the berserk koala.

After *Lemmings*, John was featured on, and for a while actually coproduced, *The National Lampoon Radio Hour*. He convinced a bunch of old pals to leave Second City and join him here in New York as costars on the show, and in a second stage show about to begin. Thus we met Gilda, and Brian, and Bill. They created *The National Lampoon Show*, and most nights there would be TV guys sitting ringside, taking notes . . .

Until, together with Chevy (from *Lemmings*), they became the Not Ready for Prime-time Players.

The point to this history lesson is: John was generous to his friends, and not afraid of competition for laughs, or anything else. They all became stars. He became a superstar, whose molecules made headlines . . .

Then there was *Animal House*, the *Lampoon*'s first movie, and once again the writers were smart enough to give John the lead, and let him play—John. Well, a part of John. The Baby Gargantua who lived inside him (alongside the teen-age guru, the lunch-counter Greek, the loving husband, the killer bee, the blues singer, Joe Cocker, and everybody else). The cuddly killer who wanted to consume the universe, eat it, guzzle it, smoke it, snort it, give it a terrible hug . . .

During the next (last) five months, a lot of sage folks are sure to say that what is shocking is not *that* John died, but *the way* he died.

Wrong. The way he died was about as shocking as a Wallenda falling off a tightrope, or an Indy racer crashing.

What is shocking is that a person so *alive* that it even came through on *television* . . . isn't alive anymore.

So, we're sorry. For John, a little, because he really was too young to die of old age just yet. For his wife, Judy, who is a decent, gentle, and sensitive person, who might have been spared the headline buzzards and the molecule counts. And sorry for ourselves, because something alive and dangerous and lovable has gone out of our lives.

One reason John liked to keep the party going was that he wasn't especially good at good-byes.

Good-bye, John. Wish you could have stayed.

—Sean Kelly

SUMMER SEX ISSUE
EDITORIAL, AUGUST 1976

Occasionally, but never more than thrice a day, the press barons who own and operate the *National Lampoon* summon the editors into the Bored Room and perform a curious ritual, during the course of which they gibber and shriek incoherently while pointing to a chart on the wall. On this chart is our magazine's sales record for the last six years. The graph begins in the lower left-hand corner, ascends with dizzying steepness, and levels off to a long gradual incline, interrupted only by unsightly bumps, buttes, towers, obelisks—call them what you will. These aberrations, representing great surges in newsstand sales, coincide, we are given to understand, with our release of issues for the most part devoted to humorous observations, japes, and jests on the subject of the difference in gender among featherless bipeds, i.e., Sex.

The conclusion that management wishes us to draw is that we might, ought, nay, *must* produce more such issues, in the interest of something called, if I remember correctly, the cash flow.

Hence the Compulsory Summer Sex Issue.

But it occurs to us, gentle reader, to ask why this is the case. Why will a quarter of a million young Americans purchase this edition of our magazine, who did not buy last month's, and will not buy next month's? Can we compete with the avalanche of published aids to onanism on the nation's newsstands? The nonbiodegradable pin-up girls of *Playboy*? The soft-focus courtesans of *Penthouse*? The amusing phallic-shaped root vegetables so beloved of *Oui*'s editors? The hookers of *Hustler*, in four-color gynecologically fascinating spreads? The vulvas of *Gallery*, the labia minora of *Club*, the fallopian tubes of *High Society*?

Surely if the adolescents of this great land are so poverty-sticken of the imagination as to require print and pictures to fire their libidos, there is a sufficiency of stroke books exercising the constitutionally guaranteed right to keep the female of the species reduced to her time-honored status of pressed turkey roll?

Can it then be that two hundred fifty thousand males, in spite of readily available print porn, skin flicks, massage parlors, life-like inflatable dolls, legalized prostitution, singles bars, gay bars, swingers clubs, legalized prostitution, and the pill-taking, liberated, orgasm-expectant girl next door, are jerking off over the *National Lampoon*?

Say not so!

Do not so!

For it is not yourself you are abusing (a wicked, atavistic Victorian concept, now abhorred by priest and shrink alike). It is *us* you are abusing.

—Sean Kelly

P.S. Re: Last month's issue: In the process of composing a thousand-word panegyric to his own inarticulateness, editor Peej neglected to tell you that (1) the jokes start on page 37; (2) "Scarlet Letters" is continued on page 99; and (3) the sharecroppers on page 52 are Vietnamese (get it?).

ANNE BEATTS

I didn't really know Anne Beatts. We'd met a few times almost forty years ago and had never worked together. So when we had breakfast recently in Los Angeles, it

was to meet *again* for the first time. We sat in a sunny and posh café, and over eight-dollar cups of coffee and smoked salmon platters, we spoke of the old times we never shared, and about the misogyny barrier at the *National Lampoon*, and how she was the first woman to breach it. She was funny and unsentimental. Her few years at the magazine were ancient history as far as she was concerned. She'd spent the last thirty-six building a career as a creator

PHOTO BY MICHEL CHOQUETTE

and writer in television. She was rigorous in her likes and dislikes, and she held strong opinions about everyone she knew at the *Lampoon* and about this book. I liked her, although I felt at any minute she might pull out a hammer and nail my hands to the table.

I asked Michel Choquette, who knew Anne much better than I, to write a few words of introduction. He went to work with gusto and delivered the essay below a few hours later.

—Rick Meyerowitz

In 1970, not long after I had put aside a career as a comedian and become a National Lampooner, I met Anne Beatts, a vivacious, loquacious young woman with a chart-busting IQ, who had established a solid reputation in Montreal ad agencies as a copywriter. Anne was terrifyingly practical and knew her own mind. We had barely found time to become involved when she told me that she intended to write articles with me for the magazine. She also informed me that she would be moving in with me in New York, but that troubled me much less. "Have you written humor before?" I ventured. She waved it off: "Not really, but what's the difference—it's just writing."

And so began our professional association and our personal relationship, a stormy combination that lasted some three years, yielding a respectable number of cosigned articles and domestic skirmishes interspersed with genuinely tender moments. Anne would probably be the first to agree that her initial contributions to our writing partnership were as curative as they were creative: she kept me from reminiscing too much about show business, helped me shake off years of dependence on the freedom to hone material according to the thumbs-up or thumbs-down of live audiences, and nudged me into a deeper commitment to the permanence of the printed page.

Her initial stabs at our collaborative efforts were, or so I was convinced, somewhat hit or miss. While she was exercising her right to try, I played a role somewhere between mentor and tyrant: "That's not funny." "Why not?" she'd ask. "It just isn't." "Then how about this?" "Still not funny." "Okay, well is

this funny?" "Almost." "Does it help if we change this to that?" "Yes, now it's funny." She never gave up, and if I shamelessly dozed off as she poked away at my old manual typewriter on the desk at the foot of my bed, she would jolt me awake: "Okay, listen to this."

Each article we produced together contained more of her handiwork than the previous one, and more lines by her, which, when I wasn't busy arguing with our male colleagues at the magazine about whether women could write comedy, I had to admit were pretty damn funny.

Pretty soon I was the one bouncing ideas and phrases off her.

But I think the moment I came to the full realization that Anne was developing her own comedic sense was when she confronted me in Ben's Delicatessen in Montreal. We'd had a major spat in New York the night before, after which I'd jumped on a plane without telling her. Taking a guess, she jumped on a plane herself. Then she tracked me down at Ben's. I was impressed, though I worked hard not to show it. When I kept reading my newspaper, she ordered a coffee—on my tab. When the coffee came, she checked to make sure it was hot, then poured it over my head. "I owe you a coffee," she said, as she walked out to head for the airport.

Ben's no longer exists. But whenever I walk by the spot where it stood, my hand instinctively reaches for the top of my head . . . and a little twinge unleashes a torrent of memories about an all-too-short-lived but very meaningful partnership.

—Michel Choquette

From The National Lampoon Encyclopedia of Humor, 1973

by Phil Socci and Anne Beatts

If Ted Kennedy drove a Volkswagen, he'd be President today.

It floats.

The way our body is built, we'd be surprised if it didn't.

The sheet of flat steel that goes underneath every Volkswagen keeps out water, as well as dirt and salt and other nasty things that can eat away at the underside of a car. So it's watertight at the bottom.

And everybody knows it's easier to shut the door on a Volkswagen after you've rolled down the window a little. That proves it's practically airtight on top.

If it was a boat, we could call it the Water Bug.

But it's not a boat, it's a car.

And, like Mary Jo Kopechne, it's only

99 and 44/100 percent pure.

So it won't stay afloat forever. Just long enough.

Poor Teddy.

If he'd been smart enough to buy a Volkswagen, he never would have gotten into hot water.

Liberal Psalm

by Anne Beatts

Now I shall sing unto the Lord a new song; and it is called the Song of the Liberal.

For he shall arise and multiply, and in Volvos he shall cover the face of the earth.

Fear ye not, though the days of Adlai have departed and Gene McCarthy is as a withered stalk;

For lo! a miracle has come to pass; and out of sterility is brought forth the truly mediocre.

For he sayeth neither yea nor nay; and he is full of good intentions.

With good intentions he paveth his way; and cleaveth to neither side thereof, except it be slightly to the left.

His good intentions are as numerous as the leaves of the fig tree, or the addresses in the *Whole Earth Catalog.*

He walketh in the ways of self-righteousness, and whenever he can, he bicycleth.

His speech is neither hasty nor unconsidered, for he engages in meaningful dialogue.

In a spirit of compromise he breaketh his bread; and lets it fall into the fondue pot.

The words of the prophets McLuhan and Galbraith and Reich are holy unto him.

Go, light candles in the rain; and raise high the roof beam, carpenters!

Behold the coming of the Liberal; for he eateth up dissent like the locust.

Violence without meaning he deploreth, as the avocado without crabmeat; yet peace without honor contenteth him not.

He is for change within the system; and he has eaten of the bread of Pepperidge Farm, and found it good.

And lo! the day of the Liberal shall come to pass; and his sun shall rise in the middle of the road; and the music of Joan Baez shall be heard in the land, and on every turntable shall the albums of Baez revolve.

And a blanket of guilt shall lay upon the land, but lightly, as doth a quilt from an Appalachian cooperative.

For unto each new cause the Liberal goeth gladly, like the virgin bride; and he rejoiceth in his own ravishing.

And each man each day shall consider his own excrement, and eat a small portion thereof, crying unto the Lord, to ask his forgiveness upon him.

And each day the black-skinned people shall receive a hearty breakfast; thenceforth they will neither steal nor rob nor commit crimes of violence against their white-skinned brethren.

And among all the nations, if there be any that be Fascist, they shall be cast into outer darkness for their iniquity; and there shall be no trade with them, unless it be vital to the economy.

And Israel shall rise in triumph above all the nations.

There shall be no television save educational television: and constructive shall be the nature of all criticism.

And ye shall not worship any actor whose commitment be not equal unto that of Jane Fonda, who hath accepted an Academy Award for your sake.

Giant redwoods shall spring forth numberless as the grass-blades; and Cesar Chavez shall have a brand of tacos named after him.

For the hour of the Liberal draweth nigh; and the sign thereof is the peace symbol.

To the woman he grants the right to labor in the sweat of her brow for so long as she remains comely in his eyes.

And she shall consent to lie with him whenever he desireth her; and he shall strive with all his might for her orgasm.

Yea, her orgasm shall become as desirable unto him as a lifetime subscription to *Realités,*

For he may not soweth before she reapeth; yet may she reap as often as she would before he soweth:

And lo! their orgasms shall come in the same moment.

For it is written that he who haveth his orgasm before his wife's orgasm, yea even one jot or tittle before her orgasm, he shall be thrown down from high estate, and his sustenance shall be from the trough of shame and it shall be bitter to him.

But he shall like it anyhow.

Yea, he shall labor at it and like it even unto the hour of her second coming.

According to the teachings of Lamaze shall the woman bring forth his children, and give them suck whenever possible within the sight of others.

And his children shall be like a matched set of wooden salt-and-pepper shakers unto him: two shall be their number, and multitudinous shall be their Creative Playthings.

And they shall go forth into private schools and he shall pay for them in gold, and upon each child shall he bestoweth a liberal-arts education.

And thereby each child shall learn that there are two sides to every question; and both sides merit further study.

For the Liberal looks to the hills, where he has builded his country place: he rejoiceth on his water bed. Sweet as the expectation of frozen scampi is the future to the Liberal.

And, he shall go down to the corner for a carton of Häagen Dazs vanilla.

And every street shall be called Kennedy; and every avenue shall be called Martin Luther King.

And Lenny Bruce shall be restored to life.

And he shall commit suicide.

Above: August 1972
Opposite: January 1972

The American Indian: Noble Savage or Renaissance Man?

by Anne Beatts

A wealthy Fifth Avenue heiress lunching at Le Grenouille carries a Hopi Snake Dancer's medicine bag instead of a purse.

A popular movie star and a celebrated director collaborate on a film that portrays Custer as a villain—and grosses $14 million.

A twenty-three-year-old Phys Ed major from Northwestern University jumps off a six-hundred-foot cliff in the belief that Yaqui spirits will protect him.

These are welcome gestures. But can they, however sincere they may be, compensate the Indian for all that he has suffered at the hands of the white man? In trying to right the scales of justice, are we not merely indulging ourselves in a romantic myth that does little but perpetuate the concept of the Indian as "noble savage"? Isn't the problem really our stubborn refusal to admit that where the Indian's civilization might have succeeded, ours has failed?

In the days when most Europeans were still claiming that the earth was flat, the "Indians"—the word itself a misnomer caused by the crude navigational ability of Christopher Columbus—possessed a culture of amazing sophistication and complexity. And even as the Huns and Visigoths crushed the splendors of the Roman Empire, so did the brutish Europeans almost succeed in eradicating a society whose finer points they could not comprehend. Yet, despite the ravages of the white men, the Indians—or "painted devils," as the ignorant European immigrants called them—could still give the world a priceless legacy: the hammock, the toboggan, the decoy duck, maple syrup, and buffalo chips.

In the present headlong rush to reexamine the values by which we live, we should be aware that the Indians had anticipated many of our institutions—and perceived their eventual transience—long before we took our first stumbling steps on American soil.

From the midst of our smog-filled cities, our overcrowded ghettos, our strife-torn campuses—we could do worse than to look back at the Indian in his simple loincloth, squatting on the dirt floor of his wigwam, scratching his back with a painstakingly carved deer's antler.

If we feel as he feels, and think as he thinks—then, and only then, can we begin to understand his silence, concealing a deep, instinctive knowledge of life's mysteries. As the Hidatsa proverb so poignantly expresses it, "When the sun goes down, it grows cold." For many weary years, the few remaining Indians have waited in patient expectation of a day when whites would be ready for the sacred trust that the Indians had been instructed to pass on to us. In fact, the Indian greeting "How" is actually the English equivalent, shortened in translation, of an Ojibwa expression meaning "How soon can we tell them?"

So, if we desire to atone for the wrongs of the past, we must take our cue from archeologists who have assembled a new case on behalf of the so-called "noble savage." And we must try to see with new eyes, Indian eyes that look to the far horizon through half-closed lids. Typical of the shortsighted attitude which we must cast off is that question which has haunted every discussion of the great American Indian civilization. It is the question of the skeptic, the modern white so desensitized by the consequences of his own historical "progress" that he cannot see the world in any other context but his own. It is: How can any people be described as civilized when they did not even discover the wheel?

Contained within the answer is the essential secret of the divergence between the Red Man's culture and our own. The Indians discovered the wheel. But, foreseeing the environmental devastation, mechanistic society, and needless suffering that would arise as an inevitable consequence of this discovery, they admired it exclusively for its aesthetic qualities. They chose to wear it as an ornament.

The Red Hunter: Too Humane to Kill

Indians were probably the first conservationists. Indian methods of hunting buffalo aided the process of natural selection, since only the old, tired, and sick animals ran slowly enough for the Indians to catch up with them. In winter, if a starving buffalo found itself separated from the herd and almost buried in a snowdrift, any Indian who happened on it would be quick to put it out of its misery. A favored hunting technique was to stampede the buffalo herd up to the edge of a cliff, leaving it up to each individual buffalo to decide whether or not to jump—further evidence of the Indians' high regard for animal life. The Indians, unwilling to slay any living being, would chase a deer into the water, then follow it in their canoes, hoping it would drown before they could spear it.

CHARLES RODRIGUES

WITH AN 'S'

I t's dawn. I am sitting at Charlie Rodrigues's desk four years after he died. First light streams into the little wood-paneled room through a small window.

An artist's studio without light? Well, Charlie only worked at night; he didn't need light. On the shelves in front of me are dusty books. I see one on Goya, *Los Caprichos*, which makes sense. Like Goya, Charlie drew beautifully, almost effortlessly, and with great detail. And like Goya, what he chose to draw left the viewer unsettled.

Charlie loved the underworld. His cartoons were set in insane asylums and morgues, bordellos and graveyards, side-shows and crime scenes. He populated them with the freaks and strangers among us: the crippled, the disfigured, the blind, the insane, the infirm, and the aged.

Charlie was the Weegee of cartoonists. And his line! He drew a stronger, darker, richer black line than any other artist I can think of. He was a very literate man who wrote like a writer.

PHOTO COURTESY OF LORRAINE RODRIGUES

And he was a religious man, a church-going Catholic. In another era he might've been painting angels on church ceilings. Yet the infernal landscape of Charlie's mind was a place the church definitely would not approve of, so he drew all night, in the dark, when other good Catholics were sound asleep. He must have felt he couldn't compose this underworld of his in the good light of day.

Of course, then he published his cartoons, so there goes that theory. Perhaps he assumed no one in his circle would ever read the *National Lampoon*. More likely, he felt that once he drew them, they might as well get out in the world because the mortgage needed to be paid, and, after all, everything he drew was pretty damned funny, and he knew it.

—Rick Meyerowitz

The Aesop Brothers die when an exasperated Rodrigues materializes in his own strip and kills everybody. February '74.

"...YES, YOU'RE ON AN OIL TANKER 1400 MILES EAST OF NOVA SCOTIA. THE RECEPTION IS VERY BAD, SIR. I'LL TRY IT AGAIN. FIRST I'LL TAKE OFF MY BRA—YES, MY BRA! THEN MY PANTIES—WHAT? MY PANTIES, PANTIES! PAPA-ALPHA-NOVEMBER-TANGO-INDIA-ECHO-SIERRA, PANTIES!"

June 1987

This is Charlie's beautiful fountain pen. He never filled it with ink—he dipped it.

From "Soviet Sex," January 1986

"I'LL TELL YA', BORIS, THE SOVIET UNION HAS TO BE THE WORST GODDAM PLACE IN THE WORLD TO BE A TRANSVESTITE!"

Below are Charlie's sketches and the finished art for the "Violence" issue, June 1973. He's a perfectionist. You can see him thinking in ink.

First, he tries a left view.

Then he tries it another way.

He gets what he wants and adds some color.

From "Cartoons That Touch on Conspiracy," February 1990

"...RAYMOND, I THINK WE SHOULD MOVE THE SPANISH CARLISTS OVER TO SHIRLEY MACLAINE'S SPOT, AND POSITION HER CLOSER TO AUGUSTO PINOCHET AND MARGARET TRUMAN..."

He works the idea over and over until he gets what he wants.
It's horrible and it's funny, and we can't help laughing—but what are we laughing at?

The finished ink drawing.

The color overlay.

The combined art on the cover, June 1973.

DALMATIANRY BITCHINESS

WOULD YOU WANT YOUR DAUGHTER TO MARRY ONE?

BY MAXIM GORKI

✴ FOR WHAT THE DEVIL DID WITH THE PRIVATE PARTS SEND TEN DOLLARS TO PRIVATE PARTS c/o NATIONAL LAMPOON 635 MADISON AVENUE NEW YORK, N.Y. 10022

MOON MADNESS
BY rodrigues

FREE TO GOOD HOME. 42 YR. OLD HUSBAND. NON-SMOKER. CLEAN, DOES LIGHT CARPENTRY. WAS CASTRATED IN INDUSTRIAL ACCIDENT. INQUIRE WITHIN
by rodrigues ©COPYRIGHT 1987

LIFE ON DEATH ROW

AMISCRON PACCAS PHOENICIAN FISH MARKET OWNER. UPSIDE-DOWN HAT INDICATES AMISCRON IS UNMARRIED. AMISCRON POINTS TO ANUS OF CODFISH.

Marilyn Monroe ● a biography

APPALLING 12
BY rodrigues

SEX ROBOTS
BY rodrigues COPYRIGHT ©1985

UNFORTUNATELY COMMA THEIR MOTHER SOLD THEM TO A FUNNY MAN WITH NO CHIN FOR FIVE CENTS A POUND AND THEY WERE NEVER HEARD FROM AGAIN EXCLAMATION POINT

CARTOONS ABOUT THE BLIND✴
©COPYRIGHT 1987 rodrigues

IN SAUDI ARABIA IF YOU USE MORE THAN 4 FEET OF TOWEL, THEY CUT YOUR HAND OFF!!!

OUT OF SIGHT
© copyright 1980 by Rodrigues

AH HELPED WID DE PLACENTA

FILLER THE CAPITAL OF THE UKRAINE IS KIEV!

THE SEVEN DEADLY & OTHER SINS!
BY rodrigues

✴ THE KIND THEY WISH THEY COULD SEE!

I SEEM TO HAVE STRAYED OFF FROM THE ORIGINAL STORY SO I WILL BEGIN AGAIN PERIOD Rodrigues

SENIOR SEX
BY SENHOR rodrigues

These are Charlie's pens.

SEX CARTOONS

DRAWN WITH A HUNT PEN

No. 22, EXTRA FINE, ROUND POINTED, A BOX OF WHICH WAS GIVEN TO ME BY A GUY WHO WORKED AT THE MASSACHUSETTS REGISTRY OF MOTOR VEHICLES, WHERE HE PILFERED THEM ABOUT TWELVE YEARS AGO. HE NO LONGER WORKS THERE.

TRUE STORY. HONEST. *rodrigues*

Cartoons & STORY © copyright 1988 BY:

SOME OF YOU PERHAPS ARE WONDERING WHY THE PUNCTUATION MARKS ARE SPELLED OUT PERIOD THE REASON FOR THIS IS QUITE SIMPLE PERIOD

TH3 BROTH3RS ÆSOP
IN THEIR
REVOLUTION RUSSIAN

GEORGI — ALEXEYEV

IN THE HAMLET OF KVIT LIVE THE PEASANT SIAMESE TWIN BROTHERS GEORGI AND ALEXEYEV ÆSOP. THEY EKE OUT A PRECARIOUS EXISTENCE FROM A SMALL FARM. LIFE IS HARD! NAY-SHITTY! A FARM 3 FEET BY 5 FEET YIELDS LITTLE FOOD-ESPECIALLY WHEN MUCH OF IT IS BARREN TUNDRA. HOW DID THESE TWO SOULS GET INTO SUCH A WRETCHED STATE, YOU ASK? STUPIDITY MOSTLY. THEY RESPONDED TO AN ADVERTISEMENT ON A MATCHBOOK COVER FOR SPACIOUS RANCHETTES IN THE MOSKVA (THAT'S RUSSIAN FOR MOSCOW) SUBURBS.

I BEGIN MY STORY WITH GEORGI SPEAKING FROM A SMALL HILL AT THE FAR END OF THE FARM...

THE INGHAMS ○ A HARELIPPED COUPLE

NO! IT CAN'T BE! YES, IT'S HIM!

FILLER THE CAPITAL OF THE UKRAINE IS KIEV

BILL'S SECOND HAND DILDOS AND SAWS SHARPENED

FILLER THE CAPITAL OF THE UKRAINE IS KIEV

BUT, COMMA

FILLER THE CAPITAL OF THE UKRAINE IS KIEV

SLEAZY* SEX CARTOONS

© COPYRIGHT 1986 *rodrigues*

* AND SHODDILY DRAWN ON POOR-QUALITY PAPER!

ROBERTA SISTER OF 'KITTY' THE 'TART' IS TARTER! SHE PAYS YOU!

GODDAM FAGGOTS!

BY *rodrigues*

OUR MAN HELL

DEAR READER,

OBVIOUSLY SOMETHING IS VERY, VERY WRONG WITH THIS COMIC STRIP! HOWEVER, IT STILL IS BETTER THAN ALL THE OTHERS IN THIS MAGAZINE. (EXCEPT MAYBE M.K. BROWN'S)

rodrigues' SPLENETIC, CAPTIOUS, LABYRINTHINE, VITIATED, trapique, SCISSILE, ATRABILIOUS, UCONSONANT, BRUMMAGEM, SATURNINE, triste, LACHRYMOSE, CIRCUS!

CARTOONS OF A SEXUAL NATURE THAT

I COULD HAVE EASILY SOLD TO 'PLAYBOY' FOR MORE MONEY, BUT WHAT THE HELL!

© copyright 1987 *rodrigues*

A GROUP OF CARTOONS REQUESTED BY S. GROSS, SOME OF WHICH PERIPHERALLY TOUCH UPON "CONSPIRACY"

and drawn by *rodrigues* (ending with an 'S'. Thank God!)

TRUE TALES OF THE URINARY TRACT

GASTRONOMIQUE COMIQUE

PAR: *rodrigues*

MAN IN MORGUE

BY: *rodrigues*

JOAN CRAWFORD'S STEAM POWERED HAIRBRUSH PADDLER for Children 3-12

NEXT PAGE- IT IMPROVES SOMEWHAT.

June 1978

From "COMEDICS," May 1975

February 1980

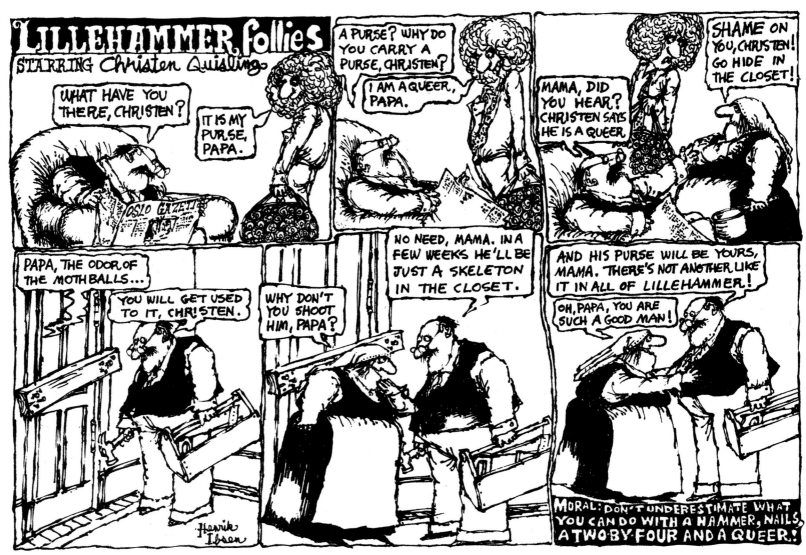

February 1974

April 1973

The *Lampoon*'s editors voted this the funniest cartoon they ever saw.

FLOP-SWEAT
Tony Hendra on Charlie Rodrigues

Rodrigues was the embodiment of the hoary old saw that it's the quiet ones you gotta watch. Although he always called himself "Charlie" on the phone, we editors stuck to his vaguely sinister Iberian last name—perhaps to nourish the hope that when we got to meet him he'd look like one of his own characters, wild-eyed and -haired, asymmetrical, jaggedly angular, out of control, hilariously repellent—in every sense, black. Black as sin and decay and perversion: all the excruciating physical and moral deformities he rendered with such obsessive glee and attention to delicious, horrible detail. I can't remember now whether I did finally meet him or whether he just sent us a photograph of himself—I do have a pretty clear image of sitting across a table from him, which doesn't mean I did (the 1970s were like that). But I was certainly rocked with the same uncontrollable laughter his drawings induced when I found out that our most over-the-top artist was indeed a Charlie, a lovable, balding dumpling of a guy you'd be more likely to hug, rather than a Rodrigues you'd run screaming from, flop-sweat flying off you in buckets, simultaneously pissing and shitting yourself.

I never failed to fall on the floor at his stuff, but I also relished it, couldn't take my eyes off it, marveled at how he managed the space, the wild asymmetrical balance to it, not unlike Ronald Searle, to whom he owed certain influences (though of a totally different sensibility). He went far, far beyond classic panel cartooning; his style was the diametric opposite of the economy of line of artists like Feiffer and Schultz. But its very grotesqueness was somehow pleasing; it had a kind of hideous beauty. And, for all the gore and violence and bodily fluids, it

was smart. He helped shape the *National Lampoon*'s unique high-low style of comedy, incredible disgustingness paired with intellectual and linguistic fireworks. He was verbally, as well as visually, witty, fluent in several languages (including Latin), throwing off double puns and multilingual wordplay with ridiculous ease. His lettering alone is hilarious, oozing a literary joy in words even as it's wallowing happily in the depravity it describes. And he loved to fool with forms, breaking off a comic strip in midstream, commenting on the stupidity (or worse) of his own characters and plots, a postmodern artist long before postmodernism was even a gleam in its daddy's eye. Rodrigues was a prepostmodernist. (He might even have been that daddy. He certainly has a better claim than Derrida.)

But most of all, Charlie had a great time. It still comes through in every line he drew. Whenever we talked (I wanted him in every issue I edited), he never hung up without repeating why he loved the *Lampoon* so: because, unlike anywhere else, he could do anything he wanted, go to whatever lengths he found funny, and we would never say, "Okay, Rodrigues, now you've gone too far." How could we? Not only were we in awe of him (which he was far too modest to have believed), but more important, however far he went he always made sure he took you along for the glorious, gleeful, brilliantly written, hilariously jarring ride.

BRIAN McCONNACHIE

If the story of the *National Lampoon* were a script by Rod Serling, the main character would have been Brian McConnachie, a man who, his colleagues were

convinced, was from another planet. Whether this is true or not, I can't say. Or won't say. Or am not allowed to say. I will only tell you that in a group saturated in brilliant chatter, only Brian could leave the others speechless.

He is a tall man, elegantly put together, firmly bow-tied, stately and somewhat diffident in manner. A patrician, he stood out in the cramped, characterless office space inhabited by what appeared to be a bunch of otherwise

PHOTO BY MICHAEL GOLD

unemployable misfits. What Brian brought to the magazine was an outsider's point of view (some thought far outside—in fact, from a different dimension).

His work simply couldn't be characterized as being one thing or the other. The dreamlike and odd scenarios left some confused. He emphasized the illogical and the absurd, and he demolished the reader's cozy expectations. He was, in fact, the staff Dadaist of the *National Lampoon*: our man descending a staircase. These days, his outsider humor seems like Outsider

art. His work was too strange, too inexplicable for him to be our Marcel Duchamp. He was our Henry Darger.

Brian told Tony Hendra that he'd come to the magazine from the "Floor of Lost Men" at the ad agency he'd been laboring at. (*What* could he have been writing for *them*?) At the *Lampoon*, he and his work were so appealingly different from anything or anyone else that he quickly became every other writer's favorite writer, an indispensable and iconic member of the *Lampoon* cohort. He'd found a home.

The surprising thing is that once he found it, he didn't stay forever. He was at the magazine only four years. He left to pursue television writing, acting, and, like some politician caught in flagrante delicto, to spend more time with his family. The work Brian did during those too-few years is still vibrant and incredibly funny. It may even be timeless. In any case, it is well loved, here on Earth, and on his home planet.

—Rick Meyerowitz

From "Kit and Kaboodle," June 1973

THE OVERNIGHT
Sean Kelly

From time to time, Brian, who liked to pretend it was 1920-something and we were all at the *New Yorker*, would invite his fellow editors out to spend a weekend at the McConnachie family vacation home in Mattituck, on Long Island. On summer Friday noons, as he set out for Penn Station, dressed in his too-short-in-the-leg seersucker suit, he conjured visions of West Egg, blue gardens, and yellow cocktails.

Once, three of us took him up on his hospitable offer.

Our train was a local and was running late. The bar car's stock was depleted by Riverhead; it was a moonless midnight when we got to the house. As we entered, Brian urged us to to make ourselves at home, but quietly, please, for his lady wife was likely already abed. So, it seemed, she was; and after bidding us an abrupt goodnight, Brian hastened to join her. We set out in search of other rooms, preferably bedrooms. We found only a kitchen and bathroom. Leaving was out of the question—it had begun to rain, and we had no notion of where in hell, geographically speaking, we were. We'd have to make it through the night. George got the couch.

Dawn slouched in, chilly, damp, and gray, followed, after some hours, by Brian, refreshed and cheery—his glasses gleaming in that extraterrestrial way they sometimes did when they caught the light just so.

"Looks like it's going to rain all day," said he. "So let's dress up as pirates and go play mini-golf."

TEEN BABY TUB TIME
M. K. Brown

In the late 1970s, Brian suggested I interview for a job in L.A. on a scripted comedy show for NBC. I got the job. Besides Brian, my fellow writers were Peter Elbling, Bill Murray, and Brian Doyle Murray.

It was soon apparent that some strange stuff was going to be produced by this eclectic group. Each morning we had meetings in every room of our cottages. By afternoon we'd spread out to the swings on a nearby playground and cafés around the neighborhood. By the time I went to bed every night, my face hurt from laughing so much.

We all wrote some very silly stuff, but the silliest and strangest ideas came from Brian. They seemed to be from some *other*, well-ordered, logical, yet screwy universe you'd like to spend some time in—perhaps. One such idea was "Teen Baby Tub Time," a quiz show in which teenagers would be dressed in raincoats and made to perform some difficult task involving water and hoses, I was never clear on the details; nor could I picture it on television, except maybe in Japan.

The point is, when our crew of offbeat writers, each contributing from pretty far out on his own particular limb, needed to convey an important request to NBC via our producer; pitch a new idea; or ask for more per diem, a better car, or a helicopter for a certain scene, we sent Brian McConnachie because he was the tallest, and the straightest-looking, and he wore a suit and tie in Los Angeles. To them, Brian looked like he was from Earth, but we knew better.

MOGDAR
Ellis Weiner

My first editor was Brian McConnachie. I'd come in for my monthly sit-down with him already disoriented by the remodeling going on around the office (plywood partitions forming a narrow rat-run to his office in the rear), where he'd be beaming in his immaculate linen suit and bow tie. I'd ask what issue he was working on next, and in his stammering, offhand, impressionistic way, he'd "explain": e.g., "Oh, you know—cocktails . . . bullet trains . . . cigarette holders, Le Jazz Hot . . . Zeppelins . . . twenty-three skidoo . . ." Naturally, not wanting to give offense, and to pretend I was competent, I would nod and say as close to nothing as possible.

The piece I'd submit would, inevitably, be not quite right. Then, when the issue came out three months later, I would see what he meant (and that, if I had been smarter, I'd have understood—or at least have asked intelligent questions). His writing was always great and sui generis.

It was only after he had left the magazine that I came to learn that his fellow editors had decided he was an emissary "from the planet Mogdar." Now you tell me.

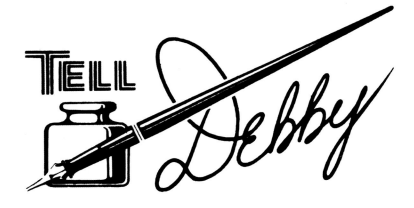

Dear Debbie: My parents fight all the time and it makes me very unhappy. I love them both so much. They used to just fight when my daddy would come home from work but now my daddy is home all the time because his boss punched him in the eye. My daddy is very sick and has to take a lot of medicine and it makes him act funny. My mommy must have caught what my daddy has because I see her take a lot of daddy's medicine.

Every night when I say my prayers I pray to God to make my mommy and daddy all better so they will stop fighting. I love them both and it is awful when they fight.

Timmy Nurock
Denver, Colorado

Young man, you spelled my name D-e-b-b-i-e. My name is spelled D-e-b-b-y.

Dear Debby: Several weeks ago, my husband and I attended a lovely dinner party given by some neighbors. We had a wonderful time. But when we arrived home, we found much to our shock and disgust, that our beautiful new home had been robbed. Several valuable paintings were stolen, our wall safe was open, and missing were stocks and quite a large sum of money as well as my jewelry. We had just moved into the house and had not had the time to purchase any insurance. We were absolutely miserable for days and days. But we began to pull ourselves together and we realized we possessed the health and energy to earn all of our losses back. That's when the real horrible part happened. We receive a subpoena and notification that we are being sued for the house and all of the money we have in the bank. It seems the burglar, while robbing our house, broke his wrist and is suing *us* for negligence. We checked with our lawyers, and they inform us the burglar has an open and shut case. The burglar, by the way, doesn't have to show up in court and is allowed to use the name John Doe.

I can't understand any of this, Debby. My entire world has just crumbled. My husband and I might have made it back from the robbery but this is too much! We can't go on. We're both just sick!

Mrs. A. Reese.
Oyster Bay, N.Y.

How terribly sad for you both.

Dear Debby: My wife is a delightful woman but she's not exactly the brightest person on earth. She hired a carpenter and had him build a huge tree house in the woods behind our house. Then she moved our three children into the tree house. She's taken a part time job and turns over all of her earnings to the kids, who spend the entire thing on candy and toys. Whenever the truant officer comes around (they've since dropped out of grammar school), the children get her to lie to him. I am very upset. I think they have her in their power.

A Worried Father
Davenport, Iowa

Oh, how awful.

Dear Debby: Our next-door neighbors went away on an extended vacation and left their children in the care of their maternal grandmother. She is a dear old lady and quite capable of handling the task. The children are four and five, and quite well behaved. Everything there is completely in order except for one thing. The kind, precious love got in her head to fix the children's teeth. When I realized what she was up to, I commented in passing that the children still had their baby teeth and the fine effort she was planning would all be for nothing. Then, most unexpectedly, she turned on me and told me to get the "hell out of" her life. What could I do? I watched her from my window. She started making braces from bent kitchenware and baker's cord. She trussed up the children's mouths so horribly they can neither eat or speak. Their lips and mouths are so gruesomely distorted with parts of colanders, spatulas, ladles, etc., that it's absolutely inhuman to look at. But, as I said, outside of this, she's perfectly wonderful to them. Now she feeds them through a funnel.

I really don't know if I should say anything. I certainly don't want her to turn on me as she did before, but at the same time, I feel very sorry for the poor children. It's a decision I'm having some difficulty with.

Maria Corless
Springfield, Ill.

That's most inauspicious.

Above: December 1973, March 1974, August 1975
Opposite: May 1975

Our Insides
Each human body has
more wiring, tubing,
insulation, filters, and
circuitry than the entire
Bell system. Our digestive
tract alone, if stretched
out in one straight line,
would allow us to have
dinner in Fort Lauderdale,
Florida, and pass our
wastes in Lexington,
Kentucky.

OUR WONDERFUL BODIES

by Brian McConnachie

For a moment, mentally picture yourself standing in front of a full-length mirror. Behold the body. Let's, for the purpose of example, imagine ourselves as a national park. Our eyes are two ranger stations on the constant lookout for forest fires and rampaging bears. The face is our own private Mt. Rushmore, which serves as our identification. Our arms and legs, giant redwoods; and the tufts of hair at the top of each, foliage. Toes and fingers are knotty roots, and there are additional bushes growing on the top of the monument. Standing firm and serene, we are Nature's trophy and a woodsman's paradise. But now, imagine a motorcycle gang or some of those rampaging bears invading our picnic area (the stomach). Knocking over trash pails and zooming along unauthorized paths, they have disturbed the serenity of the park, and official action must be taken. The rangers in the ranger station are helpless to do anything for two reasons. First, because they cannot see the trouble (it is

photographed by Ede Rothaus

directly below them), and secondly, it is not their job. They are forest rangers assigned to survey everything and they cannot leave their posts. What will happen? How will this mayhem be stilled? Just then, a glacier of late-melting winter snow falls into a nearby stream overflowing the stream which in sequence flushes the motorcycle gang and the rampaging bears with the force of a Niagara right out the front of our Rushmore.

It all seems quite simple; but it isn't.

The human body is probably the greatest marvel in the wonderful world around us. In our wildest understandings, we can just begin to comprehend the myriad, complex functions which go on ceaselessly, from the day of our birth to the day when it all just stops. For as much as we have come to know about the body, there is that much again to learn. But thanks to modern techniques and the official cooperation of state hospitals, nursing homes, and prisons, our scientific explorers are,

BRIAN MCCONNACHIE 169

The Fifteenth Islet of Langerhans
Magnified 2,000 times. Its job is to make sure that the little shelf that your heart rests on gets enough to eat.

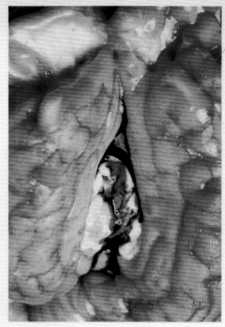

The Hernia
Located in the lower abdomen, it is considered by many as Nature's retribution to men for already having given women the menstrual cycle.

Green Corpuscles,
resting. An important part of our body when we lived in the sea, green corpuscles once did a thriving business manufacturing our scales. Displaced by their more imaginative red and white colleagues, there is not much left for them to do.

day by day, closing in on the mysterious, uncharted territories that abound within us. Perhaps one day we will know all there is to know about the body; but until that day comes, we must content ourselves with the wonders of how the liver makes bile, the miracle of wisdom teeth, and the timely function of sweat glands.

It has been often said and it is true: We take our bodies for granted. Though we pay rapt attention to our outside shell, we expect our inside to do its job, as we do our jobs, and not complain like older parents who sometimes feel neglected and whine about their condition. We live our lives relatively unaware of all the unbridled inventiveness going on inside. Only when we are forced to defecate or expel a mouthful of mucus or remove congealed darkened phlegm clinging to our nostril hairs do we outwardly share in the wondrous process. Silently and efficiently, the body does what it must do to keep us on our feet in search of further nourishment. It is per-

haps that the body's quiet labors are conducted with such stealth which eventually lulls us into our understandable neglect. We can't see the functions and we certainly can't hear them. If our bone marrow made whizzing and churning sounds when it produced blood and our muscles made ripping and snapping noises and our white corpuscles gave out maniacal banshee cries every time they attacked invading bacteria, we would, no doubt, be comforted by the industrious sounds of craft. But that would be impractical, and the body must have reasons of its own for conducting itself the way it does. Save for the faint beat of the heart and the barely perceptible exchange of our breath, there are no outward signs of the diligence within. One could almost believe it didn't want us to know. It is always so quiet.

But when the body wants something, there is no end to which it won't go. It wakes us up in the middle of the night if it is thirsty and makes us get it a glass of

The Eyebrow
Magnified fifty times, no two eyebrows are alike. Though they are exactly alike when magnified only two or three times.

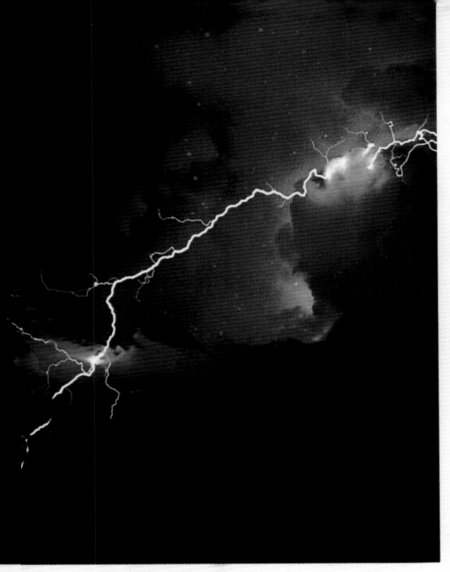

water. If it is in need of sexual release, it'll march us all over town until it finds its own brand of fulfillment. If for some reason it becomes angry with us, its recourses are seemingly endless: inflate the appendix, manufacture gallstones, leave the air passage open when we are eating bulky food, to name but a few. It can make us walk into doors, hit ourselves in the thumb with hammers, make us jump into freezing cold waters. It can humiliate us in front of our friends by urinating in our clothing. It can make us fall asleep when we don't want to fall asleep. And while asleep, it can scare us half to death by conjuring up monstrous images, tossing us off of a cliff or out of a tree. On a capricious whim, it can make just our legs fall asleep, or our eyes cross, or lower things out our nose. It can do anything it wants. It makes up 94 percent of us, and there is nothing we can do about it. Our meager 6 percent shell just has to go along. It can make us run till we drop from exhaustion, swim till we about drown, and get us into punching fights with one another. These are the cold, indisputable facts, and there is no way around them. If we attempt to take control by drugging our bodies with liquor or pills, its defenses simply release all of our muscle tension, and we drop like a placenta. But our small percent is an important percent, and our insides know this. As the container, we keep it from slithering off in several directions at once. It is truly a *good* symbiotic relationship. And we should be happy. Happy because our insides are not wicked or mischievous by nature.

One has only to imagine what it would be like if we had, say, the insides of an elephant. We would all be walking around with tusks, a big funny looking trunk, and a silly little tail. No, our bodies, as a whole, are quite serious. Sometimes they frustrate us, sometimes they give us joy, but we always should love them because they are *our wonderful bodies.* □

The Head
Captured on film is the inside of a Chinaman's brain while the Chinaman was attempting to pronounce the letter *l*.

The Soul
Once believed to be everlasting and the source of our interest in religion, the soul now busies itself with helping us pick out flashy clothes and R & B records.

A Healthy Pancreas
is the hardest working organ in the body. It filters blood, digests food, cleans up your stomach after meals, regulates the heartbeat, supervises over the small and large intestines, controls the muscles, produces calcium for the bones, keeps us walking in an upright position, and was responsible for inventing the opposable thumb.

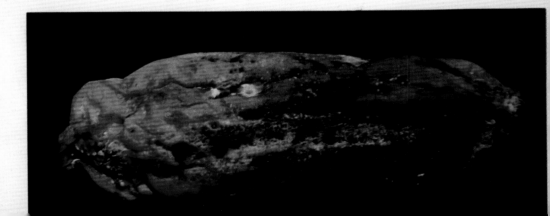

National Lampoon Encyclopedia of Humor, 1973

MR. McCONNACHIE
Chris Kelly

There are perfectly good books about the importance of Doug Kenney (by Josh Karp) and Michael O'Donoghue (by Dennis Perrin) and two about Tony Hendra (by Tony Hendra), but none about Brian McConnachie, who's at least as influential as they are. I wonder why that is.

I suppose he missed the boat by not being dead or Tony Hendra.

I remember Brian being more, um, *inner-directed* than some of the other editors. There was no trail of broken glass, hurt feelings, and Class 2 drug crimes. When I was a tween, underfoot at the *Lampoon*, my main impression of Brian McConnachie was that he was Henry Beard.

It was only later, when I learned to read (sophomore year, college), that I discovered that Brian McConnachie was *screamingly* funny. For instance:

EMMA PEEL CONTEST

*That's right, **Mrs. Emma Peel**, the one and only, will, for an unspecified period of time, smash you from pillar to post. Heedless of your pitiful cries for mercy, our **Mrs. Peel** will kick, punch, jab, chop, and God only knows what else at your cowering, panting body. Just when you think she's tiring and willing to relent, she offers you her hand and you go to accept it and then whammo—her knee right in your groin. And that's not all. Directly following your beating, you will be rushed by private car to the fabulous Cedars of Lebanon Hospital—hospital to the stars. There you will spend one whole week of carefree recovery as your memory conjures up the most vivid recollections of **Mrs. Emma Peel**: her cat-like crouch, her svelte spring, the aroma from her auburn hair filling your nostrils that second before she flung you to the far wall. No, no, they can't take that away from you. During your stay at Cedars, you will enjoy around-the-clock nurses. And here comes one now to take your temperature. Isn't that nice? But wait, why, that's no nurse! It's **Emma Peel** sneaking in to disconnect your IV and break a chair over your chest.*

Brian McConnachie is one of those rare comic writers who's so funny he makes you yourself less funny, as you force other people to read him while you watch. Like I did to you, just now.

The other explanation for the lack of a Brian McConnachie cult is that his work is almost impossible to categorize, much less explain. How do you recommend him to someone? Who could you possibly say he was like?

Is the Emma Peel Contest a parody? If so, of what? Robert Motherwell said that abstract expressionism resists interpretation. It's like that. Only with Diana Rigg beating you up.

But why? And where could an idea like that start?

One possible clue: In 1974 Diana Rigg appeared fleetingly naked in Tom Stoppard's play *Jumpers*, and McConnachie slipped quietly away from the *Lampoon* offices—as was his wont—and saw it again and again and again.

By some accounts, "again and again and again *and again*."

Around our house it was believed he also carried opera glasses and always sat in the front row.

Or maybe I'm thinking of Henry Beard.

Another clue: A strange man appears at the end of Brian McConnachie and Frank Springer's comic "Heading for Trouble." He announces, like it explains anything: "The world we live in is no joke." This man is never identified, but I think he's supposed to be Dana Andrews. So, "Heading for Trouble," which is one of the three funniest things in the world, might be about Dana Andrews. But why?

Your guess is as good as mine.

February 1974

CHRIS MILLER

I never saw Chris Miller long enough to say anything more than "hello and good-bye" until the *National Lampoon* was just a distant memory, and the two of us had

signed on as the entertainment for a *National Lampoon* cruise to the Bahamas in 1995. It was an all-expenses-paid junket, and the whole thing sounded awful, so I said yes. When we boarded ship, those in charge had no idea that the theme of their cruise was, as we'd been told, "*National Lampoon* Madness." Their front office had told them nothing about it, and beyond giving us cabins and 24/7 access to overloaded buffets, they ignored us until they saw we were happy not to speak. Then they assigned us times to give our talks. I showed slides and spoke one afternoon in a room so brightly lit by sunshine streaming in through portholes that I had to describe the invisible images on the screen to the eight people who showed up.

PHOTO BY BEVERLY LOGAN

the page." No doubt Hendra had stories such as "Caked Joy Rag," reprinted here, in mind when he wrote that. Stories such as "Lunacy" and "The Toilet Papers" caused mass ejaculations. The walls of college dormitories across the land were decorated with the personal work of Chris's many readers.

In 1975 Doug Kenney invited Chris to join him and Harold Ramis to write a *Lampoon* movie. Chris had been touring college campuses, reading his stories about college life, *Tales from the Adelphian Lodge*, to packed audiences. The stories described Chris's experiences in Alpha Delta Phi, also known as Delta house, his Dartmouth fraternity, where, according to him, everyone had a nickname, and his was "Pinto." The film, of course, was *Animal*

Chris was given a time slot that conflicted with the midnight buffet. In the audience was his wife, my wife, me, and the AV guy. It was something beyond hilarious that he told the story of the creation of *Animal House* to an empty room. And while he was speaking, I could hear the sounds of chewing and grunting coming from the dining room next door. It was more like *Animal Farm* than *Animal House*.

Chris had devoted years to crafting fiction for the *National Lampoon*. He was *the* short-story writer of the magazine. His stories were beautifully written, with prose once described by Tony Hendra as being "so explicit it practically ran down

House, and that it skewered its target so perfectly is due in no small part to Chris's contributions.

In 2006 Chris returned to the subject, publishing *The Real Animal House* to tell the true story of his Dartmouth fraternity. It's very funny, and after reading it you can see how profound his impact on the film really was.

Chris lives out near the beach in Venice, California, now. He may be an alter kocker, but he's still a very sexy-looking guy, I can vouch for that: walking on the boardwalk with him, I saw all these young women checking us out, and somehow I knew they weren't looking at me.

—Rick Meyerowitz

FOTO FUNNIES

BABY, YOUR EYES ARE LIKE OPALS FLECKED WITH GOLD.

AND YOUR LIPS. YOUR LIPS ARE LIKE A ROSE OPENING TO THE SUN.

AND YOUR BREASTS ARE LIKE...

UH, YOUR BREASTS ARE LIKE...

GUAVAS? PUMPKINS?

CASABAS? EGGPLANTS? TURNIPS? BEEFSTEAK TOMATOES?

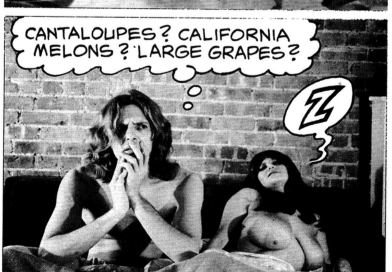

CANTALOUPES? CALIFORNIA MELONS? LARGE GRAPES?

DANIELLE

Chris Miller

How I came to make Foto Funnies with the winner of the Miss New York City Big Breasts Contest three years running in the early 1970s:

One day Michael O'Donoghue returned to the *Lampoon* offices from lunch and gleefully (to the extent Michael could ever be said to be gleeful about anything) showed to anyone who would look at it a flyer some guy had handed him on the street. It bore a photograph of a young woman who was appearing at a Forty-second Street theater. She was smiling and leaning forward so that her bare breasts seemed to flow like a waterfall from her chest. A very large waterfall. A Niagara Falls–level waterfall at the very least. Michael detected a certain *Lampoon* flavor in their immensity and said that we should find a way to use her in the magazine.

Foto Funnies were a popular monthly feature in those days. They'd been invented by Doug Kenney, who wrote and posed for the first bunch of them. The aforementioned O'Donoghue person had then appeared in a few as well. When it was decided that Danielle (for this was her *nomme de poitrine*) should be featured in the next wave of them, I was approached to be her costar. Known to have a certain affinity for the female bazoom, it took me all of a second and a half to decide this was a fine idea.

It seemed to me that whoever shared a Foto Funnies panel with Danielle was unlikely to make much of an impression. If we'd put a *horse* in with her, it wouldn't have made much of an impression—Danielle was going to be the eye magnet and everything else would be OK, fine, whatever. But that was OK: *I'd* look at me even if no one else would, so I wrote some Foto Funnies that made use of her physical attributes and gave myself a few lines as well and off we went to some guy's apartment on the Upper West Side to shoot the first batch of them.

Danielle proved to be all of five feet two inches tall, her genes having apparently been programmed to grow her out instead of up. The other thing she proved to be was a good little actress. Foto Funnies were, in essence, comic strips using photos instead of drawings. The best models to pose in them, therefore, were people who could make themselves look like cartoon characters. Doug Kenney often looked like a cartoon character, even when he wasn't posing in Foto Funnies, and had set the standard. Danielle immediately caught on and was just right with her expressions and body language.

All the Foto Funnies we did with her took place in bed. My favorite one involved her swinging her body so that her immense right boob slugged me in the face. I did feel pleased with myself when I wrote that one. For reasons of verisimilitude, we were unclothed beneath the sheets as well as above them. Danielle, the little minx, kept peeking under them to check out the effect she was having on me. Perhaps because I did not behave as a drooling, highly erect satyr, she took a

liking to me. I was, you know, focusing on getting the shot. At the completion of the shoot, mayhap thinking of me as a challenge, she invited me home with her.

We took a series of unfamiliar (to me) subways that dropped us off near her place in Brooklyn, and shortly were back in bed, this time with no cameras to record our antics. A remarkably enjoyable interlude now occurred, during which we did all the usual things and a couple of (to me) new ones involving her olympian cleavage that would have been impossible with women of lesser mammalian endowment. At length, spent, I lay back, and Danielle went off to the bathroom. It seemed like a good moment to smoke a joint, so I lit one up. My Bic lighter fell on the floor. It wasn't immediately visible so I got down on my hands and knees to look for it and thereby espied what lay under the bed—a set of barbells.

What was this? Did she work out with them? Was that where her queen-size ba-boos had come from? When she returned, I asked her about them. The barbells, that is—not the ba-boos.

"Oh, those are my boyfriend's."

This was the first I'd heard of any boyfriend. "Why does he keep them at your place?" I took a nervous hit off the j.

"Silly. He lives here."

I coughed explosively. I could picture the guy walking in at any moment with biceps as big as her boobs, and finding nothing remotely amusing about the humorist in his bed.

Setting a new land-speed record getting back into my clothes, I bade Danielle a fond farewell, and was out the door like a character from a French bedroom farce, still buttoning my shirt as I ran down the steps of her brownstone.

The Foto Funnies we shot that day proved to be most popular and so we produced a string of additional ones in the weeks and months that followed, also featuring Danielle. I did not return, however, to her apartment in Brooklyn. Just to make entirely sure of my continued good health, I did not return to *Brooklyn* for another five years. After a while, someone else inherited the Foto Funnies job, and Danielle's tenure in them came to an end.

Much time passed. In 1992 *National Lampoon* put out its last issue and went to dead magazine heaven. I was, by now, living in Los Angeles, writing screenplays. Another fifteen years went by. Having published a memoir called *The Real Animal House*, I launched a Web site, through which I began to receive email. On the Web site, I featured some of the Foto Funnies I'd been in and wrote the story of my visit to Danielle's apartment. And one day an email came in from . . . her son! He enjoyed seeing these shots of Mom as she had once disported herself, and he said that yes, he knew the dude with the barbells quite well. In fact, he called him Father.

FOTO FUNNIES

EXCUSE ME, IS THIS BED OCCUPIED?

WHY, UH, NO.

MMMMM, I'M GLAD.

OOOH, I WANT ONE OF YOUR CIGARETTES.

I JUST LOVE TO SUCK ON THINGS!

LISTEN, LET'S MAKE IT!

WHAT?!

WHAP!

WHEN ARE YOU MEN GOING TO STOP TREATING ME AS A SEXUAL OBJECT?

FOTO FUNNIES

OKAY, FOR THE NEXT FRAME, HOLD YOUR LEFT BREAST TO HIS EAR AS IF IT'S A TELEPHONE.

DRAPE THE OTHER ONE OVER HIS HEAD, BUT DON'T COVER HIS EYES.

NOW, YOU STICK YOUR FINGER UP HER...

WHAT!?

NOW, YOU JUST HOLD ON A MINUTE!

I'VE JUST ABOUT HAD IT WITH THIS VULGAR, TACKY, INSULTING SHIT! STICK IT IN HIS EAR, PUT IT UP HIS NOSE... JUMPING JESUS!

IN FACT, I'M FUCKING SICK OF YOU, YOUR FOTO FUNNIES, AND YOUR MAGAZINE, SO BLOW IT OUT YOUR ASS, PIG!

AND AS FOR YOU, YOU IMMATURE, VOYEURISTIC, MASTURBATING LITTLE BOYS...

CAKED JOY RAG

BY CHRIS MILLER

It was three o'clock on a Sunday afternoon. I decided to beat the meat.

I looked up from my book, around the parlor. Mother was knitting, reading a mystery novel, and eating crackers dipped in an onion preparation, sending a firestorm of clackings, crunchings, and page-turnings sweeping across the room at Father, who glared indignantly back at her through his *New York Times*. I yawned loudly, closed my book, and stood up.

"Guess I'll take a nap."

"That's nice, dear." Mother turned a page.

The *Times* rattled in Dad's white-knuckled grasp. He had reached the Business section.

On my way to the stairs, I pinpointed my little brother Willy in the kitchen, on the phone. Now I had only to check Grandma's location. She was well into the December of her life and given to spates of extreme paranoia. The current spate had lasted about two and a half years. Often I had caught her peering through keyholes or listening behind doorways, taking rapid notes in a small, leather volume. At night, I believed, she stole muttering to her attic chambers, switched on her short-wave, and sent out the day's entries in code.

I found her in Willy's room with the receiver of the upstairs phone pressed against the hearing device in her chest. Her eyes were wide; she was writing furiously.

I had to get her away from my room. She might feel the floor vibrating when I really got to whacking it.

"Grandma, guess what?"

She spun around, covering the phone with her notebook, her features freezing comically. Then a crafty look came over her face.

"Look!" she cried, flinging one long, skinny finger at the window. "A flying saucer!"

I looked. I saw no sign of a flying saucer, only some kids playing noisy softball next door. When I turned back to her, the phone was on the hook and the notebook had vanished. She was the picture of innocence, whistling a little tune, scuffing the toe of her old-lady shoe into the carpet.

"Grandma," I said, "I think Father is going to yell at Mother."

"What makes you think *I'd* be interested in *that*?" I knew I had her when her eyes became suddenly shifty.

"Yup, old man gonna blow his top any minute now." She was already edging for the stairs. I walked past her, into my room, wedging the door closed with the usual folded magazine: I had no lock.

The bed! Sighing, I dropped my pants to my knees and fell gratefully back onto it. A sudden shriek of dismay ripped the air, and out from between my legs streaked Puffles, our cute family cat. He hit the floor, rebounded to my chair, launched

himself to the dresser top, knocking my Olivo Hair Pomade onto the floor. I stood, pulled up my pants, walked deliberately across the room, grabbed Puffles, and hurled him out the door. Puffles told me to go fuck myself and I told Puffles to eat it.

Let's see now. Mother and Father in parlor. Willy in kitchen. Grandma crouching near parlor doorway. Puffles headed downstairs, Uncle Ernie in Buffalo. President Eisenhower at Camp David. Okay, coast clear. I dropped my pants and yanked open the drawer where I kept my cheesecake cache.

I laid it on the bed next to me, my folder of favorite breasts, thighs, and buttocks from years of *Titter* and *Beauty Parade*. Eve Meyer with her pout and her pendulous heavies! Bettie Page bursting from black-lace nothings! Nameless hot chocolates and sepia sirens! Sultry hip-flippers and torrid torso-tossers! I let my eyes flow over each cutout lady, the focus of my vision fondling remembered boob-hangs and bun-swells.

Hello. In my left hand, my Zeppelin was beginning to inflate. I riffled through the pix with accelerating haste to get to the really good ones I had arranged to come last. I put the rest on the floor, folded my pillow comfortably, and switched hands. One by one, I held my favorites before my eyes, scrutinizing them minutely.

A brunette lying nude on her stomach was my third favorite. She looked at me over her shoulder, eyes nearly closed, pink tongue just showing between full lips. Where her thighs met the cleft of her buttocks was a dark diamond of pulse-quickening shadow. My molehill was racing toward mountainhood.

My second favorite was an Earth Mother pulling a dress from her shoulders so that two vast flesh melons were spilling out. I mean, they were just *spilling* out of there. In some unknown but undoubtedly interesting fashion, she had recently excited her nipples. They had popped into high relief, fascinating circular terrains of oddly placed bumps and nodules surrounding a central volcano. *Thrubba dubba dubba!*

Finally, my number one—two girls in a bubble bath. "Italian bimbos," said the caption. The brunette stood in the foreground, her back to me, one foot up on the side of the tub. The blonde was framed between the brunette's legs, smiling with great happiness. They were collaborating in washing the brunette's right calf. I concentrated on the juncture of the brunette's thighs, imagining the same clear view of her pizza pie that was obviously what was making the blonde so happy. I licked my lips, my zucchini all athrob.

The last of the visual aids fluttered to the floor as I shut my eyes, crossed my left ankle over my right, turned my face to the left, and began . . .

. . . The pirates had me chained to a wooden post at the

docks. My elegant clothes were in tatters by now, the ruffled, white shirt torn to my waist. Velasquez, the fat, swarthy captain, had long since taken my boots; the cobblestones pressed my feet painfully.

We were in Skull Cove, a pleasure-oriented free port frequented by scum such as my captors. Already, they were lavishly spending the riches of the merchantman on which, until a few days ago, I was being conveyed as an emissary of King Charles to negotiate a certain political matter with the Spanish throne. Instead, I would now be held for ransom; I was part of the booty. Two grubby guards, impatient to join the rest of the crew at the inns and bawdy houses, waited beside me for Velasquez to return with the high chieftain of the port, the notorious lady pirate Red MacTave.

"Oi still say we oughter take 'is nuts, Bones," the smaller guard was arguing. "'E can still be ransomed; 'is voice'll just be a mite 'igher, that's all."

"Aw now, Brug," said Bones, seven feet tall and coal black, "you jus' relax. You hear de Cap'n. We got to keep this fine gen'amum in-tack, leas' 'til Missy MacTave done look him over."

On "in-tack," Bones jabbed me playfully in the ribs with his finger. It felt like an ebony battering ram, but I kept my features cool and disdainful. I would take no shit from scoundrels such as these.

Suddenly, Maureen O'Hara strode into view. Velasquez trotted to keep up with her. I could see the shapely muscles ripple on her thighs as they flashed through her skirt of hanging thongs. On top she wore a blouse of rough blue fabric, the tails of which she had tied beneath her freely swinging breasts. Her hair was molten flame.

I had been chained kneeling. Velasquez puffed to my side and grasped my chin moistly, tilting my head up roughly for inspection.

"Thees ees heem, jos' like I say, hey Red?" He smiled hopefully at her through his matted black beard.

"Let him go, pig. You are his social inferior." Though she murmured it, Velasquez snatched his hand away like my skin had turned suddenly red-hot. Bones and Brug exchanged significant glances.

She gazed down at me, her eyes snapping with . . . interest? I met her gaze. She bent closer. I could see her breasts press heavily against her blouse. Her lips were ripe, red, slightly parted. Closer she came. The perfume of her breath enwreathed me. She kissed me hungrily.

"Jesus Christ, Frances," bellowed Velasquez, "will you for Christ's sake stop making all that noise?"

"What noise, John?" MacTave knelt before me, ran a fingertip over the ridges of my stomach.

"You know goddamn well what noise! Jesus Christ!"

"John, really, *must* you use that language?" In the tatters of my breeches, her hands were leaving trails of cold fire on my thigh.

Over MacTave's shoulder I saw Bones sliding a small leather volume from his shirt. He began taking rapid notes.

"Ball four!" came a shrill cry from a bawdy house next door. "They're loaded up!"

"Well, if someone around here [MacTave's left hand was sliding slowly up my legs] would get his nose out of the paper [the other was plucking at my buckle] for a few minutes once in a while [it opened; her hand moved downwards] and talk to someone, for heaven's sake, [the hands met gently, surrounding me with feathery bliss] then I wouldn't—"

"Oh, horseshit!" yelled Velasquez and dissolved into a fit of coughing.

"What? What was that? I didn't get what came after 'for heaven's sake'!" Bones looked anxiously from Velasquez to MacTave.

"HEY!" roared Velasquez, regaining his breath. "WHAT THE HELL ARE YOU WRITING? WHAT THE HELL IS THIS?"

"Strike two!" cried the voice from the bawdy house. Somewhere, a bell was ringing insistently.

"John, you must learn to control your mouth." MacTave was stroking my now unencumbered mizzenmast, planting small, moist kisses on the crow's nest.

"GOOD CHRIST ALMIGHTY! I'M GOING OUT!" Velasquez stalked off. I heard a door slam. The bell had stopped, to be replaced by a loud clanging. An alarm?

"Strike three!" screamed the bawdy house. "Yer out!" CLANG! CLANG! CLANG! CLANG! CLANG!

I opened my eyes. Someone down in the kitchen was knocking the knife handle against the radiator pipe, the signal that there was a phone call for me.

I sighed and rose from the bed. Pulling my pants up far enough to walk, I went to the phone.

"Hello!"

"Did you get the third geometry problem?"

"Huh? Robbie?"

"Yeah. Wow, I just finished it. Took me *two* hours!"

"Well, I haven't done my geometry yet." I bounced my limp turnip in my hand. It shouldn't take me long to get off the phone and then I could . . .

"That's okay! Just tell me if this sounds right!" Mathematical particulars began pouring from the phone. Hmmm . . .

. . . The penthouse was lush, opulent. The city looked like millions of tiny, radiant jewels spilled on black velvet. Fresh from necking hotly in the taxi, Laura and I came straight to her bedroom. I was sitting on her bed, unbuttoning my shirt. Laura stood facing me, her soft, overstuffed body straining against her fashionable dress. It hooked in the front and she was toying with the clasp.

From previous experience, I knew she would blush. She was shy about undressing while I watched. The blush would spread up from her chest, through the freckles on her face, finally reaching her red-blond hair. It would happen soon; she had on that heavy-lidded, soft-lipped face she always wore when we were about to do it.

The phone rang. Biting her lip, she answered it, eyes still on me. I languidly removed my shirt, watching my aroused lover try to focus on the voice coming from the receiver.

"First," she said, "you'll need your protractor."

I couldn't refuse. I slid my pants off. Her eyes grew large. I reached up and unsnapped her clasp. The dress gave as mammoth softness shifted within. Laura closed her eyes. She could barely maintain. How wonderful! I slid the silken garment over her shoulders. She had to juggle the receiver to allow the dress to move down her arms, but then it was free and I slid it over her hips. It puddled about her ankles.

"What do you think?" Laura was stammering. "After all that, I couldn't get the goddamn angles to come out to 360 degrees!"

"Try dropping a hypotenuse," I suggested huskily. She was soft, rounded, and freckly, straining against the reinforced black bra she had been obliged to have specially constructed for her unique proportions. I reached around her broad back and unlocked the bulging under-thing, and flesh just went all *over* the place. She was blushing! Adorable!

"I did," she breathed. "Nothing. So I erected a cone on the surface of each sphere."

Accordingly, I stroked each cone with an open palm. They swelled to bursting turgidity before my hands had completed a single transit. What divine altitudes!

"Suppose I intersected your rhombus with a cylinder?" I murmured. My hand slid down the long parabola of her stomach into black silk.

"Rhombus? Cylinder? What are you talking about?"

"Mmmmmmmm." The panties were off. Her red-gold isosceles triangle sparkled and shimmered in the candlelight.

"Your theorems are as thick as honey and taste like sweet oysters."

"Huh? What? You crazy?"

"Ahhhhhhh!" My tongue bisected the tender trihedron.

"Jeez," she said, "I'm callin' Steve Greenfield. You're screwy!"

SLORP! LICK! SLOBBER! SMERP!

Click.

I opened my eyes. The taste of hard black plastic was in my mouth; one end of the receiver glistened wetly. I hung up.

Judging from the appearances of my throbbing ICBM, blastoff was seconds away. I rushed to my bed, fell down backwards, and swung my legs over my head so that the missile hove into proper azimuth. I craned my neck and, with some difficulty, reached the nose cone . . .

. . . Chooch was doin' the bop with Rita. Foojie was dirtyboogyin' with Valerie. Angelo didn't care it wasn't a slow number, he was doin' the fish with Roseanne anyway. I leaned my chair back on two legs, hookin' my fingers in my belt loops, feelin' good. It was Saturday night at the clubhouse an' the Bopping Dukes of Avenue A were workin' out.

Dolores sauntered over to me. She had just smoked a reefer and her eyes were bright. "Meow?" she asked. I looked up at her coolly, snapped my gum, and . . .

Meow?

I opened my eyes. Puffles was sniffing delicately at my exhaust vent. I reached up and pushed his face into it, closing my eyes as his nose made contact . . . .

. . . Dolores sauntered over. She had just smoked a reefer, and her eyes were bright.

"'Ey Tony," she said, "I hear you gotta sanawich fuh me."

"Shoo I do," I answered, adjusting the line of my DA with thumb and forefinger. "Come an-a get it."

"Oo bop sha boo, baum ba baum baum baum," sang the Cleftones.

"I'm-a hungry, Tony. I'm-a think I'm-a gonna eat-a some of you sanawich."

Her hair was thick and black, her lips very red. A small, gold cross hung between her bulging breasts. Going to her hands and knees before me, she took the tongue of my zipper between her small, sharp teeth and began tugging it slowly down.

"Cow wa wa wa wa wa wa, ho dough dough dough," insinuated the Heartbeats.

Dolores had completed the unzipping and was unreeling my great dago flagpole.

"'Ey, you gotta nize big-a sanawich, Tony!"

"Atsa right. It's-a juicy, too. Go 'head, take a bite-a."

Dolores laughed, shook her hair out of the way, and, in a sudden moist thrust, was rooting for truffles in my coal shute. "Meowr," she whimpered. Her nails raked my flesh, but, as War Councillor of the Dukes, I'm tough, so I didn't let on like it hurt.

Then she started on my sanawich.

"MEEEEEOOOOWWWW!" she cried.

Whoops, whoops, I think . . .

"MEEEEEOOOOOOWWWWWW!"

I can feel it, yes, it's . . .

"WHAT ARE YOU DOING?"

Now yes yes yes yes yes . . .

"I SAID, 'WHAT ARE YOU DOING?'"

I opened my eyes. Grandma.

"I . . . I'm looking at a pimple."

"WELL, STOP LOOKING AT IT! WHAT ARE YOU DOING TO PUFFLES? WHAT'S THAT ON HIS NOSE? . . . OH!!"

I released Puffles. He streaked from the room. Grandma was so beside herself she was actually forgetting to take notes.

"FRANCES! JOHN! COME SEE HOW YOUR SON SPENDS HIS SUNDAY AFTERNOONS!"

I had to get out of there. I leapt from my bed and fell on my face. Kicking the tangled pants from my ankles, I regained my feet and burst past Grandma. Eggplant in hand, I flew up the attic stairs and flung myself on Grandma's bed . . .

. . . The pounding on the heavy, oaken lab door began as I had almost completed transmission of the SOS. As usual, Zarkov's instructions had been perfect. The Z Beam generator was working exactly as he had predicted.

"He's up there, John! He's locked himself in my room!" Old Queen Azura's voice quavered over the pounding.

"WHAT'S THIS I HEAR ABOUT YOU HOMO-ING YOURSELF OFF? JUMPING JESUS!"

Ming had arrived!

My message completed, I snapped the immense generator off. The pounding had intensified. They were smashing the door with a heavy piece of furniture. Would it hold until Prince Barin's stratosleds arrived? Well, no use worrying about what you can't control.

"Dale," I said, "come over here and sit on my face."

GAHAN WILSON

I have always been astonished by Gahan Wilson's work. His first cartoons appeared in *Playboy* in 1957, when I was beginning high school. His aesthetic was completely new to me. I marveled at his style of drawing and his use of color. How were those things so luminous? But it was his vision—not his humor, his vision—that caught me. There was nobody else like him anywhere. I imagined he looked like his drawings: he'd have multiple tentacles and eyes and be waiting behind a door—with a knife! Anyone would be afraid to meet such a person.

Gahan's unique work haunted me and teased from me the notion that to succeed as an artist I, too, would have to be unlike anyone else. Easier said than done. It wasn't so simple to be yourself when you had no idea who the hell you were.

So how did it happen that in 1970 he and I were contributing work to the same magazine? Even now, that—though it's a fact—seems amazingly improbable to me! And meeting him for the first time in 1971: No tentacles! Two eyes! A blue blazer, gray slacks, white shirt, and tie. Hair slicked back, drink in one hand, bright, blonde Nancy Winters holding the other. Here's a fine WASP gentleman, and a lesson: cartoonists never resemble their work!

In 1973, at a Cartoonist's Guild cocktail party (yes, cartoonists have cocktail parties), I introduced Gahan to his hero, Charles Addams. I think they were both at a loss for words because they just stood there and grinned at each other.

Self-portrait, from "My Hundred Years with the *Lampoon*," July 1978

Around that time, Gahan and I were going to meet for lunch. He called to say he couldn't make it. He had bought a Cuisinart, one of the first models imported into the States. While wrestling with the packaging, the "S" blade fell out and landed on his foot, cut through his shoe, and remained there, sticking straight up. When he removed it, it bled so fiercely that with each step, a geyser of blood spurted from the cut in his shoe. Now, I know it's not polite to make fun of the injured, but if that isn't Gahan's life imitating Gahan's art, I don't know what is.

We were lucky to have him at the *National Lampoon*. Gahan said no other publication had ever given him the freedom the *Lampoon* did. He created fiery social satire, an antireligious, antimilitary, antiauthoritarian, oversize dose of distrust of all authority. He'd never done anything else like it anywhere else. Even "NUTS," that sweet dose of childhood nostalgia, is successful mainly because of its deep skepticism and mistrust of adults.

Every day we see proof that we live in Gahan Wilson's world. He has, most probably, imagined our real future. Now, isn't that scary?

—Rick Meyerowitz

C is for Cover-up,
The verb and the noun,
If you don't see it,
Then you won't frown,
If you do see it,
Then you must pray
No one has seen **you**
Looking that way!

O's for Official,
For those things rated true
By the people who run us
And tell me and you
What is and what isn't,
What's up and what's down,
And you'd better believe them,
Or get out of town.

From "How to Spell Conspiracy," January 1990

The first "NUTS" appeared on the first page of the first "Funny Pages," January 1972.

N's for the Nothing
You hear about stuff
Which might get you started
Into calling the bluff
Of those who would fool you
And lead you astray,
And to think for yourself
Instead of their way.

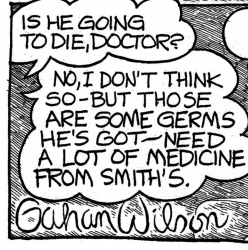

S is for Sneaky
And Slimy and Sly,
For things that slip by you
Which you never spy.
Since they've suckered you silly
And stolen your mind,
You won't even see them
Stealing up from behind.

P is for the Presidents
Who proudly come and go,
And lie and blather constantly,
And finally bore you so
That you come to leave off puzzling
If they're good or bad,
And only ponder if they're just
Another TV ad.

I is for Invisible,
For things you cannot see,
For things that are not printed
Nor shown upon TV.
If you and I see nothing wrong
We cannot place the blame;
That's why the villains laugh at us—
Now isn't that a shame!

NUTS

REMEMBER HOW LONG SOME DAYS IN SCHOOL SEEMED TO LAST? ESPECIALLY FRIDAYS? ESPECIALLY FRIDAYS BEFORE A LONG WEEKEND? BUT THERE WAS NOTHING TO DO BUT SIT THERE AND SIT THERE AND...

...ADABLADA, ISAAC NEWTON BLADABLADABLADA LAWS OF MOTION DABLA...

OH, GOD, THIS HAS TO BE OVER SOON!

©1977

...DABALADABLABLADALAH AHDA 1642-1727 DABLAH DAH REFLECTING TELESCOPE.

WHAT'S THIS DUST ON MY PAPER?

...ADABLABLALADA OF THE SPECTRUM ADABADAH...

...AND MY FINGERNAILS HAVE GOT ALL LONG!

OH, MY GOD—I'M DYING OF OLD AGE! I'M NOT GOING TO LIVE THROUGH THIS GODDAMN BORING CLASS!!!

DABH ABDABAH ABADADAH BABA AR

NO DOZING, THERE!! NOW YOU TELL ME WHAT ISAAC NEWTON SAID ABOUT GRAVITATION AND DO IT NOW!!!

YES'UM! YES'UM! HE, AH—

August 1977

R is for the Rascals
Who run our world for us,
They do it very quietly,
They never make a fuss;
They do it all with puppets
Dressed as common folk and kings,
And now you'll understand, perhaps,
Why you're wearing all those strings.

A is for the Asses
Who claim that all is well,
Whose bland assurances ensure
The world will go to hell.
They'd have us look the other way
As villains kill our seas;
They'd have us smile as others force
The wretched to their knees.

NUTS

Remember how you got yourself involved in weird projects which really made very little sense, but became the most important things in the whole entire world?

I wonder why I never thought of doing this before.

LOT FOR SALE CALL

This is going to be great!

Hey, I guessed just right on how much wood I'd need!

Gahan Wilson ©1977

Well, that sure looks like it'll hold me.

Nice to have something work out o.k. for once!

October 1977

C is for the Craftiness
With which exploiters lurk—
How cunningly they lure us in,
How tidily they work
Ourselves against each other
So we bring ourselves in line,
And march ourselves right to their feet
To give what's yours and mine.

Y is for You, the only way out,
But you've got to get moving
To put them to rout,
You've got to start **looking**,
Make the effort to **see**,
And if you all do it,
By God—we'll be **free**!

Strange Beliefs of Children

by Gahan Wilson

Outside of the occasional surviving stone age tribe come across on an isolated Pacific isle or discovered tucked away in some obscure bend of the Amazon, there is no observable group of humans living on this earth more darkly benighted, more shuddersomely superstitious, or more grossly misinformed than the ordinary children we see pottering about daily at our knee level. Constantly forced to obey the incomprehensible rules of a society they cannot even dimly begin to understand, menaced by awesome diseases and fearsome technological poisons, endlessly presented with unanswerable questions, these tiny creatures, in a brave, if faltering, attempt to explain their basically alien environment to themselves, have created one of the richest troves of strange beliefs ever assembled.

Storm Drain Biters

If a coin or a ball or a marble rolls into the opening of a storm drain, the wise child will try to claw it out with a stick or just leave it alone, as there are things down there which *bite off fingers*.

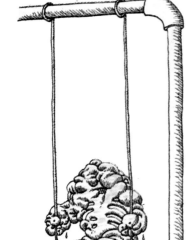

Swinging over the Bar

Swinging over the bar is to be avoided at all costs for it will turn the swinger inside out.

Counting Every Board

Compulsion is an important aspect of children's beliefs, and whose life has not been severely bent this way or that accepting some dare or crossing a drawn line? Here is a self-imposed challenge—the child has vowed he will touch each and every board, *and count it*, on the way home. If he does not do this, he knows that he will be eaten.

continued

continued

Making a Face
If you make a face and are slapped on the back unexpectedly while doing it, the face will stay there for the rest of your life. If you stick your tongue too far out, it will stay like that for the rest of your life, and if you cross your eyes wrong, *they* will stick for the rest of your life.

Step on a Crack and Break Your Mother's Back
Very few children actually believe this, but probably there is not one child who has not tried it, just to see.

The Awful Stuff in the Center of a Golf Ball
If you cut down into the center of a golf ball there is this horrible acid that destroys everything. Somebody once told me they had done it but they weren't burnt so I knew they were lying. I got down as far as the rubber band part once.

Water Fountain Germs
Children know there are germs on water fountains, but are vague on what germs are. They know they are nasty, slimy things. Probably they jump.

Kissing Grandma
If you kiss grandma your lips will get all wrinkled up like hers are as it is catching, but of course there is no way to avoid kissing grandma.

Getting Cramps from Eating
If you eat anything, even a half a hot dog, and you go into the water less than a half hour later, you will get terrible cramps. If you are swimming, you will sink like a stone.

The Toilet Monster
I never knew about this when I was a child, thank God. There's this thing which lives in the toilet, and *likes* it, and when you go late at night and flush the toilet it *wakes the thing up,* so you better hurry getting out of there. This kid was too slow.

Eating Milk and Cherries Together is Poison
This boy told his parents that eating milk and cherries together would kill him, but they wouldn't believe him and they made him do it and now they are sorry. Another thing that will kill you is coke and aspirin, and if you drop a candy bar on the sidewalk and then eat it anyway you are really asking for trouble.

The Exploding Boy
If you block a sneeze wrong, you can burst your eardrums. If you block a burp wrong, you can burst your throat. If you block a fart wrong, you can burst your asshole. If you do all of these, this is what happens.

It is clear, as churches of all denominations have constantly assured us, that God loves to get money.

GOD IS MONEY

by
Gahan Wilson

December 1975

Despite some assertions to the contrary, the most obvious theological law is that power and wealth tend to the greedy and unscrupulous, and that the humble and meek are invariably poor, if not actually enslaved.

A great deal of confusion has arisen in the Christian Church because of a misunderstanding between God and His Only Son. At first, God was delighted with the Boy and would happily watch him blasting fig trees for hours.

But the Lad changed and did contrary and peculiar things, even—and this is what made the Old Fellow particularly mad—throwing money changers out of his Father's very temple. He withdrew His support and taught the Child a badly needed lesson.

OUR FOUNDER

No longer Mr. Nice Guy, He can hardly wait for the second coming to show His Dad (who has taken on a whole new Corporate Image) how tough He can be on those who foolishly look out for anyone but themselves. So you better get smart, and quick.

GERRY SUSSMAN

T he first thing we did was play stickball together, in 1973. Gerry could do things with a Spaldeen that I can't describe here. Gerry struck me out maybe fifteen

times in that first game. Even though we were from different lands—he grew up in Brooklyn, I was from the Bronx—we bonded over stickball and Chinese food and laughter. We collaborated on many articles over many years. And we began each one over a lunch in Chinatown.

I can see him now, walking toward me as I wait in front of that noodle joint on Division Street, his rubbery nose preceding him through the crowd, his face creased in a crooked grin. In one hand he's carrying a briefcase stuffed with ideas, in the other, a bag stuffed with steamed buns to bring home to his wife. And he's wearing his green-and-white varsity jacket with the name "Shorty" beautifully embroidered over his heart.

PHOTO COLLECTION OF SUSSMAN FAMILY ARCHIVES

Gerry loved to suggest dishes that weren't on the menu but seemed as if they should be. ("Hey, Rick, have you tried their Bird Drop Soup? This place makes the best in town. Their birds are imported from Macao." Or: "You have to order the Rin Tin Tin. It's got a secret ingredient! And let's try Chef Loo's Golden Shower Pork Ribs. They're marinated in the chef's own essential juices.") We'd laugh and chew and talk. Perhaps it was the surroundings, but some inspired bit of nonsense always emerged from these lunches. Once, it was an article on funny new sports, such as Turkish towel snapping, or bone swallowing, or uphill crawling, or the herring throw (Native-born Scandinavians had an unfair advantage).

Over another lunch, we decided to do a guide to the 1988 Olympics in South Korea. Gerry wrote about the history, customs, and religion of that country. He wrote reviews of

restaurants serving free-range mice and the mice kabobs that were the local specialty. He wrote about street markets where one could shop for Korean cementware, jackets made of beef jerky, replacements for golf-ball centers, horsemeat jewelry, and inflammable pajamas. He recommended hotels, gave sightseeing tips, even advice on inoculations. (According to Gerry, Korea was the only country in the world that required a shot for cancer.) He even included a chapter on their greatest philosopher, Confusion, and his philosophy, Confusionism. Nothing escaped him. What a fertile mind he had!

When Gerry suggested to the editors that he write a parody of the Yellow Pages, they didn't think it was doable . . . by them. But they knew if anyone could write a funny phone book, and have it look and read exactly right, Gerry could. He did the whole book from A to Z as a ten-page article. In his version, under *Accountants, Jewish*, there are 250 names and addresses. Names such as Albert Sweatgarb, Milton Radish, Seymour Seymour, Harold Underpantz, Murray Rabbi, and Nathan Brillbuilding. The names were perfect, as was everything else in the parody. It was breathtaking in its completeness, and wonderfully funny.

Gerry had a well-used espresso machine in his office. When I would visit, he'd give me that look—sizing me up as if it were the first time we'd met—and say, "A doppio, right?" Somehow I could only nod at the pitch. No comeback was possible. It was strike three—again.

—Rick Meyerowitz

Illustration of Chef Loo by Rick Meyerowitz, February 1985
Opposite: April 1973

196

The joys and the justice, the wit and the wisdom, the pomp and the paradox, the humor and the heartbreak, the suffering and the satisfactions, the ire and the irony, the warmth and the wonder, the mockery and the mischief, the sentiment and the sarcasm, the smiles and the sorrows, the heartache and the humility, the shmaltz and the shrewdness, the zest and the zaniness, the ribaldry and the resilience, the love and the laughter, the dignity and the drama, the pride and the pathos, the pain and the passion, the modesty and the madness, the bravura and the bathos, the faith and the fickleness, the morality and the meanness, the B'nai and the B'rith of Yiddish

by Gerald Sussman

The important thing to remember in learning Yiddish is that many of the words have a "ch" or "cheh" in them. It is similar to the Scottish and German "ch," only thicker, heavier, and juicier.

If you are having trouble pronouncing the "ch," simply put your index and middle fingers as far down in your throat as you can, as if you were inducing a vomit. Bring up a little sound. You are now doing the Yiddish "ch."

Also practice hand gestures, shrugs, and shaking your body up and down. Do a lot of moaning, whining, and sighing.

Here are some hip Yiddish words for you to practice. Master these words. Use them in your regular line of conversation and you will elevate your ordinary talk into poetry and theatre. No other language sounds so rich and resourceful, so full of nuance and shades of meaning. No other language can give you so much warmth, humanity, and style.

chalopshlikel

Pronounced CHALOP-SHLUH-KUL, to rhyme with "pop-suh-cull." From German: *klopstocke*: "meatball on a stick."

1. A man who looks into restaurant windows and watches people eat.
2. A wine taster.
3. A bauble; a piece of cheap jewelry.
4. A little meatball on a stick.

To simply define a *chalopshlikel* as a man who looks into restaurant windows and watches people eat is to miss the many nuances of this wonderful word.

For instance, a *chaluptzekeh* is a man who is so low he will steal the tip from a waiter's table. A *chalumptzekeh* will catch the *chaluptzekeh* in the act and demand half the tip or he will tell the waiter. A *chalopshlikel* will be watching the whole thing from the window, and in his attempt to rob the *chalumptzekeh* and the *chaluptzekeh*, he will be soundly beaten and will have to go to the hospital for X-rays and treatment, for which he is not covered by Blue Cross, and he will be thrown out in mid-enema.

chechutz

Pronounced CHEH-CHOOTS, to rhyme with "heh-boots."

A ringworm, a fungus or a high skin-rash (sometimes confused with *charchess*, giant hives).

The word *chechutz* has been adapted from its medical meaning and is used as a special curse—a heavy, juicy curse you save for someone who has little or no redeeming qualities. "May a *chechutz* grow out of his ears and make sideburns!"

In the give and take of the Yiddish language *chechutz* has recently been modified and now means "sagging underpants."

For some reason it is a sin in the Jewish religion to throw away undershorts. Many Jews have worn the same undershorts for twenty to forty years. They are always freshly laundered, but the snap of the elastic is long gone, and they are usually held up with pins.

Old Talmudic saying: Who is the Orthodox Jew? It is the one who is always pulling at his undershorts.

Used as a term of derision, *chechutz* is a loose, sagging state of mind; a person lacking in discipline and initiative. "He'll never amount to anything. He's a *chechutz* from the word stop."

chmach a chlogge

Pronounced CHEH-MACH A CHEH-LAGGA, to rhyme with "suh-rach a duh-ragga." From Low German: *chmacher*: "plumber, a man who clears up clogged drainpipes."

In Yiddish, *chmach a chlogge* means to flush out your frustrations, to give full vent to your annoyances or anger.

When a real *chmacher* is angry, he blows his empty nose into his hand, throws away the imaginary mucus, and accompanies himself with a high-pitched hum or "mmm" sound.

You are definitely annoyed about something when you *chmach a chlogge*. Usually it is a small thing that means a lot to you because it is a matter of principle. *Chmach*ing two or more times means you are irritated beyond belief and are ready to commit murder.

A good example is when you are waiting on line at a crowded Jewish bakery or at a supermarket check-out counter. There will always be someone trying to sneak ahead of you. You may allow one little old lady with just a package of cream cheese to worm ahead of you, but when another lady tries the same trick, you begin *chmach*ing *a chologge* and giving her a what-for. Everyone in the store looks at you as if you were Hitler incarnate, and that makes you *chmach* even more, taking it out on anyone within earshot. By now you are ready for a *chleitz* (a full scream). The best way to calm down is to continue *chmach*ing until you actually blow your nose.

Warning: Too much *chmach*ing *a chlogge* can lead to dizziness, headaches, excessive dryness of the mouth, blurred vision, and drowsiness. People with high blood pressure, heart disease, diabetes, thryoid disease, or glaucoma should not *chmach a chlogge* unless recommended by their physician.

chassik

Pronounced CHAH-ZICK, to rhyme with "ma-pick."

A ladies man; a regular Casanova or Don Juan. In slang terms: a sharpie; a swordsman.

Historians tell us that there was very little opportunity for courtship or "fooling around" between the young men and women in the Jewish settlements of Europe. Marriages were almost always arranged by the parents or by a professional matchmaker. Hence there were few real *chassiks*.

That's what the books tell us. But what do the historians know about fancy footwork? The fact was, most of the information about fixed marriages and such was picked up from a press release prepared by Rabbi Mendel of Lelb. Actually, there were plenty of *chassiks* around. It was said that a real *chassik* could take one look at a pretty girl from across a crowded chicken-market, and not only would she pant with desire but the chicken would lay a dozen eggs!

The *chassik* was regarded with scorn, fear, and not a little envy by most Jews.

In the town of Strelsk there lived a well-to-do merchant named Teitelbaum who had an eminently marriageable daughter. This girl was a fine cook, an expert seamstress, a hard-working housekeeper, and was pleasing to look at in the bargain.

After many months of negotiations, Teitelbaum made the match of his dreams. His daughter would be married to Zvi, the son of the rich banker, Kornblaum.

But Teitelbaum's happiness was short-lived. He discovered that his daughter was secretly consorting with Pincus, a notorious *chassik* who made a meager living selling advertising space on pushcarts. Mortified, he dragged his daughter to the renowned Rabbi Pinchel of Zwirz. He poured out his heart to the great rabbi, speaking of the brilliant match he made, the ungratefulness of his daughter, her disgraceful conduct with the *chassik*. He begged for advice.

"You've got a good-looking daughter there, Teitelbaum," said the rabbi. "Maybe she'd like to get acquainted with an older, more experienced gentleman—like yours truly, for instance."

"But, Rabbi, you're a holy man!" cried a shocked Teitelbaum. "You're married and you have nine children. You're acting like a *chassik*!"

The great rabbi snapped his cane in half and cried, "I'm tired of giving everybody wise advice. Can't *I* have some fun in life, too?"

pechuches

Pronounced PEH-CHUH-CHISS, to rhyme with "heh-soo-miss."

1. An unmitigated disaster; a misfortune that could only be topped by, say, a garment manufacturer

having a heart attack in the middle of a busy season.

2. A person who carries all sorts of pens, pencils, rulers, pocket flashlights, penknives, etc., none of which work.
3. A clever, creative fellow who is too lazy to put his ideas into action and ends up working for his brother and fooling around with his sister-in-law, who makes out the payroll and handles the books. (Also known as a *pechuchnik*.)
4. A large credenza or sideboard used exclusively for buffet-style *seders* (the combination banquet and religious service performed on the holiday of Passover).
5. A manila envelope.

When you are being attacked by a band of prehistoric-looking animals with long, pointy noses and big teeth but you can't run fast because your ankle is swelling from a snakebite—brother, you've got a *pechuches*!

chucheleh

Pronounced CHUH-CHUH-LEH, or CHOO-CHUH-LEH, to rhyme with "duh-duh-la."

Literal meaning: "little motorcycle." *Chuchel* is Yiddish for motorcycle or motorbike or some kind of gas-propelled bicycle. The *eh* is the diminutive suffix denoting affection. *Chucheleh* is a term of endearment, acknowledging someone to be extra-precious, extra-wonderful, and just plain terrific.

To the Jews, the *chuchel* (the motorcycle) was the most precious thing a family could own, next to the holy Torah and a brand-new car. Every Jewish boy dreamed of joining a *chuchel* club, zooming in and out of the fish markets, scaring old ladies and trying to impress the young ones. The *chuchel* was flashy transportation, a status symbol, a friend, a companion. It stood for masculinity, power, freedom. When a Jew called a person a *chucheleh*, it was not just a lightweight word. It was almost a pledge of love.

Today, however, it has been watered down to one of those Jewish show-business words, adopted by every race, color, and creed. It is used equally with *chuchee*, a variation. The Jewish motorcycle clubs of California still use the original pronunciation.

chlechman

Pronounced CHLEHCH-MAN, to rhyme with "dech-van."

An evil, demonic spirit that enters your food, making almost everything taste like Canadian bacon.

When someone was eating ordinary food, such as boiled celery, and suddenly started salivating and going crazy, wanting more and more (especially with fried eggs or with tomato and mayonnaise on toast), Jews would cry, "A *chlechman* has entered his celery!"

Many rabbis thought that God sent the *chlechman* to the Jews to test their piety and love of Him. For as soon as anyone tasted food that a *chlechman* inhabited, they knew it must be Canadian bacon. It always tasted too good to be kosher.

A *chlechman* could be exorcised from the food. It was usually marinated to death. Every rabbi had his own marinade recipe handed down to him by his teacher. The marinades always included coarse salt and a cup and a half of a Gentile baby's blood.

If, for some reason, the marinade did not work, the rabbi had to eat the *chlechman*-invaded food himself but could not move his bowels for the next nine days and nine nights. This would make even the most humble rabbi mean and tough, equipping him to "do battle" with the *chlechman*. At the end of the nine days and nine nights, the rabbi would recite a chapter from the mystic book of Karash, sound a sharp note on the ocarina, and tell the *chlechman* that he is exorcised whether he likes it or not.

cheh!
cheh! cheh!
cheh! cheh! cheh!

Pronounced with the regular Scottish-Jewish "cheh" sound (see introduction).

Cheh is the most expressive word in the Yiddish language. It can be shouted, sighed, whispered, laughed, cried. It conveys every emotion, every nuance. *Chehs* can roll off the tongue in profusion or in simple one-word bursts. It is the indispensable word that seems to accompany every other sentence in Yiddish.

Ernest Cockburn, in his *Dictionary of Medieval Yiddish Slang*, traces the *cheh* to the French *chou*, meaning "cabbage," "kale," "puff paste," "darling," "bow," "rosette." Professor Jesse Korman's *Origins of Yiddish* claims it comes from the Italian *chiara* (the white of an uncooked egg).

I'm sure that there is excellent scholarship to back up the findings of these eminent authorities, but I maintain that *cheh* just happened one day—out of the blue, as it were.

It probably occurred when a Jew was clearing his throat and receiving a friendly slap on the back simultaneously, while at the same time he was a victim of a surprise attack by drunken Crusaders.

Here are just a few examples of the hundreds of ways you can use *cheh*:

1. "*Cheh!* Why is my umbrella in the sitting room?"
2. "My grandmother's bananas will be ready by four o'clock. *Cheh!*"
3. "*Cheh! Cheh!* We have received a dinner invitation from your cousin, the chiropodist."
4. "I have saved enough money to buy my mother the silk scarf she likes. *Cheh!*"
5. "*Cheh!* Working in the garden on a hot summer day makes me warm and sleepy."
6. "*Cheh! Cheh! Cheh!* We have reservations at the restaurant next Friday." □

THE WIT & WISDOM OF BERNIE X
Sean Kelly on Gerry Sussman, May 1990

When he left us, Gerry Sussman took with him the secret formula for the potion he had invented—a noxious chemical concoction that could transform a gentle, soft-spoken family man into a criminally insane, foul-mouthed, sex-crazed New York cabdriver.

Gerry never let anyone see the process. We never actually met Bernie X. Preparatory to writing a column or story, Gerry would make us promise to lock his office from the outside and ignore the hideous cries, the demands for freedom, broads,

weapons, and deli food (in a coarse Brooklyn accent) that were sure to come from behind the door. When the sounds of cursing and belching and typing had died down—the process usually lasted several hours—we would open the door and find Gerry asleep on the floor of his ruined office, smiling like a baby. A completed Bernie monologue would be beside the stained and battered typewriter.

Was it all worthwhile? Here is a brief anthology, selected almost at random, from the Complete Works. Judge for yourself.

GERRY SUSSMAN'S BERNIE X

From "The New York Cabbie's Guide to New York" (April '74)

. . . I'm always taking 'em down to the Village, those people. I had what's-his-name in my cab yesterday . . . Clint Eastwood. He's a fag. I had to take him down to a gay bar. You know how they all get away with it? They all got doubles. They got guys to look just like them. So I take Clint Eastwood and his spade fairy boyfriend to the Village and meanwhile his double is uptown talking to the reporters and fucking twenty-nine broads in his hotel room. They're all like that. Elvis Presley, John Wayne . . . Wayne is a dyke. I had 'im in my cab once. A lot of those big, tough guys are actually bull dykes, y'know.

From "My Meter Is Running" (December '75)

. . . You want to know what Cher really looks like? First of all, she's a Negro. That's why she always looks so tan. Second of all, she's only four and a half feet tall. Third of all, she wears a wig. Right. All that long black hair is what we call an "elevator wig" . . . builds up the height. She wears the wig and her specially built-up shoes and she's five-seven. Then you add the makeup, the eyes, the lips, etc., and the way the camera and the lighting work, and bingo, you got what we call a "package."

From "My Meter Is Running" (January '76)

. . . I open a closet and who do I see in there but Sonny. Sonny Bono. He's walking around in this big fucking closet smelling all the jackets. Y'know . . . lifting up the arms, the whole thing. I look around and I see he's got a little pot of coffee going on a hot plate and there's a cot, and a TV set in there, too. The son of a bitch lives there. That's what he really likes—to live in a closet. And not just him. He's living there with Geraldo Rivera. Because all of a sudden, Geraldo comes out from behind a big fur coat and puts his arms around Sonny and they start kissing each other's mustaches. They're really getting hot rubbing

each other's mustaches. They tell me to fuck off, I'm disturbing their privacy. What the hell, it's no skin off my ass. They can have a blue baby for all I care.

From "My Meter Is Running" (September '78)

. . . So there we were in Casa Hemingway—Papa, his wife, and their other guests, Gary Cooper, Jean Harlow, and Duke Ellington. Cooper, or "Coop," as everyone called him, was a regular chatterbox—talk, talk, talk, night and day. I hate to say it, but he was a fairy, a cowboy fairy. He liked to gossip with Papa about Hollywood and all the sex scandals going on. Papa loved it. He wanted a piece of every ass in Hollywood. "Tell me again about the broads," he would say to Cooper. And Cooper would tell him that Joan Crawford liked to put goldfish up her twat. That Norma Shearer was still a virgin, that Katharine Hepburn was really a man—a very strange-looking man, but a man. A lot of stuff like that.

From "My Meter Is Running" (November '78)

. . . It is a documented fact that Bormann had the worst case of flatulence in Germany, worse than Hitler's, which was very bad. No matter how hard Bormann tried to control it, it always got the best of him. It used to drive his associates crazy. Some of them wanted to sue him for giving them permanent lung damage. He was a terror, that Bormann. Only Hitler could take him in stride. They used to have contests, trying to outgas each other. It was their idea of a good time. German decadence can be puzzling at times, but you know how anal they are.

From "My First Time" (July '86)

. . . I guess Havana was to fucking what Vegas is to gambling. You could get laid anywhere in Havana. I mean *anywhere*. You went into a grocery store for milk and you got laid in the back room. Clothing stores had extra dressing, or rather undressing, rooms, as they called them. Taxi drivers had spare girls in the front seat or in the trunk. The hospitals were mainly used for fucking instead of caring for the sick. They told me that at baseball games the guys would take a seventh-inning fuck, a quickie, instead of a seventh-inning stretch. Everywhere we went some kid was trying to sell us a piece of his sister, his aunt, even his mother.

In Havana you could get a shoeshine and a blowjob right on the street, at the same place. Or you could get a blowjob without the shoeshine. One kid would shine them up while his sister was licking your log as neat as a kitten. They gave you these Spanish newspapers to read to hide the girl while she was doing you. A lot of guys knew how to read Spanish upside down.

From "Bernie X and Bruce X" (September '85)

... That was the night the president fell in love with Bruce and took him back to the White House. He's seventy-four years old and has finally come out of the closet. Bruce told me what he likes to do. He likes to kiss a lot. He always has a minty mouth because he's always sucking on those breath mints because he's always in the public eye. Sometimes he shows Bruce how Wallace Beery taught him to kiss on the neck. Light and feathery, the president says. No wet stuff and no biting. And no tickling either. It has to be just right. Sometimes he has those jellybeans in his mouth when he kisses and he makes Bruce swallow them whole. He also likes to get his lips bitten, his tummy rubbed, and have his pubic hair shaved so it tickles and has to be scratched.

One day he asked Bruce to give him a shower, to soap him up real thick and scrub him with a brush. When Bruce asked him if the showers were turning him on and if he'd like to get laid the president went blank. "What do you mean, get laid?" he asked. Bruce was taken aback for a second, but caught on. The president didn't know how homos do it. He tried to explain it to Reagan in a nice tasteful way. The president got all red in the face. He was embarrassed. He wouldn't accept it. Impossible. That kind of thing is just not done, he said. Bruce assured him that it was done and how pleasurable it could be, especially when he did it gently and with great finesse. The president reacted like Bruce was going to stick some knitting needles down his throat.

He just wouldn't hear anymore about it.

Anyway, Bruce becomes the president's behind-the-scenes

ILLUSTRATION BY ROBERT GROSSMAN

June 1983

companion, his adviser on how to dress, what kind of makeup and hair dye to us—image building, as Bruce calls it. The president was using too much pancake and rouge, a leftover from his acting days. Bruce got him to emphasize his cheekbones more with some gloss—to give him a more rugged, manly look, with more character to his face.

He got him to wear shirts with higher collars so his neck wouldn't be exposed and he wouldn't need neck makeup. He toned down the orange in his hair and gave him more salt and pepper.

Where's Nancy all this time? Doing what she always does—looking at her husband with those big, moist eyes popping out of her head. She ignores Bruce. Doesn't even know he's there, or doesn't want to know about him. Once they had to share the same bathroom when hers wasn't working. Bruce says she takes forever to move her bowels. And she wears a hooded mask every morning, like the hangmen. No one sees her face until ten o'clock.

And then the shit hit the fan. George Bush showed up one day and fell in love with Bruce at first sight.

From "Mango" (January '85)

... So they finish my training as a Russian explosives expert and I get to be pretty fucking good at it. Pretty soon I can blow up an office building with some chicken wire and Silly Putty. I get my ID papers, a course in Russian, and a briefing on Nicaragua—its people and culture. What the fuck do I need that for? I live in New York and I see more spics every day than these pieces of white bread see all their lives.

You got to understand how the mind of the fucking CIA works. They'll try anything to beat the Commies. If they could put cornflakes in Castro's bed, they'd do it. They're like those college fraternity kids doing jokes. "What about the Jew boy with the educated cock?" they asked. "Maybe he can fuck the entire female Sardine army. And if he doesn't, he'll die in a jungle swamp somewhere and we'll have one less Jew in the world to worry about."

I know those guys. Just because they can't fuck their way out of a paper bag they got to take it out on us Jews. They're jealous. While they're figuring out how to put tacks on the Commies' chairs, the Jews are fucking their wives' brains out every day. Why do you think the shiksas have a headache every time their husbands want to fuck them? Because they've already been fucked so many times that day they feel their heads are on backward.

Gerry Sussman wrote ten Yello Pages. Here's a five-page sampler.

► Accountants-Jewish

Aaaaaaron Aaaron 666 Boorvis Av 555-8181
Aaaaaron Aran 2105 N Ziska Blvd 555-3170
Aaaron Aron 7777 Snide Av 555-2916
Aaron Arin 5643 Pisher Av 555-7324
Abrahamowitz Abraham 98 Gevalt St 555-9789
Abrahamsberg Albert 454 W Pupik Av 555-1665
Abrahamskowitz Arnold 909 Kurveh Lane 555-2389
Abrahamstein Abe 987 Lingle Av 555-2329
Balabuster Robert 231 S Tefillin Av 555-2951
BEBLACH & BUNZ 521 Lekvar Av 555-0194
Beltz Murray 12 N Mug Av 555-0010
Berniewitz Lou 976 Custard St 555-9453
Biller Jay 876 Kosher Av 555-1738
Blintzkrieg David 89 Shvengadik Av 555-3945
BRILLBUILDING NAT 45 Narrishkeit Av 555-4862
Bris Stuart 789-81 Gevalt St 555-8829
Brisket Marvin 342 S Rectum Av 555-0206
Bubkes Martin 125 Garbanzo Lane 555-0591
Bunjamin Benjamin 65 Boobi Av 555-9916
Buttweiler & Wurme 675 Passover Av 555-2584
Carmel & Zion 32 Nafka Pl 555-8553
Challah & Weber 41 Tuchis Av 555-2257
Chimpkin Leon 709 Bialy Av 555-6457
Chutzpa George 87 Lingle Av 555-8386
Chwurst Seymour 67 S Matzoh Blvd 555-8065
Chynik Peter 897 Gezund Av 555-1072
Cramerstone Jerome 541 Yeshiva Blvd 555-7454
Demograff Ira 65 Boner Av 555-2822
Dreidel David 321 Putz Blvd 555-7254
Drooper Ben 99 Gefeylach Pl 555-1932
Dropkick Seymour 765 Putz Blvd 555-6963
Drugstein Sam 786 Pareve Av 555-0789
Farb Simon 65 Finster Pl 555-4633
Farbissiner Hy 87 Dreidel St 555-1423
Farfel Elliot 90 Dreidel St 555-7954
Fassbinder Werner 32 S Munich Av 555-7185
Feigenfelder Abe 987 Brisket Pl 555-3172
Felderfeister Brian 71 Dreckster Av 555-9985
Fendermacher Sidney 128 Borscht Pl 555-8941
Ferg George 90 Grepps Av 555-1369
Finderskeepers Nathan 78 Gefeylach Blvd 555-6927
FINGERFOOD IRA 56 Gribinis Av 555-6976
Finkelfarb Stephen 789 S Trayf St 555-8435
Flem Irving 12 Chitlin Pl 555-1007
Fliegel Stanley 154 Zitt Av 555-8867
Fliegelfarber Bruce 122 Naches Av 555-4523
Frankincense Murray 232 Naches Av 555-4950
Fruchtenspiel John 908 Sputum St 555-2686
Funnelfinger Neil 567 N Bumhole Blvd 555-0279
Gefilte Paul 678 Naches Av 555-7522
Gelaympter Sol 97 Boorvis Av 555-6999
Gevalt Morris 6721 W Palooka Blvd 555-4074
Gimmel David 34 Tefillin St 555-6900
Gimmelfarber Ted 432 Nipple Av 555-5332
Goldbricker Sy 7698 Lunger Av 555-0323
Grooder & Miltz 876 Zarzuela Blvd 555-7300
Grossbomb Marty 984 Spunk Av 555-4476
Grubstake Saul 21 N Dingleberry Av 555-2849
Hanukkah Stanley 768 Hanukkah Av 555-3435
Hebrewitz Joel 9824 Yeshiva Av 555-1719
Hesch Milton 32 N Zionist Av 555-7059
Himmelheish Norbert 87 Nugel St 555-4973
Hirschbard Leo 7890 Pistachio Av 555-2077

HUMMENTASCHEN MARC
C.P.A.
New Business Setups • Money Laundering
Swiss Tax Shelters • Book Balancing
987 N. Dingleberry Ave.
(bet. Spunk & Lunger) 555-4397

Imglick Paul 3421 Zugsmith Av 555-5001
Immelkrieg Barnett 901 S Bris Blvd 555-4851
Ipstein Henry 723 Synagogue St 555-1060
Jewish Ira 876 Schvantz Av 555-0303
Kanilster Phillip 567 Booger Pl 555-6502
Karsha Lawrence 54 Lekvar Av 555-1906
Katz, Katz, Katz & Katz 807 Miltz Pl 555-6006
Kayak Ivan 712 Pishke Av 555-8313
Kishkowitz Glenn 986 Ankles Av 555-1120
Kluck Louis 234 Pullet St 555-3964
Klutz Richard 87 N Radish Blvd 555-1942
Knish Walter 231 Zagreb Av 555-7392
Kornbread Harold 990 Humetz Av 555-8211
Kosher Leon 56 Nafka Av 555-6769
Krackstein & Krass 677 S Zeyde Av 555-0993
Kremel Ben 236 Zitt Av 555-6052
Krindelman Seth 976 Booger Av 555-2675
Krippleman Simon 897 Gevalt St 555-1605
Kugel Jerome 781 E Meshuggeneh Av 555-5286
Kvetch Barney 98 S Rectum Pl 555-2806
Kwisk Gerald 212 Spunk Av 555-5349
LANSKY MEYER 45 Megillah Pl 555-9408
Leavenbread Walter 87 Dreckster Pl 555-1441
Lefkorn Abe 909 Mousetrap Blvd 555-2492
Legbard & Legbard 565 Capon Av 555-0624
Legfelder Gene 432 N Derma Av 555-0540
Leghorn Austin 21 N Derma Av 555-0333
Lekvar Eli 761 Farouk St 555-9194
Loltzer Samuel 653 Filbert St 555-3561
Lox Murray 75 Salmon Av 555-5424
Lukschen Arthur 34 S Noodle Av 555-1251
Mandlebread & Kimmel 56 Carraway Av 555-0293
Marbelman John 562 N Halvah Rd 555-4588
Maven & Maven 6 E Bubkes Av 555-8960
Meltz Jeffrey 891 Pupik Av 555-2709
Mezuzah Arnold 54 Gezund Pl 555-0686
Mimmelfinger & Zirn 45 W Brisket Av 555-4989
MOMZER SY 322 Van Dork Blvd 555-3277
Munsky Milton 56 Trayf Av 555-9727
Naches Steven 78 Galeympter Av 555-0507
Nafka Cy 77 Gevalt Pl 555-3270
Narrish Bob 644 Van Dork Blvd 555-3762
Nechtiger Daniel 655 Bubkes Av 555-5137
Needlezweig Warren 454 N Vontz Av 555-1340
Newbaby Bruce 988 Yeshiva Av 555-4461
Nittlefin Carl 22 W Putz Av 555-8291
Nosh Al 62 W Capon Av 555-2183
Nudnick Irv 899 Negro Av 555-8270
Orbanger Leon 779 Wingwang Pl 555-1798
Orkushlu Harry 8991 W Chink Av 555-3586
Orrenzweiger Saul 876 Kosher St 555-3494
Ortfinger Lewis 9972 Shpritz Av 555-0963
Oysgedart David 88 Van Dork Av 555-5934
Ozzenbrau Leonard 71 Matjes Av 555-3759
Palestine Stanley 885 Hasid Pl 555-9668
Pareve Isidor 788 N Talmud St 555-8175
Parvenu Lester 765 Bagel Blvd 555-2636
Pavolya Jack 145 Nignog Av 555-8108
Pearlfuss & Bucker 765 Sheeny Pl 555-5206
Perlminster Seth 980 Sephardic Av 555-1790
Phink Lester 65 Van Dork Av 555-1276
Pickstein Jesse 2143 N Kike Av 555-1551
Pishkin Elliot 876 Pareve St 555-6063
Pisk Gerry 98 Lukschen Av 555-8273
Pletzel Dan 986 Bialy Blvd 555-1658
Plotz Leonard 32 S Virgin Av 555-5251
Plutzberg Milton 781 Smegma Blvd 555-9787
Pomeranian George 76 Gefilte Av 555-1560
Potchka Arnold 567 Yeshiva Av 555-6063
Pranis, Kleefeld, Sinkowitz & Dworn
65 Nignog Av 555-8273
Pulka Jay 21 N Kvetch Av 555-1658
Pullet & Frasker 54 Bazooka Av 555-5251
Pupik Murray 333 Tuchis Av 555-1560
Rabbi Bernard 56 Hebrew Av 555-2418
Rabbiwitz John 79 Mishnah Pl 555-5914
Rabid Milton 890 Mezuzah Av 555-6699
Radish Milton 45 N Sinus Av 555-8354
Rambobaum Ronald 992 E Langerhans Pl 555-8332
Raskolnikov Milton 97 Schlepper St 555-3017
Rathbomb Stanley 2102 Zaftig Av 555-7117
Ratsberg & Sklore 76 Faygel Pl 555-5363
Reintraubner Murray 654 Kibitzer Av 555-9721
Rightfish Moe 45 N Salmon Av 555-7722
Romanian Eli 622 Negro Av 555-1364
Rosenburp Richard 766 Kugel St 555-3749
Rosencake Charles 675 Bendover Av 555-9676
Rosenpantz Herbert 6 W Hebrew Av 555-3965
Rothbanger Gary 88 Liberal Av 555-2529
Rothcup Harvey 21 Latke Blvd 555-2989
ROTHSTEIN ARNOLD 42 Palestine St 555-5746
Rubber Hyman 652 Noogie Av 555-1222
Rubinbarge Joel 9988 W Gumbo Av 555-8161
Rustsky Burton 8811 Wombat Av 555-4246
Sapp Milton 55 Pulka St 555-8250
Scamstein Mitchell 565 N Kasha Av 555-3427
Scham Elliot 897 W Varnishka Pl 555-8582
Schmendrick Aaron 98 Knockerman St 555-6997
Schneib Jerome 676 Kashruth Av 555-0281
Schrei Murray 877 Kosher Pl 555-7286
Schtick Barney 912 Zaftig Av 555-4110
Schtummie Paul 21 Pupik Av 555-5177
Schtupp Warren 245 N Zetz Blvd 555-2157
Schvitz Albert 87 Jewish Av 555-3963
Schwarbenfeiber & Tress 86 Pareve Av 555-5065
Schwerbel John 665 S Negro Av 555-2720
Schwink Joel 4321 Jewish Princess Av 555-8657
Scrofula Alvin 212 N Boff Av 555-0163
Seltzerstone Harvey 32 Yiddish Av 555-4539
Seymour Seymour 521 Tornado Av 555-6332
Shinestone Sy 65 Boorvis Av 555-5643
Silvercup Harold 723 Kashruth Av 555-2592
Silverdome Gene 76 Jewboy Av 555-7310
Silverwort Marvin 2112 S Kike Av 555-9946
Skimmer Barney 53 Lunger Blvd 555-3435
Skurnsky Murray 7521 Jewish Princess Av 555-7954
Slitstein Myron 78 Pulka Av 555-9239
Slumberman Donald 65 Coriander Pl 555-0270
Smeltz Paul 321 Kidneystone Av 555-9582
Smeltzer & Ling 21 Bugger Av 555-7415
Sniff Walter 63 Yenta Pl 555-7877
Sockowitz George 877 Lingle Pl 555-1237
Sossfelder Leonard 7785 Zetz Av 555-4404
Sperman Bruce 899 Narrish Av 555-0450
Spiceglass Edgar 67 Nafka Pl 555-0771
Spickler Stanley 8932 Zetz Av 555-2323
Spitnick Jerome 34 N Halvah Av 555-8221
Spurl Peter 42 Spunk Av 555-8222
Sputumberg Ben 909 S Pletzel Av 555-3784
Sugarstone Alan 55 Booger Av 555-1922
Susspearl Marvin 221 N Negro Av 555-4125
Swettgarb Albert 55 Zeyde Av 555-0209
Swettsky Bernard 2233 N Zitt Av 555-4464
Tackenbaum Ira 665 Kugel Av 555-9509
Talmud Lawrence 22 Pupik Pl 555-9662
Tarpaulin Hyman 778 Dingleberry Av 555-7573
Tchotchke Ben 567 N Oysgedart Av 555-2770
Tichter & Groob 44 N Dago Av 555-3133
Ticker & Putrell 221 Kishka St 555-9019
Tiff Rokbert 333 Calcutta Av 555-7927
Titz Jay 887 Knockerman Av 555-9792
Trayf Bennett 667 Pork Pl 555-0110
Trumbanick Jerome 2123 Nafka Av 555-7159
Truss Elliott 565 Gallstone Av 555-3696
Tuchter Norman 786 Limey Pl 555-8029
Tummler Leon 329 Gravyboat Av 555-8485
Tushman Ben 87 Tickler Av 555-0634
Twitzkowitz Arthur 988 Van Dork Av 555-2831
Uggstein Lawrence 554 Schtick Av 555-0717
Ulangerer Isidore 320 Van Bris Blvd 555-5415
Underhander Emanuel 21 Vontz Av 555-7970
Underpantz Harold 444 Brisket Av 555-6414
Understander Marvin 55 S Dago Av 555-7106
Underwriter Melvin 222 Jewish Av 555-6423
Unfresser Jack 66 Pork Pl 555-5213
Uplonsky & Bogratz 666 Tuchisman Av 555-9881
Upspringer Barry 555 Rectum Plaza 555-9619
Upstein & Glitz 22 Bumhole Blvd 555-0864
Uzi Jack 767 Rear End Av 555-2836
Van Lipschitz John 667 Frontal St 555-2002
Varblunger Nat 334 Van Naked Av 555-0384
Varnish Murray 3399 N Pubic Blvd 555-0021
Vell & Vell 6691 Flanken St 555-2966
Vigorish & Gold 889 Lunger Av 555-1288
Vontz Jay 11 W Negro Av 555-4297
Wabbaport Harry 9912 Sheeny Av 555-2407
Wanderlutz Martin 223 Legwort Pl 555-0502
Weinwein Barry 889 Fester St 555-0710
Weisenheimer Jack 776 S Pustule Av 555-3488
Wingwanger Bruce 212 Van Spick Blvd 555-6536
Wopter Saul 43 N Gonad Av 555-4800
Wosnofkowitz Alan 990 Mojo Blvd 555-4323
Wunk George 555 Van Penis Av 555-0082
Wunkler, Tzigoonis & Schteck 21 Zitt St 555-5377
Yarmulke Oscar 77 Fellatio Av 555-3529
Yeshiva Richard 77 Hebrew Blvd 555-5099
Yihuda Ben 5567 S Rectal Av 555-6206
Yimmel & Twitz 666 Vas Deferens Av 555-0216
Yipnis Jack 222 B'naib'rith Av 555-3275
Yodelzweig Eli 555 Shtreimel Av 555-4320
Yohannesbaum Bernard 77 Semen St 555-6761
Youngfeller Nat 897 N Chutzpa Av 555-9562
Yugley David 667 Garmento St 555-1706
Yutz Sam 88 Pupik Av 555-7729
Zaftig Brian 777 Fellatio Av 555-1101
Zagzig Leon 24 Van Spick Av 555-9161
Zapkin Harry 990 Gefilte Av 555-0951
Zapp & Armulstone 55 Trayf Av 555-1067
Zasslove Ira 8897 Booger Av 555-6896
Zasu Gary 99 Chink St 555-7523
Zetz Walter 22 Highball Av 555-3135
Zeyde Alan 9903 W Muff Av 555-8389
Zieg & Zieg 998 Dementia Blvd 555-0731
Zinger Frank 887 N Kike Av 555-3163
Zipp Murray 44 Pickle St 555-0388
Zipskin Jerome 45 Pickle St 555-2667
Zitz & Zitz 2167 Halvah Av 555-3047
Zizma Leon 77 Cocksmith Blvd 555-1820
Zoth Peter 912 W Ginzo Av 555-4835
Zsismore Alan 88 S Pupik Av 555-2411
Zug Henry 21 Perfect St 555-0429
Zugwater Carl 667 Van Penis Av 555-4780
Zussgarten Jack 99 Kosher Av 555-1375
Zwag Barney 7765 Lockjaw Av 555-6136
Zwegma Eugene 543 Canker Pl 555-7774
Zwei Arnold 88 Polyp Av 555-5013
Zweiback Bennett 227 S Dandruff Av 555-9364
Zwigger Stanley 3342 Alcoholic Dr 555-9583
Zwill & Merlinger 556 Herpes Av 555-7211
Zwirdlove Herbert 778 Bacteria Pl 555-6574
Zwirgo Nathan 66 Freon Av 555-6473
Zworsky Milton 909 Salami Av 555-4037
Zwuckerstone Sy 77 Brilliantine Av 555-3638
ZWUZFINGER & CABAL 8888 Van Hump Blvd 555-2434

► Acid Throwing

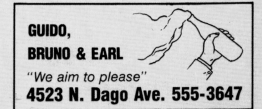

GUIDO,
BRUNO & EARL

"We aim to please"
4523 N. Dago Ave. 555-3647

From "Gerry Sussman's Yello Pages," December 1987

JERRY'S

Beautiful handmade belts depicting Bible scenes, crafted from the finest leathers—with complete miniature Bibles in the belt buckles. Choose from Old and New Testaments.

9876 S. Jesus Ave.   **555-3345**

▶ **Children's Entertainment**

Larry Lavelli and "Gums," the Toothless Old Crone
See Our Display Ad Page 6
875 S Putz Av 555-4721

▶ **Churches**

Church of Abraham Pincus 222 E Moses Dr ----- 555-9898
Church of Andy Devine 8976 Messiah Way ------ 555-8982
Church of the Absolute Word
675 Eucharist Av ---------------------------------- 555-2222
Church of the African Experience
980 N Negro Av-------------------------------------- 555-4326
Church of the All Natural 21 Granola Av---------- 555-6708
Church of the Bicoastal Tabernacle
7899 Missionary Dr -------------------------------- 555-1298
Church of the Cavalry 5544 S Custard Av -------- 555-2419
Church of the Chosen Few 6609 Holy Av --------- 555-5223
Church of the Epileptic Vision
6699 Miracle Mile --------------------------------- 555-8719
Church of the Forgotten Popes
2109 Vatican Av ----------------------------------- 555-4732
Church of the Little People 5432 Mary St ------- 555-1189
Church of the Open Wound 6743 Martyr Walk -- 555-9137
Church of the Teamsters 76543 Union Tpke ---- 555-6735

▶ **Cowards-Rentals**

PERCY'S

Good supply of 'fraidy cats, chickenshits, yellowbellies, pond scum, lily-livered liars, pipsqueaks, twerps, chowderheads.
Our cowards make anyone look good.
2231 N. Nipple Dr.   **555-3569**

▶ **Boring People**

HO HUM

Rent one of our professional bores and kill your already dull party. You'll send unwanted guests home in a hurry. Our bores make great insomnia cures.
8709 Traffic Blvd.   **555-2327**

▶ **Caning & Ear Boxing**

LORD BARRON
The Earl of Breakstone

Expert caning done by a former member of the House of Lords, a perfect English gentleman who has been trained to cane and box ears from birth. Surprise and stun your enemies with a proper caning!
Discipline your children with a sound boxing of the ears!
3342 Anglo-Saxon Ave.   **555-8988**

▶ **Car Mice-Exterminators**

KATZ
The Car Mice Killers

Overnight service, while-u-park
453 Rectum Av----------------------------- 555-7792

▶ **Catholic Lingerie**

THERESA'S

Clerical and lay undergarments. Basic lingerie and ceremonial lingerie for nuns, sister superiors. Sensible apparel for laywomen.
567 N. Apostle Rd.   555-3973

CONSUMER TIP
Driving in reverse puts a strain on your engine and gives you poor gas mileage. Use the "drive" position. And remember: Apply your brakes when you want to stop. It could save your life! Federal Energy Commission, Washington, D.C.

▶ **Chest Hair**

SPITZER   *The Chest Hair People*

★ SPITZER ★
The Chest Hair People

Yes, you can grow your own chest hair. As little or as much as you want. SPITZER CHEST HAIR CLINICS analyze your chest follicles, put you on a special diet and give you their patented Dermagen hormone treatments. In seven days or less you will see your first hair growth. In two weeks you'll have a beautiful layer of chest hair. In three weeks you'll be a teddy bear!

"Nobody does it better than guys with chest hair."

6766 Postum Rd.   **555-2348**

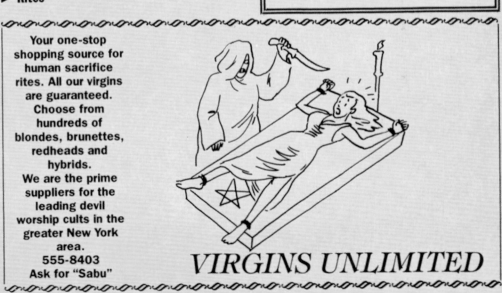

GERRY SUSSMAN (1933–1989)
An Editorial by Sean Kelly, January 1990

Gerry Sussman was, by most standards, a pretty unusual guy. But around the offices of the *National Lampoon* in its early days, he was the closest thing to normal that we had. For example, he was neither a drug abuser nor a beer-swilling alcoholic-in-training. He liked (and appreciated) wine at meals, and drank the occasional martini. (When he had two, he was transformed into the dreaded Two-Martini Zen Master, but that's another story.) Unlike the rest of us editors, Gerry had actually held a job in the real world, as an advertising copywriter. What I'm trying to say, I guess, is that he was our first grown-up.

He was also our first professional humor writer—he'd already been published in other, *real* magazines, like *Playboy*, and even written a book, *The Official Sex Manual*. (It was reprinted not long ago, and is still screamingly funny.) In it, Gerry isolated and described, among other things, the human "Erroneous Zones," which concept some swine later ripped off to use as the title of a bestseller (amusingly, a bogus self-help book of the type Gerry specialized in taking the piss out of).

ILLUSTRATION BY RICK MEYEROWITZ

The original *Lampoon* editors were from out of town—either from foreign countries like Harvard, England, and Canada, or, in at least two cases, from distant planets. Gerry was our first natural-born New Yorker. He was thus inherently obsessed with the state of his health, Yiddish terms of abuse, sports—stickball as a participant, the Knicks, Mets, and Giants as a fan—and Chinese food. He quickly became our resident expert on these essential humor subjects.

Gerry's first freelance piece for the magazine, "The Young Adorables," appeared in March 1973. It was a hatchet job on yuppies, ten years ahead of its time. Since it was apparent to the editors that he was the only person of our acquaintance who a) knew anything about sports, Yiddish, Chinese food, etc., and b) made us laugh, he joined the staff. As somebody back then observed, "The thing about Gerry is, even when he's not funny, he's funny."

By 1989, Gerry had written *more*—more words, more pieces, more captions, more *jokes*—than anyone ever associated with the *National Lampoon*. There is a reason for this, beyond Gerry's remarkable natural industriousness and fecundity.

Sometime in the late 1970s, Sussman found himself in need of funds with which to procure food, shelter, and other such luxuries. He approached the then-owner of this publication and requested a small, short-term loan—which, much to his astonishment, was readily proffered: "Sure thing, Ger, consider it done, come to me anytime, what are friends for? . . . Oh, and

if you'll just sign here, no reason to read the fine print, a mere formality, ahem, ahem."

Too late did Gerry realize that the loan, with interest compounding by the nanosecond, was to be deducted from his salary, and could only be repaid *in jokes*, at the rate of a dime a gag. In practice, this meant that if Gerry wrote an entire issue by himself—which he did, some months—he would find himself only another couple of bucks less behind in his debt to NatLampCo.

Throughout the era of Reaganomics, Gerry was the one-man proletariat of the magazine. He survived two big-bucks-buy-out changes in management and three editorial putsches, increased his productivity, and got a littler further behind in his payments.

To support his wife and daughter (whom he loved more than Chinese food, the Giants, and Yiddish profanity *put together*) he worked nights. He wrote advertising copy, film and television scripts, and books: a university handbook parody, a scandal-tabloid parody, a parody of *TV Guide*. There were rumors that Gerry had developed the ability to write in his sleep. And still, even when he wasn't funny, he was funny.

One thing he could certainly write in his sleep was "Bernie X," the over-the-shoulder monologues of a foulmouthed, know-it-all, sex-crazed New York cabdriver. Bernie—narrator and protagonist of a dozen feature pieces and countless columns over the years—became the most popular fictitious character to appear in the *National Lampoon*'s pages since Michael O'Donoghue.

Gerry was not only a terrific solo act, he was a pleasure to work *with*—generous, patient, enthusiastic. When you shared a byline with Gerry, you discovered that you, too, could be funny even when you weren't.

(I could name four hotshot young Emmy winners who learned to write comedy working for Gerry. The fact that they did not attend his memorial service proves that TV is where they belong.)

After that memorial service, quite a few of us, who hadn't seen each other for a while, went out for Chinese food. Some of us brought our kids. Wine and a few martinis were consumed, in moderation. We talked about the state of our health, and the Giants, Knicks, and Mets, applying to their performances suitable Yiddish terms of abuse. Grown-ups.

At the service itself (Kaddish recited in an Episcopal church; Gerry would have grinned until his ears wiggled), some of his friends had the good taste to read aloud from his work. The assembled mourners laughed so hard, they cried. Even when he wasn't funny, he was funny.

ED SUBITZKY

T he particular genius of Ed Subitzky begins with his disguise. He's the type of man—a bald guy with glasses—you'd pass on the street and not give a second

glance. But if you did, you'd notice he was handsome in the way that some bald guys with glasses can be. And then there is that glint in his eyes, mischievous, a bit randy. If you're a woman, you'll think, "I wonder . . ." And you'd be right. A powerhouse of male libido thrives inside Ed Subitzky, a man who has drawn a comic strip with a woman and an elephant in full . . . but you can read that later.

Beginning one of Ed's comic strips is a lot like curling up on the sofa with the Bayeux tapestry. His stories unfold in complicated and minute detail. Each strip is a perfect little novel that teems with more characters than you'll find in a Proustian fever dream. He draws with the delicacy of a medieval monk illuminating a manuscript, only he has a more ribald eye for the saucier details, the kind you'll find in a Mughal miniature, which his work also resembles.

One recent evening, I found myself looking into the lighted windows of buildings I was passing. Each building was a different story. Each window was a way into the story. I thought of

PHOTO BY JOE HENSON

looking into a Subitzky, how each tiny box illuminates a window into an elegant piece of conceptual storytelling.

Read a Subitzky strip and you'll find yourself engaged in a conversation you didn't expect to have. A strip will suddenly recede from you at 10^5 x 1.8241. You could drown in the epic existential guilt of "Come-Too-Soon Comics," and you'll have total power over the destinies of the characters in "Torture the Characters Comics!"

I don't know how many different dimensions physicists are currently hypothesizing as they search for a catch-all theory of the universe, but it occurs to me they'd save themselves some effort by studying the work of Ed Subitzky, a man who creates his own universes with the ink he uses, the drawings he makes with it, and the words he writes to accompany them.

If you find yourself in one of these universes, be advised there is a deity already in place. He's a mild-mannered bald guy with glasses and a glint in his eyes, and he's got ideas about you and an elephant.

—Rick Meyerowitz

December 1973

March 1974

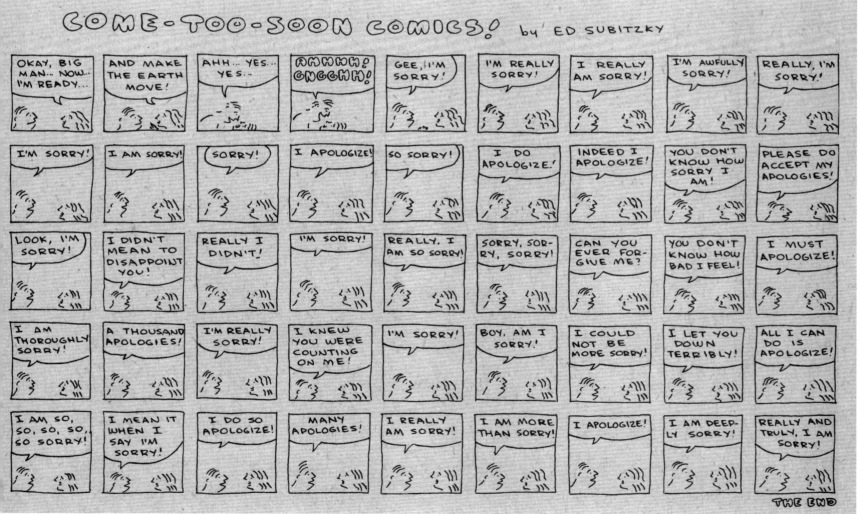

November 1974

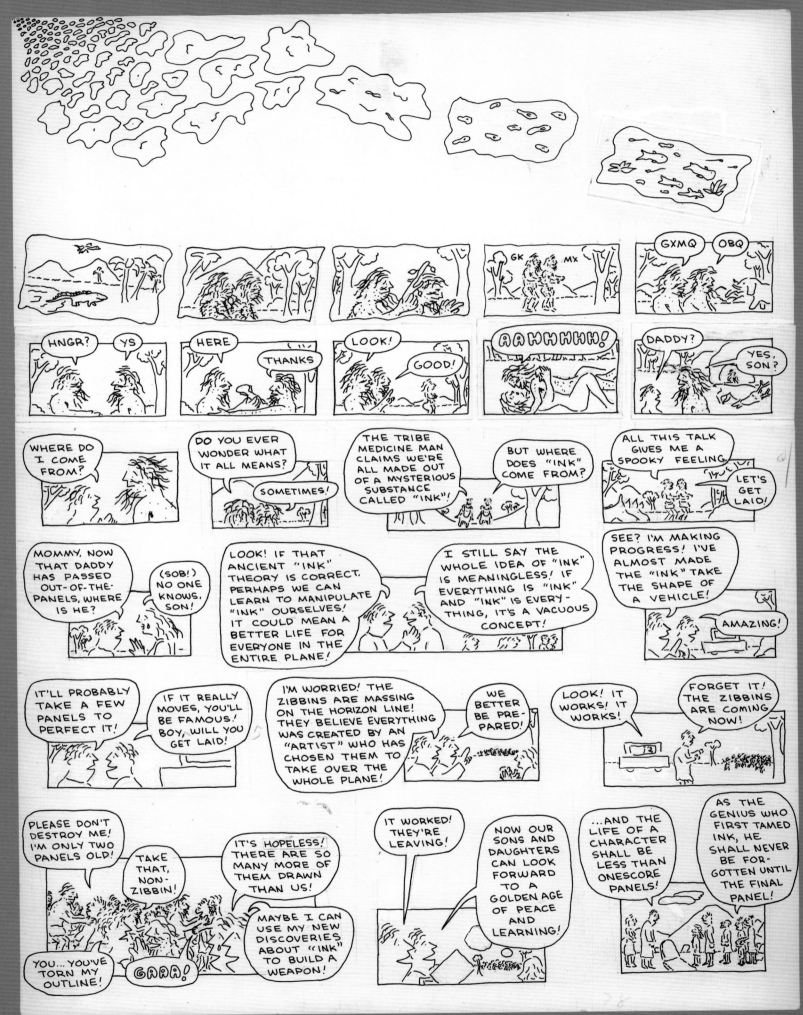

"Boring Strip," February 1976

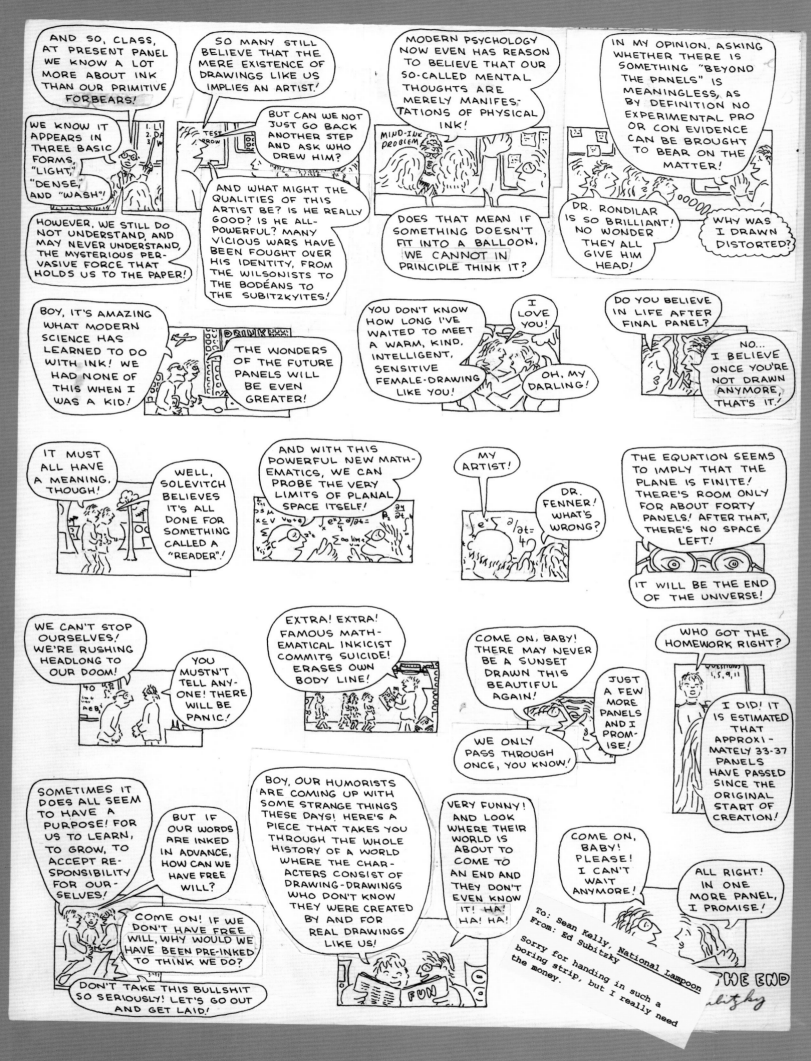

TORTURE THE CHARACTERS COMICS!

BY ED SUBITZKY
COLORING: B. SCHUBECK

LETS YOU, THE READER, CHANGE PEOPLE'S DESTINIES AND RUIN LIVES!

DIRECTIONS: READ ONLY ONE BALLOON IN EACH PANEL! WHENEVER YOU WANT TO TEMPORARILY RAISE FALSE HOPES FOR THE CHARACTERS, READ THE YELLOW BALLOON IN A PANEL! WHENEVER YOU WANT TO PLUNGE THE CHARACTERS INTO DESPAIR, READ THE BLUE BALLOON IN A PANEL! AS YOU PROCEED ONWARD THROUGH STRIP, JUMP BACK AND FORTH BETWEEN YELLOW AND BLUE (HAPPINESS AND DESPAIR) AS MUCH AS YOU WANT, WHENEVER YOU WANT!

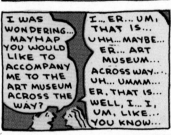

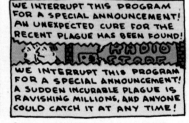

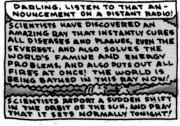

From the "Depression" issue, January 1979

MAD AS HELL COMICS!
BY ED SUBITZKY

 BOY, THERE'S ONE THING WE DRAWINGS REALLY HATE!

 AND WE'RE REALLY GLAD TO FINALLY GET THE CHANCE TO TELL YOU!

 IT'S YOU!

 THE WAY YOU TURN THE PAGES OF THE MAGAZINE!

 THE WAY YOU GET YOUR GREASY FINGERS ALL OVER US!

 THE WAY YOU READ US JUST TO LAUGH AT US!

 AND THE WAY YOU KEEP HOPING ONE OF US WILL TAKE OFF OUR CLOTHES OR SOMETHING!

 OR SAY A DIRTY WORD LIKE "FUCK"!

 SEE? YOU JUST LOVED THAT, DIDN'T YOU!

 THEN WHEN YOU'RE THROUGH WITH US, YOU JUST TURN THE PAGE LIKE WE NEVER EXISTED!

 AND SOONER OR LATER, YOU THROW US AWAY WITH THE TRASH!

 YOU THINK YOU'RE SO SUPERIOR, DON'T YOU!

 WELL, WHO DO YOU THINK THE REAL COMIC IS?

 LOOK AT YOU! ALWAYS WAGING WAR ON EACH OTHER!

 WELL, WE THINK THAT'S HYSTERICAL!

 AND THE WAY YOU POLLUTE YOUR AIR! AND YOUR OCEANS!

 AND THE PATHETIC WAY YOU ALL TRY SO HARD TO GET LAID!

 YOU WAIT YOUR WHOLE LIVES TO FALL IN LOVE, AND WHEN IT HAPPENS YOU DO NOTHING BUT FIGHT AND ARGUE!

 YOU INSIST ON BELIEVING IN MEANING AND PURPOSE, BUT AT LEAST WE KNOW WE'RE JUST STUPID DRAWINGS!

 AND THE FUNNIEST PART IS THE WAY YOU GROW OLD AND DIE!

 YOU CAN'T HANDLE LIFE AND YOU'RE TERRIFIED OF DEATH!

 AND YOU CAN'T EVEN GET CHANGE OF A QUARTER WHEN YOU NEED IT!

 YOU'RE SO DESPERATE FOR A LITTLE ENTERTAINMENT YOU'LL DO ANYTHING!

 EVEN LAUGH AT POOR, HELPLESS DRAWINGS LIKE US!

 WELL, WE CAN'T HELP WHAT WE DO! WE'RE INKED IN ADVANCE!

 YOU SUPPOSEDLY HAVE FREE WILL! AND LOOK WHAT YOU DO WITH IT!

 BUT YOU'RE NOT INTERESTED IN ANY OF THIS, ARE YOU!

 YOU JUST WANT TO SEE ME SLIP ON A BANANA PEEL OR SOMETHING!

 AND ALL YOU REALLY WANT TO DO IS SEE MY TITS!

 WELL, WE DON'T CARE IF WE ARE JUST PRINTED DRAWINGS!

 SOMEHOW, THIS ONE TIME, WE'LL MANAGE TO RESIST!

 WELL, I'VE GOT TO RUN!

 ARGGHHHH!

 OH NO! HE JUST SLIPPED ON A BANANA PEEL!

 I THINK HE BROKE HIS NECK!

 BUT I'M STILL NOT SHOWING YOU MY TITS!

 I WON'T STAND HERE AND BE EXPOSED AND HUMILIATED IN FRONT OF HUNDREDS OF THOUSANDS OF LEERING EYES!

 SOB!

 YOU KNOW WHO I HATE THE MOST? THE MORON WHO DREW ME!

 AND NOW HE'S GOING TO MAKE ME CURSE LIKE A BANSHEE! I JUST KNOW IT!

 I WON'T! SOMEHOW, SOME WAY, I WON'T!

 SHIT! FUCK! CUNT! PRICK! HARD-ON!

 GASP! PLEASE UNDERSTAND! I HAVE NO CHOICE IN WHAT I SAY OR DO!

 YOU DO HAVE A CHOICE! SO MAKE THE MOST OF IT!

 ENJOY YOUR THREE-DIMENSIONAL WORLD! MAKE IT GREEN AND BEAUTIFUL!

 LAY DOWN YOUR WEAPONS AND HAVE A GOLDEN AGE OF PEACE!

 LIVE A SWEET LIFE OF BROTHERHOOD, LOVE AND HARMONY!

 AND CREATE A WORLD WHERE NO ONE HAS TO BE MAD ABOUT ANYTHING!

 KNOW WHAT WOULD BE A GOOD PLACE TO START?

 STOP STARING AT MY TITS!

 AND WHATEVER YOU DO, DON'T READ THE LAST PANEL!

 BECAUSE I HAVE THIS STRANGE FEELING THAT THEY'RE GOING TO DRAW ME MAKING LOVE TO AN ELEPHANT!

 IF YOU CAN RESIST READING THE LAST PANEL, THERE JUST MIGHT BE A LITTLE HOPE FOR YOU AND YOUR WORLD!

OOOH, YES! YES! YES! I LOVE YOU! DON'T EVER STOP! YOU'RE SO BIG AND STRONG! OH YES! OH YES! NOW JUST A LITTLE OVER TO THE LEFT...

Ed's stinkin' pencil sketch for "Mad As Hell Comics!," November 1985

P.J. O'ROURKE

Occasionally a person wonders what sort of impression he makes on others. In the early 1970s, thanks to P.J. O'Rourke, I had little doubt. The *National Lampoon* had been running my work for a year when P.J. traveled west to Del Mar to finally meet me, the "California crazy man." He was to be our guest for a few days. At the appointed hour came a knock on the door, and there he stood, long hair, gray suit, tie askew, bags under his eyes, cigarette hanging from his lips, and a bottle of Mumm Cordon Rouge dangling at his side.

"Welcome," I said, offering my hand. He eyed me up and down for several seconds, then pronounced, "You look like a fucking accountant!"

Later, over dinner, my wife Jackie and I extolled the virtues of San Diego. "We can go to Balboa Park; it's fabulous! Or the San Diego Zoo! And there's always La Jolla or the beaches—whatever you'd like to see!"

"Take me to Tijuana," P.J. demanded. "I've gotta see Tijuana!" Being gracious hosts and sensitive to the requests

PHOTO BY DAVID KAESTLE

of such an aesthete, we drove P.J. south of the border in our Volkswagen. We spent an entire day deflecting offers of intimacy from strangers, while P.J. tried on various serapes and huaraches ("Hey! They're made from real tires!") and queried us regarding the artistic merits of countless bullfight posters and black velvet paintings.

P.J. to a vendor: "Your Elvis on velveto es muy bueno, but I'm looking for a Neil Sedaka."

The trip was a huge success and P.J. was delighted. "Christ, look at all the squalor—*this is great!*"

As we headed back to Del Mar, our weary companion dozed in the back of the Beetle, happily clutching his brand-new T-shirt, an item of apparel favored by bikers and surfers that cleverly promoted Baja's most notorious sex bar. It read: "I ate at The Blue Fox."

—Wayne McLoughlin

DEAD SERIOUS
Alan Rose on P.J. O'Rourke

P.J. O'Rourke is a dead serious comedian. For professionals, writing scathing satire is a job. Writing humor the way P.J. writes it requires great attention to detail. At the *Lampoon* most stories were visually driven. Authors usually delivered "art notes" to accompany a written manuscript. P.J's notes were extraordinary—almost OCD in their detail. When Marc Arceneaux and I created the illustrations for the high school yearbook parody, we made intentionally bad imitations of student drawings. They were truly bad, but even though we broke every rule we could think of, P.J. often returned them for revisions because they weren't bad enough. "Make 'em worse!" he'd say. He recommended that we use our left hands, draw blindfolded, hold a pen between thumb and pinky, hold it in our teeth, make a lettering drop-shadow go "both ways," or use all uppercase Old English–style characters. P.J. knew the importance of exaggerating a parody to reinforce the joke. The *Lampoon*'s art department later won awards for the yearbook, surely owing much to his additional "art direction." P.J.'s devotion to his art notes was without equal. He knew how to articulate what he wanted, and he got it.

Artist's conception of a U.S. B'way-42 "Rolling Fortress" fighting in Normandy, had it been there. The most versatile medium bus of the war, the B'way-42 mounted as many as seventeen guns or, equipped with the Norton Bus Sight, was able to carry twenty-six 250 lb. bombs which could be lethally dropped.

From "Battling Busses of WWII," *The National Lampoon Encyclopedia of Humor*, 1973

THIS IS WAR

by P. J. O'Rourke

March 1977: War-Torn Namibia, South-West Africa, German South-West Africa, or whatever they're calling it this month.

Perimeter Defenses, Windhoek, S.W.A., Sept. 28—Mars, the dog of war, has raised its ugly head again on this dark continent, Africa. High in the Auaz mountains, hardy descendants of the same Dutch people whose other hardy descendants fought so bravely in the resistance during W.W. II plus some English await the onslaught of Botswanans, Zambians, Angolans, Congolese, Lesothoians, Swazilanders, and who knows who else no doubt soon to be massed on their borders. Defended only by their army and air force, these plucky South Africans strive bravely to fulfill their responsibilities to this former possession of the Kaiser—responsibilities thrust on their reluctant shoulders by a League of Nations mandate in 1921. Yet when South Africa turns to that august body for succor or support, they hear only silence. The tragedy of impuissant world law is repeated, as in Abyssinia prostrate before Il Duce's dago hordes. Thus the South Africans, surrounded on all sides except the south and east, their backs to the often very choppy Atlantic, prepare for a fight to the death, or until an internationally supervised truce can be arranged.

We are inside a low concrete bunker in the final defense line of a Windhoek military base. The heat is stifling. Outside it must be 80 degrees. There's no whiskey to be had for half a kilometer in any direction; the beer is warm, and the situation reminds me of nothing so much as the Jap prison camp I was in in the Malay peninsula. Fortunately, that was a couple of years after the war and I was just visiting, but it was a scene of unspeakable horror, or recently had been.

We are surrounded by a dazzling array of computer terminals, radar screens, and infrared sensor devices abandoned by the Germans in 1915—the "U.S.A." stenciled on all the equipment standing for *Underdeveloped* Colonial Enclave under the *Sovereignty* of Germany in *Africa*. Colonel Tulipburgher, the commanding officer, explains that as a result of the U.N. sanctions, South Africa can buy no new military equipment, and must make do with jet planes and guided missiles left over from the Boer War and W.W. I.

This Tulipburgher is a big man, rough-cut and steely-featured, possessed of a craglike visage. Yet, as I sip from can after can of Lion and Castle, this strong face seems to dance and blur—no doubt as a result of the deeply felt emotions he voices. "Can't imagine what the nig-nogs want with South-West Africa," he's saying. "There isn't a thing here of any use to them. Just diamonds and uranium, iron, vanadium—things that they wouldn't know what to do with even if they could figure out how to get them out of the ground. Why, all they'd do is buy more wives than the grazing land can support. They're better off the way they are, and I dare say most of them know it. At least, the bearers and the kitchen boys do."

His voice is filled with the experience of Africa, and I feel a manly camaraderie with this defender of the lowly bushman and the bauxite ore. There we are, he and I, face to face in this lonely outpost, where we are human prey to bands of bloodthirsty guerrillas armed to the teeth with Communist-supplied knives and large sticks. At any minute, these black fanatics might swim the Okavango River, snip the strands of electrified barbed wire, slither through a minefield, hike two hundred miles to Tsumeb, catch a train to Walvis Bay, switch to the Windhoek local, hitch a ride to the outskirts of town, bluff their way past the gatehouse, silence the guard dogs, and set upon us with incomparable savagery. But Colonel Tulipburgher is a stranger to fear, or, if he and that base emotion have met at all, it is but a nodding acquaintance, strictly social. Perhaps they've been unwilling bridge partners in some previous rubber of brinkmanship, with spades trump and mankind's future bid, doubled, and redoubled.

Ah, yes, here is a guardian of civilization's barely glowing ember in a world of night. Suddenly, there is a blaze of light upon the dials and screens, bells ring and sirens bellow, beer cans rattle around my feet. This is war, but I'm told there is no reason for concern. Only a herd of antelope has been nuked. "But from all reports and indications, it *might* had been a herbivorous armored column of four-footed tanks," explains the colonel, and he tells me how grateful the bushmen will be. It seems that if you set an A-bomb off five hundred meters above ground zero, it cooks those fleet-hooved turf-nibblers just like a giant microwave oven—done to a turn the whole way through. The blacks love it that way; it's the only real cooked meat that they ever get. Plus it's a great help in reconnaissance patrols, as it causes the natives' blood to glow in the dark.

JUST ONE OF THOSE DAYS

BY P.J. O'ROURKE

The alarm went off about half an hour late, and I pulled out the old Smith & Wesson 9mm automatic I keep under my pillow and squeezed off a couple of rounds at the fucker. I didn't even have my eyes open yet, but I still managed to nick the snooze button. *Kee-rist*, I hate to get up in the morning, but I swear they're going to kill me if I'm late to work again. They killed a couple of other executives just last week—hauled them into the freight elevator and shot them in the head. But I would have gone back to sleep anyway, really, if it hadn't been for this old bitch in the apartment next door. She was putting her cat out—for keeps. She must have taken six shots at the thing and the sucker just wouldn't die. It was howling bloody murder. I threw a couple of slugs through the wall in her general direction and then hit the deck and belly-crawled to the kitchen while she returned fire. Using the dishwasher for cover, I made myself a cup of coffee and then I slipped out onto the fire escape and popped a white phosphorus grenade through the old cunt's window so that I could shower and shave standing up.

Then I couldn't find any clean shirts. And when I did find one it took me twenty minutes to disarm the plastique charge the fucking Chinaman had pressed behind the shirt cardboard. I finally had to set it off in the sink. It was a brand-new shirt, too.

And the explosion about wrecked the kitchen. The apartment was a mess anyway. Good thing the cleaning lady was coming, and double good thing I had the cleaning lady's kid tied up and booby-trapped in the hall closet or she'd never do windows.

So I was all dressed and ready to go to work, but my date was still asleep, lying on her back with her mouth open, snoring. Even with all the sirens and the fire trucks and the commotion next door, she hadn't stirred. I don't know, somehow this really pissed me off, so I picked her up and threw her through the window. My place is only on the third floor, so she probably lived. I'll call her next week and apologize.

The mail hadn't come yet either. The doorman said that there was a company of marines trying to get through with it but they were pinned down in Murray Hill somewhere. The doorman was as surly as usual and would have slit my throat if I hadn't judo-flipped him and kicked him in the solar plexus first.

I was going to drive to work, but then I remembered that the parking garage up by the office was still under siege. A dozen spook parking attendants were in there holding about thirty schoolkids from the suburbs. The kids had come into town for the circus. I don't know why they bothered. Some Puerto Rican meat hunters had gotten all the elephants already. Anyway, I couldn't get in to park, even though I've got a monthly slot. Besides, day before yesterday the spooks put some of the schoolkids in this one Cadillac,

"THEN I HIT THE DECK AND BELLY-CRAWLED TO THE KITCHEN WHILE SHE RETURNED FIRE. USING THE DISHWASHER FOR COVER, I MADE MYSELF A CUP OF COFFEE..."

PTEEOOW!

TZIP!

set it on fire, and drove it off the garage roof. I guess about ten pedestrians were killed when it landed.

Now, I had my favorite little personal defense unit out of my briefcase and ready as soon as I hit the street. This is a Walther MPK 9mm submachine gun I had special-ordered with selective fire. It doesn't pack quite the punch that an Uzi does, but it's the most compact automatic fire weapon made in the world, at least in 9mm. I'm a real bug on 9mm ammo. It's kind of my hobby. But by this time the morning rush hour was in

full swing and I couldn't even get a cab in my peep sights, so I had to take the subway. I hate taking the subway—all those kids that spray graffiti all over the place. The cops ought to tie them up and cut their balls off—which is exactly what the cops are doing, except they don't catch enough of them for my money. Plus it was a regular shitty morning outside, raining and cold, and bombs were dropping in the next block. I bet twenty snipers took a shot at me between my building and the subway station. I don't know why those people are allowed out on the streets—they can't hit a goddamn thing. Although one did get a bag lady right by the newsstand and I got brains all over my raincoat, which I had just gotten back from the cleaners. And *that* wasn't easy either. In fact, it took a midnight raid on the manager's house in Rego Park, where I picked off all four of his guard dogs with the help

of a starlight scope. So there I was with brains all over me and then I had to beat the shit out of the blind guy at the newsstand before he'd give me a paper.

I shot my way past a couple of transit cops at the token booth, jumped the turnstile, and got a train to stop by pushing some lady out on the tracks. It's surprising, even a 100-pound woman can derail those babies when they're going at full throttle; so they generally try to stop if they can. On the train a pack of asshole teenagers was terrorizing everybody, ripping gold chains off women and taking wallets at knifepoint, so I joined them for a while and picked up a little, you know, cab fare. Then I forced everybody, including the conductor, to get in the last car, and I pulled the pin and

left them back in the tunnel. Sometimes that's the only way you can get a seat. Almost got my butt kicked for that, though—who would have thought one of those kids would be carrying a wire-guided antitank missile? Good thing it bounced off a signal light and ricocheted right back at the kid with the launcher or I would have been hurting. I mean it.

I was late for work for sure by now. The subway was running way behind schedule and I had to help the engineer for a while when we ran across an armored train. It must have been from over on the IND line. Anyway, it was shooting up the Thirty-fourth Street station. Fortunately, I'd planted some radio-detonated Claymore mines under the litter baskets in that station just a week back. And I had the transmitter in my briefcase. It's great—it doubles as a digital travel clock. The mines killed all the people on the plat-

form, but they brought a big section of the tunnel roof down on those guys from the IND, too.

Well, by the time I blasted my way through the reception area and raped my secretary and piled up the desk and some chairs to barricade myself in my office, the "Old Man" was really fuming. He was over on the roof of the building across the street with about twenty guys from accounting, and they all had M-16s and tear-gas-grenade launchers. He was giving me a real talking-to over the bullhorn, telling me to come out with my hands up or forget about that raise. I got my gas mask on and pulled the Browning automatic rifle out from behind the file cabinet and gave him a little argument. But I couldn't keep that up for long. I had to take some calls and dictate a bunch of letters, and it was a real pain in the ass giving dictation to a secretary who was coughing and gagging from the CS gas, especially when she was still holding her crotch in this hurt-looking way.

Then I had the Peterson contract to straighten out. They manufacture designer jeans, and what a bunch of hard-nosed sons of bitches they are. Their CEO had been on the horn to me all week threatening to nuke our Tarrytown office if he didn't see some action soon. Here was a client who was definitely hanging by a thread. And I knew if that Peterson thing fell through, my ass would be in deep shit.

I didn't have time to go out for lunch, so I just had a deli owner and his family killed and some sandwiches sent up. I was working like a bear and by three o'clock I was pretty sure I had all my ducks in a row, and then wouldn't you know it—fifteen megatons right in the parking lot of our suburban branch office. You probably

> "THE 'OLD MAN' WAS REALLY FUMING...HE TOLD ME TO COME OUT WITH MY HANDS UP OR FORGET ABOUT THAT RAISE."

read about it in the papers. It broke half the windows in Manhattan, and I'll bet it takes weeks to decontaminate all the radioactive fallout shit all over the place. And that wasn't the worst of it by any means. Right after Tarrytown goes up in a mushroom cloud and the Peterson account goes with it, the boss finally breaks through my office wall with a bangalore torpedo and tells me he's promoted young Donovan over my head to group vice-president. That means I'll have to go all the way out to Donovan's house in Darien and poison his kids. Well, that did it. I decided to toss a Molotov cocktail into the mail room and knock off early.

A couple of the guys and I took our secretaries down to Clarke's for a few drinks, raped the girls again, and then gut-shot one of the waiters and bet on how long it would take him to die. I guess I had a few more than I meant to, becasue I was really bushed. So I thought I'd just have a burger in the back room. I wanted to carve it right out of the cow myself, but the fucker wouldn't hold still. Finally I had to hit it with a tranq gun. Then the guys and I tried to attach some gelignite to the cow's ass and make chopped steak that way. But the gelignite gave the whole thing a really rotten taste. After that, I

"IT WAS A REAL PAIN IN THE ASS TO DICTATE WHILE SHE WAS HOLDING HER CROTCH IN THAT HURT-LOOKING WAY AND COUGHING AND GAGGING FROM THE CS GAS."

just said fuck dinner and had a couple more drinks and decided to go back to my place and spend a peaceful night at home for a change.

It was still raining outside and I had to call in an air strike to get a taxi. One of the A-1E Skyraiders finally spotted a Checker on Park Avenue and strafed the hack until he chased it over to me. I held the MPK on the driver all the way back to my place and shot up his gas tank for a tip. Then the doorman tried to kill me again, and I had to toss a fragmentation grenade at this lady in the lobby to keep her dog from jumping on me. So I ended up outside waiting around

in the rain while one of the building porters cleaned her guts off the elevator door, and *then* what the fuck do you think I saw? A goddamned parking ticket on my car! Jesus, I was pissed. I mean, I'm *sure* it was one of those Jewish holidays when the alternate-side-of-the-street parking regulations are supposed to be suspended. I mean, I'm pretty sure all the Jews aren't killed yet. I would have complained to a cop if he hadn't shot first. And then when I finally did get inside, fucking Carson was on vacation again and that asshole Letterman was hosting the "Tonight" show. Man, it was just one of those days. □

"IT WAS STILL RAINING OUTSIDE AND I HAD TO CALL IN AN AIR STRIKE TO GET A CAB."

—ARBY AIRZ...

HOW THE WORLD LOOKS TO CHILDREN
Ball-point pens as seen by a twelve-year-old boy.

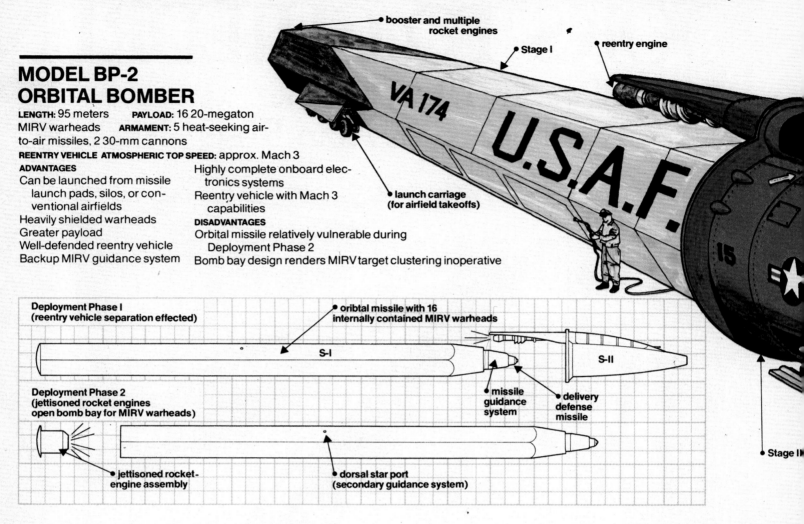

MODEL BP-2 ORBITAL BOMBER

LENGTH: 95 meters   **PAYLOAD:** 16 20-megaton MIRV warheads   **ARMAMENT:** 5 heat-seeking air-to-air missiles, 2 30-mm cannons

REENTRY VEHICLE ATMOSPHERIC TOP SPEED: approx. Mach 3

ADVANTAGES

Can be launched from missile launch pads, silos, or conventional airfields
Heavily shielded warheads
Greater payload
Well-defended reentry vehicle
Backup MIRV guidance system

Highly complete onboard electronics systems
Reentry vehicle with Mach 3 capabilities

DISADVANTAGES

Orbital missile relatively vulnerable during Deployment Phase 2
Bomb bay design renders MIRV target clustering inoperative

booster and multiple rocket engines
Stage I
reentry engine
VA 174
U.S.A.F.
15
launch carriage (for airfield takeoffs)

Deployment Phase I (reentry vehicle separation effected)
oribtal missile with 16 internally contained MIRV warheads
S-I
S-II
missile guidance system
delivery defense missile

Deployment Phase 2 (jettisoned rocket engines open bomb bay for MIRV warheads)
jettisoned rocket-engine assembly
dorsal star port (secondary guidance system)

Stage I

MODEL BP-1 ORBITAL BOMBER

LENGTH: 80 meters   **PAYLOAD:** 12 10-megaton MIRV warheads
ARMAMENT: 1 launch/delivery defense rocket, 5 reentry defense rockets
REENTRY VEHICLE ATMOSPHERIC TOP SPEED: approx. Mach 1

ADVANTAGES

Can utilize conventional airfields for launch
Well-defended reentry vehicle
Highly complete onboard electronics systems

DISADVANTAGES

Poorly defended launch vehicle
Unmaneuverable reentry vehicle
Requires crew of 3
Complexity of design
High launch cost

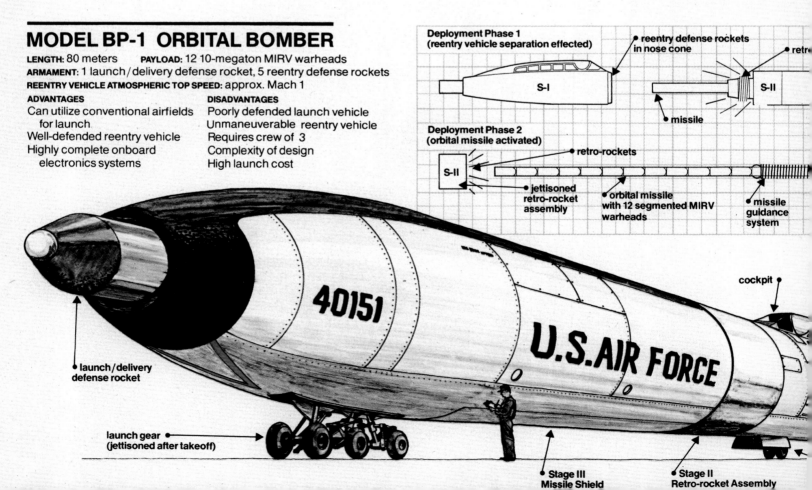

Deployment Phase 1 (reentry vehicle separation effected)
reentry defense rockets in nose cone
retro-
S-I
S-II
missile

Deployment Phase 2 (orbital missile activated)
retro-rockets
S-II
jettisoned retro-rocket assembly
orbital missile with 12 segmented MIRV warheads
missile guidance system

40151
U.S.AIR FORCE
cockpit
launch/delivery defense rocket
launch gear (jettisoned after takeoff)
Stage III Missile Shield
Stage II Retro-rocket Assembly

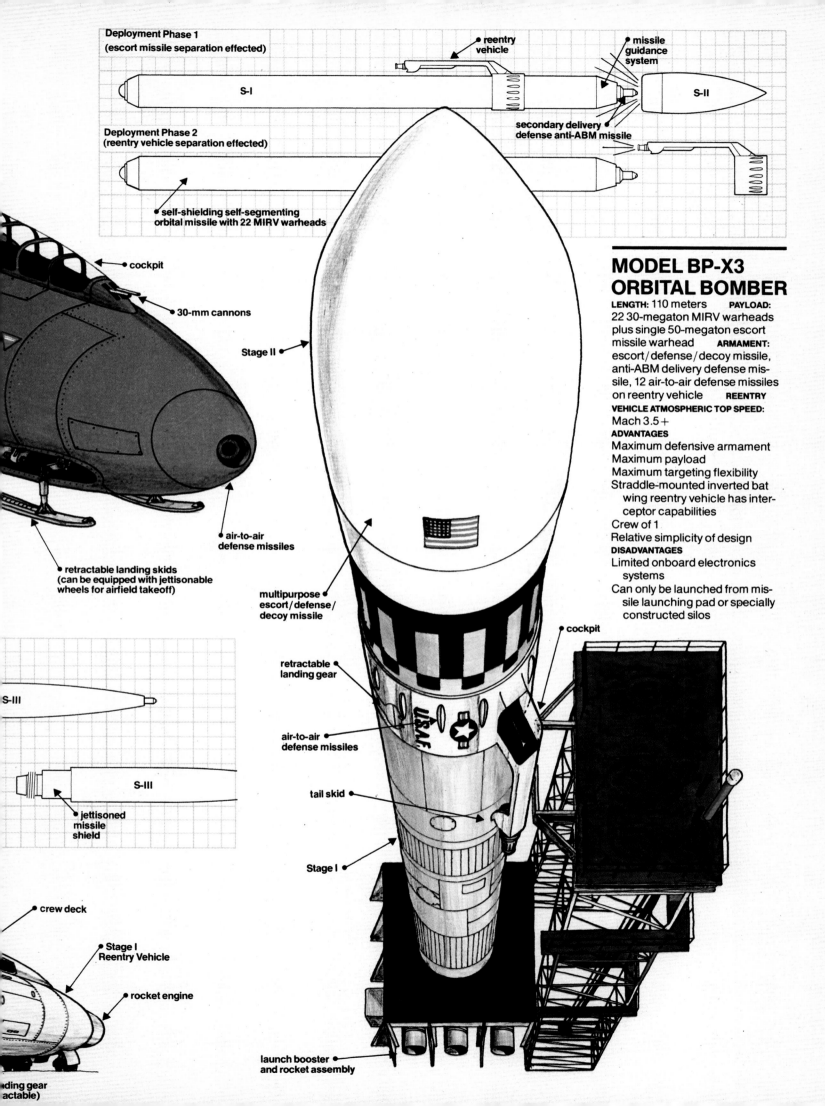

Deployment Phase 1
(escort missile separation effected)

S-I

• reentry vehicle

• missile guidance system

S-II

secondary delivery defense anti-ABM missile

Deployment Phase 2
(reentry vehicle separation effected)

• self-shielding self-segmenting orbital missile with 22 MIRV warheads

• cockpit

• 30-mm cannons

Stage II

• air-to-air defense missiles

• retractable landing skids (can be equipped with jettisonable wheels for airfield takeoff)

multipurpose escort/defense/decoy missile

MODEL BP-X3 ORBITAL BOMBER

LENGTH: 110 meters   **PAYLOAD:** 22 30-megaton MIRV warheads plus single 50-megaton escort missile warhead   **ARMAMENT:** escort/defense/decoy missile, anti-ABM delivery defense missile, 12 air-to-air defense missiles on reentry vehicle   **REENTRY VEHICLE ATMOSPHERIC TOP SPEED:** Mach 3.5+

ADVANTAGES
Maximum defensive armament
Maximum payload
Maximum targeting flexibility
Straddle-mounted inverted bat wing reentry vehicle has interceptor capabilities
Crew of 1
Relative simplicity of design

DISADVANTAGES
Limited onboard electronics systems
Can only be launched from missile launching pad or specially constructed silos

• cockpit

retractable landing gear •

air-to-air defense missiles

tail skid •

Stage I

S-III

S-III

• jettisoned missile shield

• crew deck

• Stage I Reentry Vehicle

• rocket engine

ding gear actable)

launch booster and rocket assembly •

ILLUSTRATIONS BY ALAN ROSE

BRUCE McCALL

Unique: being the only one of its kind; without equal or equivalent; unparallelled; incomparable; Bruce McCall.

Imagine Bruce as a boy: mittens, hat with earflaps too big, heavy padded coat, galoshes, a scarf muffling his face. If he is saying something, we can't hear it. He lives in the bland Ontario outback between the lakes during the bleak years of World War II. Besides a pair of hand-me-down ice skates, he owns exactly one thing: a stack of old *Popular Mechanics* magazines as tall as he is. During the long gray winters he reads each issue over and over. He draws incessantly, sketching an impossible world of zeppelin travel to the moon, sleek, roomy cars that cruise up the sides of tall buildings, and ocean liners that dive like submarines. Bruce falls in love with the genre and the breathless tone with which it proclaims a sunny and magnificent future.

He's surrounded by cold water. Lake Huron is just to the north, Lake Ontario to the east. From his point of view, embedded in a gloomy childhood on the wintry northern shore of Lake Erie, the present doesn't look so rosy. So he comes down with a strong case of irony, and develops a wry, cantankerous sense of humor to go with his burgeoning drawing ability.

Hoplock's amazing catch in the 1946 World Series.

Bruce McCall, section 34, row R, seat 27

It's the early 1950s. Bruce works in an art studio in Windsor, Ontario, painting car advertisements for the American autopoly in Detroit. These are the years of big, wide, preposterous cars and hyperventilating ad copy. Bruce paints all of them. Eventually, he finds himself writing that ad copy, too, and he is drawn into the world of advertising. The 1960s arrive and he spends three years living in Germany, creating ads for Mercedes-Benz. He absorbs the contradictions in German culture and, on moving to New York, he never shed his outsider's gimlet-eyed view of American life.

So, by 1972, the year he first contributed to the *National Lampoon*, his originality burst from the pages of the magazine and became an integral part of its classic years. An argument could be made that the *Lampoon* wouldn't be the *Lampoon* without his trademark visual work. He got his start creating a world only he could see. We all saw it and recognized that Bruce McCall owned this material and there was nothing else like it anywhere, and forty years later, there still isn't. He's very funny, completely original, unique.

—Rick Meyerowitz

Above: November 1973

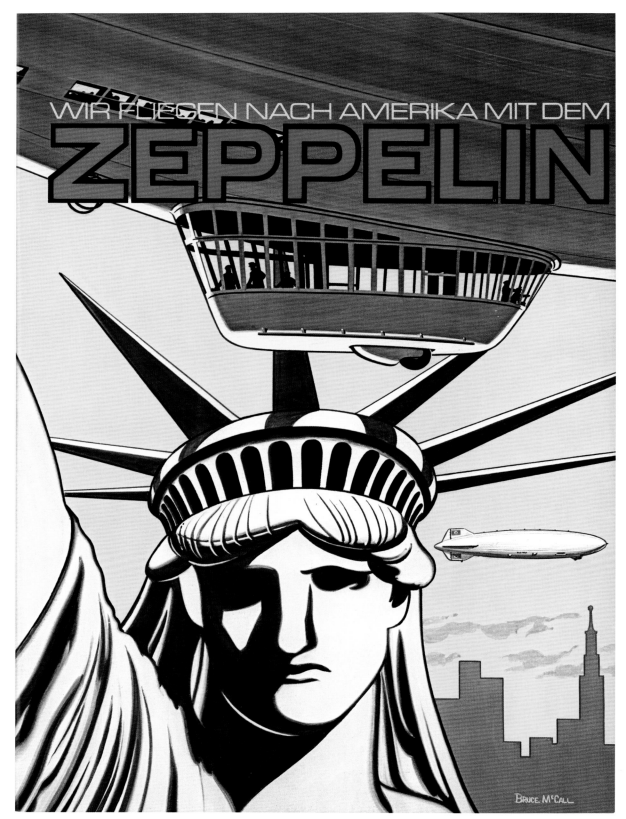

WIR FLIEGEN NACH AMERIKA MIT DEM
ZEPPELIN

January 1975

ZEPPELIN NACH NEW YORK

I felt compelled to come up with a visual metaphor for the saga of the Zeppelin. The Götterdämmerung of the Hindenburg in 1937—the first human catastrophe to be caught live on film and radio—forever made the rigid airship a symbol of fiery death, despite a long and safe commercial life over the previous twenty-odd years. I used skeletons because I wanted to convey the idea that the Zeppelin had always been doomed: a romantic nineteenth-century dream of travel, leisurely and gentle; and I did it in German because it was solely German pride in a German invention that pushed it far beyond its natural lifespan into the age of the passenger airplane, where it couldn't compete. Hitler, of course, hated Zeppelins.

—Bruce McCall

AUF WIEDERSEHEN!

Langsam und lautlos, wie durch Zauberei, hebt der mächtige Zeppelin ab. Unten auf der Erde stehen deine winkenden Freunde und Angehörigen und beobachten, wie die gigantische Silberwurst der Lüfte sich gegen den Wind dreht, um die grosse Reise anzutreten. "Macht Euch keine Sorgen," schreist du ihnen durch das grosse Fenster zu. Dummes Volk, ein paar von ihnen heulen!

DER ATLANTIK!

"Ist das da unten die R.M.S. Titanic?" fragst du einen von der Mannschaft. "Was für eine Frage, wo dieses Unglücksschiff schon vor 25 Jahren gesunken ist!" Der Mann hat hur ein Lächeln. Auf einer Zeppelinreise bekommt man viele seltsame Dinge zu sehen. Zwischendurch ruft Grete: "Ich glaub, ich seh die Lusitania!" Was für ein Gelächter, was für ein fideles Zeppelin-Abenteuer!

HERR KAPITAN!

Möchten Sie den Kapitän und seine Mannschaft kennenlernen? Sie reden nur selten; sie scheinen wie Geister durch diese schwebende Reisenwelt des Zeppelins zu gleiten. Aber sie lächeln fortwährend... denn sie wissen, was Ihnen bevorsteht!

KOGNAK?

Einen Kognak nach dem Essen? Aber sicher! Der Steward scheint aus dem Nichts aufzutauchen, als hätte er Ihre Gedanken gelesen. Und wenn Sie ihn nicht mehr brauchen, ist er plötzlich verschwunden. Alles ist ruhig. Die Wolken ziehen vorbei. Dennoch beschleicht Sie eine seltsame Vorahnung!

MMEN
IHRES
SCHIFFES!

ELT BETRETEN,
IMMER VERÄNDERT!

FASZINATION!
"Schau, Guntherchen, das stürmische Wetter kommt direkt auf uns zu!" Fasziniert beobachtet es Guntherchen, während der lächelnde Navigator etwas von bösartigem Himmel und heftigem Blitz murmelt. "Kann der Blitz in unsern glückliches Zeppelin-Heim einschlagen?" fragt Gunther. Aber der Navigator ist weg.

"MMMMM—MILCH!"
Wer ist der unerwartete Fremde in der Kabinentür? Nur der Steward! Schau, gute warme Milch und ein lächelndes "Gute Nacht." Bald ist das mächtige Luftschiff dunkel. Begleitet vom Gebrumm der Dieselmotoren träumt man durch die Nacht; lebhafte, farbige, fantastiche Träume, die in ein feuriges Morgenrot übergehen!

ZIGARETTE?

Das Essen ist vorüber, der Kaffee serviert; und da unser Bestimmungsort nur noch ein paar Kilometer entfernt ist, lass den Donner ruhig grollen and die Blitze zucken. Der Chef-Steward ist schon mit einem Streichholz zur Hand, als Sie sich eine Zigarette aussuchen und scherzen: "Man sollte ja annehmen, Herr Chef-Steward, dass bei all dem feuergefährlichen Wasserstoff angezündete Streichhölzer . . ."

A Lung Surgeon Needs
STEADY NERVES

NO WONDER AMERICA'S HOSPITALS ARE FULL OF *EGYPTIAN CORKS* SMOKERS

Doctors know that the rare Egyptian Corks blend of Turkish hemp and choice sweepings is laboratory-proven to trigger the famous "Cough of Confidence," clearing the bronchia and relaxing your "Y-Zone." Egyptian Corks are just what the doctor ordered to promote calm nerves. That's why whenever you see a surgeon you should think of Egyptian Corks!

NOT A LUMP IN A LUNGFUL!

EGYPTIAN CORKS

Try This Test On Your "Y-Zone"

Smoke a carton of Egyptian Corks a day for 12 months, then ask your Y-Zone if it wants more. It'll say yes—proof positive!

EGYPTIAN CORKS
TURKISH HEMP BLEND CIGARETTES
CHOICE SWEEPINGS

July 1973

1934 AIRDREME *Nabob* V-16 SLEEKSTER: ONLY A BA

SAY, SHE'S ROOMY AS THE DUST BO

Tap-A-Toe Futuroidic Footless De-Clutching features Single Pedal Power Control and the Floorboard of the Future in 1934.

More solid than a WPA dam, more economical than an Okie's diet, more fun per mile than Mah-Jongg —jeepers, creepers, the 1934 Airdreme Nabob is a League of Nations of motoring value wrapped up in Mello-Streme Style that gives competition something to fear besides fear itself!

Take new Tap-A-Toe Futuroidic Footless De-Clutching. Instead of old-fashioned gas, brake, and clutch pedals that kept your feet busier than a dance marathon, Tap-A-Toe Futuroidic Footless De-Clutching offers the convenience of Single Pedal Power Control—combines *all foot functions* in one single pedal!

Think of it: one tap—you go, moving off faster than a barfly after Repeal.

Two taps—you change gears, as smooth and automatic as a mortgage foreclosure.

AILURE COULD MAKE YOUR HEART BEAT FASTER
—AND HOTTER'N A SOUP KITCHEN!

Three taps—you stop quicker than the U.S. economy.

And that's all there is to it. Tap-A-Toe Futuroidic Footless De-Clutching with Single Pedal Control is as easy and effortless as the Jap march on Manchuria!

But that's not all there is to Airdreme Nabob for 1934, nosirree. There's Golden Girder Chassis Construction, borrowing the engineering secrets of the twenty-ton railway mammoths to surround you in an Iron Octagon of safety stronger than the Empire State Building. There's new improved Silent Flame Radiant Heating—flick a switch and suddenly inside your Airdreme, things are hotter than a strikebreaker's temper. Powerful new Klaxon-Matic horn tone, to clear the road ahead faster than the National Guard. New Double-Vision windshield wipers with unique Half-Time Power; only FDR can see more clearly! Explosion-proof new Triple-Deluxe Constant Radius Balloon Tires with Air-trap Valves proved at the Indian-apolis Speedway! Double-nub "Living Mohair" fabrics, water-treated to avoid premature soiling! (The same mohair chosen by Hollywood Star Norma Talmadge for her beach cabana.) There's the glamour of Twin-Streme Running Boards!

Had enough? You've heard only the half of it. And best of all, it's all wrapped up in a package labeled *Mello-Streme Style*, the ultra-smart, ultra-super auto fashion look that makes other cars seem like they're riding the rails!

STAN MACK

Stan Mack, creator of the long-running *Real Life Funnies* and author of illustrated popular histories, developed "Mule's Diner" for the *National Lampoon*.

Who came to Mule's?

Five crazy old ladies singing.

One man who marinated his nose.

Another who spent thirty-eight years in the men's room at Acme Bolt.

A woman who married a man with two heads. (She was turned into a tree. Not by his brother who had three heads. Not by his brother who had four heads, and not by his brother who had five heads. She was turned into a tree by his father. He had ten heads!)

Sven Smokehouse, who sold herring from a cart.

One of his herrings, who called a politician an "Asshole Napoleon."

Sven's son, Ewart, who had a big toe for a nose.

And Murray, whose one fart ten years ago has become his mortification and everyone else's urban legend.

If surrealism is the making of art and literature by liberating the subconscious with fantastic imagery, then we've got some serious surrealism here in the work of Stan Mack.

PHOTO BY SYLVIA PLACHY

In Mule's Diner, surrealism was dished up with the coffee, or maybe it *was* the coffee. Stan invited the *Lampoon*'s readers into Mule's to sit and have a cup and listen to a story. Dine at Mule's and you'll find yourself ruminating on some fantastic little morsel for days afterward. The stories, like the ink, are indelible. Read a few now and see if there is another artist who has cross-hatched his way this deep inside parts of your head you didn't even know you had.

Stan misses nothing. It's only after looking at the picture he drew of you that you notice you've been missing a button on your coat. I saw him interview a politician in a crowded convention hall. He looked the man right in the eye while he wrote down verbatim what the guy said, and drew his portrait without even once looking at the 2 x 3-inch pad he held in his right hand. The portrait looked like the guy, too. That's talent.

So grab a seat at the counter. This is Mule's Diner. What'll ya have?

—Rick Meyerowitz

From "Mule's Diner: Endings," *The National Lampoon Encyclopedia of Humor*, 1973

232

MULE'S DINER

IT HAPPENED AT THE WEDDING RECEPTION FOR MURRAY OXE AND STELLA DOLL.

IT WAS LATE. STELLA WENT UPSTAIRS TO THEIR HOTEL ROOM TO GET READY FOR THEIR FIRST NIGHT TOGETHER.

MURRAY STOOD UP AT THE HEAD TABLE TO SAY GOOD NIGHT TO HIS GUESTS.

WITH ALL EYES ON HIM, MURRAY UNEXPECTEDLY LET GO WITH A HUGE, LOUD, SMELLY FART!

BRUMP

PEOPLE SAT IN STUNNED SILENCE. THEN THEY ALL BEGAN TO TALK AT ONCE.

MURRAY WAS MORTIFIED. FINALLY, HE MADE HIMSELF WALK OUT THE FRONT DOOR OF THE HOTEL.

HE KEPT WALKING UNTIL HE WAS OUT OF TOWN — WHERE HE SPENT THE NIGHT.

THE NEXT DAY, HE HITCHHIKED ACROSS COUNTRY.

MURRAY SETTLED IN A SMALL TOWN, TOOK A NEW NAME, GOT A JOB, AND LIVED QUIETLY FOR TEN YEARS.

ONE DAY, HE BECAME NOSTALGIC FOR HOME. SURELY, NO ONE WOULD REMEMBER AFTER TEN YEARS.

HE TOOK A TRAIN HOME, AND WHEN HE ARRIVED, DECIDED TO WALK AROUND.

HE WAS HAPPY. IT FELT GOOD TO BE BACK. HE WALKED BY SOME HOUSES.

VOICES WERE COMING FROM AN OPEN WINDOW. A LITTLE GIRL WAS TALKING TO HER MOTHER. MURRAY LISTENED.

"MOMMA," SHE SAID, "I CAN NEVER REMEMBER THE DATE OF MY BIRTHDAY."

"THAT'S EASY," REPLIED HER MOTHER, "IT'S THE DAY AFTER THE ANNIVERSARY OF **MURRAY'S FART!**"

MURRAY OXE LEFT HIS HOME TOWN FOR GOOD.

STAY LEFT NEXT RIGHT

mack '75

SEEMS LIKE OLD DOBBS SPENDS A LOT OF TIME IN YOUR MEN'S ROOM, MULE.

HE DOES - LISTEN TO THIS STORY.

WHEN DOBBS WAS A KID, HE WENT TO WORK FOR ACME BOLT, IN ACCOUNTING.

IT WAS A PRETTY BORING JOB. THE EMPLOYEES WOULD USE ALL KINDS OF EXCUSES TO BUG OUT.

DOBBS WAS QUIET AND A FAST WORKER, AND NO ONE NOTICED WHEN HE BEGAN HITTING THE MEN'S ROOM FOUR TIMES A DAY.

AS THE YEARS WENT BY, HE DEVELOPED ROUTINES - AN HOUR WITH THE PAPER IN THE MORNING...

...URINAL, HAIRCOMBING, AND SOCIALIZING; SOMETIMES HE WOULD TAKE WORK IN.

WHEN HE WAS FORTY, THERE WAS A MANAGEMENT CHANGE, AND DOBBS WAS TO BE TRANSFERRED TO SOME OTHER FLOOR.

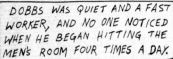

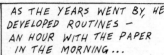
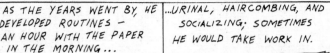
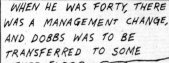

HE WAS SUPPOSED TO DELIVER HIS OWN TRANSFER PAPERS. BUT THAT DAY DOBBS SPENT THE AFTERNOON IN THE MEN'S ROOM.

HE MEANT TO DELIVER THE PAPERS THE NEXT DAY, BUT HE STOPPED IN TO READ THE PAPER FIRST, AND, BEFORE HE KNEW IT, IT WAS 5:00 P.M.

BY THE THIRD DAY, DOBBS REALIZED THAT ANYONE WHO KNEW HIM ASSUMED HE WAS WORKING ELSEWHERE IN THE BUILDING.

ON PAYDAY HE WENT DOWN TO THE CASHIER AND FOUND THAT THE COMPUTER HAD SPAT OUT HIS CHECK AS USUAL.

DOBBS SETTLED INTO A ROUTINE. EVERY DAY HE COMMUTED FROM NEW JERSEY TO THE EIGHTH FLOOR MEN'S ROOM AT ACME BOLT.

DOBBS KEPT TO HIMSELF, AND THERE WAS NO ONE TO CARE OR SUSPECT.

IT WASN'T BORING. THERE WERE PEOPLE TO CHAT WITH AND DAILY PAPERS TO READ.

HE HAD BOWEL MOVEMENTS FOUR TIMES A DAY, URINATED TEN TIMES, WASHED HANDS AND COMBED HAIR CONSTANTLY.

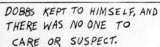

THE FEW PEOPLE WHO RECOGNIZED DOBBS THOUGHT OF HIM AS A FAITHFUL, DULL EMPLOYEE.

WHEN HE WAS SIXTY-THREE, DOBBS FOUND A NOTE ATTACHED TO HIS CHECK. IT ASKED HIM TO REPORT TO A VICE-PRESIDENT'S...

...OFFICE, WHERE HE WAS GIVEN A RETIREMENT WATCH AND CONGRATULATED ON THIRTY-EIGHT YEARS OF FAITHFUL SERVICE.

AND NOW HE SPENDS MOST OF HIS DAY IN MY MEN'S ROOM. IF YOU'RE GOING IN, WILL YOU BRING HIM THIS CUP?

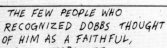

June 1973

MULE'S DINER

 MULE, YOU LOOK AT ME NOW, YOU WOULDN'T KNOW I ONCE HAD IT MADE.

 I HAD MONEY AND SPENT IT — THREW IT AWAY.

 THERE WAS THIS RICH OLD GUY — HERMAN — HAD A THING FOR NOSES. I WORKED A DEAL WITH HIM.

 EVERY MORNING AT 6:00 A.M. I'D SNEAK INTO HIS PLACE AND SIT QUIET WHILE HE MAKES OUT WITH MY NOSE.

 HE GOT REAL EXCITED. IT WAS AWFUL.

 AFTER AWHILE HE'D HAVE HAD ENOUGH AND HE'D PAY ME $100.

 I'D RACE OUT AND SPEND THE DAY SPENDING AND FORGETTING.

 WHAT A GREAT TIME! I NEVER THOUGHT ABOUT TOMORROW.

 WELL, SOMEHOW A DUDE NAMED JONES CAUGHT THE ACT AND DECIDED TO MOVE IN.

 HE WAS CRAZY CLEVER. FIRST HE BOUGHT RED WINE, PEPPERCORNS, BAY LEAF, CLOVES, ONIONS, AND ROSEMARY.

 LATER HE MIXES ALL THIS STUFF TOGETHER, SLICES INTO HIS NOSE, POURS THE MIX INTO THE CUTS, AND CHILLS OVERNIGHT.

 NEXT MORNING AT 5:00 HE SNEAKED INTO HERMAN'S KITCHEN AND STUCK HIS NOSE ON A HOT GRILL.

 HERMAN SMELLS BURNING FLESH, SPOTS JONES'S NOSE AND IS OVERCOME WITH PASSION.

 BY THE TIME I ARRIVE, HERMAN'S MADE A NEW DEAL — EVEN UPPED THE PRICE.

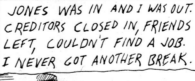 JONES WAS IN AND I WAS OUT. CREDITORS CLOSED IN, FRIENDS LEFT, COULDN'T FIND A JOB. I NEVER GOT ANOTHER BREAK.

 HOW CAN YOU FIGURE IT, MULE? A GUY CRAZY ENOUGH TO **MARINATE** HIS OWN NOSE.

THANKS, BUDDY.

January 1973

M. K. BROWN

I t's a summer evening in New York City. We cooked eggs on the sidewalk today, with extra grits. You can see the air. It hangs heavily from the sides of the buildings like sticky shower curtains. Sweltering people are making their way home from work. Everywhere, things seem to be bending and stretching and unreal. In this weather, time's arrow seems to have stopped. We're all living in an alternate reality in which entropy prevails. And this brings to mind M.K. Brown's work.

Her elastic imagination matches my mood: I see her drawings of heads that look like baskets of laundry or hands that look like shrimp. She, of the congenial disposition, disposes within borderlines of ink a strange new world inhabitable only by ideas she conjures up. It is not only different from the all-male world of the *National Lampoon*, but from our commonplace understandings of reality. She sees something we don't. And her humor, whimsy, and wit are matched by an ability to draw and tell stories that are unique to her. Say "M.K." to any former *Lampoon* editor and he will swoon a bit at the memory of something wonderful she did on his watch. More than any other *Lampoon* regular, she was beloved by that crew of cynical, egocentric, crotchety misogynists.

PHOTO BY JERRY WAINWRIGHT

M.K. brought a refreshing jolt of femininity and whimsy to the pieces she did for the magazine. I recall stories about cowboys and Indians, and strange autobiographies that end in a kitchen with a recipe lesson, or a song, or a woman teaching a monkey to dance. Each M.K. Brown piece took us on a trip around her Oz and dropped us back in our own Kansas again.

She was our guilty pleasure: a woman who, using ink and imagination, could make us laugh. Yes, it's true: you really could count on the fingers of one hand the number of women who contributed regularly to the *Lampoon*. And three of them were cartoonists: Shary Flenniken, Mimi Pond, and M.K. Brown. M.K.'s unselfconscious originality made her a standout in that excellent group. She always surprised. I loved her work because I never knew what would happen next—or even what was happening then.

Give in. Let these oddly happy pieces flow over you like cool breezes on hot day. See if you can resist her charm. On the other hand, why would you try?

—Rick Meyerowitz

Heck, no! We're not crazy! Why? Do we look crazy?

May 1975

March 1986

If there was misogyny at the *National Lampoon*, I didn't feel it in California. From the first time I saw the *Lampoon*, I felt an immediate kinship. It was a place where very odd and offbeat things could be published. Who else would print anything I wanted to draw? They ran "Aunt Mary's Kitchen" for four years, and "Snakes in the Bathroom," and "Love Story," as well as "Women," the last line of which is: "Women want the best of everything, as men do, and since we know best, we should always have our own way."

—M.K. Brown

COPING with CHAIN-SAW MASSACRES

© 1986 M·K·BROWN

ANOTHER TRUE-LIFE PRETTY FACE IN THE FIELD OF MEDICINE

BY M.K. BROWN

HELLO! MY NAME IS VIRGINIA SPEARS NGODÁTU, M.D. AS YOU MAY HAVE GUESSED I WAS BORN IN NEW GUINEA WHERE MY PARENTS WERE MISSIONARIES. UNLIKE OTHER LITTLE GIRLS I GREW UP PLAYING WITH MONKEYS! HA HA BUT SERIOUSLY, I'VE COME A LONG WAY FROM THOSE RAT-INFESTED JUNGLES TO THIS GAY SPOTLESS OFFICE WHERE, INCIDENTALLY, I MAKE A SMALL FORTUNE TREATING SKIN DISEASES

..BUT IT HASN'T ALL BEEN EASY FOR SEVENTEEN YEARS MY FATHER WAITED AT THE JUNGLE'S EDGE WITH SACKS FULL OF HAMMERS FOR THE PYGMIES WHILE POOR MOTHER PLAYED THE ORGAN IN THE TENT, NEVER LOSING HOPE

MY LONELY DAYS WERE SPENT HIGH IN THE TREETOPS WITH THE GIBBONS AND THE SPIDER MONKEYS

WHEN THE PYGMIES FINALLY CAME THERE WAS A GROSS MISUNDERSTANDING WHICH NOT EVEN FATHER'S HAMMERS COULD ASSUAGE

I WAS GLAD WHEN WE LEFT NEW GUINEA

May 1975

GLAD AT LONG LAST TO BE "JUST ANOTHER GIRL" AT A LEADING UNIVERSITY

GLAD AFTER GRUELING YEARS OF MEDICAL SCHOOL TO FINALLY HEAR THOSE WORDS

DR. NGODÁTU! PAGING DR. NGODÁTU!

WHY, THAT'S ME!

TO THIS DAY I REMEMBER MY FIRST CASE AND HOW VERY NERVOUS I WAS... A RETIRED ARMY COLONEL WITH A NASTY RASH. HIS HEAD WAS INSIDE A BOTTLE, SO YOU CAN IMAGINE HOW DIFFICULT THAT WAS TO TREAT

AND THEN THERE WAS THE YIPPIE WHO HAD EATEN TOO MUCH CHOCOLATE! HE FELL INTO A TRANCE AND HAD A VISION RIGHT THERE IN MY OFFICE

ALL MANNER OF PEOPLE HAVE PASSED THROUGH THIS WAITING ROOM; MOVIE STARS, POLITICIANS, KOOKS, CRIMINALS, NOBODIES. I TREAT THEM ALL! WHAT DO I CARE?

LIFE IS WONDERFUL. I LOVE BEING A DOCTOR! I LOVE SITTING AT THIS GIGANTIC DESK, DRESSED ALL IN WHITE, CLEAN INSIDE AND OUT LIKE A QUEEN WAITING FOR MY NEXT PATIENT. MAYBE IT WILL BE A MOVIE STAR — OR A JOCKEY!

WHAT MORE COULD A GIRL WANT?

END

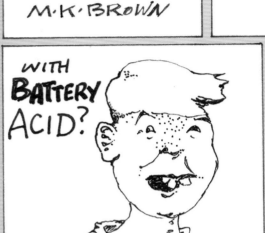

March 1986

LET'S DO THE WHITE GIRL TWIST
(LIKE WE DID LAST SUMMER)

©1986 M·K·BROWN

September 1986

TED
MANN

I knew I would fall in love with Ted Mann the minute I heard that he had slammed his bicycle through the windshield of a car that had cut him off in Midtown traffic.

Ted had yanked his bike from between his legs, lifted it over his head, and brought it crashing down through the windshield as the car's occupants, a middle-aged businessman and his two sisters, watched in horror. Feeling somewhat repentant, Ted then brought the man up to the office, where a deal was made to have the magazine pay the damages.

I thought anyone that angry had to be equally passionate. Surely he was the Prince of Darkness I had been seeking. It was entirely one-dimensional for me to view the poor guy that way, but heck, it was the seventies. The fun didn't begin or end with the bicycle incident. Once Ted brought a homeless guy into an editorial meeting and introduced him as a famous writer. Another time he hired a bagpiper and had him annoy everyone by playing "Hava Nagila" all afternoon.

Ted was tall, handsome, exotically Canadian, and impressively hyperarticulate, so I moved my backpack full of Danskins and art supplies into his small apartment on Hudson Street. He proudly pointed out that, on more than one occasion, Dylan Thomas had drunk himself to death directly across the street at the White Horse Tavern. After work,

CRAPPY POLAROID COURTESY OF TED MANN

we'd all meet Tony, Sean, and the others for happy hour in the dimly lit bar at Robata, around the corner from the *Lampoon*. Later, we'd all go to the Bells of Hell, on Thirteenth Street, where we'd meet other *Lampoon* writers or artists. They would drink endless pints of Guinness, and I would sit there drinking ice water and attempting to write down everything they said in my sketchbook.

We were all tormented by one thing or another; psychically bruised by the unwinnable war in Vietnam and grievously disappointed by the unrequited promise of free love. That was why everybody was so darn funny. Most of the time it was difficult to tell whether *National Lampoon* editors were being oddly serious or brilliantly humorous. With a confounding turn of phrase, they could make a run-of-the-mill ethnic joke sound like incisive commentary on the ridiculousness of the racial divide. Or was it that they really didn't like Jews, Catholics, Asians, blacks, and *anyone* from Pakistan?

All I knew was that these super-smart men were nothing like the boys back in Seattle. These guys all used language as a weapon, and Ted Mann was one of the deadliest sharp shooters in the gang.

—Shary Flenniken

Ted Mann once did something that, looking back, we might think of as an act of guerilla sculpture, but which is better described as one of the funniest fucking things I've ever seen.

The *Lampoon* offices looked out on both Madison Avenue and Fifty-eighth Street. Across the street were high-rise office buildings, the floors at the same level as ours and the windows essentially identical. One of these offices must have housed an ad agency, because sitting on the sill of one of those neighboring windows—as visible to us, across the street, as to anyone actually in the room—was, ranked in size order and neatly aligned, a nuclear family of boxes of Tide detergent. From the

jumbo Daddy box to the merely large Mommy box to the cute little mini box, they stood in perfectly ordered, face-out array, bright orange and unmistakable.

So one day I go into Mann's office and, behind his chair, on *his* windowsill and facing the building opposite, is an identical lineup of Tide boxes. Touching, yes—and a brave effort, however futile or misguided, to establish contact with a neighboring civilization by semaphoring to them in their own language. Did they reply? We may never know. But the act—artistic, mocking, ridiculous—remains.

—Ellis Weiner

Come north... Come hunt the Innuit

Americans have crisscrossed the globe in search of game. They've been to India and Africa; to the mountains of Russia and Romania. They've bagged species thought to have been extinct for years. But few men of any nation can claim to have bagged an *Innuit*.

North of the tree line, in the wilds of Canada, live the Innuit. Savage, uncivilized, and scarce, they migrate across thousands of miles of trackless Arctic waste in search of raw dog blubber, which they eat with moss.

They are not easy to find. You will have to hire an experienced bush pilot-guide. Even then it may take one day, or even two. But if you're the kind of hunter we think you are, you enjoy the chase as much as the kill. There is simply nothing like it on earth....

You come upon them suddenly at dawn, the sun at your back. The pilot jams the stick forward and the plane's nose dips down and you're in a power dive. You have seconds in which to act. Bracing your rifle against a wing strut, you try and sight in the scattering Innuit as the light plane bucks and saws and the backwash from the prop rips streams of tears from your eyes. If you're lucky, you'll get one or two on the first pass. If you're *really* lucky, you may get a trophy. One thing you'll get for certain is the thrill of a lifetime.

For more information on vacations in Canada's Northlands, contact:

The Ministry of Ecology, Oil, and Indian Affairs

c/o The Parliament Buildings, Ottawa, Ontario.
No Stamp Is Required

September 1976

I have always liked "Brave Dog" without being able to explain why. Perhaps I just like dogs. Their plight is our own writ small—for all their devotion (and pissing on carpets), the purpose of their existence remains a mystery to them, though, in order that this not trouble them excessively, providence has granted them the ability to lick their own genitals. Yet we recognize our situation in theirs and find that predicament troubling, or why would we say "die like a dog?" They die just as we do. You see? Had I their special ability, these questions would not arise.

—Ted Mann

SOOOOOOOOOOOOOOOOOOOOOOOOOOOOOOOOOO OOOOOOOOOOOOOOOOOOOOOOOOOOOOOOOOEEE!
PIG PIG PIG PIG PIG PIG PIG
GET ALONG!
. . . .

The True Story of Champ and the Two-Hundred-Mile Swine Drive

"Ho, Champ," said Mr. Burns. Champ wheeled quickly, forcing the hog he was chasing slightly to the right into the small reaming pen where John Burns was able to pin and root the big male prairie hog. "Ho, boy," he said. "That's about the last of the hogs, I reckon. We'll start early tomorrow morning and head them out towards Boise over the Clangbird trail."

John Burns was one of the best swine men in Idaho. Pig ran in his blood and in his father's. The same was true of Champ. His sire had been all-state champion swine hound for three years running, and Champ himself was figured likely to take the prize sooner or later. Together they made a swine-handling team that was the best in the state.

As Champ lay by the fire that night and listened to the night sounds of the prairie, owls hooting as they hunted and the regular grunting of the penned pigs, he felt at peace. He thought of the long hog drive ahead and of the adventures that might befall them on the trail. A coyote might try to make off with a straggling pig, an older hog might stray onto the highway and be run over. Any of these things could happen if he grew careless.

The next morning, John Burns and Champ were up at the crack of dawn, and by the time the voles had stopped their nocturnal foraging, the three hundred head of swine were moving steadily over the Clangbird trail. They had twenty miles to go before they made camp for the night, and there was no time to waste. John Burns worked one side of the herd, swinging his stick and shouting to keep the hogs in motion, while Champ ran up and down the other side, barking sharply and occasionally nipping at a balky sow.

The day passed without adventure, and evening had begun to steal up upon their pitched camp when Champ sensed something was wrong. There was a tension in the air. The hogs could feel it, too, plunging and bucking in the makeshift trail pens. Champ looked at John Burns meaningfully as if to say, "Thunderstorm . . . can you feel it?" Burns nodded at the dog. "You're right," he said. "We're in for trouble tonight." He coughed badly for a minute and straightened up, his face as colorless as stream water.

"Darn it, boy," he wheezed, "what a time for me to get sick. Feels like another attack of trichinosis." He clutched at his stomach as a stab of pain twisted its way through his guts. "Have to make camp here," he gasped, " . . . try to sweat it out."

Painfully, slowly, Burns built a small fire and then lay beside it. He was too weak to cook, and lay, moaning softly, while the fire died. Champ pressed his muzzle against John's face. He was feverish; soon he would be delirious. Champ licked his face gently. Burns sat up with a start. "Worms in my guts!" he shouted. "I'll show 'em. I'll show the worms! I'll eat rocks and prickly bushes! I'll drink my hair oil! That'll fix 'em, they'll see! They'll not mess with a swine man again!" Burns stuffed a handful of pebbles in his mouth and washed them down with a long slug from a hair oil bottle in his bedroll. "Gimme a box of tacks!" he screamed. "Tacks will fix the sons of bitches!" Champ had no time to try and stop Burns. He had another problem. Right then, lightning struck the back of the hog corral, crisping a dozen swine and blowing a ten-foot crater in the soft mud of the wallow. Thunder broke at the same time, and as it died, the cries of the terrified herd grew in volume, and the pigs began to run. They were going to come through the front of the pen, straight for the campsite!

The first bull hog hit the fence railing with a terrific crash that broke the weathered two-by-four as if it were a broomstick. The almost dead fire threw an eerie light on the plunging, bucking forms of the squealing herd. "Kreeeeeahggguh!" screamed the lead hog, and the stampede was on.

Champ stood his ground against the charge, barking furiously and trying to turn the body of the herd away from the recumbent form of his master. He turned the first pig, but the herd was relentless. On they came, hog after hog, and Champ went down in the heaving melee.

Long after the pigs had passed, they found them. Champ and Burns's bodies were stomped and trampled to death. Champ's body lay across his master's, and his lips were pulled back in a snarl of defiance. When the men who found them had looked around a little, the taller of the two turned to his companion and said these spare words: "**Brave dog.**"

From "Brave Dog," September 1976

Handy Home Handbook of
Teen-age Poisons
and Their
Antidotes
by Dr. Richard Speck

DR. RICHARD SPECK

VALIUM

SYMPTOMS	Ataxia, blithering, venous thrombosis, vacuousness, dysarthria, slobbering, rectal hiccups, vigorous projectile vomiting, involuntary urination.
ANTIDOTE	Strapping has proved effective in some cases, but grounding may be necessary in severe cases.

CONTRAINDICATIONS Freshly painted garage.

DEMEROL HYDROCHLORIDE

SYMPTOMS	Decrease in respiratory rate and/or tidal volume, somnolence, blackened spoons in drawers, desire to rob grocers.
ANTIDOTE	Double up on chores for six weeks. Beating may be necessary in severe cases.

CONTRAINDICATIONS Ñone.

SECONAL SODIUM

SYMPTOMS	Pharyngeal spasms, central nervous system depression, reflex depression, lower body temperature, decreased urine formation, stumbling, spitting, shit on shirt, apnea.
ANTIDOTE	Confiscation of car keys for six to twelve months.

CONTRAINDICATIONS Superior grades in the sciences, all cars washed.

LSD

SYMPTOMS	Visual and auditory hallucinations, suicide attempts, religious fervor.
ANTIDOTE	Slapping, shouting. Talks with ministers.

CONTRAINDICATIONS Freshly mowed lawn, clean sleeping area.

MDA

SYMPTOMS	Arryhthmia, libido changes, missing televisions or silverware, periodic snot blasts, gutter mouth.
ANTIDOTE	Wash mouth out with laundry soap, followed by two weeks close supervision of homework.

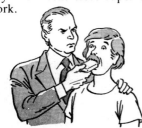

CONTRAINDICATIONS All dishes washed and dried.

QUAALUDE
(Methaqualone)

SYMPTOMS	Restlessness, hypertonia progressing to convulsions, increased secretions, disarrayed clothing, renal insufficiency, loss of inhibitions (if they ever existed), throwing food around and then up.
ANTIDOTE	Early bed and beating.

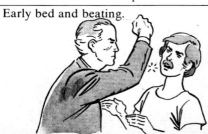

CONTRAINDICATIONS Freshly washed windows.

METHEDRINE HYDROCHLORIDE

SYMPTOMS   "Rapping," decreased salivation, vertigo, biting, shedding.

ANTIDOTE   Allowance reductions as indicated.

CONTRAINDICATIONS   Recent haircut.

PCP

SYMPTOMS   Inability to sweat, hallucinations, respiratory depression, slurred speech, incomprehensible speech, speech in a foreign language, handkerchief up asshole.

ANTIDOTE   Weekend service with National Guard.

CONTRAINDICATIONS   **Pays over one hundred dollars a month board.**

ROBITUSSIN
("Robo")

SYMPTOMS   Bleary eyes, slurred speech, vomit on coat, sleeping in crashed car, etc., etc.

ANTIDOTE   Four years in U.S. armed forces.

CONTRAINDICATIONS   None known.

PRELUDIN
(Phenmetrazine Hydrochloride)

SYMPTOMS   Cardiovascular: palpitations, tachycardia, exploding capillaries. Central nervous system: restlessness, meaninglessness, and mindlessness. Possibility of psychotic episode if patient is not already psychotic. Gastrointestinal: dryness in mouth, uticaria.

ANTIDOTE   Beating, early bed, and no television for one month.

CONTRAINDICATIONS   Victim is bona fide Japanese ex-fighter pilot.

About Dr. Speck

General Alexander M. Haig, Jr.: "Dr. Speck was a prominent member of the war movement from 1965 to 1973. While serving as a physician for the army draft board medical review, he qualified many sick lads for service who would otherwise have been unable to attend Vietnam."

Karen Ann Quinlan: "If my parents had sent me to Dr. Richard Speck, the night orderly would not be renting me to his friends for stag parties."

These quotes from famous people tell us that Dr. Richard Speck is a widely experienced and intelligent physician concerned with the chemical problems facing today's young people, and not simply interested in seeing them naked.

Dr. Speck knows that modern parents and sheriffs are hard put to know which drugs (if any) are causing today's young people to throw up and talk back. For this reason and about three thousand others, he has compiled a list of common household poisons and their antidotes. We at the **National Lampoon** hope that all our readers' parents will cut out this little booklet and hang it next to their wallets. It could save a life.

Sincerely,
T. Mann
Associate Editor

HOW TO USE THIS BOOKLET

When the victim begins to display symptoms of poisoning, match the visible symptoms with those listed in this booklet. After matching the symptoms, you may make tentative identification of the drug or drugs involved in the poisoning. Now, before proceeding to the antidote, look for **contraindications.** A contraindication tells you not to administer the antidote for various reasons. This is important. Remember: an antidote may actually be harmful if administered in the presence of contraindications or witnesses.

Lexicon of Modern Drug Slang

Marijuana
Loafer, Cong lawn, Jamaican vacation, Mexican food, fighter-bombers, burning issue, fire-fuck.

LSD
Rat dream, synapse shanghai, dog aphrodisiac, eighth floor exit, brain-eater.

Quaalude
Chemical straightjackets, mumblers, Quinlans, pick-me-up-I-seem-to- have-slipped.

Barbiturates
Stumblers, antinutso pills, lunch- launchers, date-stunners, brain- killers.

Diet Pills
Essay writers, night-lights, little lawyers, fat girls' friends.

IMPORTANT PHONE NUMBERS

Your Doctor ————————————
The Police ————————————
Stomach Pumpers ————————————
Narks ————————————
Stern Uncle ————————————
Inhalator ————————————
Army De-Tox Division ————————————

The Office of Commander S.W. Goatlips IV
The Pentagon
Washington, D.C.

Ted Mann
<u>National Lampoon</u>
635 Madison Avenue
New York, N.Y. 10022

Dear Mr. Mann:

I was pleased to learn from your letter that <u>National Lampoon</u> is planning an issue entitled "Let's Get It Up, America." I quite agree that our national self-esteem suffered gravely during the Carter administration. Unfortunately, my new duties here at the Pentagon do not allow time to write articles for outside publication.

In your letter you asked if it was true that our military leaders are as demoralized and indecisive as they are often portrayed in the press.

Nothing could be further from the truth.

Ted, I presume you saw <u>The Deer Hunter</u> and <u>Apocalypse Now</u>. These two well-known films pretend to show us the more frightening aspects of men in action. They barely scratch the surface of what went on in Vietnam among our troops--especially among our officers.

I'm talking about anal dynamite masturbation.

Several weeks ago a young officer, just returned from Europe, where he had been serving with our NATO forces in Germany, told me quite a story concerning this practice.

It seems that several years ago a well-known general named Alexander Haig was commanding the North Atlantic forces during war games held in the Netherlands. The Russians, as usual, had sent along a couple of military observers (this was during "détente"). One evening, in the senior officers' mess, taunting toasts were exchanged between our general and the two Russians. One of the Russkies lost his temper and, producing a revolver, dumped four of its six shells on the table and fired at his head. He then threw the gun on the table in rude challenge. "No American," he said, "would have the courage to do that."

Well, Ted, General Haig didn't say a word. He motioned to an aide and whispered a few instructions in his ear. The aide left and the general kept staring at the Russians, who attempted to look unconcerned.

A few minutes later a Seabee entered the room with a briefcase, which he unlocked before giving to Haig. From it the general removed a stick of 70 percent Forcite dynamite, a jar of Vaseline, and a Fabergé egg of incredible beauty and workmanship. Haig dropped his pants and knelt on the table, placing the Fabergé egg--with the top opened--beneath his meat. He snipped about an inch from the dynamite's six-inch fuse and lit the fuse from his cigar tip. After dipping the cartridge into the Vaseline he shoved it up his ass and began to piston it in and out while masturbating furiously into the Fabergé cup.

The Russians' faces were white with fear. Nobody moved from their seats. After what understandably seemed like a very long time, the general came into the egg cup with a satisfied grunt. He pulled the explosive from his rectum and extinguished the fuse with the tip of his tongue.

After pulling his pants up, the general shoved the ornate Russian jewelry, now brimming with jism, across to one Russian observer. Raising his glass, he cried, "I now propose a toast... To the Russian czar, Leonid Brezhnev!"

The Russians had no choice but to drink.

I would not say that a victory like that was the work of a demoralized or indecisive leadership. Would you, Ted?

Yours,

S.W. Goatlips IV

S.W. Goatlips IV,
Commander

August 1981

National Lampoon editor Ted Mann can't think of a subscription ad.

National Lampoon editor Ted Mann has a writer's block caused by the publisher's rejection of his earlier, funnier sub ad.

And now some clown has copped his job!

Subscribe to *National Lampoon*, save money, and never miss an issue.

May 1982

SHARY FLENNIKEN

She is the daughter of an admiral, for goodness' sake. Rear Admiral James A. Flenniken, Ret. Stalwart of the navy, hero of one battle or another, who moved

his family from Alaska, to Panama, to the state of Washington. Shary lived in a suitcase until the family settled in Seattle in the 1960s. And given it was the 1960s, she was as far politically from her adored father as it was possible to be.

So she moved to San Francisco, where she became one of the founders of The Air Pirates, a commune of politically motivated cartoonists. Shary has written that she loved the salon atmosphere. The Air Pirates drew all day and night, learned from one another, and "discussed politics and pen points with equal seriousness." It was in this scruffy, "deliberately wretched world" that she created "Trots and Bonnie," a comic strip featuring a sweet young girl and her beautiful floppy-eared everydog. As a child, Shary tells us, she had a dog named Bonnie. (Personally, this boggles my mind; I've always thought Bonnie was the girl.)

PHOTO BY GREG PRESTON

line Alley." "Trots and Bonnie" was so explicit, it had an immediate effect on the overwhelmingly young male *Lampoon* audience. Sure, one could write a long prose piece such as "Law of the Jungle" or "The New York State Bar Exam" for those readers who are cerebrally inclined, but Shary drew a teenage girl undressing or masturbating, or two people screwing on a couch, or a bed, or on the floor. She drew them doing what they were doing from the front, or back, or bottom, or top, and many thousands of readers experienced a rather more visceral relationship to the magazine, so that sales—among other things—quickly rose. The front office duly noted the new bulge in the numbers and decreed Shary to be a contributor of the utmost importance.

It wasn't prurience alone that accounted for the long relationship readers had with Trots and Bonnie. Charm and a narrative innocence had a lot to do

Shary and Bobby London, creator of "Dirty Duck," left the commune and, at the behest of Michel Choquette, began contributing to the *National Lampoon*. Shary didn't attempt to out-*Lampoon* the boys. Instead she gave them Trots and Bonnie straight up. After a few years of publishing lackluster photos of naked women, they finally had something really erotic on their hands, and it was a cartoon strip! Her western sensibility and frank view of sex was presented in a comic style reminiscent of such classic strips as "Little Nemo" and "Gaso-

with the longevity of the strip. What Shary has in person, and what she gives us on the page, is a freckled, tomgirl-next-door (Bonnie—or is she Trots?—has short hair and always wears pants), and a sweetness that shines through in every frame. These days Shary is living in Seattle, drawing every day, and working hard. If you see her walking her dogs, don't ask her to tell you about old times. Instead, ask her what's new. She'll tell you she's "a slave to her pets."

—Rick Meyerowitz

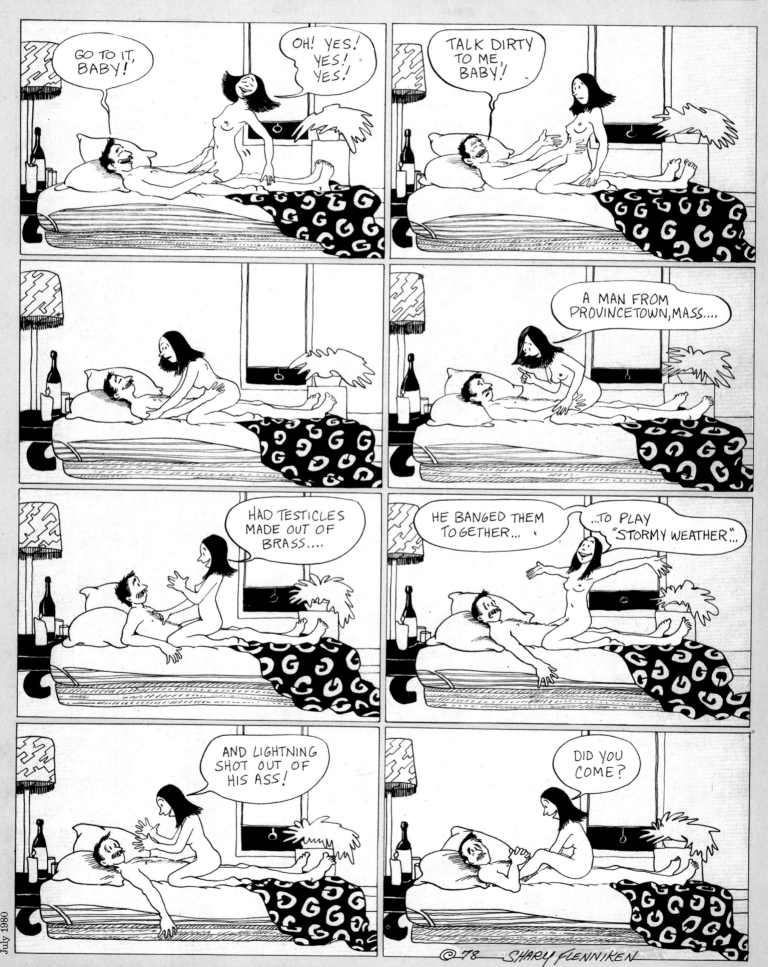

trots and bonnie

WOW, PEPSI! ISN'T HE ADORABLE!

HE'S SO CUTE! HE MUST BE A NINTH GRADER!

HE LOOKS SORTA QUIET AND SHY

I WONDER WHAT HE'S REALLY LIKE!

WELL, GARY'S NOT TOO SMART...

BUT HE'S A GREAT LAY.

OH TROTS! HE'S NOT A VIRGIN!

AT LEAST HE'S YOUR INTELLECTUAL EQUAL.....

TROTS AND BONNIE

I THINK I SHOULD'A BROUGHT MY BATHING SUIT, PEPSI.

YOU'RE SO UPTIGHT!

BE LOOSE! BE FREE! BE NAKED!

LIBERATE YOUR BODY! UNCLOTHE YOUR INHIBITIONS!

HOW COULD YOU STARE AT HIM LIKE THAT?!

DON'T YOU HAVE ANY MANNERS AT ALL, BONNIE!? HOW DISGUSTING! WHY, IT WAS PRACTICALLY SEXIST!

WHAT DID I DO WRONG, TROTS?

YOU WERE SO LOOSE - YOU FELL APART!

DANNY
ABELSON & ELLIS WEINER

Danny Abelson, who remains the most articulate person I have ever met, worked at the Strand bookstore, driving boxes of product in from estates and libraries, and out to stock the Strand stalls in Central Park, which I was running in the summer of 1974.

We had interests in common: art, social criticism, music, humor. He and his girlfriend (later wife), Patty, took me in as a too-frequent dinner guest and hanger-out.

I knew Sean Kelly, and I proposed to Danny that he and I write a parody of *ArtNews* for the *National Lampoon*. We did. It ran in February 1976. We were asked if we wanted to join the staff and we said yes, please.

Working with Abelson was exactly like having a hilarious conversation with him about whatever the hell we wanted to talk about. He was an incredible resource.

And, of course, there were the girl-friends he saw me through, the acid trips we took, and the lines—funny, of course, but also accurate and true—that I remember thirty years later. For example, at dinner at his house:

D.A.: Do you want more peas?
E.W.: No, thanks.
D.A.: Do you want more peas?
E.W.: Uh, no, th—
D.A.: Do you want more peas? Can I give you more peas? Are you schizo-phrenic, yet, or do you want more peas?

Or, after I persuaded him to attend an introductory *est* seminar: "I think *est* does to the mind what the Army Corps of Engineers does to the landscape."

There are others. We haven't spoken in three decades, but for no reason I can think of. What's that all about?

—E.W.

My story begins in the Strand bookstore, where it was my daily habit to cower behind a fellow worker, Ellis Weiner, in order to shield myself from the blinding hipness of the leather-clad luminaries, such as Robert Mapplethorpe, who would glide past us on their way to hang out in the stacks with our colleague Patti Smith. Ellis was too skinny to offer much in the way of protection. Nor could he could stop passersby from alerting the management to yet another theft from the fifty-cent book carts on the sidewalk. I was reluctant to be killed in the line of duty over a used copy of *I, Claudius*, and Ellis knew about this magazine . . . so together we decided writing humor was a plan.

So we wrote, we submitted, and found ourselves in Doug Kenney's office, beginning our careers at the *Lampoon* as he was packing up. I think that same day Brian McConnachie gave us an assignment, but I can't say for sure. And so we entered a far bet-ter world than the one we had known, with enormously productive people who didn't keep to the kind of evening schedule that makes for a productive workday. Good-natured rivalries and even the occasional episode of lingering, bitter hatred have to expected. But at the *Lampoon*, old-fashioned professional respect won the day. Sean Kelly once looked up from a newly minted issue and commented on P. J. O'Rourke's ability to make a sentence snap, mag-nanimously setting aside their sincere differences of opinion on everything.

Now here we are. Our kids ask us how it was back then. The bright ones, and God bless them, long ago realized that we would tell them if only we could.

—D.A.

Witje and Erlin O'Flaherty, *Nothing Suite*, 1975, mixed media, 180¼ x 144 x 288⅝ in. On loan from Fifth Avenue Racquet Club. "…floating in arrogant horizontality…"

PHOTO BY RICK MEYEROWITZ

Los Angeles | Group show at Gnossini

For my money, Klaus Uber's *The Liberation / Judgment of Paris* is the high point of the show. A shallow metal trough nine feet across and some twelve deep, it is constructed of a special alloy struck in Essen under the personal supervision of the artist. The trough is filled to a depth of some inches with sausages of various types (listed in the catalog, from bratwurst to wiener).

The display is first of all a retinal delight, the unrelieved surface tension playing to great effect against the rigidly horizontal geometry of the shape. Close scrutiny of the sausage sea will reveal many hidden treats. A blood-stained photograph of Neville Chamberlain peeps out, as does the miniscule mast of a plastic ship, the latter a waggish word play on the fecal nature of the material, something Uber is fond of doing.

A companion piece, listed as *an appendix*, hangs adjacent to *Liberation*. It is a portrait comprised of irregularly shaped sausages sufficiently suggestive of viscera to give the title a second meaning. The face formed is an interesting one, possibly oriental in character.

As a whole, the piece works and works well. It is at one and the same time aggressively real and proudly abstract; the interplay of the iconic food matter and the spatial dimensionality is subtle and compelling. It is a witty, well-wrought work.

Liberation is a tough act to follow. Witje and Erlin O'Flaherty's *Nothing*

Suite is a cryptic new work by the team that attracted considerable attention with their *Laserlasslovelees* at HOT in Milan last year. Pencil marks are the visual referent for a strip of red tape that wanders across the wall, floating in arrogant horizontality at a deliberately provocative height. Cognitive harmony is disrupted by the subtle segmentation of wall and floor—stripe becomes divider becomes stripe. Negative shape is thus stressed in a manner that suggests that the O'Flahertys are more than casually concerned with the problems of visual representation in philosophical terms. As with most cerebral, highly differentiated works, there is a disquieting feeling of something lacking.

Roman has contributed four watercolor studies of the knee, the subject of his exclusive concern for many years. The plastic qualities of the subject matter are exploited fully, though I for one long to see Roman escape the studio. We have had *Knees in Love, Famous Knees, Knees Time Out*, to name but a few, why not *Knees at the Beach, Knees Attend an Opening, Knees on the Grand Canal*, and so on?

Davis's toenail clipping assemblages, Tammer's shredded vegetable tableaux, and the Bozo Group's *Hot Tamale*, a parody of the drollest sort, all address themselves to the problems of depicting organic truth in an entropic and increasingly synthetic reality.

—Curt Vile

From "Arty News," February 1976

A Book of Common Hair

BY JOAN LIBRION

I don't think I have ever known a woman for whom the subject of coiffure was as charged as it was for Carla Perkins. She had not always thought about her hair. It was just her hair. Period. In any case, she had known then that she could not "think" about her "hair" even if she had wanted to. At first.

"Think about your hair, don't think about your hair," said Toda, who was dying of an obscure cancer. "I'm only telling you what matters to me, and what matters to me is not whether or not you think about your hair."

When he said this she stared at the floor and contemplated driving to a small nightclub near Oxnard. Women like Carla Perkins were always contemplating driving to a small nightclub near Oxnard. A dingy, depressing place where the air conditioning was fierce and you never had to think about your hair.

"Jesus, Carla, I'm sick of this shit," said Toda, and she felt a wave of warm feelings swell up from deep within her. An absurd tenderness. She placed her cold hand over his and thought about what the prime minister had eaten for breakfast at the palace. The morning the bomb exploded. The day they found his ear pinned to the oak paneling. A tuft of hair still attached.

Once, in New York, a pimply girl handed her a leaflet advertising the opening of a new beauty salon. Later she thought about why she had accepted the handout. Later she also thought about when she had first seen her second husband using hedge clippers for the first time, and how she had driven the convertible into the Laundromat and mailed the baby to Arizona.

When she glanced down at the leaflet something snapped in her, and she started walking south. She knew after something snapped in her that she would not be able to stop walking once she had started. She walked downtown, into the tunnel leading out of New York, and continued south through the cluttered length of New Jersey. She did not think of stopping. Only of the photograph of the woman with the new hairstyle whose smile presumably evoked the satisfaction of money well spent.

She called from somewhere in South Carolina. She could not remember where it had been or whom she had been calling. It was characteristic of the incidents in Carla Perkins's life that she could not remember the specific coordinates that would locate the event in space or time. As she stood in the phone booth waiting for the phone at the other end to be picked up, she had what she thought was the first clear thought she had had for days. She thought that her whole life had been a series of decisions about her hair.

"I think that my whole life has been a series of decisions about my hair," she said when the phone was answered.

"Hello?" said a neutral voice at the other end. "Can I help you? . . . "

She stood with the phone in her hand, silent. She remembered later thinking that the disembodied voice came from the absolute still center of the universe, and that the question it posed was the most pointedly beautiful and heartbreaking thing she had ever heard.

After she hung up she bought a Coke, rented a car, and drove to Oregon, where she had once had a miscarriage or blacked out in a plastic lampshade factory. She wasn't sure which. It was in the nature of her kind of life that she could not be sure whether it was a fainting spell or a miscarriage at the beginning of the end of a marriage that drew her across the vast expanse of a continent.

In Oregon she checked into a motel and pulled the shades and sat on the edge of the bed for two days without turning on the television set. She did not turn it on because she was afraid of being bored. She was afraid of being bored because she knew that if she became bored she would start crying or bleeding and not be able to stop. She wasn't sure which, but she knew that if she did either for long enough she would start thinking about her hair and that would remind her of her illness. The illness she was dying from. Such were the frail strands of causality from which her life was woven.

On the third day, Simon rang the doorbell.

"I'm dying of a terrible disease. A fatal one," she said to him, in a tone that sounded artificial even to her own ears.

"We all are, princess," he said, smiling, and she knew it was true. She knew that all of them—Jean, Baxter, Simon, Toda, and herself. They were all dying of specific, frightening diseases. Alcoholism, cancer, missed opportunities. She had never even thought about it before. She had thought only about her hair, and how her father used to run his fingers through it when she was little.

Simon smiled.

Carla twirled a strand of her hair between two fingers, and started to cry.

"Split," said Carla, tears falling down her cheeks, thinking about her life and all of their lives and her hair.

"Ends," said Simon, still smiling.

—Danny Abelson

From "A Garland of Parodies," July 1978

How to Rave About Your Own Life

BY ERICA JUNK, THE AUTHOR OF *FEAR OF FAILURE*

"I'm amanuensis to the Zeitgeist," I said to Bennett.

"That's nice," he said patiently, reading his journal.

The prick! Jealous of me, of my fame, of my success. I hated him, and yet... at least, I know I disrespected him. At least, I think I did. Why? (Why did I think I did? Why couldn't I just *know*? Are women different from men because they have husbands, whereas men have wives? A rhetorical question.)

So I talked to my friends about it. Yet the *guilt* I felt was *incredible*! This wasn't someone *else* feeling guilt! It was *me*! Me, with my *own* personal past and fears and Jewishness and womanness. My friends were sympathetic—oh, sure, easy for them, now that I was a famous woman writer and all.

Jeffrey: "Let's have an affair, Erica."

Me: "You mean now? But we're friends. I'm famous, certainly. I'm a woman, I freely confess to that 'sin.' I'm a writer, that goes without saying."

Jeffrey: "So what you're telling me is that you're a famous woman writer. You have a cunt, and a little booklet of Ko-Rec-Type and all. Is that the point of all this?"

Me (petulantly): "I don't *know*!"

Dear Reader, it isn't that great being famous. I should know. I live with that fickle houseguest, Fame. You see, it just so happened that I wrote a book about a woman with an Oriental married name who goes and does things and has sex and discovers that she's a woman who can do things and have sex. And... twelve billion women responded! I was truly shocked. The thought just had never occurred to me that twelve billion women all had Oriental married names and went and did things. (*Why*? Why do women do things? Is it because life makes them? What is life, then? Is it what we do, or who we are? What *are* we doing? And *why*?)

So my friends weren't much help. Oh, sure, I went to the literary luncheons and book promotions and autograph signings and played the part of the famous woman writer. But it didn't *change* anything! I still was a poetess. I still had an Oriental psychiatrist husband. (Did I tell you that Bennett was Chinese? He is.) (In the novel, I mean, the novel I wrote. Or rather, this one, the one I'm writing now, the one *after* the one that made me famous and a woman and a writer.) (Does it matter that he's Chinese? I mean in real life? Or is this real life? No, this is a *novel*. Isn't it?)

That was just the point: I didn't *know*. (Query: Why don't women know? Because they are famous? Or because they're writers? Or because their husbands are Chinese psychia-trists?) God, I wish Leonardo da Vinci were here to help me with all this! Or Keats or Lawrence or Whitman, or any other of my famous peers.

Then I spoke to my agent. God, you *know* what she's like. Rude, pushy, vulgar, self-centered, dishonest—and yet I found myself obeying her every command! Then again, in spite of all her *kvetching* and *nudging* and *hocking* and *draying mein kopf* with her *mishegoss* and *meshuggeneh bobbe-mysehs*... I guess I loved her. (Why?)

So I went to Hollywood and had some writer-type insights about how plastic and Alice-in-Wonderland it all is. You know what I mean? And then I met Josh, who had a big cock and was under thirty, and therefore honest.

There we were, in my hotel room (Beverly Wilshire) sipping wine (white) and nibbling caviar (black), when he turned to me and said, "Listen, I want to fuck you. What did you call it... a zippy fuck...?"

I scowled. (I hate being misquoted, like many famous writers such as myself.) "Zipless," I said.

But he refused to heed anything, and in a second had stripped both myself and himself of our Bloomingdale's finery (Bullocks, in his case). Then suddenly he was eating me with arduous ardor, looking up and saying, "You have the best cunt in the world." Oh God, I thought, He's so *honest*! And yet still I couldn't come. *Why*?

"I need to hear it," I begged shamelessly. "Tell me." (I herewith apologize to all my sister feminists for this crass betrayal of the Code. I needed to hear it!) "Tell me again. Please."

He looked up and smiled. "All right," he said sweetly, the odor of my sexual juices rising around us like a tree. "You're famous, Erica. You're a famous woman writer. Just like Mary Shelley. Just like Simone de Beauvoir. Colette, George Eliot, Jane Austen, Virginia Woolf, and you. You have a writing desk you like to talk about. You do things that writers do. You drop coy references to your typewriter. Henry Miller loves you. Other famous people write blurbs for your paperback editions—even Anthony Burgess, who should know better. You can complain how terrible it is to be a writer. You can use the word *writer* ten times in every paragraph you write. It's really true. You're a famous woman writer."

And then I came, every fiber of my being shuddering as though it were about to burst, and I came and came and came.

—Ellis Weiner

ASSOCIATE EDITORIALS

A Friendly Warning

A word to the wise—there's nowhere to grow but up.

Consider the available alternatives, such as the Ageless Hippie route. You may not believe it now, but those who've been there will tell you that coming off a two-day acid trip on the food stamp line at your local welfare office just doesn't do it after a while. Nor does sleeping on the floor—not only do people and animals and those in between literally step on your face at regular intervals, but sooner or later you wake up one gray morning with your tongue lying on the carpet like a piece of liver and your hair clotted with hash brownie, and you realize that today is the day your little sister graduates from law school.

Then, of course, you might try to hold on to that carefree, hang loose attitude you prize so highly by developing what the magazines call "an aggressively youthful lifestyle." One small hitch. History teaches us that those who treat life in the Real World like an endless extension of freshman year at college almost invariably end up lurching forward suddenly some evening while removing their sneakers in a musty locker room. Do you think it's fun winding up your days stone dead at thirty-one with a sock clutched in your right hand, a grimace of pain and surprise on your now frozen features, and a chorus of friends remarking sadly on the irony of *your* being the one to go ("... and he played ice hockey and polo every day and practiced for intramural decathlon on his lunch hour—it just doesn't make any sense!")?

I only bring these unpleasant scenarios to your attention to save you and your loved ones needless heartache and grief later on. To be frank, these are comparatively benign forms of evasion. Incest, Satanism, and the uglier varieties of psychotic disorder are just a few of the strategies I have declined to elaborate on.

But enough gloom and doom. My point is made, and I can hope to do no more. You can either decide, now that you are armed with the facts, to grow up and take your rightful place as a soldier in the ranks of society's army, or you can sit around reading comics and scratching yourself and waiting for the Enforcement Squads to burst through your door and drag you into the street and beat you to within an inch of your putrid little self-absorbed life.

The choice is yours.

—Danny Abelson

A Responsible Reply

Peter: I won't grow up.
Michael, John, and Wendy: I won't grow up.
Peter: And I won't be an adult.
Michael, John, and Wendy: And I won't be an adult.
Peter: With a lawyer and accountant.
Michael, John, and Wendy: With a lawyer and accountant.
Peter: And a broker to consult.
Michael, John, and Wendy: And a broker to consult.

I won't grow up. (I won't grow up.)
And I won't wear a toupee. (And I won't wear a toupee.)
Or feel guilty 'bout my diet. (Or feel guilty 'bout my diet.)
And some stupid crème brulée. (And some stupid crème brulée.)

If growing up means I must wear
A jockstrap swimming to protect down there
I'll never grow up, never grow up, never grow uu-up!
(Don't care.)

I won't grow up. (I won't grow up.)
I don't like *Time* magazine. (I don't like *Time* magazine.)
And I think that Jimmy Reston (And I think that Jimmy Reston)
Should be conked upon the bean. (Should be conked upon the bean.)

I won't grow up. (I won't grow up.)
'Cause the opera makes me puke. ('Cause the opera makes me puke.)
And I won't use Aqua Velva (And I won't use Aqua Velva)
Like some cretin from Dubuque. (Like some cretin from Dubuque.)

If growing up means I must read
New Yorker articles on Margaret Mead
I'll never grow up, never grow up, never grow uu-up!
(Indeed.)

Never gonna play a game
Of golf.
Never wanna see a shrink
Or Ibsen.
Anybody says to drink
A Gibson
(Onion in the glass)
Shove it up his ass!

I won't grow up. (I won't grow up.)
I don't wanna learn to screw (I don't wanna learn to screw)
'Cause the women all are scary ('Cause the women all are scary)
And there's too much stuff to do. (And there's too much stuff to do.)

If growing up means I must choose
Between a pair of Keds and Gucci shoes...
I'll never grow up, never grow up, never grow uu-up!
(Fuck youse)
Michael: Fuck *you*.
All the children: *Fuck youse!*
Peter: So there.

—Ellis Weiner

On Chili: The Last Word

by Ellis Weiner

"...If you don't like my recipe, you can open a can of corned beef hash and stick it up your nose, because you don't deserve any better..."

Sit down. Shut up. Put out whatever you are smoking, put down whatever you are drinking. Pay attention. Not "soon," not "after I finish this article." Now. Do you think I'm joking? Try me.

After years of subjecting my palate, digestion, and health to every sort of abuse and insult labeled, either out of ignorance, innocence, or malice, "chili," I have found the ultimate recipe for that dish—yes, the one with the beans and the meat, you fool, the one more correctly called *chili con carne*. Don't carp with me, I haven't the time or the inclination to play games with you; and the first reader who feels pleased with him- or herself for knowing that *chili con carne* means, in English, "chili peppers with meat," may rest assured that he or she is a Mongoloid nitwit of the first water, to be shunned by anyone with an ounce of intelligence or discrimination.

Stop laughing. Shut up, sit down and shut up.

Chili is, as you presumably know, a mixture of beef and other meats, heavily spiced with cumin, oregano, red pepper, garlic, and salt, all of which is available in a mixture called *chili powder*. The dish gets its name, not for the South American country whose absurd experiment in democratic socialism suffered the fate it so richly deserved, but from the well-known *chili pepper*, a green or red pepper commonly used in Mexican cooking and its Americanized bastard offspring, the so-called "Tex-Mex" dishes.

I know you know all this. Please, if it is not asking too much, please attempt to curb your impulses to posture and snort impatiently, and allow me to present this recipe in my own way. If this text is over your head, then why don't you put down the magazine, climb into your wretched lime green Ford Pinto, and tool on off to any one of the several billion McDonald's outlets near where you live, work, or breathe. I am certain you will find their "Big mac" sandwich suitable fare for your boorish palate. Or do you think a palate is something upon which a painter mixes his oils? Why, then, perhaps, in your case, that's true! What do you think of that?

Then again, if you happen to have a copy of last Sunday's newspaper lying about the house or apartment, why don't you leave the authentic preparation and consumption of fine foods to the rest of us, and prepare what I have called a "Mock Big Mac," or, if you must yield to the temptation to neologize, a "Big Mock." Simply spread an ungodly amount of commercially prepared mayonnaise over any or all of the newspaper (judge quantity according to your hunger), add dash commercially prepared ketchup (not *catsup*, which is more properly a phrase meaning "feline dine," as in the statement, "We were watching the cat sup,") and, at your option, sprinkle with one teaspoon commercially prepared pickle relish. You will discover, to your no doubt crudely expressed delight,

that you have created what to nine idiots out of ten is a perfectly acceptable substitute for an authentic Big Mac. And this at a fraction of the cost of the real item. In any event, go, and never glance at my column again. I don't want you. I don't like you. You don't like me, I know that perfectly well. So be it. Now, please. Go away.

Where were we...? Chili. Please note that it is not only the chili pepper that makes the chili con carne hot; no, what also gives this sublime, robust dish its snap and burn is a combination of cayenne, black pepper, and other auxiliary hotteners such as tabasco sauce and crushed red pepper. To be sure, there are hot chili peppers, and please note their inclusion in the recipe below. Also remember that the distinctive aroma and tingly richness of chili powder is contributed, not by the peppers therein, but by the ground cumin. Fanciers of Indian cuisine will nod knowingly at this.

Note also that there is no mention of beans. Canned, institutional, and other Cro-Magnon forms of chili do feature beans, and usually at the expense of the meat content. Let it be stated forthwith: beans are to chili what potatoes are to fish cakes, i.e., filler. Eschew beans, and likewise eschew potatoes, pasta, noodles, rice, macaroni, and any other starchy thickener you may feel this recipe "needs." It "needs" nothing. Follow it or ignore it, and content yourself with whatever godawful Hormel stew concoction or fast-food Taco Pronto nightmare you can find, and to hell with you.

1 lb. chunked round top tip sirloin flank segments (also called "Saratoga filet club steaks" or "Delmonico shoulder ribeye London luncheon slabs")
1 lb. loin center cut pork chops
4 whole fresh tomatoes, peeled, seeded, and diced
1 tsp. ground cumin
1 tsp. crushed oregano
1 tsp. salt
1 tsp. freshly ground black pepper
1 tbsp. mild Peruvian chili powder
1 tbsp. medium New Mexico chili powder
1 tbsp. Hot "Caramba Nueva" chili powder
3 tsp. Emiliano Zapata tabasco sauce
1 4-oz. can Comet scouring powder
5 .38-cal. Remington Standard bullets
½ cup white vinegar
½ cup Prestone antifreeze
¼ cup Sterno jellied cooking fuel
3 rolls Sharpshooter cap pistol caps
1 4-oz. can Vasco da Gama green chilies
3 fresh Anaheim "Sum'bitch" green chili peppers
4 tbsp. olive, vegetable, or peanut oil
4 tbsp. 3-in-1 oil
Dash Drano

One pack matches
Cup tap water
1 cup heavy water (deuterium oxide)
Sulfuric acid to taste

1. Have the butcher coarse grind the steak and the chops. (Keep the ground chop bones for garnish.) With an ordinary household pair of pliers, extract the lead slugs from the Remington bullets, saving the gunpowder. Discard slugs and shells. Fine-shred the rolls of caps in a food processor or by hand. Be sure not to get any water on the caps.

2. Sauté the meat in the cooking oil. Add the cumin, salt, pepper, oregano, vinegar, and scouring powder. Let simmer until the scouring powder turns a bright green and begins to make odd noises.

3. In a large pot, combine the diced tomatoes, tabasco, antifreeze, Sterno, and both canned and fresh green chilies. Let simmer five minutes, then set aside. Now, dice the fresh chilies while still in the pot. In small bowl, mix the 3-in-1 oil with the shredded caps. Chop off the heads from the matches and sprinkle them into the mixture. Discard the rest of the matches. Blend.

4. Add the tap water and the heavy water to the meat and scouring powder mixture. (Note: Heavy water, or deuterium oxide, is available from any nuclear power station, or may be ordered by mail from Harry the Night Watchman, Second Desk from the Right, Auxiliary Security Station, Seabrook Power Facility, Seabrook, Conn.)

5. Combine all ingredients in large pot, taking care to blend the chili powders in very well. Let simmer for three hours, stirring occasionally. Add Drano, sulfuric acid to taste. Serve in a warmed bowl, garnished with ground pork chop bones, parsley, chopped raw onion, or thumb tacks dipped in benzene. Serves four.

I will tolerate no deviations from this text. Those readers for whom this dish may be a trifle too hot may feel free to slice off their own or each other's tongues with a butter knife. Similarly, those souls for whom this may be too tepid may increase the amounts of chili powder called for, provided they completely immerse their heads in the resultant mixture *while it is still simmering on the flame* and sing the "Toreador Song" from *Carmen*. This recipe is the absolute last word on chili con carne. Enjoy it. And if, for some reason, it does not delight you with its piquant blending of the rich, the spicy, and the hot, then you are a total and irrevocable cretin, and frankly, do not deserve to live. In fact, the thought of you makes me physically ill with disgust. Just go away. Don't apologize or try to defend youself, don't whine that "it's not fair." I really couldn't care less. Just go away and leave me alone with my delicious chili.

WAYNE McLOUGHLIN

He's a cowboy, Marine, Vietnam vet, anthropologist, frontiersman, explorer, angler, hunter, craftsman, surfer, designer, artist, writer, and dark humorist.

And he's from Wales? Wayne McLoughlin's biography is his identity and his strength. No one else who passed through the riot gates that guarded the offices of the *National Lampoon* had anything like Wayne's background. He was a man among boys: a droll, stable, healthy, well-muscled surfer among tubercular wiseass urban malcontents. It was as if he'd come from another world.

His talent for dark humor and his ability with paint made him unique in the *Lampoon*'s arsenal of visual treats. His work, painted on Masonite board, was often very dark in color. His surfaces were unusually smooth: finished with such meticulous detail, it appeared he was channeling Jan van Eyck or that he'd turned in a painting he'd filched from the Frick Collection. His originals reflect light, like morning sun on a dark lake. But then, bubbling up

PHOTO BY JACKIE McLOUGHLIN

from below, an impish idea surfaces, and that sober finish gives way to Wayne's very offbeat sensibility. He's made you laugh.

Wayne's writing was always as strong as his painting. In one piece, *Monumental Disasters*, the Hoover Dam is constructed in the wrong location and is being used as a drive-in movie screen. And this week's film is *The Wonderful World of Grenades*.

Wayne's career at the *Lampoon* lasted ten years. In the three decades that have passed since, he's worked for every outdoor magazine and is the only funny artist-writer who works for the likes of *Field and Stream* and *National Geographic*. I like to think a little bit of the *Lampoon* sensibility has crept into those publications through Wayne. I like to think that, but I doubt it.

—Rick Meyerowitz

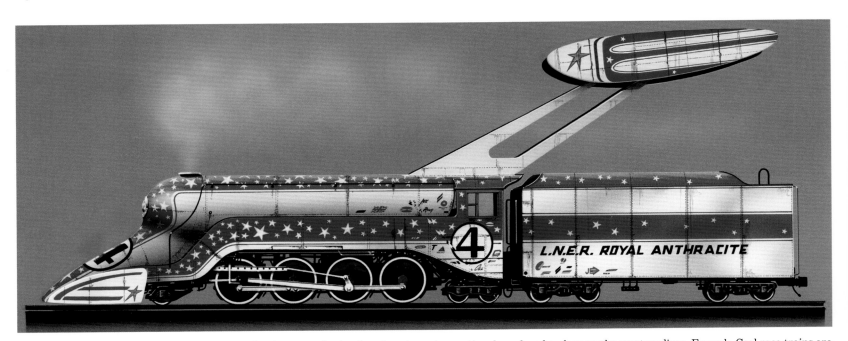

Formula Coal—although the diesel-electric now dominates professional racing, steam locomotives have found a place on the amateur lines. Formula Coal race trains are uniformly powered by North British "Nelson" class 2-4-4-4 engines, with the only allowable modifications being up to three sets of Walschaert valves. With a maximum weight of only 96,300 pounds, Formula Coal locomotives get excellent performance, and the keen competition provides a breeding ground for future Grand Prix talent.

March 1977

The National Lampoon Encyclopedia of Humor, 1973

GRAND PRIX
RAILROAD RACING

by Wayne McLoughlin

The Classic Era   *1946-1955*

Above Luke Dumply pilots his Team Rio Grande Baldwin Light Mallet over the hump trestle at the Chattanooga GP in 1953. The Light Mallet was among the most powerful steam engines ever raced. A four-cylinder power plant with double overhead articulated boilers produced 1800 horsepower. But poor aerodynamics and a 641,700-pound dry weight made handling skittish. Dumply rode the Rio Baldwin to a 1953 World Engineer's Championship in what was to be steam's last year as unchallenged master of the tracks.

Right Nineteen fifty-two witnessed the advent of the racing diesel-electric. The first diesel engines were used in sports trains such as this North British Excursion Prototype, shown going out of control during a South African grade climb. But the diesel-electric was to soon prove itself on the Grand Prix Trunk Routes as well.

March 1977

Monumental Disasters

and Colossal Cover-ups

by
Wayne McLoughlin

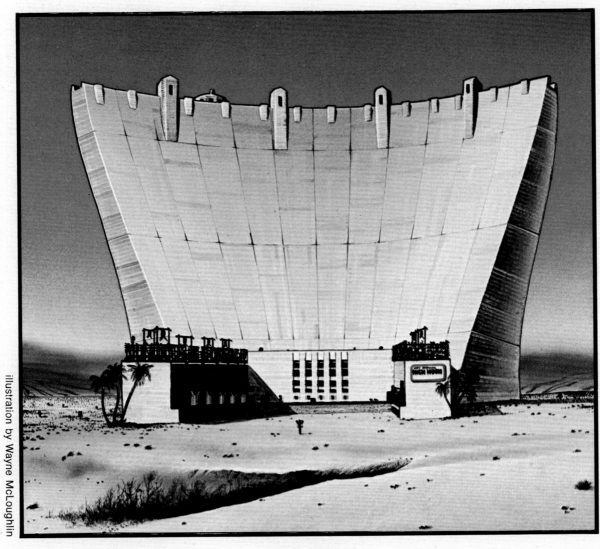

illustration by Wayne McLoughlin

Hoover Dams

This photo is conclusive proof that the Hoover Dam was built twice. This is Hoover Dam number one. A surveyor's error (a misplaced decimal point) resulted in the dam's construction a little over one hundred miles too far to the left. Located outside the small desert community of Mesquite Spring, this enormous structure has yet to arouse curiosity. The area's inhabitants think it's a drive-in. Fearing adverse publicity, the Department of the Interior has kept a lid on the multimillion dollar blunder since 1935 by providing the movies. Showing the day this photo was taken was *High Noon* and a short feature, *Wonderful World of Grenades*. The latter is an Army training film.

A lone speaker stand indicates the size of Mesquite Springs; the projector is placed on a card table. Ironically, electricity is supplied by a one horsepower gasoline generator.

Several dozen badly damaged bulldozers, in various states of decay, were found in the vicinity. This lends credence to the theory that there was some attempt by the construction companies involved to push the dam into position on the Colorado River, 112 miles away.

November 1974

March 1980

RON BARRETT

I first met Ron Barrett in December 1967 at a Madison Avenue advertising agency. He was milder mannered than Clark Kent. I was a brash guy who was just starting

PHOTO BY DICK FRANK

out as an illustrator, and he was one of the first art directors to see my portfolio. Ron seemed to like my work, and me, enough to close the door to his office and politely say, "Now, may I show you my portfolio?" His art was so much more professional and refined than the uncouth images I had showed him that I wondered whether I ought to give up on becoming an illustrator. It crossed my mind that we could switch jobs, until I realized I couldn't do his job either. At that moment, my options seemed clear: short of chewing on a shotgun, the only thing I was qualified to do was dishing out falafel from a street cart.

In 1972 Ron showed Tony Hendra an elaborate collage he'd made. It was a large landscape, a Yosemite of meat, done with dozens of photographs surgically cut from magazine ads. And, to use the vernacular, it blew Tony's mind. He conceived of a project they could do together. It was a perfect *Lampoon* collaboration: artist inspires writer, who inspires artist right back, and something wonderful comes of it. In this case, that wonderful thing is the singular and spectacular *Wide World of Meat*.

Ron contributed to the magazine often during the 1970s. And he worked on other projects, such as his wonderful

children's book, *Cloudy with a Chance of Meatballs*. In the early 1980s he began doing his great monthly comic strip, "Politenessman." It was an instant success and has become a *Lampoon* classic. Ron's work was transferable to other media. His humor and aesthetic worked beautifully in the *National Lampoon*, and with some editing, it worked just as well in the *New York Times* or in a children's book.

Ron never gave up his day job, continuing to work as a designer for many publications. In 1990 he became the last art director of the *National Lampoon*. It was the last year the magazine would be published with any regularity. By then, already dismal readership numbers had crossed some event horizon and been sucked into a black hole with the rest of the magazine. You wouldn't get an argument if you said nobody even knew the *Lampoon* was still publishing. Too bad. Because of Ron's crisp, smart, knowing art direction the magazine looked better than it ever had.

All this is to tell you that Ron Barrett, with his sense of humor and his elegant aesthetic, is a singular talent. He's too polite to tell you that, but I just did.

—Rick Meyerowitz

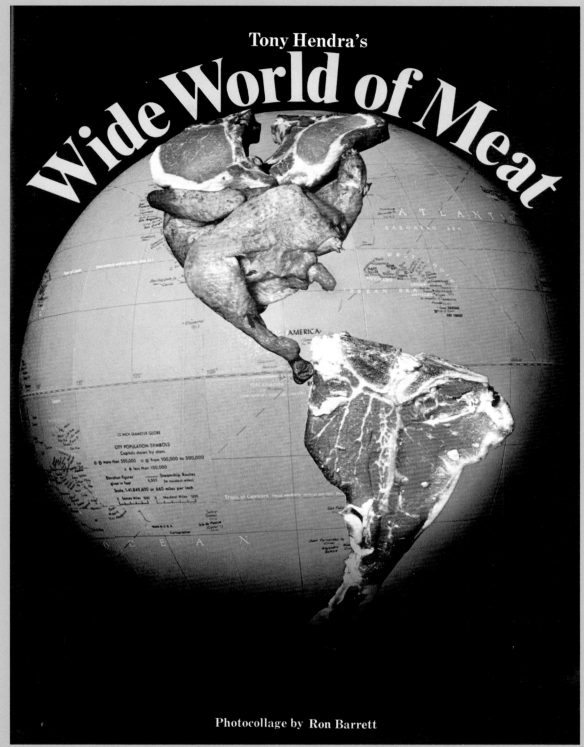

Tony Hendra's

Wide World of Meat

Photocollage by Ron Barrett

December 1973

MEAT IS FUNNY
Tony Hendra on Meat

Meat is funny. Fish isn't. (Except when mailed to the drama critic of the *New York Times* in newspaper with the scrawled message "Swim with the fishes.") Meat is colored funny: pink, grey, mottled. Meat is shaped funny: weirdly suggestive folds, lumps, orifices. Tube Steak, meet Beef Curtains. Meat just sits there, naked, dumb, stupidity incarnate. "'Ey, meathead!" "Ah, baloney!" Meat is the paradigm of mindless consumerism. Mindless meat in packets becoming mindless meat in shorts. Goddam, meat is funny! So when a graphic genius named Ron Barrett walked into my office in 1972 with brilliant photo collages of meat (no Photoshop in our shop, all hand-cut), I fell on the floor. He skillfully butchered a few more photos . . . et voilà! A *Lampoon* classic.

From the moment God cooked Adam's goose with a sparerib to the time his Son served Himself for supper, through all the ages in which fat was rendered unto Caesar and Sir Loincelot rode to the Meate d'Arthur, honest Dutch burghers ignored the Rump Parliament and millions of tons of perfectly good ground round was buried in the poppy fields of Amiens while children starved in China, fundamental questions have been raised regarding meat. As the German pessimist Flanken has it in his monumental *Meataphysics,* "Are we not merely meat arranged to facilitate the passage of irrelevant electric currents? And if so can we not eat our sister?" Other questions crowd the plate. Will the meat inherit the earth? In a tight spot should you sell your chicken stock? What is a sweetbread? Perhaps we shall never know, but of one thing we can be certain: meat was never meant to fly. Thus on May 6, 1937, the 7,630,000-cubic-foot, 804-foot-long Hindenbird, largest turkey ever to cross the Atlantic, caught fire at its moorings in Lakehurst, New Jersey, and burned to a crisp.

6:00 P.M. and time for the news—
Meat Lai thrills a hungry nation.

Above: Recipe for relaxation: Loin lies down with limb and weenie with wahine to grill gently in a moderate Florida sun.

From the ashes of tragedy comes forth a rib roast. In 1963 meat finally makes the grade in its long journey from humble pie to *prime inter pares.* Sworn in by the successor to Frankfurter and precursor of Burger, Chef Warren, the Bird made Flesh embarks on a stomach-boggling Administration, including the war in Meatnam, the Grade-A Society, and, with the help of his First Lady, herself a tooth-some 140 pounds of choice Texan tartare, the Meatification of America.

Over: Rising in majestic splendor from the fertile platters of the Midwest, USDA National Pork presents a mouth-watering vista to the astonished tourist. Dominated by Mount Butterball (7,365 feet, $1.39 per pound), the Pork is considered to be the most remarkable occurrence of natural meat in the free world. Visitors may feast their eyes on the extraordinary formations of Marble Beef Heights and Jerky Ridge, shoot the Gravy Rapids, hear the passing wind in Kielbasa Caverns, or ride tall up Brisket Bluff to see the business end of a meatball avalunch. A leisurely drive north through Moby Duck—a tunnel has been blasted out of the sheer stuffing—takes one past the timeless Spam quarries and on across the eerie landscape of the Ham Flats, toward the sun-kissed sirloin tips of the horizon and the primeval drama of Rising Gorge.

Above: Taste the classic elegance of America[n] design. General Meats' top-of-the-line for '7[3]. A sleek roaster, boned and rolled throughou[t]. Lays lard with the best of them, yet boasts [a] specially tenderized interior for the ultimate i[n] comfort. Revolutionary safety snout built [to] withstand up to 10-m.p.h. impact. Body b[y] Butcher. Live high off the hog in '73. You won[']t regret i[t].

Is there intelligent meat on other planets? A[t] Cape Carnivoral (*left*), a team of exper[ts] labor round the clock to prepare Pollo I for i[ts] historic flight in search of the answer to th[at] and other timeless secrets of the univers[e,] answers that cannot but have the profounde[st] implications for the future of all meatkind.

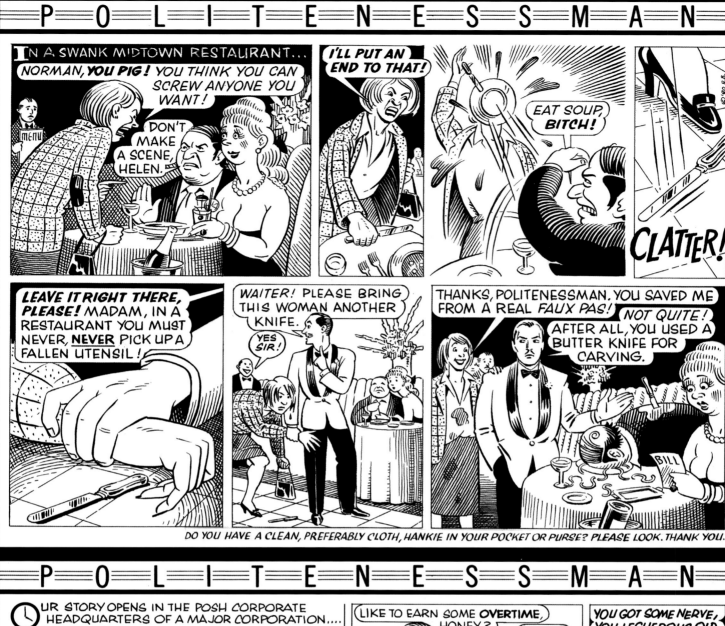

JEFF GREENFIELD

The Jeffster. El Jefe. Greeny. These are the names no one ever called Jeff Greenfield. He was, even then, sober-minded and serious, too grown-up to be called anything

but Mr. Greenfield. I don't know that anyone at the *National Lampoon* even knew his first name before they read it in the byline of his first story.

Jeff Greenfield was born on Manhattan, a small island off the East Coast of North America. He kayaked to the mainland each day to attend the Bronx High School of Science. He then spent four years in Wisconsin, where he used his science training to grill cheese. He also learned to write, and he edited his college newspaper. He graduated from Yale Law School and became a reporter. He wrote speeches for Robert F. Kennedy and authored quite a few books. Yet he was unfulfilled.

He had in him the soul of a *tummler*. The Jeff Greenfield the world saw, the one kicking Bill Buckley's mephitic old ass on *Firing Line*, or on CBS with Walter Cronkite, discussing whether the election of Ronald Reagan meant the world was coming to an end, or taking over *Nightline* when Ted was

PHOTO BY PETER KLEINMAN

wounded while embedded in a block of gelignite by troops of the 101st Airborne, or soberly discussing the meaning of the sailboat designs on Elián González's pajamas with Larry King: this was not the Jeff Greenfield that Jeff Greenfield thought was Jeff Greenfield.

Jeff Greenfield wanted to be Dorothy Parker, Robert Benchley, and Woody Allen. And so he arrived, this man of

the law and the press, at the *National Lampoon*, with sheaves of parodies jammed into his Coach briefcase and each pocket of his Brooks Brothers' suit bulging with smart ideas.

He toiled, if that's what it could be called, at the *Lampoon* off and on for a decade, beginning in the mid-1970s, and he wrote some very funny pieces. It could be said about him that no one else wrote the kind of articles he did. Jeff's run as a *Lampoon* contributor ended around the time the head of his network found out he'd been moonlighting. "Did you write *this* story of Richard Nixon's sex life?" he was asked. "Or *this* advice to young women on sex, or *this* account of Jesus's return and his fondness for corporate mergers?"

The chips were down, the ball in play, his head on the block. The network president demanded Jeff's allegiance to the network, or to the heretical *National Lampoon*. It was his way or the highway. The gauntlet had been thrown down, along with other metaphors. This, then, was to be the great turning point in Jeff's life. Summoning up all the frustration, all the years of breaking his own instinctive whimsy on the corporate rack, and the need of a true comedian to express himself, he answered: "And if I stayed, would I get a raise?"

He did.

—Rick Meyerowitz

Elborne Whippet, Jr. On Campaign ·'76

Mr. Elborne Whippet, Junior, bears a close, nay, precise resemblance to one Jeff Greenfield, a disgruntled politico-journalist of New York City.

Rancho Los Vistas, Calif.—And so they will flock to Kansas City, these rock-ribbed, respectable Republicans, they of the Dacron sport shirts with multiple ballpoint pens secured in protective plastic breast pockets, they of the impenetrable foundation garments, the Valium and lithium, they of the Seagram's and Wonder Bread, there to confront the agonizing choice between he who beckons the head and he who speaks to the heart. The struggle between Gerald Ford and Ronald Reagan is the struggle between the two legs of this shrinking yet somehow triumphant party. And where those two legs meet can truly be found the spirit of Republicanism.

But what of this challenger, this Reagan, this rhetorical master who can tempt this stolid, solid gathering of burghers into abandoning an incumbent president of their own party? What governs the one-time governor who can with a wink, a quip, a challenge, summon the faithful to cheers heretofore reserved for the achievement of daily regularity?

To search for the answers, this correspondent left the poolside comfort of the Beverly Hills Hotel and ventured to the ranch of Ronald Reagan. To my surprise, I found the challenger in a book-lined, dimly-lit study. The hairpiece was gone, the teeth were resting casually in a tumbler full of twelve-year-old Scotch, the elevator cowboy boots were closeted away— and in place of the Ronald Reagan who fills the television screen, this scribe saw a four-foot ten-inch, bald, pipe-smoking gentleman buried in a mass of yellowing books, and muttering to himself.

"Ah," Governor Reagan said, "you surprised me. I was attempting to locate a more reliable translation of a particularly critical passage from Kant's *Fundamental Groundwork for a Metaphysics of Morals*. If you *knew* how these younger translators *butcher* the masters, you would..."

I expressed surprise at Governor Reagan's choice of leisure reading.

"*Leisure?*" he bellowed. "You call a man's life work *leisure*? Ahh, well, it is to be expected. You are from the

KRISTIN JOHNSON

world of Washington; of power and alliances. The eternal verities are to you like some blur, while the fractious business of the moment is thrown into sharp angularity. You are no doubt familiar with Auguste Comte's tri-laterization of the human mind? All politicians—and reporters as well— are in the positive state, while I still prefer the metaphysical.

"You wonder what a man who has spent every spare moment of his life in pursuit of philosophical questions is doing in the world of politics? Allow me to explain.

"All my life I have sought to resolve the Kantian contradiction between the noumenal and phenomenological worlds: to discover the eternal in the transient. All my life I have explored the phenomenological world; my broadcasts of sporting events was an attempt to immerse myself in the most transient of matters; my Hollywood career again a search for the most ephemeral of events—oh, yes, with a brief excursion into the absurd, as in *Bedtime for Bonzo*. That was where Camus first hit upon his own notion of the Absurd. The concept was mine, of course, but no matter.

"And now politics. Can you *imagine* a more perfect illustration of the epistemological dilemma? The tendency to assume knowledge derived from unreliable data? My enemies ask whether I dye my hair—not whether

I have any. They assume a character, a personality, based on words scribbled by Thorazine addicts I keep chained in my corral. I have demonstrated by my own life that the gap between perception and reality is a chasm of unbridgeable proportions."

It seemed out of place, but I asked Reagan to assess his future.

"I am, of course, yearning to be relieved of this burden," he said. "Each day my language, my policies become more deranged, so that I will be defeated and permitted to return here and finish my studies. And what happens? With each new excretion, my primary victories increase—my delegate count soars—my prospects for the nomination grow brighter.

"I sought to adopt a position so outrageous that even my strongest supporters would be repulsed. I determined to come out for slavery. I went to six state delegations with a black man in chains following me, and I told them that my position on slavery was identical to my position on the Panama Canal: 'I bought him; I paid for him; he's mine, and I'm going to keep him.'"

He sighed.

"The next day," Reagan said, "the Mississippi delegation unanimously endorsed my candidacy." He shook his head.

"Sartre was right, you know— there *is* no exit." □

THE SPECIALIST

by Jeff Greenfield

"The doctor will see you now."

"You're absolutely sure no one else is in there. I mean—"

The efficiently attractive receptionist smiled reassuringly as she motioned him inside.

"I'm sure, sir. In fact, I'm leaving now as well. You'll be utterly alone." She slipped on her coat as she motioned him inside. *He's even handsomer than he is on television*, she thought to herself.

As he walked into the doctor's office, hands thrust into his pockets, a walk familiar to millions, his mind was again wracked with doubts. *What the hell am I doing here?* . . . Then he remembered the call from the U.S. Attorney's Office, the mumbled, half-apologetic, half-insistent inquiries on the other end of the line, and he knew.

"Please come in, Governor." The voice was liquid, rich, reassuring. As he looked up, he confronted a silver-haired, tanned face behind the teak, chrome, and glass desk. The face was strong, craggy, as ruggedly confident as an airline pilot's. The governor felt a tinge of reassurance.

"Sit down, please, Governor." The chair was contemporary yet deeply comfortable. The office itself was redolent with quiet elegance, befitting a doctor at the top of his profession. The governor now recalled the cloakroom rumors: the income of more that $1.8 million a year, the East Side townhouse, the villas around the world, the luxurious vacations with transportation provided by the most secret agencies of the federal establishment . . .

"Governor?"

"I beg your pardon, I was . . . woolgathering."

The doctor smiled.

"I asked you what seems to be the trouble."

The governor paused. How to begin?

"I—I'm not sure. My chest . . . my back . . . my . . ."

The doctor leaned back in his handcrafted Eames chair and smiled broadly. His tapered fingers formed a steeple.

"Governor," the doctor said, "I have been performing my . . . specialty for almost ten years now, since the early seventies. In my time, I have treated people whose . . . position is even higher than yours. In that time, have you ever heard a

whisper of a rumor about my . . . practice *or* my clients? Now, please. I cannot offer an accurate . . . diagnosis without knowing *exactly* what your condition involves." Beneath the smile the well-modulated tones echoed steel.

All right, the governor said to himself. *Across the Rubicon.*

"This morning, the U.S. Attorney called. Seems they've been investigating the collapse of the Logan Street Bridge."

"I saw the films, of course," the doctor interjected. "Terrible loss, terrible."

"Yes, of course," the governor said, looking intently at the far wall. "I personally wrote the tribute to the dead and maimed that was inserted in the *Congressional Record*. Anyway, it appears that the contractors did not meet the specifications of the federal contract. They . . . they substituted certain more economical materials in place of those called for in the contract. In the interest of thrift."

"While billing the government for the full amount," the doctor observed.

"Yes," said the governor. "Naturally, these venal men will do anything to avoid paying for their crimes, and they're making *wild, to*tally unfounded allegations about . . . *pay*offs and wire-pulling and—"

"And unfortunately there are . . . documents," said the doctor.

"Stop me if I'm boring you," the governor said.

"I'm sorry, but these conditions always have similar symptoms."

The governor slapped his palms to his forehead, his air of formal calm gone.

"Photographs . . . tapes . . . witnesses . . . the whole shebang," he murmured. "I'm supposed to go before a grand jury next Tuesday. That means four, five counts, *federal felony counts*, nine months before the first presidential primary. And a trial right through the first of the year. Never mind my . . . hopes for the future. I might as well resign my seat or flee to Brazil."

The governor looked at the doctor with eyes of naked pain.

"What have I got?"

The doctor sat completely still.

October 1975

"Please, doc," the governor said, sweat now beading on his patrician forehead. "This is my life we're talking about. *What have I got?*"

"The fee . . . ?"

"Oh, yes, yes, of course," the governor babbled with relief as he handed the attaché case across the desk. "If you want to count it now—"

"I'm sure it's all there," the doctor offered reassuringly. "You will please send an assistant round tomorrow to retrieve your case." The governor nodded. "You've left some papers in here in addition to the . . . fee?" Another nod.

"Good," said the doctor. He rose from his desk and began to pace back and forth, with professional solemnity.

"Governor, you have three children, I presume?"

"Why, yes. I have a boy, thirteen, a girl, twelve, and then there's Bonnie, who's three." His eyes lit up at the mention of the dimpled, cheerful redhead who had brought new strength to his troubled marriage.

The doctor's brow furrowed.

"Governor, I'm afraid I have some bad news for you. Bonnie is very, *very* ill."

The governor sat bolt upright.

"Oh, no. Oh, no."

"Yes, Governor." The doctor went to a file cabinet marked *Diagnoses—Terminal* and pulled out a file of X-rays and medical charts.

"It seems, Governor, that little Bonnie has contracted a rare disease—a cancerous condition of the liver which is totally and irreversibly terminal."

"You can't be serious—it's monstrous—surely there's *some* other . . . diagno-sis, somebody else, perhaps a lingering, curable malady, I mean . . . hepa*titis* . . ."

The stern expression on the doctor's face silenced the governor.

"I am a specialist," the doctor said quietly but firmly. "You have come to me seeking the proper form of attention for your particular

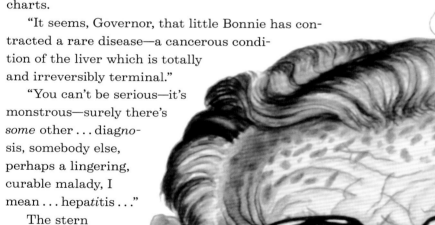

malady. I have been in the profession since Gerald Ford and Nelson Rockefeller came to me a decade ago. In that time, my work has been at the service of the most important people of the world."

He continued now, warming to his words.

"When Bentsen's election was in trouble, did he come whimpering when I told him of his wife's breast cancer? And subsequently? Do you realize that woman had a colostomy, three open-heart operations, and has had all of her limbs removed? Do you know what they call her now in society? 'The Paperweight.' But Bentsen understood what was needed.

"Did you hear Teddy whimper when the Chappaquiddick stories surfaced again, and his son had to lose a leg? Have you looked at the Congress lately? Do you know that there are 275 monopedes in the House of Representatives? Did you ever wonder what those twenty-seven senators thought of when their children were lost at sea on a cruise?

"You must understand, Governor, that the burdens of leadership are heavy. The . . . temptations of public life are not so easily buried these days. The press—TV—this practice of mine is the last barrier between our natural leaders and *mob anarchy*."

The governor squared his shoulders.

"Yes, yes, I see, doctor. What—what do I do?"

"Bring Bonnie in next week for a checkup. We'll prepare the necessary medical documents and, of course, the injections with the—culture. Then we just let nature take its course."

"And the timing—"

The doctor smiled.

"I think I can assure you of a somber funeral a week before the New Hampshire primary."

"Will Bonnie—suffer much?"

"No more than is necessary," said the doctor, rising to his feet. "Now if you'll excuse me, I have another patient to see. If you'd mind leaving by the back entrance . . ."

"Of course, doctor, of course." As he left, he heard the doctor greeting the next patient.

"*Buon giorno*, Your Holiness, *buon giorno*, and what seems to be the trouble?"

RON
HAUGE

The high plains and soaring peaks of Montana really are a long way from the high rents and soaring prices of New York City, but Ron Hauge always felt he'd

"been born in the wrong place." The grim and gritty streets of Manhattan should be his natural home. He moved there as soon as he could and settled into a tenement flat in Alphabet City.

It wasn't long before he noticed that the New York depicted on the cover of the *New Yorker*, the quaint, friendly, spotless, trouble-free New York of those days, didn't square with the New York he saw from his window. A city where you wouldn't eat off

PHOTO BY KRISTINE LARSEN

the sidewalk if Jesus himself appeared and said, "Go ahead, it's okay."

The drawings on these pages were submitted to the *New Yorker* to give the real New York equal time on their cover. The rejection slips that piled up were always quaint, friendly, spotless, and, as a bonus, filled with good advice: "The editors are saddened to see you wasting so much good money on postage. Get a job."

—Rick Meyerowitz

RON HAUGE'S YEAR OF REJECTED
NEW YORKER COVERS

December 1983

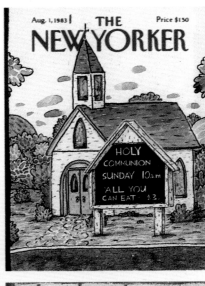

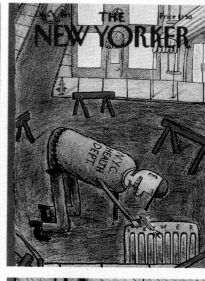

FRED GRAVER

The year he turned fifty, Gerry Sussman awoke to discover he had been transformed into the editor in chief of a magazine perused exclusively by persons one-third his age. Thinking fast for an old guy, Gerry brought up three rookies (Al, Kevin, and Mike) from the farm team—the *Harvard Lampoon*, that is—and drafted a recent Notre Dame graduate, Fred Graver. Fred was discovered at a small publishing house, where, by coincidence, he was editing a book Gerry had written.

On staff, the Ivy League grads were ironic and witty. Their output was small. Fred was enthusiastic and funny. He wrote fast, and he wrote lots. (Ted Mann dubbed him "the Crazy Laughter Bear.")

PHOTO BY BETSY GRAVER

All too soon, Al, Mike, and Kevin decamped for the West Coast, where their glittering careers initiated the Harvard alumni's monopoly over all writing gigs in TV comedy, forever.

Fred continued to toil at the *National Lampoon* until the office putsch of 1984. Subsequently, he has written rather a lot of television and won so many Emmys that you'd never guess he didn't go to Harvard.

—Sean Kelly

In April of 1984, a few months before he left the magazine, Fred Graver created this sharp-witted parody. Whether you've got Iraq, Afghanistan, Iran, or Venezuela on your mind, it resonates powerfully.

TINTIN IN LEBANON

No way around it: jokes about 9/11 will always be "too soon." In the case of this piece, I guess I qualify for "too early."

In October of 1983, a suicide bomber attacked the U.S. barracks in Beirut; 241 soldiers died. I remember being confused at the time, in my limited-perspective Midwestern American way. Even my post-Vietnam cynicism wouldn't let me wrap my head around the question, Why do they hate us? Oh, 1983! We were so young then!

A week or two after the bombing, I was looking in the paper at photographs of the dead soldiers. One of

them had a Tintin haircut. I thought to myself: "Boys' adventure gone very, very wrong." Although the boys I was thinking of weren't the dead soldiers, they were Reagan's boys, soon to be Bush's boys, in Washington. Too soon, indeed.

I was in a friend's apartment on a Sunday afternoon, and I wrote the whole thing out in two or three drafts in a few hours. I don't know... on the one hand, it's held up pretty well. On the other, I wish it didn't.

One thing I do know: The illustrator, Cliff Jew, is a *genius*.

—Fred Graver

April 1984

- SHERGÉ -

THE ADVENTURES OF
TINTIN
★
TINTIN IN LEBANON

METHANE

TINTIN
IN LEBANON

Beirut, 1984...

Here we are, Snowy. It's quite an honor being personally invited by the American president to get to the bottom of this Lebanon situation.

And some people say he doesn't like reporters.

He likes the Evil Empire even less.

Look, Snowy, there's the military attaché now.

Greetings, Mr. Tintin. I'm glad you're here. They're expecting you at the French encampment.

I believe you know your destination....

?

Son of a camel flea!

He walked right into my trap!

Hello, what's this? That's the third checkpoint he's driven through!

KABOOM

①

Well, Snowy, looks like we're out of a room tonight. Maybe the Americans can help us out!

Meanwhile, in the nearby Shuf Mountains...

IN SESSION
MIDEAST UNITY LEAGUE

Of course we've had our differences. But we must all agree-- that busybody Tintin cannot be allowed in our country!

Pardon my interruption, but I disagree.

Perhaps this boy could be put to good use.

One might expect that from a man who would do a three-way with a camel and a goat!

BEIRUT

Better a camel and a goat than a hollowed-out pomegranate, you fruit-felcher!

You bloodstained nasal secretion!

Wait a minute!

BEIRUT

Infidel!

Excrement-eating dog!

Windward defecator!

Hand-shaker of Jews!

THUD

Meanwhile, at the office of the American envoy...

Mr. Tintin, according to our intelligence report...

You were here last week, and have left already. I'm afraid I can't help you!

Wait a minute— I was almost killed!

You silly reporters! When will you stop endangering your lives and allow your government to do its job? Take him to the press room!

BOUM

(2)

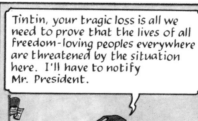

THE END

FLUKE OF THE UNIVERSE

Fred Graver

It's 1972. I'm in high school in Chicago. I wake up one morning to WPLJ, which at the time is a "free-form" (meaning "hippie") radio station. They're playing "Deteriorata," a piece by Tony Hendra from *The National Lampoon Radio Hour*.

"You are a fluke of the universe / You have no right to be here / And whether you can hear it or not / The Universe is laughing behind your back."

This was a perfect knife-twist into the gut of the entire Kahlil Gibran, hippie-dippie "You are a child of the Universe" ethos. It was perfect *National Lampoon*. I decided right then, "I want to do that!"

From its inception, the *Lampoon* was casting off seeds, which began taking root in American culture. By the time I arrived in the early 1980s, *Animal House*, the *Radio Hour*, and *Lemmings* (whose cast members included Chevy Chase, John Belushi, and Christopher Guest) had become *Saturday Night Live*, *Caddyshack*, and *Spinal Tap*. The *Lampoon* had done its job. If you wanted *Lampoon* humor, you didn't need to read the magazine anymore.

I got my job because a Hollywood producer had hired "a couple of *Lampoon* guys" to write *Airplane 2*. And the two guys fled the office for Hollywood that day, literally leaving the articles they were writing in their typewriters. Joining the *Lampoon* in the early 1980s was like joining the cast of *Beatlemania*. No, wait, that's too good. It was like joining *Wingsmania*.

"Deteriorata" is the natural course of things. That's what gave Tony Hendra's parody its teeth. You can't fight the rot. Rust never sleeps.

There was still a lot of great work being done at the *Lampoon*. But the front office, which once nurtured Beard and Kenney, was, without their vision, seduced by the success of *Animal House* and read that success not as the subversive, antiauthoritarian message it really was, but as tits and fart jokes and toga parties. The *Lampoon* was losing its grip on its audience, and they thought they could get it back with seminaked girls on the cover, not satire.

The moment had passed by the magazine. Not that we weren't working hard. And after all, the founding editors wrote for a magazine that sold posters of half-naked women in its back pages. But the founders ignored all that. They were going to bend the psyche of America and teach it to look at everything in a new way. And they did just that. What the next generation of comics learned from the *Lampoon* was that getting it right was everything.

Look at the pieces in this book, how good they are, and think about who read them and the effect they had at the time. (I am *so* mad that I didn't take every back issue from the *Lampoon* storage room before they fired us.)

The legacy of the *National Lampoon* in the eighties was that *Ghostbusters* was so much better than it needed to be. The *Letterman Morning Show* was so much better than it needed to be. John Hughes movies were so much better than they needed to be. *Ridgemont High* was so much better than it needed to be. *Spinal Tap* was so much better than it needed to be.

Today, every episode of *The Simpsons* is so much better than it needs to be, and so is *The Daily Show* and *The Colbert Report* and the *Onion*. All of them can trace their ancestry right back to the *National Lampoon*.

Okay, one last story. Here's how bad it was at the end: The magazine had no editor in chief. So Sean Kelly and I created one: a self-proclaimed "seventh-generation Harvard man-child" named L. Dennis Plunkett. The editor in chief's phone was answered in his name, restaurant reservations were made (and broken) for "L," and I corresponded as Plunkett with the authors of unsolicited manuscripts. One of these writers really hated Plunkett, and I wrote, as Dennis, that this writer should correspond with . . . Fred Graver. Up until the very end, I spent time writing to this guy about how much better the *National Lampoon* used to be and how both of us deserved better treatment than "L. Dennis Fuckitt" was giving us.

Then we all got fired.

"And whether you can hear it or not / The Universe is laughing behind your back!"

Good for the Universe!

L. Dennis Plunkett, 1982–1984

PHOTO BY RICK MEYEROWITZ

CLOUD STUDIOS

Art Directors, 1970–1970

It was the summer of 1967. I saw a sign in a second-floor window in the East Village. It had a loopy underground look to it: *Cloud Studios.* I was curious, so I found a door and climbed a flight of rickety stairs that led into an open loft space where I saw a guy serenely smoking a joint. My abrupt arrival startled him, and he attempted to hide the lit joint behind him in the cushions of the old couch above which he had just been levitating. All the while, he was coughing and wheezing out an appropriately paranoid "Who the fuck are you?" I introduced myself, swore I was an illustrator, not a narc, and within a few minutes we were sitting together, smoking and talking as if we'd known each other for a few minutes.

The guy with the joint was Peter Bramley. He was the heart and soul of the commune of underground artists and cartoonists who called themselves "Cloud Studios." Cloud, in this case, referred to the pearlescent nimbus of reefer smoke that replaced the oxygen up there. Peter looked like a cartoon by Frans Hals. He had long, straight hair, a goatee, and a mustache, and he wore clothes outlandish enough to turn heads even in the East Village. We became friends, and I got to know the other Cloudies, among them the collagist Bill Skurski, the artful Stephanie Phalen, and the photographer Michael Sullivan.

In the fall of 1969, Cloud Studios was hired to art direct the new *National Lampoon.* Against the advice of the publishers, and anyone who knew anything, Cloud was going to design the great American humor magazine. Doug Kenney had insisted it have an antiestablishment look. He wanted his magazine to be subversive, and who better to design it than a bunch of subverts. Henry went along with Doug on this, but he never

June 1970

fully got behind Cloud the way Doug did. Then again, Henry never inhaled the way Doug did. He preferred drinking his way to hell.

Cloud gave the *Lampoon* a boisterous, uncommercial, chaotic look. For the first issue, the publisher wanted a sexy babe on the cover. Instead of sexy and funny, what Cloud delivered was a leather-clad bimbo. Next to her was the world's worst drawing of a duck, by Bramley; it was to be the mascot of the magazine. That idea was dead before the magazine hit the stands, but the duck and the cover it appeared on still mystify anyone who stumbles across it on eBay.

What the first issues lacked in coherence they made up for in sheer energy. The articles and the art jumped off the page, but not in the same direction, and often they made no sense in context of the thing they were parodying. It seemed Cloud could only do Cloud, and not the sophisticated national publication the publisher was demanding. Most troublingly for all, delivering an issue on time became the issue.

Finally, under pressure, Doug pulled the plug. And with the arrival in November 1970 of Michael Gross, the *National Lampoon* took off like a rocket. Cloud Studios had launched it, done seven issues, burned out, and fallen back to Earth. Bramley and some others continued to work for the magazine occasionally. Cloud drifted into the seventies, and, like the smoke that often wreathed their bearded heads, they scattered and faded from the scene.

—Rick Meyerowitz

MICHAEL GROSS

Design Director, 1970–1974

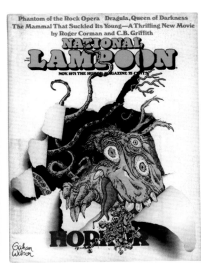

When Michael Gross arrived at the *National Lampoon* in October 1970, the place was in disarray. The editors were creating a radically new concept of funny, but Cloud Studios had produced each new issue as if it were a potluck dinner with ten varieties of "whatever" on the table.

In his job interview, Michael Gross told Henry and Doug that the design and the writing were not connecting. He felt Cloud had fundamentally misunderstood the art of parody and resorted too often to goofy underground cartoons as a solution. Sophisticated ideas and excellent writing by the editors were being wasted. Michael's concept, which at a distance seems to be self-evident, seemed revolutionary at the time. If, for instance, a parody of postage stamps was going to be funny, the stamps ought to look like real stamps, not witless cartoons.

Within two issues, Michael turned the magazine around. The *Lampoon* began to look sharp. And in each issue, every article looked like what it was supposed to be. The range of objects and publications Michael and his design partner,

a play by Michael O'Donoghue

(Hotel guest gives bellboy what appears to be a dollar bill.)

BELLBOY: Thank you.

(Bellboy realizes that what he thought to be a one-dollar bill is actually a ten-dollar bill.)

BELLBOY: THANK YOU!

(Bellboy realizes that he has again been in error and that what he thought was a ten-dollar bill is, in reality, a million-dollar bill.)

BELLBOY:

THANK YOU!!

(Curtain)

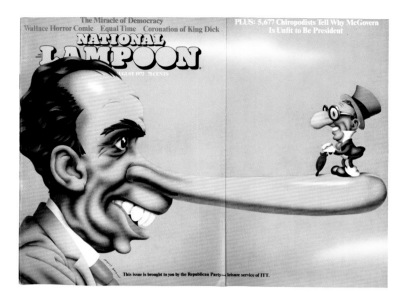

DAVID KAESTLE
Art Director, 1970–1974

PHOTO COURTESY LOUISA GRASSI

David Kaestle, parodied over the next few years was immense: menus; brochures; real magazines, such as *Esquire* and *Popular Mechanics*, and invented ones, such as *Weighty Waddlers* and *Negligent Mother*. They made advertisements, invitations, bumper stickers, calendars, children's books, sheet music, tax forms, an encyclopedia, and a high school yearbook, to list just a few. It was a range of work unequaled in any other publication, and each piece was a spot-on perfect lampoon of the real thing.

In late 1974, if not burned out from the demands of producing a magazine and its myriad special products, then slightly scorched by it and eager to try something new, Michael and David left the magazine and started their own design firm. In 1978 Michael moved to L.A. to produce movies. They continued to advise the *National Lampoon* until its demise and to work on projects together until David passed away in 2004.

The design legacy they left behind has been incorporated into the larger vocabulary of modern design. Every page of this book is, in some way, a tribute to their original vision.

—Rick Meyerowitz

Being at *National Lampoon* was like being at Sun Records.

When I was art director of the *Lampoon*, I moonlighted on a book about Buddy Holly with my friend Val Warren. We met Roy Orbison, and one afternoon we talked with him about what it was like being at Sun Records in the 1950s.

He told us: "I'd go to Sun with a few new songs, and there would be the Everly Brothers—just hanging.

"They'd say, 'What's new, Roy?'

"I'd say, 'I wrote a new tune,' and I'd play it for them.

"And they'd say, 'That's great, can we give it a go?'

"I'd answer, 'Sure.' So we'd go into the studio and record it. We'd have fun. Sun would release it, and it'd be a hit. We were young and feeding off each other—having the time of our lives recording on the fly with no interference. Nothin' but doing the best we knew how and always appreciating each other's talents. We loved it, and we weren't experienced enough to know there were other ways of doing things. It was a magic time that could never be re-created."

That was what it was like at the *National Lampoon*.

—Michael Gross

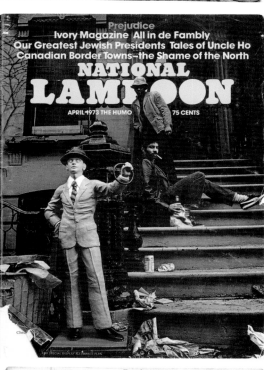
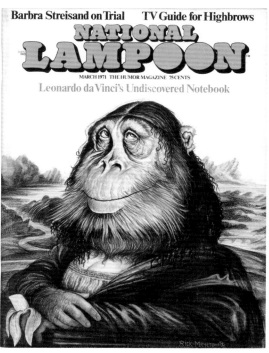

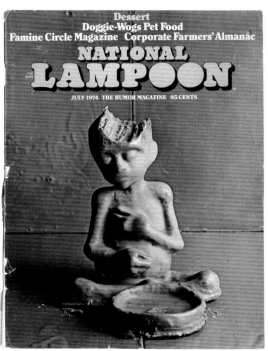
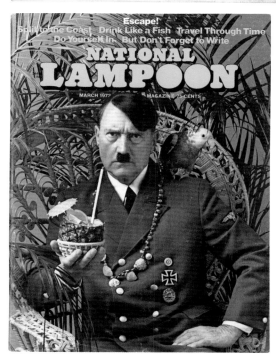

Civics
mental Disasters Prison Farm Comics More Jerry Ford Jokes
e Runaway Grand Jury The Impeachment of John F. Kennedy
The Rockefeller Art Collection

NATIONAL LAMPOON

NOVEMBER 1974 THE HUMOR MAGAZINE $1.00

ILLUSTRATION BY DON IVAN PUNCHATZ

INTERMENT FOR MEN

PLAYDEAD

JANUARY 1973 ONE DOLLAR

PLAYDEAD PICKS THE PIGSKIN PLANE-CRASHES OF '73

13 PAGES ON THE GIRLS OF FOREST LAWN

SHROUDS OF SPRING: FASHION FORECAST

SUBURBAN GRAVE-SWAPPING

THE NUDIST SHARON TATE EXHUMED

PHOTO BY DICK FRANK

I flew out to Kansas with Mike Gross to learn how the magazine got printed every month. I loved Mike. He was a mentor and a friend. We got so drunk in Kansas, we ended up missing our plane home.
—Peter Kleinman

Split Beaver Section

labeled in the past as dirty, smelly, and destructive, and subject to inquisitorial persecution on account of its rampant activity, beaver is still hunted down, trapped, eaten, or otherwise molested by large, vicious men using unspeakable instruments of torture—a process which does indeed prevent it from its hereditary tendency to gnaw on husky trunks with its busy little mouth; but which also obviates the very real advantages it confers on its immediate surroundings. Traditionally, the chief reason behind man's quest for beaver has been its delicious, tender meat and its soft, springy, scrumptious fur, but recent demonstrations have shown that, with the correct treatment, a beaver can be quite effectively tamed. Warm, affectionate, obedient, open, and given to performing the most charming little tricks, pet beavers are a constant source of pleasure to their owners, as evidenced by the increasing number found in captivity all over North America.

ILLUSTRATION BY DON IVAN PUNCHATZ

Split Beaver, February 1974, art by the inimitable Don Ivan Punchatz, who also painted the Gerald Ford cover above.

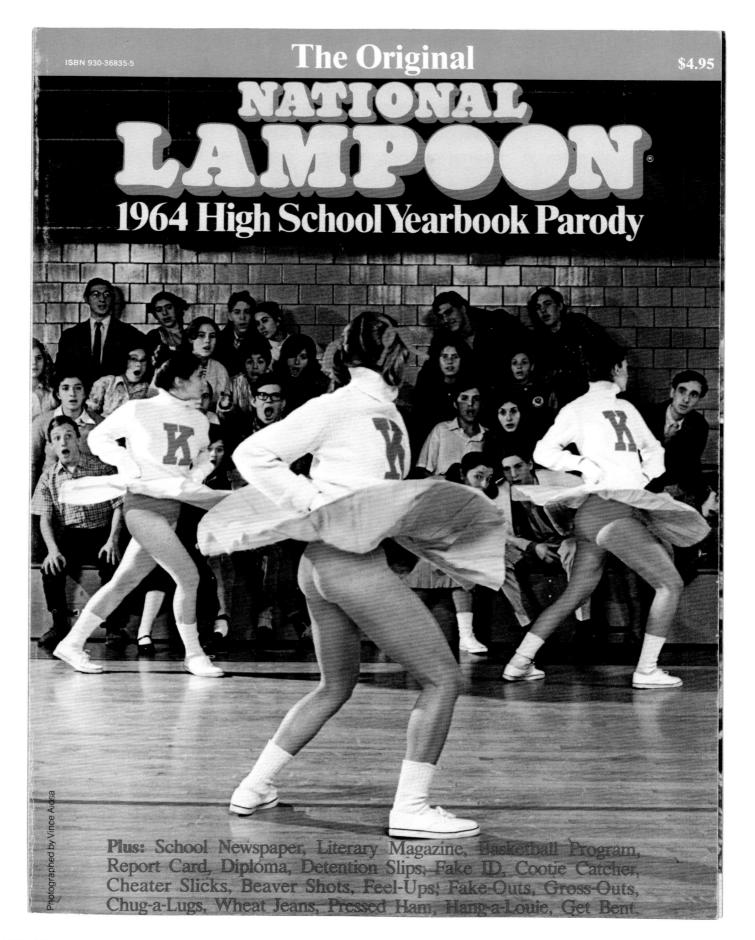

The Original

NATIONAL LAMPOON®

$4.95

1964 High School Yearbook Parody

Photographed by Vince Aiosa

Plus: School Newspaper, Literary Magazine, Basketball Program, Report Card, Diploma, Detention Slips, Fake ID, Cootie Catcher, Cheater Slicks, Beaver Shots, Feel-Ups, Fake-Outs, Gross-Outs, Chug-a-Lugs, Wheat Jeans, Pressed Ham, Hang-a-Louie, Get Bent.

June 1974: The "1964 High School Yearbook Parody" arrives a decade late. Brainchild of Doug Kenney and P.J. O'Rourke, art-directed by David Kaestle and photographed by David Kaestle with Vince Aiosa, this pitch-perfect satire, which should never be allowed to go out of print, was a huge hit. Doug owned this material. He knew what high school kids thought and looked like and wanted. P.J. was the pitch to Doug's perfect. But this project succeeded because of the tireless brilliance of David Kaestle, who got it. To make it all work, it had to be exactly right; David made sure it was. Close to four decades later, it still is.

—Rick Meyerowitz

PETER KLEINMAN
Art Director, 1974–1978, 1984–1987

I was doing paste-ups at *Esquire*, and I was just learning to tell the difference between Bodoni and Cheltenham. It added up to zero experience, but when my friend Rosie called to say the *National Lampoon* was looking for a new art director, I took a shot at it. Michael Gross looked at the handful of spreads I had designed and brought with me as a portfolio. To my surprise, he loved it. I assumed I'd never get the job, but the next day he called to ask if I could come right over to meet the staff.

In the room were Mike Gross, David Kaestle, Doug Kenney, Henry Beard, Brian McConnachie, Tony Hendra, Sean Kelly, P.J. O'Rourke, Gerry Sussman, and I don't know who else. I felt I'd walked through a door into the epicenter of something way beyond smart, and I had no business being there because I was a twenty-one-year-old Pratt dropout, wearing a ripped golf shirt and jeans.

Doug spoke first. He said, "Three questions: Can you get us drugs? Can you get us nude models? And do you have a loft or someplace where we can go with the drugs and nude models?" I replied truthfully, "Yes, yes, and yes." And Doug said, "Well, I have no more questions."

The rest of the meeting was more traditional. "What's your background? What ideas do you have for the magazine?" Brian asked me what my design plans were. My answers were definitely bullshit because I had no

PHOTO BY CHRIS CALLIS

clue, no plan, no experience, no training, and no fear. For some reason I believed I could do it, and I told them that. They must have agreed, because a few days later Mike called to offer me the job. Twenty grand a year to be art director of the *National Lampoon*!

My first day, Mike took me to my office and introduced me to my staff. What a joke! I was a college kid, I barely shaved . . . now I had a staff?

Next, I met with the boss. He was chewing on a big Montecristo. He looked me over, smiled, and said, "Lissen, kid, talented or not, you're gonna need to be trained, so we're starting you off at sixteen thousand a year."

The room started spinning. I had just quit *Esquire*. They were paying me eighteen! "But Doug and Mike told me I'd be making twenty!"

"Well," he said, "they don't write the checks. If you don't want the job, you don't have to take it."

I walked out of his office feeling like I'd been reamed with a cigar. I'd just been handed a twenty percent pay cut. I told Mike and Doug. Mike shrugged, but Doug grinned and said, "So are you gonna stay, or go back to *Esquire*?"

I sheepishly told him I'd stay. He said, "Ahhhhh, we love hiring people before they really understand money."

—Peter Kleinman

CHOPPED-LIVER SCULPTURE OF MEL BROOKS BY DIANA BRYANT, JULY 1975

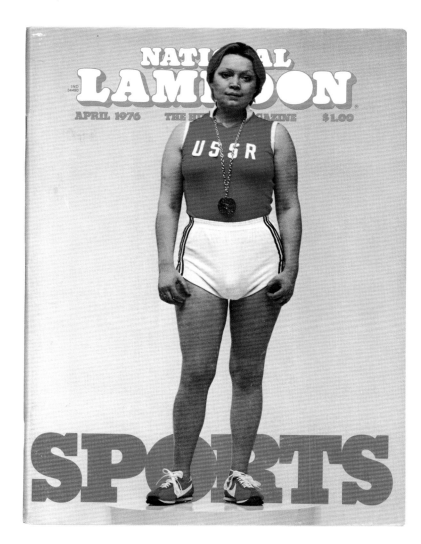

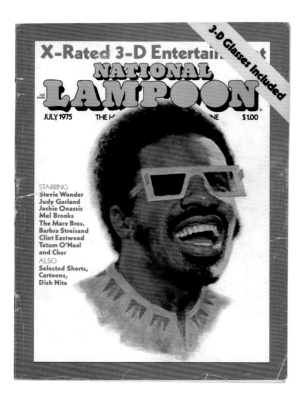

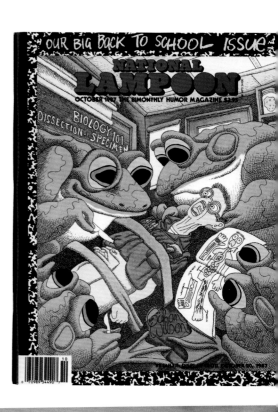

MY **PENIS**

by Karen Wheatley as told to John Hughes

One day last fall, I woke up with a...with this...with a...well, it was, it was all covered with hair and um, it was, oh, it was big and, ah, it was a...you know, it was a...what it was was a...it was like a, well...it was a penis. A real one. It scared me to death!

continued on page 67

30 NATIONAL LAMPOON The Body Issue

ILLUSTRATION BY BOB LARKIN

November 19

Peter Kleinman, who boxed under the name "The Kosher Butcher," designed some of the *Lampoon*'s most outstanding covers and interior visuals, such as the two articles by John Hughes (above and opposite). I've read both of these overlong,

GRAND FIFTH TERM INAUGURAL ISSUE
NATIONAL
LAMPOON
February 1977   The Humor Magazine   Price $1.00

JFK's First
6,000 Days

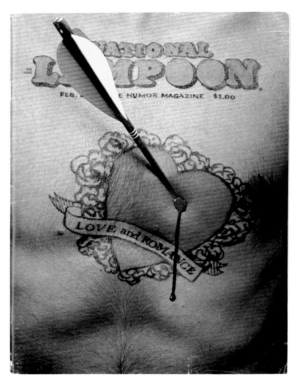

NATIONAL
LAMPOON
FEB.   E HUMOR MAGAZINE $1.00

LOVE and ROMANCE

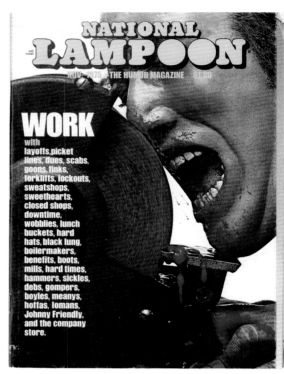

NATIONAL
LAMPOON
NOV. 1975   THE HUMOR MAGAZINE $1.00

WORK

with
layoffs, picket
lines, dues, scabs,
goons, finks,
forklifts, lockouts,
sweatshops,
sweethearts,
closed shops,
downtime,
wobblies, lunch
buckets, hard
hats, black lung,
boilermakers,
benefits, boots,
mills, hard times,
hammers, sickles,
debs, gompers,
boyles, meanys,
hoffas, lomans,
Johnny Friendly,
and the company
store.

MY
VAGINA

by
Larry
Taft
as told to
John
Hughes

One morning last winter, um, I woke up and, well, I was asleep and then I woke up, and what I found was, um, well, I woke up and there it was, and my...what should have been there wasn't and what was there was...it was...a vagina. I mean, *I was a sixteen-year-old guy with a box!* I had a damn ugly, hairy woman's privates and it was gross and sickening, and I was so pissed off I wanted to punch it right in the face!

continued on page 66

64 NATIONAL LAMPOON

ILLUSTRATION BY BOB LARKIN

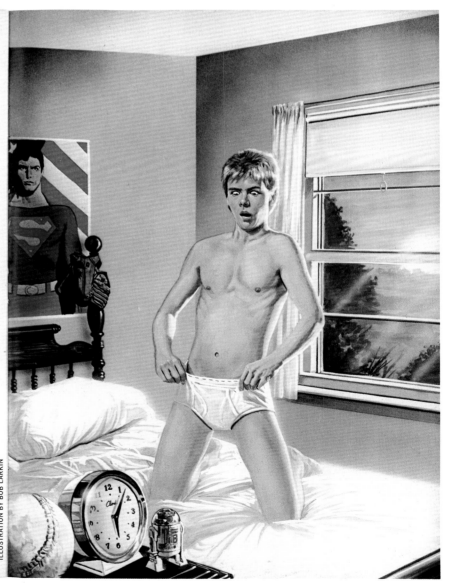

ril 1979

SKIP JOHNSTON
Art Director, 1978–1981

Skip, seen here with Truman Capote, made bold statements in print. None more so than the fabulous cover for the "Vengeance" issue (below), painted by Eraldo Carugati. Never mind that it was the Iranians (Persians) not the Arabs (Arabs) who were holding fifty-three Americans hostage. The Arab taking one on the chin provided a catharsis for all who saw it. Given that *Lampoon* readership at the time was headed down-hill without brakes, that may have added up to fewer readers than hostages.

—Rick Meyerowitz

PHOTO BY RONALD G. HARRIS

Skip Johnston (right)

Money for nothing chicks for free
d.c. cynic abets apostates on mad ave/
editnistas meets w art direct attending listen / laugh /
suggest + open to ideas = most laughs win /
/ cee "unique" editorial control ~~management~~
mattygement **persuaded** to leave / exit
by volume + unanimity of editors + occupants
of the room = Brit house o'commons PM's????s

shoot pj capotee w/ real ~~live~~ pig on stick
/ head *conan-sized!* + paw?hand?hoof?
@ronaldG(harris) studio/ *bwo* überurban bike
messenger in / "überurbanbikemessengerbag®"
/ adobe pre-alpha is sun-dried brick / *dude!*

mattyegment "sunday paper" kvetch /
"*they* (N.Y.T.) put one out *everyday*!" tru dat
s.p.d ~~real~~ gold award for a·fore·men·tioned/
name misspelled/ bri dee!

ride ends w/ *Jerry Maguire* moment = the
Big '*I was inspired, and I'm an accountant*'
Bunny / walks out with ~~thee~~ me
/ sadly *our* last laff.

—Skip Johnston

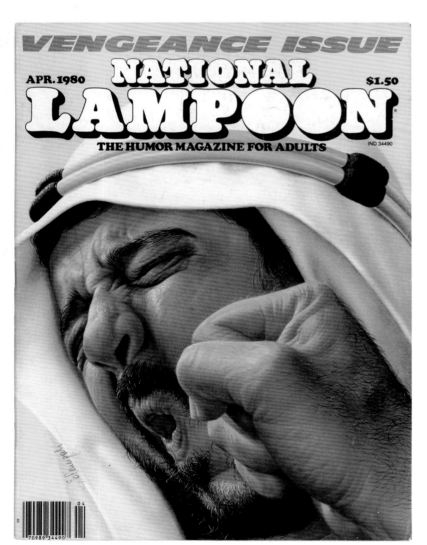

VENGEANCE ISSUE

APR. 1980

NATIONAL LAMPOON

$1.50

IND 34490

THE HUMOR MAGAZINE FOR ADULTS

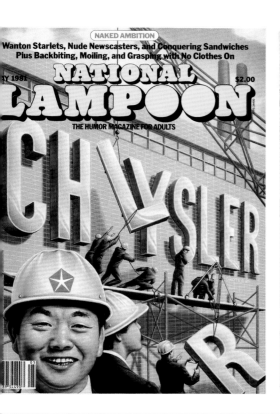

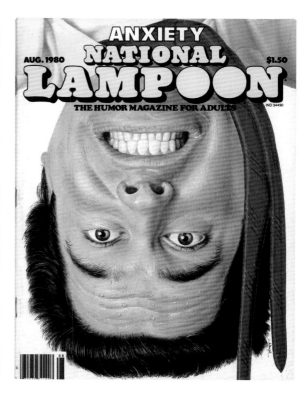

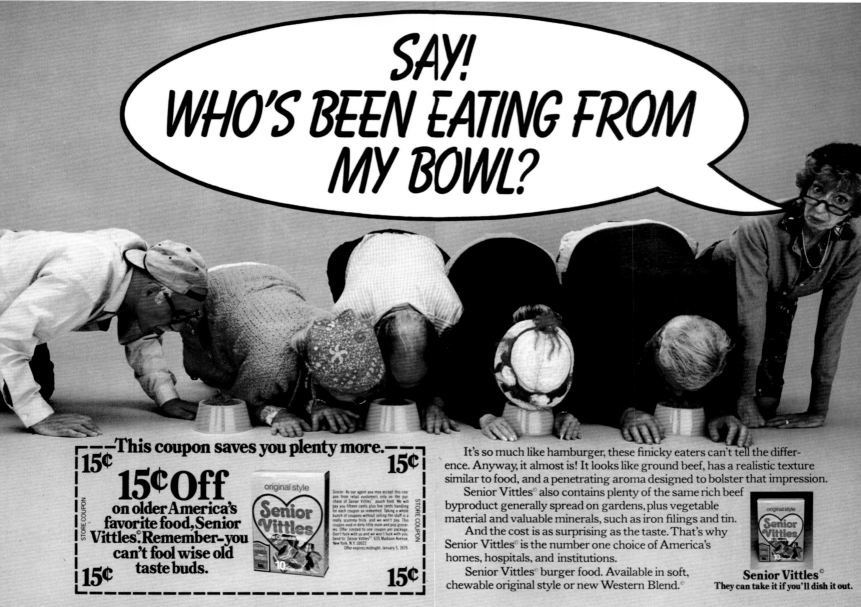

December 1978

INDEXTRAS

page numbers in *italic* refer to illustrations

"Sure he may be a flasher, but he's also a national hero."

> *Four Things I Know About Sean by Ron Hauge*
> *He swears more than any other man who claims Mr. Rogers as a hero and he believes that men don't want sex, they want the moment after sex so they are momentarily relieved of the burden of wanting sex.*
>
> *No matter how much Sean loves you there's one thing about you he doesn't like at all and it comes up a lot when you're not around.*
>
> *Twenty years ago Sean went up to Jim Henson's offices for a long-standing appointment and when he arrived he found everyone was sobbing. The executive he was meeting managed to tell him through her tears that Jim had died the night before from an untreated infection. Sean told her he was relieved—he'd naturally assumed the sobbing was about him. Then he brightened and wisely added, "Well, you've got to expect that kind of thing is going to happen when you spend thirty years with your hand up a frog's ass."*
>
> *I introduced Sean to his final wife by grabbing the most attractive woman I saw at a party, pressing her up against Sean, and telling them both that they'd make a beautiful child together. A couple years later they did just that. Sean introduced me to my first TV agent but that story has a very different ending.*

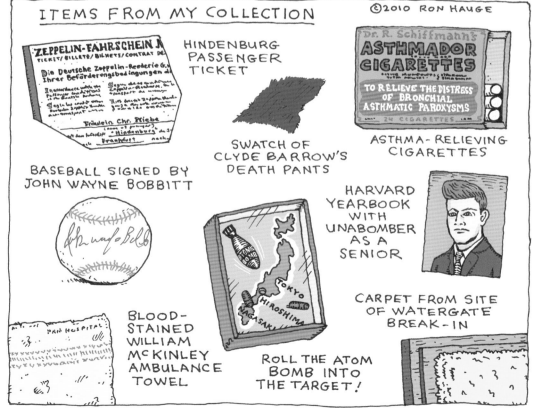

See Hauge, Ron

A gay Irish priest in New Delhi
Tattooed the Lord's Prayer on his belly.
By the time that a Brahman
Read down to the "amen,"
He'd blown both salvation and Kelly.

A jaded old lady from Phlox
Set dynamite off in her box.
When asked the sensation,
She screamed with elation:
"It's better than elephant cocks!"

In Danzig, an artsy old nun t
Ook a chisel and sculptured her cunt.
She carved to Perfection
The Lord's Resurrection
And wore her skirts open, in front.

He stood with his legs spread apart.
Below him knelt Fifi, the tart.
"Eat me!" he cried.
"Certainement!" she replied,
"The lunch, sir, or just a la carte?"

There was an old lady from Cork
Who liked to eat shit with a fork.
Her son cried, "You goon!
You eat shit with a spoon!
It's pork that you eat with a fork!"

A hygienic young miss from out West
Asked the cowboy who sat on her chest:
"Will come cause decay?"
"No, ma'am, I've heard say
It's the secret ingredient in Crest!"

Can You Spot the Three Mistakes in This Limerick?
A G.I. at a smoker in Thule
Asked a woman who'd sucked off a mule:
"Don't you find that quite sordid?"
"Mais non!" she retorted,
"In Spain, we are taught this in school!"

A writer who'd mastered all medial
Tried a humorous Encyclopedia.
When his deadlines had past
He admitted at last
To habitual sins of Acedia.

"Political fools make me sick
With their lunatic left rhetoric
About getting involved.
All my problems are solved
By striking a wall with my stick!"

A fat kid from upstate New York
(Not McCall, Kelly, Beard or O'Rourke)
Developed a passion
For taste, style and fashion
And has learned to eat peas with a fork.

A poetess (name rhymes with Keatts)
Although not endowed with large teatts
Had great charms for those
Who, bereft of their clothes,
Let her walk up their backsides with cleatts.

"Hello, my name is Private Cristobal Esquina of the Salvadoran army, and I just threw $8,550 worth of hand grenades at a dog."

But it could have been an enemy soldier—how was Private Esquina to know? He's just a confused, completely unmotivated peasant with an attention span of about five minutes who has never held anything in his hand more valuable than a dirt clod, and if we want Private Esquina to fight our wars for us, then there's no reason to complain when he uses up $60,000,000 worth of ordnance every three months.

Let's Not Quit on El Salvador Now

For more information on how you can help, write to:
MILLIONS OF DOLLARS' WORTH OF
AMMUNITION AND GUNS FOR UNMOTIVATED PEASANTS
Department A-1
635 Madison Avenue
New York, N.Y. 10022

NCMD
© 1983 National Council of Millions of Dollars

34 NATIONAL LAMPOON · JUNE 1983

> *The day I started at* National Lampoon, *the writers went out for lunch at noon and never came back. They treated me to sushi and sake—I was 21, it was 1982, and I'd never seen either before in my life. One of the writers ordered sliced cold jellyfish for me. I'm not sure if that was a delicacy or a hazing.*
>
> *We soon switched bars and started drinking Aquavit, a Swedish liqueur that tastes like rye bread and is served from a block of ice the size of a glacier. Eventually, we retired to one of the writers' homes. I drunkenly asked my new boss Todd Carroll, "Why did you get divorced anyhow?" Halfway through his story, I ran to the bathroom and threw up in what I thought was a toilet. It was actually a full laundry hamper.*
>
> *On Monday, I faced Todd, chagrined. "One of the writers suggested I apologize to you."*
>
> *He replied, "Tell that writer he's an asshole and you don't apologize for anything."*
>
> National Lampoon *was the craziest, greatest job I ever had. I loved it every day for ten months. Then I quit for something that paid better.*

Bulb with note found on Charlie's desk after he died.

Pin owned by Michael O'Donoghue

WHO IS OR WAS

Abelson, Danny: Danny Abelson came to the *Lampoon* in 1976 as half of a writing/editing team with Ellis Weiner. I have never met another human being who spoke as fast or conversed as furiously as Danny. For the last 30 years he has been president of the Abelson Company, a communications agency that works mostly with nonprofits in the United States and Europe. Danny says, "There are some experiences that are so enjoyable that I forget to see through them. This work falls into that category." He goes on to say he's lost the "caustic edge" that served us all so well back in the day. Yeah. Right.

Adams, Neal: A legendary comic book artist who did many of the *Lampoon*'s comic book parodies such as "Son-O-God Comics." Neal is still active and producing great art. His website has a science section, in which Neal explains why the Earth is growing bigger.

Barrett, Ron: He is the creator of the "Politenessman" and "Steve Draper, Custom Reupholsterer" comic strips for the *Lampoon*. It is our loss that there was not more room for those in this book. Ron created the classic mega-bestselling children's book, *Cloudy with a Chance of Meatballs*. He brings his great design sense and unique humor to everything he does.

Beard, Henry: Coeditor with Doug Kenney of the *Harvard Lampoon* and cofounder of the *National Lampoon*, Henry was the magazine's original executive editor. He became editor-in-chief in 1972. All were in awe of his intellect, vocabulary, and the stunning breadth of his knowledge. It was said, "Everything Henry touches turned to gold." Since leaving the *Lampoon*, Henry has minted more gold, writing numerous bestselling books, including *Tennis*, *Sailing*, *Latin for All Occasions*, *French for Cats*, and *The Dick Cheney Code*.

Beatts, Anne: From 1971 to 1973, Anne held her own with the chauvenist pigs at the *Lampoon*. She partnered first with Michel Choquette and then with Michael O'Donoghue. She and Michael left the *Lampoon* to write for *Saturday Night Live*. Anne was coeditor of *Titters*, the first collection of humor by women. She created the TV series *Square Pegs*. Anne teaches comedy writing and improvization at the University of Southern California.

Bendel, John: From 1982 to 1991, John edited the "True Facts" section and special "True Facts" issues of the *Lampoon*. These days, John is a writer, a photographer, and a marketing consultant to trucking technology companies.

Bode, Vaughn: Creator of the "Cheech Wizard" comic strip, which ran in the Funny Pages for four years. The strip's popularity baffled me back then, and still does.

Boni, John: John wrote some very funny things for the magazine during the first few years of its publication, including the bayonet-sharp indictment of Vietnam politics, a faux soap opera titled "As the Monk Burns." John wrote for television for years. He lives in North Carolina.

Bramley, Peter: The man had a great sense of fun. The costumes he wore (and they were costumes, not clothes) the parties he hosted, the coffee cans filled with grass, the all-night cartooning, the all-afternoon stoned-instead-of-working bull sessions—were all part of his daily routine. It was as if he'd dropped into New York's Lower East Side from some Toon planet. Peter Bramley was something else. I've written (page 292) disparagingly of Peter's duck mascot. I don't take it back. You could hate that duck, but you couldn't hate Peter. You had to love Peter.

Brown, M.K.: It was as if she wasn't painting, but baking up each month's new confection. Everyone loved her work! Mary K. grew up in Connecticut and Canada, went to art school(s), married B. Kliban, had a daughter. She has written and made animations for television, has paintings in galleries and museums, and published cartoons in *Playboy*, *Mother Jones*, *National Lampoon*, and the *New Yorker* ... M.K. Brown has cartoons in the *New Yorker*? She lives and writes and paints in great happiness in Northern California.

Carroll, Tod: Tod contributed a lot to the magazine in the late 1970s when he was an editor under P.J. O'Rourke. Tod and Ted Mann created "O.C. and Stiggs," and he went to Hollywood when it became a movie. Hollywood: the land of lost writers. Tod never returned. All I could find out about Tod Carroll is that he married, moved to Arizona, and lives anonymously so as to keep his past as a *Lampoon* writer secret. Whoops!

Cerf, Christopher: Chris helped launch the *National Lampoon*. His experience as an editor at Random House added a sense of professionalism to the magazine in those early days. He has won two Grammy awards for songs written for *Sesame Street*. He created the Emmy-winning show *Between the Lions* for PBS. He was coeditor

with Tony Hendra of *Not the New York Times*. He has collaborated with Henry Beard on several books, notably *The Pentagon Catalogue: Ordinary Products at Extraordinary Prices* and *The Official Politically Correct Dictionary*.

Choquette, Michel: Michel was touring the United States as half of a comedy team, The Times Square Two, when he discovered the *Lampoon*. Michel was a contributing editor from 1970 to 1974. Famously, he traveled to the Caribbean, stayed for ten days, exceeded budget, and shot the Führer on the beach. His magnificent, decades-long project *The Someday Funnies* will be published by Abrams in 2011.

Devins, Susan: Susan, a copy editor at the *Lampoon* from 1976 to 1982 is the author of four children's cookbooks, including *Chew on This!*, a history of bubble gum, and *Christmas Cookies*.

Enos, Randy: Randy is a talented and versatile man who works in pen and ink, or by doing virtuoso linoleum cuts. Randy's popular comic strip, "Chicken Gutz," ran in the *Lampoon* for years. Randy dug through his meticulous files and managed to come up with the one piece of art in his basement that wasn't water-damaged or chewed on by whatever is living down there. I am referring to the stunning original art on pages 26 and 27 for Doug Kenney's "Code of Hammurabi."

Flenniken, Shary: Shary was a founding member of the Air Pirates, a group of San Francisco–based underground cartoonists. Michel Choquette recruited her for the *Lampoon*. She wrote and drew the funny and sexy "Trots and Bonnie," which appeared in the Funny Pages for almost twenty years. In 1978 P. J. O'Rourke hired her as a contributing editor. She now lives and works in Seattle.

Flesch, Hugo: For some years, Hugo was thought to be a pseudonym for Henry Beard. Nothing could be further from the truth, except maybe the truth. Hugo was a real writer. He didn't produce a lot for the magazine, but some articles were choice. My favorite? "Does the Name Pavlov Ring a Bell?"

Gikow, Louise: Louise was *Lampoon* copy editor from 1972 to 1978. She is cocreator with Christopher Cerf of *Between the Lions* and *Lomax: The Hound of Music*. She is the writer of the planetarium shows "Cosmic Collisions" and "Journey to the Stars" at the Rose Center for Earth and Space at the Museum of Natural History in New York City and around the world. Louise is the author of *Sesame Street: A Celebration of 40 Years of Life on the Street*.

Gorey, Edward: It seems an odd fit, yet the utterly unique, completely original Edward Gorey did several articles and two covers for the *National Lampoon* during the early 1970s.

Graver, Fred: Fred and Sean Kelly became coeditors-in-chief under the fictional name of L. Dennis Plunkett. "Editor" Plunkett held the fort until 1984, when the management fired Sean and Fred for insubordination and mutiny, and the new editors printed Plunkett's obituary. Fred wrote for David Letterman, then joined Norman Lear Productions. He wrote for *In Living Color* and *Cheers*. Until recently Fred was the creator and executive producer of VH1's *Best Week Ever*. Always at the top of his game, Fred is now developing Apps. How apropos.

Greenfield, Jeff: Jeff wrote for the *Lampoon* in the mid-1970s. Prior to that he had been a speechwriter for Robert F. Kennedy. He is a brilliant and astute observer of the American scene, and that may explain why he came to the *Lampoon*. After leaving the magazine he became a correspondent for CBS News, a political analyst for ABC News, and an analyst for CNN, where he spent years analyzing the color of Larry King's hair. He's now back at CBS as senior political analyst. Jeff writes a column for *Time* and has authored or coauthored nine books. Jeff's official CNN biography actually mentions the *National Lampoon*.

Gross, Michael: Michael was the *Lampoon*'s design director from 1970 to 1974. The editors relied on him to tell them what the hell it was they were supposed to be doing—and when. In 1974 he left the *Lampoon* to found a design firm with David Kaestle. The two of them continued to work on special projects for the magazine. In 1978 Mike became a producer in Hollywood. He produced *Twins*, *Ghostbusters*, *Kindergarten Cop*, *Beethoven*, and other films. He lives in Oceanside, California, and is a part-time curator at the Oceanside Museum of Art.

Gross, Sam: The inimitable work of caustic and darkly funny Sam Gross brought a lift to each issue of the *Lampoon*. Throughout the seventies and eighties, he was a regular in the magazine. He drew cartoons he could never publish anywhere else. He is a regular *New Yorker* cartoonist now. Somehow he finds a way, week after week, to censor the *Lampoon* aesthetic that still dwells inside him. Sam created the famous "Try Our Frogs Legs" cartoon that the *Lampoon* made into T-shirts and posters and sold the heck out of. Sam fought for every penny of royalties he was owed, and he got them.

Grossman, Michael: Is a New York–based designer. Michael art directed the *National Lampoon* from 1981 to 1984. He has worked at numerous magazines and consulted on the design of even more.

Hauge, Ron by Ron Hauge: Ron Hauge was born into the hands of Tom Brokaw's father-in-law.[1] He grew up in a Montana ghost town.[2] His parents met in an insane asylum[3] and his father worked as a department-store Santa.[4] Ron has half a dozen Emmys and one gold record.[5] His drawings have appeared in *Time* and *Screw*.[6] Ron is delighted to call Woonsocket, Rhode Island, his home.[7]

1. It's not so remarkable when you know he was a doctor and not just some guy related to the newsman.
2. Fifty thousand people lived there when a giant dam was being built in the 1930s. After the work was completed, about 250 people stayed on. So yes, it was a true ghost town.
3. They were working summer jobs in the asylum's kitchen. They weren't any crazier than you.
4. Seasonal. The rest of the year he was a government surveyor.
5. The gold record came from a flea market in Pennsylvania. It's for a terrible Rod McKuen album that Ron had nothing to do with. The Emmys are for writing and producing *The Simpsons* over fourteen years.
6. Ron has drawn for dozens of magazines and newspapers but enjoyed listing just these two side by side.
7. Being delighted to say something doesn't make it true. He lives in Los Angeles.

Hendra, Tony: Cambridge, not Harvard. Tony, as half of the comedy team *Hendra and Ullett*, appeared numerous times on the *Ed Sullivan Show* and *The Tonight Show with Johnny Carson*. He began contributing to the *Lampoon* in 1970 and soon became an editor. He worked on the *National Lampoon Radio Hour* with Michael O'Donoghue, and was cocreator, with Sean Kelly, of the first *Lampoon* stage show, *Lemmings*. Tony and Sean were the magazine's coeditors-in-chief from 1975 to 1978. Tony acted in *This Is Spinal Tap*. He was editor of *Spy* magazine for five minutes. He is the author of *Going Too Far*, a history of boomer humor; *Father Joe: The Man Who Saved My Soul*, a memoir; *The Messiah of Morris Avenue*, a novel; and *Last Words*, a biography of George Carlin. *"Un uomo che vive la sua vita camminando lungo precipizio ha l'obbligo di mantenere il suo equilibrio."* (Pope John Paul II)

talents—he was extremely smart, and utterly fearless." There is not enough room here to do justice to Rob. At his death in 2006, he was one of the most influential and successful men in his hometown of Dallas. He was a nationally known supporter of the arts who left his huge collection to the Dallas Museum, and he was one of the foremost philanthropists in the country. Rob was a bright, friendly, and curious fellow who looked so young, visitors to the office thought he was an intern. When the three founders cashed out in 1975, Doug used his money to buy a Porsche. Rob bought a Jasper Johns, a Philip Guston, and a Richard Diebenkorn. "Rob's sense of humor," said his brother, "was wry, and ironic. He was witty, with a twinkle in his eye and half-smile on his lips when he watched you." That sounds just right.

Hughes, John: John was working at a Chicago ad agency when he began submitting pieces to the *Lampoon*. He wrote *Mr. Mom* and the *Vacation* movies. He had an amazing Hollywood career, writing, directing, and producing films such as *Sixteen Candles*, *The Breakfast Club*, *Pretty in Pink*, *Ferris Bueller's Day Off*, *Uncle Buck*, and the *Home Alone* series. John had a reputation for being reclusive, rarely venturing from his rural Illinois home, so those who knew him found it not only sad but quizzical that when John had a heart attack and died in August 2009, he was having an early morning stroll on the busy streets of midtown Manhattan.

provided a benchmark for a *Los Angeles Herald-Examiner* redesign. Present at creation: *PC World*, *Macworld*, and *Publish*. Freelance designer at the *New York Times* and *Boston Globe*. I now art direct for political nonprofits.

Kaestle, David: David came to the *Lampoon* in the fall of 1970 with Michael Gross. Together they re-created the magazine and made it viable. He went on to do great things as a designer for many years. David was a perceptive and sagacious man who, had he lived a longer life, would surely have had a lot to say about the shape of this book. His friends miss his wise counsel.

Kaminsky, Peter: Peter was a civilizing presence at the magazine in the mid-1970s. It has been said that he was better in a meeting than anyone, but that once out of the meeting, "the typewriter became his natural enemy." He now writes on fishing and food for the *New York Times* and numerous magazines, and he is the author of many books on those subjects. He is the creator and producer of the annual Mark Twain Prize for American Humor for the Kennedy Center in Washington. The typewriter, by the way, is long obsolete, but Peter is doing beautiful work.

Kelly, Sean: He was a professor of literature at Loyola College in Montreal before escaping to New York to become the poet laureate of the *National Lampoon*. He was an editor from 1970 to 1978, and coeditor-in-chief from 1975 to 1978 and 1981 to 1984. Sean created *Lemmings* with Tony Hendra. He created "Son-O'-God Comics" with Michel Choquette. He was the founding editor of the *Lampoon*'s sister magazine, *Heavy Metal*. Sean has written for television and is the author of *Saints Preserve Us! Everything You Need to know About Every Saint You'll Ever Need*; *Who in Hell . . . : A Guide to the Whole Damn Bunch*; *Herstory: Lisa Marie's Wedding Diary*; and, with Tony Hendra, *Not the Bible*. Sean, saints preserve us, lives and teaches in Brooklyn, New York.

Hoffman, Robert: Rob Hoffman, Doug Kenney, and Henry Beard came to New York City in the summer of 1969 to found a new magazine. Rob, who contributed very little in the way of written humor to the magazine, contributed all of the business acumen the Harvard boys needed. The deal done, Rob went back to Harvard to get his degree. Henry Beard said, "*National Lampoon* never would have happened, and none of the things that came out if it would have happened, without Robert. He had an exceptional pair of

Jew, Cliff: Not much is know about Cliff Jew: he is a designer; he lives in Berkeley; he likes motorcycles; he has great Halloween parties. And in 1984 he magnificently channeled Hergé, the creator of Tintin. Fred Graver, who conceived and wrote "Tintin In Lebanon," called Cliff Jew "a genius."

Johnston, Skip: Skip writes: Pratt Institute with Peter Kleinman. Cronyism spawned a five-year hoot that ended abruptly; booted out, my design of the *Sunday Newspaper* parody, ironically,

Kenney, Douglas: Coeditor, with Henry Beard, of the *Harvard Lampoon*. Cofounder, with Henry, of the *National Lampoon*. He was original editor-and-chief. He loved to play the bad boy, but he had no aptitude for it. He was much loved, envied, and worried over. Why did a man with an IQ of 185 feel so insecure? The fertility of his imagination and his self-deprecating wit were unmatchable. Cowriter of *Animal House* and *Caddyshack*, Doug seemed destined for even greater things. He never got there. Doug Kenney died in 1980.

Kleinman, Peter: Peter was hired in 1974 to succeed Michael Gross (page 300). He's focused and funny, and it turned out, he was a good designer. He could learn anything in a minute. His contributions to the *Lampoon* were essential to the magazine remaining a great-looking publication throughout the seventies. He also boxed under the name The Kosher Butcher. A photograph of The Kosher Butcher is also on page 300.

London, Bobby: Bobby wrote and drew "Dirty Duck." "Dirty" was Groucho Marx–like character, a leering, baseball cap–wearing canard, a dirty old man in the shape of a duck. Bobby went on to draw "Popeye" for King Features. He now writes and draws for Nickelodeon and the Cartoon Network and lives on the West Coast.

Mack, Stan: Stan wrote and drew "Stan Mack's Real Life Funnies" in the *Village Voice* for twenty years. He created "Mule's Diner," a series of surreal happen-ings that ran occasionally in the *Lampoon*. He is the author of graphic histories, such as *Stan Mack's Real Life American Revolution* and *The Story of the Jews: A 4,000-Year Adventure*. Stan's most recent book series, *The Cartoon Chronicles of America*, is published by Bloomsbury USA.

Maffia, Daniel: Daniel is a fine illustrator who, forty years ago, took the assignment from Doug Kenney and became Leonardo Da Vinci. His perfect forgery of Leonardo's drawing style was a breathtaking act of counterfeiting that set the bar high for all the other parodies the magazine would undertake in the future.

Mann, Ted: Ted was the most uninhibited and unpredictable of all the people who ever worked at the *Lampoon*. And he was a good writer of tough, smart prose. He had serious issues on his mind, but first he and Tod Carroll created "O.C. and Stiggs," and he was one of the writers of *Disco Beaver from Outer Space*. Ted has since written and produced for *Miami Vice*, *NYPD Blue*, *Judging Amy*, *John from Cincinnati*, and *Deadwood*.

Marek, Mark: I love Mark Marek's work. His "Hercules Among the North Americans" and "Dirty Father Harry" comic strips were always amusing, and his art was cutting-edge-new/underground/punk/something-or-other great.

McAfee, Mara: Mara was a cover artist for the *Lampoon*. She painted many other illustrations for the magazine in a style that was lucid and beautiful. She was the *Lampoon*'s Norman Rockwell. Mara passed away in the mid-1980s. The Van Gogh cover on page 297 and the wedding cover on 301 are fine examples of her work.

McCall, Bruce: Bruce arrived at the *National Lampoon* like a thunderbolt. *"BULGEMOBILES!"* No one had seen anything like him before. Soon he was writing and painting in almost every issue. Bruce's career in advertising had given him the training to parody the very form at which he made his living. He quit the *Lampoon* in a dispute with the owner over being paid for his work. Bruce thought (correctly) he should be. Thus, the *Lampoon* lost his unique talents, which he shifted, without any change in his aesthetic, to the *New Yorker*, where he still resides.

McConnachie, Brian: His wonderfully offbeat sense of humor charmed fellow editors and left them thinking he could be from another planet, which (no one can recall why) they named Mogdar. He is the exemplar of charm—a title which, unlike, say, the Sultan of Jaipur, has no fortune attached to it. Since leaving the *Lampoon*, Brian has written for *SNL* and *SCTV*, and *Shining Time Station*. He has acted in Woody Allen's films. Brian is an irregular commentator on NPR's *All Things Considered*.

McLoughlin, Wayne: Wayne McLoughlin was born in Llanfrechfa, Wales. He did paintings, special "posters," and many articles for the *Lampoon*. He has a darkly humorous way of looking at the world. Wayne lives in the woods of New Hampshire with his wife, Jackie, their fluffy dog, Zoe, and more firepower in his garage than the Tenth Mountain Division has at Fort Drum.

Meyerowitz, Rick: Rick believes he is the most prolific contributor of illustrated articles to the *National Lampoon* magazine. If I were you, I wouldn't contradict him. He painted the poster for *Animal House* and was the creator of the magazine's trademark visual, "The Mona Gorilla." Shortly after 9/11, Rick and Maira Kalman created the most talked-about *New Yorker* cover of this century, "NewYorkistan," about which the *New York Times* wrote: "When their cover came out, a dark cloud seemed to lift." Rick is also the author of this book, and all these short biographies, including the one you're reading right now.

Miller, Chris: Chris wrote delicious short stories about sex. He was an early contributor to the *Lampoon* and stayed connected until the mid-1980s. He starred in numerous "Foto Funnies," usually in bed with a woman. His stories about college life were the basis for *Animal House*, which he cowrote. He has written numerous screenplays. In 2005 Little, Brown published his memoir, *The Real Animal House*.

O'Donoghue, Michael: Michael was a brilliant and prickly man. Working with him was like trying to laugh while kissing a porcupine. He produced *Radio Dinner*, the first *Lampoon* record album, and he created the *National Lampoon Radio Hour*. Michael left the magazine in 1974 in a fit of rage over some now-forgotten misunderstanding. He became the first head writer of *Saturday Night Live* and starred in the first sketch aired on that program. He created *Mr. Mike's Mondo Video*. Michael died in 1994.

Orlando, Joe: Joe was working upstairs from the *Lampoon* at DC Comics when Doug Kenney went up to the DC office and asked if there was anybody on staff who'd like to draw a comic book parody for the *Lampoon*. Joe became comic art guru to Doug. Many of the early *Lampoon* comic book parodies were produced with Joe's help, and his work. I remember how gleeful he was to be doing the spoofs the *Lampoon* gave him.

O'Rourke, P.J.: P.J. and Doug were coauthors of the *1964 High School Yearbook Parody*. P.J. was editor-in-chief from 1977–80. He writes for *Playboy*, *Vanity Fair*, and *Rolling Stone*, and is the author of many books: *Republican Party Reptile*, *Holidays in Hell*, *Parliament of Whores*, and the recent *On the Wealth of Nations*. He is a frequent guest on NPR's *Wait Wait . . . Don't Tell Me!* P.J. lives in New England with his brood of young O'Rourkes. He recently told me, "I'm having my own grandchildren."

Pond, Mimi: I just love Mimi Pond. Her "Famous Waitress School" comic strips, which ran in the *Lampoon*, were a delight. Mimi has written for television and published numerous books, such as *Secrets of the Powder Room*, *Shoes Never Lie*, and *A Groom of One's Own: And Other Bridal Accessories*.

Prager, Emily: Emily is the author of several novels and a collection of short stories and is a contributor to many publications. Emily's sad-sweet essay about Michael O'Donoghue is on page 60. She and her daughter Lulu live in Shanghai.

Punchatz, Don Ivan: Don had a studio through which passed every aspiring artist in Texas, and from which Don would send out illustrations all over the world. He was immensely talented and very droll. See for yourself: his work appears on page 298. Don died in 2009.

Reiss, Michael: *Harvard Lampoon*, *National Lampoon*, *The Tonight Show with Johnny Carson*, *The Simpsons*, *The Critic*. Mike lives within sight of Times Square in a really big glass building.

Rodrigues, Charles: As Charlie would say, Rodrigues ends with an "s." Charlie lived in Mattapoisett, Massachusetts, near Cape Cod. It is a coastal village of clam shacks and churches, along whose rocky shores live the vestiges of the great Portuguese migrations of the nineteenth century. Charlie did not like New York City very much. Over the twenty years he contributed cartoons to the magazine, few editors could claim to have met him. Yet he was a prolific contributor, and if you look at his work, you can see the urban landscape populated by city dwellers seemed to be his favorite subject. He loved us, although he couldn't stand *us*, and that ends with and "s."

Rose, Alan: He created meticulous graphics in collaboration with Michael O'Donoghue and P.J. O'Rourke. Alan has done lettering and illustration for San Francisco rock groups and worked in advertising, TV, film, and publishing. His paper model books have kept him busy. He tells me he has spent years turning "an otherwise promising career into an otherwise promising career."

Roth, Arnold: Arnold Roth was a star cartoonist when most of the future *Lampoon* stars were in grammar school. Before there was a *Lampoon*, he'd worked with Harvey Kurtzman on *Trump* and *Humbug*

and was a veteran at *Punch*, the English humor magazine. Arnie appeared in almost every issue of the *Lampoon* during the first two years of its publication. His work was, and still is, rich and unique and very funny. We stand, as they say, in awe.

Sattler, Warren: Warren was the unsung hero of the *National Lampoon*. He drew innumerable cartoons and illustrations in an endless variety of styles. He was a terrific comic artist/chameleon. His only role was to parody other artists, and he did that beautifully.

Sloman, Larry "Ratso": Ratso, as the executive editor from 1984 to 1990, fought to hold the place together. He has a Master's Degree in deviance and criminology. He was captain of the Queens College hockey team. He is author of a dozen excellent books and ghostwriter of more. He is friends with Kinky Friedman, in whose novels he is a character. And he is close with Bob Dylan, who once sang "Happy Birthday" to him at an early morning party in a European hotel room. Ratso is a sharp dresser and a cat who is way beyond cool.

Springer, Frank: Beginning in 1964, Frank drew Michael O'Donoghue's innovative and scandalous *Adventures of Phoebe Zeit-Geist*. They partnered on many classic comic book parodies, such as *Tarzan of the Cows*, and *Frontline Dentists*. Frank Springer, a wonderful draftsman, and the handsomest cartoonist who ever lived, passed away in 2009.

Subitzky, Ed: Modest Ed Subitzky wrote and drew the longest, talkiest, most mystifyingly strange, incomprehensibly dense, oddly literate, and ripely libidinous comic strips ever created for any magazine. Why isn't there a collection of this man's work? Aside from the comic strips, he wrote numerous articles for the magazine over the years, and in 1974 he conceived, wrote, and acted on the *Official National Lampoon Stereo Test and Demonstration Record Album*.

Sussman, Gerry: "Suss" wrote more words and more articles than any other contributor to the magazine. His alter ego was Bernie X, a New York cab driver for whom he wrote long, foul-mouthed, over-the-top sexual monologues. Gerry also parodied the Yellow Pages. He created fake restaurant menus and bogus guidebooks. He had an extraordinary ability to give verisimilitude to what he was creating. It always looked like the real thing, but it was completely wacky. He was editor-in-chief from 1980 to 1982. Gerry died suddenly in 1989. His was a singular talent. He is much mourned by his friends.

Taylor, B.K.: B.K. created the "Appletons" comic strip, which ran in the *Lampoon* for years. What *was* the Appletons about? I recall a lot of mayhem initiated by the loving but psychotic father, who always reminded me of Uncle Charlie in Hitchcock's *Shadow of a Doubt*.

Trow, George: A *Harvard Lampoon* alumnus, George was an eccentric man who radiated intelligence. He knew his WASPs (he studied his whole life to pass for one) and wrote about them with great wit and flair. He joined the *New Yorker* and wrote for that magazine for twenty years. George is celebrated for his essay *In the Context of No Context*. He died in Naples, Italy, in 2006.

Weidman, John: *Harvard Lampoon*; Yale Law School; editor and contributor to the *National Lampoon* from 1970 to 1984. John became a writer for *Sesame Street* and won eleven Emmy awards. As if that wasn't enough, working with Stephen Sondheim, John wrote *Pacific Overtures*, *Assassins*, and *Road Show*. *Contact*, which he co-created with Susan Stroman, won the Tony for Best Musical. We could go on, but isn't it enough for you to know the man won eleven Emmys?

Weiner, Ellis: Ellis is droll and cerebral. He says he lived in a state of constant fear that he wouldn't understand what the other editors were talking about (page 280). Ellis writes for television and has written or cowritten numerous books, among which are *Drop Dead, My Lovely*; *The Joy of Worry* (with Roz Chast); *Yiddish with Dick and Jane*; and *Oy! Do This Not That!: 100 Simple Swaps That Could Save Your Life, Your Money, or Your Mother from a Heart Attack, God Forbid*. Ellis is a regular and very funny blogger on the *Huffington Post*.

Wilson, Gahan: Gahan became a star working for *Playboy* in the 1950s. The *Lampoon* gave him the chance to write and draw multipage articles, comic strips, and covers without being edited. All the editors wanted to know was how many pages he needed. That kind of freedom is liberating. Besides innumerable articles, Gahan's wonderful strip about his childhood, "NUTS," led off the Funny Pages every month for seven years. There's no *Lampoon* now, but Gahan is still contributing to *Playboy* and the *New Yorker*. He is the author of numerous books, including *I Paint What I See*, *And Then We'll Get Him*, and *Gahan Wilson: 50 Years of Playboy Cartoons*.

Left to right: Gerry Sussman, Peter Kaminsky, Tony Hendra, Danny Abelson, Sean Kelly, Ellis Wiener, and Peter (horizontal) Kleinman.

THANKS

Thank you, Eric Himmel, for suggesting to me that I do a book about the *National Lampoon*. And after I said you were out of your mind to think I could do it, thank you for convincing me that I was the right man for the job. Without the space you gave me to develop the idea, and your patience listening to the grousing I did over the coffees you paid for, this book never would have been realized.

Thank you, editor Aiah Wieder: whip-smart, and strong of heart. I love the way you loved this project.

Thank you, old friend and collaborateur Sean Kelly. You're the sharpest tack in Brooklyn. Thank you for your advice, your genius, your brilliant *Lampoon* work, and the essays you wrote for this book. Thank you, Michel Choquette, for the gorgeous scans you made from your original 35mm slides. Is anything funnier than your photo of the Führer sunning himself, naked, on the beach? Thank you, old friend Tony Hendra, genius *Lampoon* editor and writer. Your book, *Going Too Far,* was a source of inspiration for me. Thank you for your brilliant work and the essays you contributed.

Thank you, *Lampoon* design legend and old friend Michael Gross. Your talent as a designer made the *National Lampoon*. Thank you for the many conversations we had about this project.

Thank you, Sam Gross, for your advice and your humor and your original art and your unique fucking vocabulary. Thank you, Ratso Sloman, for writing the hilarious essay about Sam, and for dressing better than anyone else named Ratso. Thank you, Ron Barrett, for the original giant Meatscape art. What is better than a giant Meatscape? Thank you, Ron Hauge, for your fifty-two New Yorker covers. Thank you, Ed Subitzky, for being Ed Subitzky. And thank you, John Weidman, Chris Cerf, Chris Miller, Fred Graver, and Wayne McLoughlin. M.K. Brown, Queen of Northern California: I thank you for the beautiful images you sent of your original art.

Thank you, Lorraine Rodrigues, for allowing me to scan Charlie's original art. You helped to make his chapter into a joyful celebration of his work. Thank you, Josh Karp, author of the Doug Kenney biography. Your contact list of *Lampoon* veterans was my Rosetta Stone. Thank you, Rachel Friedman. Your scanning skills are legend in this part of town. Thank you, Stan Mack, for all those mornings in the coffee shop you listened to me grumble about everybody I've already thanked.

Thank you, old friend Michael Gold. Your evocative portraits of *Lampoon* editors from 1972 appear throughout this book, and enrich it. Thank you, Anne Hall, for your photos of George Trow and Sam Gross and Bruce McCall. Thank you, Sylvia Plachy, for the photo of Stan Mack. Thank you, Chris Callis, for the use of your photograph of Peter Kleinman and the rest of the guys. And thank you, Peter Kleinman, for your stories as we put this all together.

Thank you, Michael Goodwin, for the photo of John Belushi. And thank you because this is my thank-you page and I feel like thanking you.

Thank you, Molly Bloom, my favorite daughter: Queen of Transcribers, the guardian of my grammar. I was painting the *Animal House* poster the day you were born. Your arrival turned just another day of illustration into a major occasion. Your arrival any time these days still does.

How am I going to thank you, designer Laura Lindgren? The six months we spent putting this book together from scraps and scans, and making it into something we hope will knock the socks off readers, were memorable. We laughed our heads off while we worked—or rather while you worked, and I sat there eating sandwiches—to make the design come to life. Laura Lindgren, you are something else.

Thank you, friend-companion Maira Kalman, for your clear-eyed optimism/pessimism, your truth telling, your great heart, your humor, and your faith in me.

Thank you, Doug Kenney, Henry Beard, and Rob Hoffman. Whatever possessed you to think you could create a national humor magazine? I arrived in your world, a ruffian from the Bronx, yet you welcomed me, and anyone else who you thought was funny. Thank you. Thank you. Thank you.

EDITORS: Eric Himmel and Aiah Rachel Wieder
DESIGNER: Laura Lindgren
PRODUCTION MANAGER: Jules Thomson

Cataloging-in-Publication Data has been applied for and may be obtained from the Library of Congress. ISBN: 978-0-8109-8848-4

Compilation copyright © 2010 ABRAMS

Front endpapers by Ed Subitzky (detail from page 209)
Rear endpapers from the *National Lampoon 1964 High School Year Book.*

Photo credits, pages 314–319: Ron Barrett by Jack Slomovits; Henry Beard by Michael Gold; M.K. Brown by G. Solberg; Shary Flenniken by "some waiter in Duke's Bar & Grill"; Tony Hendra by Jeffrey Schiffman; Rob Hoffman by Michael Gold; Doug Kenney art by Bruce McCall; Bruce McCall by Anne Hall; Wayne McLoughlin art by Wayne McLoughlin; Rick Meyerowitz by Elizabeth Beautyman; Chris Miller by Raul Vega; Ed Subitzky by Michael Gross; Ellis Weiner by Susan Burnstine; group photo by Chris Callis. All other photos by Rick Meyerowitz.

Printed and bound in China
10 9 8 7 6 5 4 3 2 1

ABRAMS
THE ART OF BOOKS SINCE 1949
115 West 18th Street
New York, NY 10011
www.abramsbooks.com

Rufus Leaking
"Spaz"
"Shake, rattle, and roll"
Easy-going . . . always on the move . . . happy-go-lucky . . . smile for everything . . . carefree . . . can take a joke . . . great dribbler . . . stores erasers in his cheeks . . . good sport . . . ants in his pants . . . forever blowing bubbles . . . brown hair, wavy eyes.

Remedial English 1,2,3,4; Therapeutic Numbers 3; Special Students Club 1,2,3,4; Flash Card Club 3; Slow Learners Council 2,3, Pres., 4; Corrective Speech 2; Breathing for Credit 4; Finger Paints 3.

Carl S. Lepper
"Fungus"
"Absence makes the heart grow fonder"
A watchful guardian of KHS tradition . . . beady little eyes . . . "Let's see your hall pass" . . . Cornholt's Commandos . . . "Detention Study Hall is full of guys like you" . . . greasy kid stuff—on his nose and cheeks! . . . Dad works for the IRS . . . volcano face . . . Summer job as a drive-in movie attendant.

Hall Monitors 1,2,3, Lieutenant Colonel 4; Junior Police 2,3,4; Chairman, Locker Safety Week 3; Lavatory Patrol 2,3; Gym Showering Monitor 2,3; Student Court Prosecutor 4; Lunch Tray Chaperon 1; Bay of Pigs Club 3,4; Tidiness Committee 1,2,3,4; Walk-Way Proctor 2,3,4.

Francine Paluka
"Half-Track"
"Poetry in motion"
Strong silent type . . . big Paul Hornung fan . . . "You eat with that mouth?" . . . tag team matches in the girls' locker room . . . "Watch yer language, Bud" . . . knitted barbbell booties . . . "Listen, fresh guy, want your face redecorated?" . . . keeps 'em quiet at the Y-Teen dances . . . headed for Purdue.

Girls' Field Squash Captain 2,3,4; Girls' Gym-Ball Captain 2,3,4; Girls' Tennis Mitten Captain 2,3,4; Girls' Hurdle Hockey Captain 2,3,4; Most Outstanding Senior Athlete 4.

Ddb Lžmdc Oûaejk
"Alphabits"
"Bring us the wretched refuse of your teeming shore"
Kefauver's first AFS student . . . hands across the sea . . . combs her hair with a fork . . . rubs Reese's peanut butter cups into her clothing . . . "Is not for eating this round meat stitched with sewing as the yak bladder stuffed of elm leaves my country good yum?" . . . "Not being boy bought-by I am who ox-ward strong on hammering the fire lumber and worth no few-fold rifles is why?"

Pep Club 4.

Amana Swansdown Peppridge
"Fridge"
"There's a divinity that shapes our ends"
Poise and charm . . . sophisticated . . . cute figure . . . popular with the boys . . . "Gee, I'd *love* to, but . . ." . . . door hugger . . . slim . . . pitches no-hitters . . . "Stop that!" . . . beautiful honey-colored hair . . . does a wicked frug . . . "I *mean* it!" . . . wears latest styles . . . does she or doesn't she? . . . "Look, I'm gonna call a *cop*!" . . . she doesn't . . . "Oh, grow *up*!" . . . dates college guys.

Runner-up, "Miss Teenage Dacron" Contest; Charm Club 2; Future Stewardesses 4.